SLEAZE CREATURES

HSD-17

ACKNOWLEDGEMENTS

Academy of Motion Picture Arts and Sciences, Paul Anthony, Richard Bojarski, Cape Copy Center, Film Favorites, Alex Gordon, Fred Olen Ray, Shock Toon Video, Something Weird Video, Gary Svehla

4

Published by Fantasma Books: 419 Amelia Street, Key West, Florida 33040
For more information, visit our website at: www.fantasmabooks.com

Printed in the United States of America
Library of Congress Catalog Card Number: 95-60148
ISBN 1-888214-02-3
First American Edition 1995
Second American Edition 2002

Cover design and layout by Chidsey Graphics

Dedicated to

My Mother, Helen, my good friends Gary Svehla and Paul Anthony, my departed father Earl and Aunt Marjorie, and the actors and technicians who I speak of most kindly in this book.

PUB-10

TABLE OF CONTENTS

I WAS A TEENAGE WEREWOLF (1957).

IT CONQUERED THE WORLD
Every man its prisoner... Every woman its slave!
STARRING
PETER GRAVES · BEVERLY GARLAND · LEE VAN CLEEF
Produced and Directed by ROGER CORMAN, Executive Producer: JAMES NICHOLSON, Screenplay by LOU RUSOFF
Released by AMERICAN INTERNATIONAL PICTURES

INTRODUCTION

by D. Earl Worth

Until splatter matter left its ugly taste, the late fifties Monster movie was held up as the most disreputable kind of horror film. Such an attitude on the fan level took shape when old classics, the revisionist Gothicism of Hammer and AIP Poe films were considered model cinema. Of course, in the Sixties, when the Puritan view prevailed, there was no Fifties nostalgia and for having built itself up on schlock of that era, AIP was meant to feel it had a shameful past to live down.

But it wasn't American-International that turned out the first mass-manufactured creature cheapies, it was Monogram Pictures and the Producers Releasing Corp. Surreal and sometimes deliberately humorous, the Monogram and PRC films were otherwise a runty collection of programmers mimicking "respectable" Universal B's. Gone by 1947, PRC never lived to see a mid-life, while Monogram, in 1953, became AIP's strongest Fifties competitor as Allied Artists (AIP itself didn't begin until 1954 and for its first two years was the American Releasing Corp.).

American-International founders James Nicholson and Samuel Arkoff were first to comprehend the emerging Fifties youth market and set out to provide the ruder, cruder brand of sensationalism it wanted. From 1956 to 1959, AIP, Allied and their imitators gave us the farthest-out fiends anyone had ever seen: A teenaged werewolf, a fifty foot woman, articulate crustaceans, flying alien brains and a walking tree man among others. AIP monsters were usually realizations of preconceived ad art images or intimations of them if low budgets or limited effects talent were technical hindrances. How a picture compared to the campaign spelled either truth in audacious advertising or deceptiveness close to outright fraud. When an emotionally disturbed high school kid turned into a wolf, you had a genuine Teenage Werewolf. Calling a mostly-invisible alien a Beast with a Million Eyes, however, could get you hung from a lamppost by strips of the celluloid that purported to show it.

Mainly pickup products, the films of Allied Artists were no better or worse than the AIP releases, but now that it had outgrown its distinctive Monogram era, its only "identity" features were the last Bowery Boys comedies. The emblem initials of Allied could have easily stood for Alcoholics Anonymous. AIP's logo of an oval-enclosed capitol backed by white clouds was as commanding a trademark as the Universal globe.

American-International's name and favorite subject matter made AIP look conspicuously derivative of Universal when it was Universal-International — and even before —since each company had its own particular wolfman and Frankenstein monster. AIP did a lot of in-house work and monsters who were Studio Pets like the Teenage Werewolf, the Teenage Frankenstein, the She Creature and the Colossal Man were sure to come around again with new faces and personalities. AIP was the Space Age Monogram while Monogram's reincarnation, Allied Artists, dogged behind the vapor trail of AIP as a PRC equivalent.

Other independents that picked up after these two were Howco-International, Distributors Corp. of America, Astor Pictures Corp., and Roger Corman's Filmgroup — the latter an AIP subsidiary. DCA was partial to foreign fare. Astor peddled the vulgarity of Richard Cunha. New Orleans based Howco commissioned a number of made-in-Hollywood movies. Filmgroup had an affinity for the avant-garde.

Until shifting standards of critical evaluation began to vindicate the undervalued and cast a sterner eye on the once overly-revered, it wasn't the thing to defend an *I Was a Teenage Werewolf* or a *Monster of Piedras Blancas*. By then, the Fifties were In again: the music, the cars, the best-loved TV shows. Pre-Hiroshima monsters had had "their" day because of assimilation into the common culture and even faded Hammer was passe, laboring to death Period stories with increased amounts of sex and blood and fumbling its attempts to go Modern.

In their series of Golden Turkey books, Harry and Michael Medved shafted films major and minor, well-liked and much-loathed, but it was their special joy of putting down monster schlock that helped put these films back in wide circulation, making them known to people other than horror scholars. Now titles like *Attack of the Fifty Foot Woman*, *The Brain from Plant Arous* and *The Killer Shrews* grace the video shelves of every Camp follower, horror completist and serious admirer of shoestring fantasy. Where a prestigious picture like *The Exorcist* must either be overpoweringly convincing or a total flop to arouse strong attitudes, something in the league of *Brain from Planet Arous* can engage several sets of reactions.

With independent monster films from the last third of the fifties, there was a bazaar of bizarreness that on purpose or by accident prompted changeable feelings. They let you go with an imperfect effect either by laughing at it or attempting to believe what it was trying to accomplish. And sometimes, incredibly, there were specks of Real Gold a better film would envy. Both the obvious and your indulgent imagination made a movie what you wanted it to be.

Horror films conform to the times and if AIP and Allied were still around today, chances are *they* would be making Jason and Freddy Kruger-type Dicearamas. Happily, they folded before they could add to the list of what passes for Monsters today . . . monsters for an age that in its depletedness, soullessness and madness *deserves* them . . . the Gray Nineties.

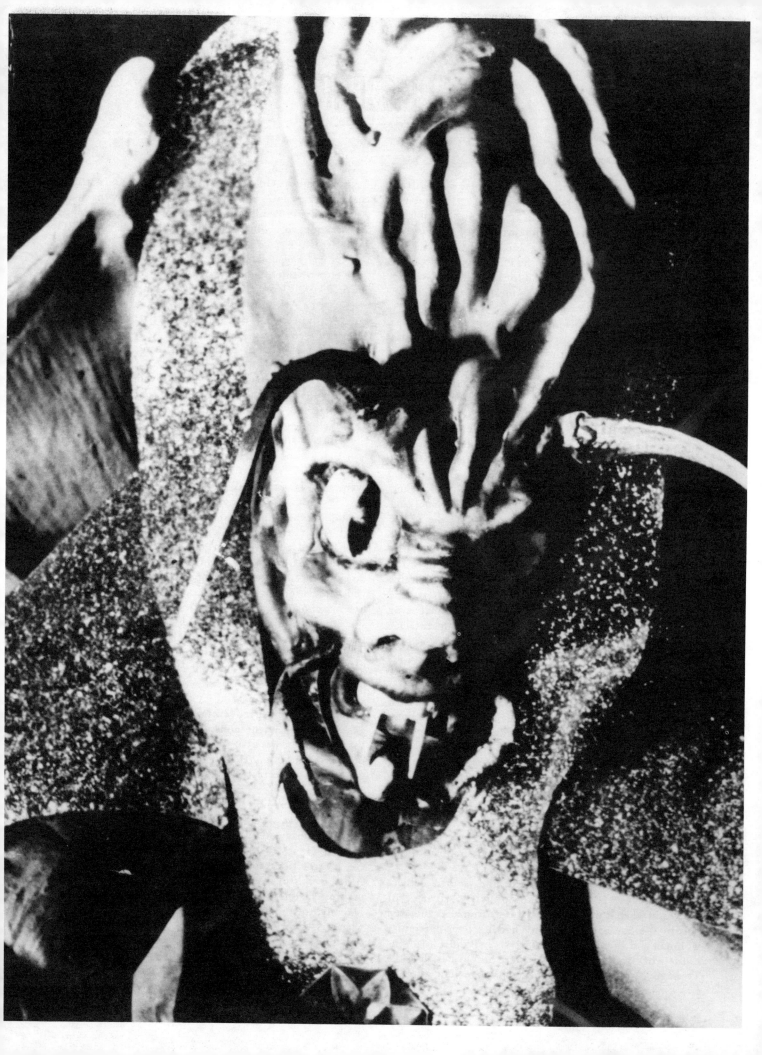

THE BEAST WITH A MILLION EYES

American Releasing Corp., 1956

Executive Producer	Roger Corman
Producer	David Kramarsky
Directors	Roger Corman, Lou Place
	(direction credited to David Kramarsky)
Screenplay	Tom Filer
Associate Producer	Charles Hanawalt
Cinematography	Everett Baker
	(and Floyd Crosby)
Film Editor	Jack Killifer
Music	John Bickford
Art Director	Albert Ruddy
Production Manager	Jack *aka Jonathan* Haze
Assistant Director	Donald Meyers
Technical Director	Sheldon Mitchell
Special Effects	Paul Blaisdell

A San Mateo Production
presented by Palo Alto Productions
Running time: 78 minutes

Cast: Paul Birch (Alan Kelly), Lorna Thayer (Carol Kelly), Dona Cole (Sandy Kelly), Richard *aka Dick* Sargent (Larry Brewster), Leonard Tarver (Carl / "Him"), Chester Conklin (Ben Webber), Bruce Whitmore (Voice of The Beast)

The *Beast with a Million Eyes* started AIP off on the wrong monster — meaning it had no visible Beast in the first cut and the effects that were added later could not satisfy a concept too high for thirty thousand dollars. Because he overspent on *Five Guns West* (1955), the first film he directed, that was all the money Roger Corman had left. A union member, Corman could not direct *Beast* officially or hire a Union crew. Better if the movie had gone by writer Tom Filer's script title "The Unseen" since the "eyes" of its alien were all the eyes of lower earth creatures the alien controlled . . . seeing everything they saw. Corman assigned the producing to Dutch-born David Kramarsky while another assistant, Lou Place, was set to direct.

To make the optical prowess of the alien appear literal, James Nicholson conceived the *Beast* title and had designed a poster entity that saw every which-way. A cluster of receding multiple orbs with a fanged mouth, cratered lips, spiked nose, tentacular whiskers, and two dominant front eyes, its face was the forefront of a shapeless black mass that constituted a "body". What the artist wrought conveyed no suggestion of anything except primal malevolence, nor was there any hint the beast was extraterrestrial.

World War II veteran Alan Kelly owns a failing California date ranch. Economics, isolation and family friction are breaking the Kellys down. Alan perceives another negative force in the thoughts he shares with us " . . . it has something to do with the feeling you get when you start thinking what's out there . . . just beyond the groves . . . a vast, cruel world . . . still, dry, deadly . . . slowly withering beneath the white heat of that desert sun . . . a place to hatch a brood of horror — or of hate . . . perhaps it began out there . . . the hate . . . something that goes far deeper than angry words . . . a growing, twisted thing that's destroying us . . . "

Most affected by all this is Alan's wife, Carol, who doesn't want their teenaged daughter, Sandy, to go to college and bitterly regrets the passing of her own youth. Sandy and her dog, Duke, go to a swimming hole and are watched from atop a tree ladder by "Him", a mute, mentally defective handyman who lives in the woodshed. In the kitchen, Carol hears the deafening hum of a UFO as a coffee pot shatters in her hand. Sandy thinks it was a passing jet showing off and lectures "Him" for his voyeurism. Carol phones the Sheriff about the damage done to all the glass in the house. "Him" comes in for lunch and frazzled Carol orders him to leave.

A blackbird bumps into the windshield of Alan's station wagon. More blackbirds led by a crow attack Alan. Sandy looks for missing Duke. Alan visits old neighbor, Ben Webber, whose cow Sara acts up during milking. Duke approaches a spaceship in a deep crater and is mesmerized by its revolving lights. Alan sees the wreckage at home and when "Him" comes in again expecting to be fed, Carol tells him in no uncertain terms never to set foot in the house again. Sandy's boyfriend, Deputy Larry Brewster, comes to check the damage. "Him" appears menacingly before Sandy and Larry with an axe, then chops wood.

While Alan and Sandy are in town buying things for Sandy's eighteenth birthday, Duke returns to the ranch, threatening Carol. She locks the kitchen door, but Duke enters through the front. Carol fires a rifle shot, drops the gun and flees to the woodshed, but "Him" has locked the door of his room. Carol grabs the axe. Alan and Sandy return to the dark house, where disoriented Carol begs Alan not to let Sandy see Duke. Alan goes to the woodshed. Sandy sees the rifle laying on the kitchen floor and rushes to the woodshed, where she screams. Because of the axe, Sandy thinks "Him" killed Duke and when she realizes Carol did, becomes furious. Carol confides in Alan her awareness of the alien power.

That night, Sandy finds herself walking in the desert. Also entranced is "Him", who feels compelled to walk further until Sandy takes his hand to go home.

When Ben goes to milk her, berserk Sara tramples him. Carol goes to feed the Kelly chickens in their coop and they savagely swarm at her until Alan fends them off with a blowtorch. Concerned about the odd behavior of "Him", Alan writes a letter addressed to the Psychiatric Division of the Veteran's Administration.

The Creature from THE BEAST WITH A MILLION EYES (1956).

All the shocks Carol has received have changed her personality. Alan leaves "Him" in the grove to do some work. "Him" wanders off while Alan finds Ben's body and notices Sara missing. "We thought it was over," Alan muses, " . . . it's just beginning." "Him" confronts the spaceship.

Sara wanders over to the Kelly place. When Sandy tries to put a rope around her neck, Sara attacks. Sandy hides in the woodshed and Alan shoots Sara. Alan phones the Sheriff's office, asking for Larry before some birds fly into an electrical control box and cut all the power. Larry learns he was called, but, not knowing by who, will have the call traced. Alan wants Carol and Sandy to drive into town. He searches for "Him" before the birds attack him.

Home, Alan is chagrined to see Carol casually preparing for Sandy's birthday party. The birds had forced them back. Alan connects everything to the UFO. "Suppose it wasn't a plane — in *our* sense of the word." "A plane from another world . . . ," interprets Carol. Again, the birds prevent the Kellys from leaving. Larry is told that Alan made the call. He picks up "Him" near the ranch. Carol remembers that together Sandy and "Him" were strong. "That's our strength, Alan . . . being together. Alone, we're nothing." "Him" slugs Larry and wrecks the Kelly car by deflating its tires.

Larry scuffles with "Him", who overpowers Larry again. Sandy leaves the house to find Larry and "Him" abducts her. When Larry appears, Alan and Carol cannot find Sandy in the house. Alan and Larry follow her and "Him" to the spaceship. Calling him "Carl", Alan talks "Him" into giving him the unconscious Sandy. The emanations of the ship destroy "Him". Carol appears because the birds forced her out of the house.

Alan and Carol hear the telepathic voice of the alien, who wants Sandy. Though he causes her intense pain to get his way, Alan and Carol refuse to sacrifice her. The alien's bodiless race feed on the brains of lesser creatures, making them their short-lived slaves. "This is a perfect testing area," boasts the alien, " — possessing hate. Hate and malice are the keys to power in my world. This one seemed easy. What went wrong?" Carl was in Alan's Army unit during the war. A snap decision Alan had made caused him injury, warranting a lobotomy. Love is the inner strength of earthlings that puzzles the alien. Its meaning touches an obscure reserve of his heritage memory. The spaceship will leave at dawn. To force Alan and Carol to provide her, the alien inflicts more hurt on Sandy. "Once his kind might have been something like us before they evolved into these superbrains," hypothesizes Alan. "They lost something along the way. For an instant there, he remembered . . . I think he remembered that he'd lost his soul."

Alan and Carol take Sandy to the ship. The hatch opens and they face a creature the alien uses to fly it. The creature succumbs to earth's atmosphere. As the ship takes off, Sandy returns to normal and the alien

enters a rodent. Suddenly, a bald eagle swoops down and devours it. Alan aims his rifle, but Carol wants the eagle spared. "Where did the eagle come from?" asks Alan. "Why do men have souls?" "If I could answer that," Carol tells him, "I'd be more than human."

At least *Beast With a Million Eyes* was able to keep the purity of its story premise. As a family feeling the strains of nuclear-age life and the eternal hardship of the desert, the Kellys were in critical transition. Business setbacks, marital woes and the imminent departure of a daughter with more advantages than what her mother had at her age all piled up at once. Distracted by their all-encompassing troubles, each Kelly was left open to the force that dominated minds in progression to the species of its subjects and certain sets of mental conditioning in people. First it was the birds, then pet animals Duke and Sara and "Him", the one human with only half a brain. As avians were the most consistently dangerous specimens, *Beast* prefigured *The Birds* (1963) — even down to the detail of select ones guiding the rest.

A peeping tom and pinup addict who made Carol uncomfortable, "Him" was a mood sustainer whenever the film did not cut to the spaceship or the uprisings of the alien's other charges (so indigenous to deserts, why were snakes excluded?). When the Kellys finally saw the light past the trees, they turned against the alien a lost asset of its own breed. Why purely negative emotion was felt by the aliens could only be explained as the corruption of the powers they correspondingly gained. The alien's chauffeur indicated that other strange worlds were also vulnerable — a refreshing switch in a format where invaders always pick on earth.

It was rather silly for Carl to be called "Him" for any reason other than having the sound of his name restore his limited senses. Why couldn't Alan have addressed "Him" by his army rank? Since the bald eagle symbolizes American greatness, the supposed demise of the alien struck a patriotic chord. Given his free body-hopping, wouldn't he have taken the eagle over from within? If the eagle was God-sent, maybe the gastric juices in the stomach of the bird dissolved the alien's essence.

Made out of random junk, the spaceship was a six-foot tank half buried in a shallow hole. To one side was a motor that powered the revolving lights on top. The crater was made to look deep by shadows and foreground placement of the actors. Expecting more than just a conjectured occupant, the exhibitors loathed what they saw. Joseph E. Levine, the Boston representative, offered to buy up the master print, burn it and finance a new film. Jim Nicholson did some impromptu surgery. With a pair of scissors, he scratched jagged lines into the film emulsion and filled them with fountain pen ink. The ship appeared to be shooting lethal rays, but the exhibitors wanted a *monster*.

Roger Corman asked Forrest J. Ackerman if he

Lorna Thayer in THE BEAST WITH A MILLION EYES.

could suggest a special effects person. Ray Harryhausen and the cheaper Jaques Fresco were too expensive. One of Ackerman's clients was sci-fi magazine illustrator Paul Blaisdell, who graduated from the New England School of Art and Design with his wife Jackie. The couple lived in a secluded home in Topanga Canyon with a workshop where Blaisdell would create his monsters, aided by Mrs. Blaisdell. Blaisdell also did technical art for Douglas Aircraft, but it was his science-fiction images that stood out. He had illustrated one of Ackerman's sci-fi stories, making him an instant fan. Corman had to raise his effects budget from two hundred to four hundred dollars before Blaisdell showed any interest. Ackerman earned a percentage of the fee.

From liquid latex and modeling clay, Blaisdell made a cute eighteen-inch hand puppet nicknamed "Little Hercules" or "Herky" to represent the alien's slave. Since the alien fed on brains, its lackey had a bulbous banquet of gray matter resting above its eyes. One of its hands held a small ray gun. The wrists wore slave-like manacles with dangling chains and the body was costumed in a suit with a high glittery collar. Herky originally had wings on his back not seen in the picture. A large crowd of onlookers made it difficult for Blaisdell to handle the puppet and most of its footage would later be cut.

Blaisdell built a miniature spaceship that was initially rejected because David Kramasrsky wanted another one to match the large mock-up. Then Kramarsky changed

his mind and the first model was used. Lou Place set up a small studio where the mini-ship was to be launched by an intricate set of wires. A technician who had just finished lunch tripped over one, sending the model to the ceiling. When the actual takeoff was shot, Forry Ackerman pulled the string that made it fly.

Kramarsky wanted the film to be darkened so Herky would be *less* visible. A hypnotic spiral and a magnified single orb were superimposed around Herky to suggest the slave was projecting the will of its master.

Scenes without the alien were messily made, too. One day before the location scenes in Indio were to be done, the Union went after Corman, who told Kramarsky to hide until he could join the Union. Two days were needed for interiors. Corman directed them on a sound stage, replacing the first cameraman, UCLA film instructor Everett Baker, with Floyd Crosby. The art director was Albert Ruddy, who would produce the *Godfather* films of future Corman alumnus, Francis Ford Coppola. The main set dressing consisted of girlie mag pages in the photo-plastered room of horny "Him".

Baker's cinematography was the most interesting. Bleached, grainy and shaky like day exteriors in an old thirties outdoor independent, some of his scenes had the same degree of suffusive starkness that hostile landscape has to a person deep in the throes of exposure. Setting the film off on a promising mood was an animated titles sequence by Paul Julian, fraught with complicity between the alien and the environment it ruled. It was here one could glimpse blinking multiple eyes.

Original music was a luxury, so *Beast* underscored scenes with selections from classic Wagner music that later found themselves in *The Brain Eaters* (the million-eyed beast and his people could have been called that).

Paul Birch, Dick Sargent and Chester Conklin were a microcosm of AIP cast types, Birch a strong character actor, Sargent a juvenile headed for fame (as Darrin Stephens on "Bewitched" following Dick York) and Conklin an old-timer in his dotage. Birch had a screen propensity for gloom and ponderous contemplation and his character, Alan, had patterns of the sterner Capt. Jim Maddison in Corman's *Day the World Ended* (1956). As in that film, the actor playing the resident freak was the most arresting performer and it was Leonard Tarver who was the Paul Dubov of *Beast*.

Preview audience comments on *Beast* were so dismal that Lou Place refused directing credit, which Corman gave to David Kramarsky. Kramarsky stayed active for a while as a copartner in two production units. Other than the undistinguished *Daddy-O* (1959), Lou Place was content to remain an assistant director.

Cheapness, fast payoff and a poster that whetted dashed expectations were all that helped *Beast With a Million Eyes* show a profit. Valuable as an object lesson for AIP, it convinced the company to stop making films aimed at supporting movies from other studios. Bankruptcy was averted when AIP began to make its own dual programs for all-or-nothing twin packages. Only a surface scratch of Paul Blaisdell's talent, Herky was adopted by Forry Ackerman, who kept him in his refrigerator. After a few years, the model deteriorated. A photo of Herky in decline was printed in Ackerman's "Spacemen" before the puppet was discarded.

14

Lorna Thayer runs for safety in THE BEAST WITH A MILLION EYES.

THE PHANTOM FROM TEN THOUSAND LEAGUES

American Releasing Corp., 1956

Producers-Film Editors	Jack Milner, Dan Milner
Director	Dan Milner
Screenplay	Lou Rusoff
Story	Dorys Lukather
Cinematography	Brydon Baker
Music	Ronald Stein
Art Director	Earl Harper
Production Supervisor	Byron Roberts
Sound	Frank Webster
Special Effects	Jack Milner
Technical Advisor	Alfred Hanson

A Milner Brothers Production
Running time: 71 minutes

Cast: Kent Taylor (Dr. Ted Stevens / Ted Baxter), Cathy Downs (Lois King), Micheal Whelan (Prof. King), Helene Stanton (Wanda), Philip Pine (George Thomas), Vivi Janiss (Ethel Hall), Rodney Bell (Bill Grant), Michael Garth (Sheriff), Pierce Lyden (Andy)

*T*he *Phantom From Ten Thousand Leagues* was the next AIP film after *Beast With a Million Eyes* hurt by subpar visuals, not enough monster and an overly exaggerated title. "Leagues" in this movie's name meant miles of descent, not travel length, and the "Phantom" appellation was odd for an marine animal menace unless it was to indicate that no one ever saw it above water. Pinched for cash, James Nicholson and Samuel Arkoff farmed the story out to film editors Dan and Jack Milner, loaning them writer Lou Rusoff, music composer Ronald Stein and Paul Blaisdell.

A fisherman casts his net near a glowing undersea uranium deposit. Guarding its shaft of light, the scaly phantom capsizes the fisherman's boat and drowns him. His radiation-burned body and the charred boat are found washed ashore by Prof. King, president of the Pacific College of Oceanography. Another man, Ted Baxter, sees King hastily leaving the scene. Ted is warned not to touch anything by Bill Grant, Special Investigator for the Defense Department. King's assistant, shifty George Thomas, approaches the spot with a spear gun.

(Above) Philip Pine and Helene Stanton in THE PHANTOM FROM 10,000 LEAGUES (1956).

Ted presents himself as a tourist. He has a letter of introduction from King and was en route to his home. Ted and Grant glimpse George lurking behind a bush and Grant orders him to show himself. Grant saw George at the College yesterday. George excuses the spear gun by saying he was going about his normal business. Grant tells him not to dive in this area or remember that Grant was ever here.

King comes home to his daughter, Lois. He has been working on breathtaking things and feels George and his secretary, Ethel Hall, have been spying on him. When Ted knocks, King asks Lois to say he has been in bed for over an hour. Meeting Lois, Ted notices King's wet shoe prints on the living room rug. The visit is an urgent one and he asks Lois to wake King up. She opens King's bedroom door, but he has left through an open window.

Ted watches King the next day as he runs a Geiger counter test on the rowboat. Grant confronts Ted, having learned he is really Dr. Ted Stevens, a known authority on radiation.

The College has been closed for vacation. Janitor Andy tells Ethel the fisherman's boat was found, but not his body. People blame the college for the Phantom killings. As King prepares to enter his locked lab, he takes two books from Ethel's desk. A slip of paper falls from one without him knowing it. George sees Ethel pick the paper up and plucks it out of her blouse pocket. It has scientific data. George compares the information to the computations of a formula. He wants Ethel to help him get into the lab. It would be worth money to her. When Ethel threatens to tell King, George levels the point of a spear gun at her as a mild threat and puts it back on the rack.

While Ted takes a test dive in the place where the fisherman died, King places a small turtle in a water tank and exposes it to radiation. Ted sees both the underwater light and the Phantom. On shore, Lois is about to take a swim, but Ted gently dissuades her.

Ethel snoops by the lab door until King tells her to get some nautical charts from the supply room. Ted calls on King, wanting a detailed study of the ocean in this area. King will bring the material to his home and Ted can wait for him there. King knows that Ted is working with Grant. Turning to go, Ted sees the shadow of eavesdropping Ethel by the office door and tells her to come in. King reprimands Ethel for her blatant prying. In the lab, he removes from his satchel a book on radiation that Ted wrote under his real name — Dr. Ted Stevens.

While Lois takes a shower, Ted knocks on the front door of the King house, but is not heard. He relaxes on a couch and Lois reacts with embarrassment when she steps out of the bathroom wrapped in a towel. Ted helps Lois zip up the back of her dress, when King arrives with the maps Ted wanted, calling him Dr. Stevens. Apologizing for the ruse, Ted mentions the atomic light and the Phantom. He has experimented with the

activation of hydrogen isotopes in heavy water. The submerged uranium deposit has created this effect on a larger scale. Some creature exposed to the light mutated and lives off the light. Ted created a mutant of his own, but destroyed it. The creator of this weapon may have offered it to the highest bidder. King feels Ted has an overactive imagination. Grant phones. He wants to take a test dive with College equipment tomorrow. King's concern for Grant belies his skepticism of the Phantom.

George rendezvous with his sultry foreign spy lover, Wanda. She is to bring information on King's work to Antwerp in two days — all the time George has to procure it. He will meet Wanda at the designated time at Colby's Point. To eliminate Ted and Grant, George puts poison in the mouthpieces of their scuba gear. Ethel meets Grant at a roadhouse to accuse King of treason. She hates King because her student son died in a squall while gathering specimens for him. Needing proof of her allegation, Grant will show Ethel how to make a wax impression of the lab locks. Wanda overhears from the next booth.

Another King student and his girl go diving while Ted steps out with Lois. Returning to their boat, the kids are killed by the Phantom. Ted and Lois find the bodies and Ted tells Lois to get Grant. George fires his spear gun at Ted, but misses and escapes. Ted collects the spear. At the County Morgue, Grant and Ted view the dead youths. Grant has learned that Washington had also assigned Ted to this case. Initialled as College property, the spear will be dusted for fingerprints. Ted discloses to Grant the existences of the light and the Phantom.

Before Ted and Grant can enter the water, Grant reacts to the poison capsule meant for him. He gets his breath back as Ted instinctively removes the capsules from both sets of mouthpieces. Bringing a Geiger counter, Ted tests the light before he and Grant brush with the Phantom. Grant fires a spear at it. On shore, Grant decides to arrest King and George both, but the knowledge that went into the light is the real danger.

Ethel notices that George's spear gun is missing. George says King took it out. Ethel knows he is lying and still refuses to help him enter the lab. Ted tells King about the Phantom, but King still feigns disbelief. At Colby's Point, Wanda tells George she saw Ethel with Grant and heard his name mentioned. Ethel is working late at the College. In the lab, King sees keys lying on the floor and realizes someone else has been here. He shows the keys to Ethel, who defensively exits. King becomes aware of the missing spear gun. With it, George kills Ethel on the beach. King joins Ted and Lois at home, where Grant and the Sheriff report Ethel's murder and what device was used. Although under suspicion, King is not formally charged.

While Ted and Grant await the Sheriff's report on the spear prints, Grant resolves to get into the lab. He presents the notes Ethel copied from King's paper. The

Sheriff says the fingerprints belonged to missing George. The spear gun was left in his car. The Sheriff knows how to get George. Wanda is arrested. When a tanker passes over the light, Ted and Lois witness its explosion. King sees the glare from his office window. Ted confronts King about his Phantom cover-up, expecting him to surrender in one hour.

Guilt-wracked King burns his papers and wrecks his equipment. Andy enters the lab and sees the stillborn mutant King created from the turtle. George goes to Colby's Point to see Wanda. Grant jumps out from behind her beach parasol and hits him. The Sheriff charges George with homicide. King places an underwater bomb near the light. The Phantom grabs him and the blast kills them both, burying the uranium. Ted makes Lois understand King's sacrifice.

Like the mutants of *Day the World Ended*, the film *Phantom From Ten Thousand Leagues* supported, the Phantom subsisted on the same atomic poison that created it . . . taking energy in a purely concentrated form the way plants thrive on sunlight. The Phantom killed mainly to protect its food source, so its attacks were adequately motivated, but preferring to stay close to the light, the Phantom had to wait for its prey to come close to *it*. The thing was too sequestered to be a threat to anyone else. In all this muddled spy-ence fiction, which took off from a cleverly conceived relationship and the power that gave it birth, the *cause* of the Phantom's being was more important than the product.

Edgy, irritable King was painted as a gruff eccentric — yet his science, at least at the outset, was no more "mad" than the prototype experiments of Ted, who doused the light of his "phantom" before it could do any harm. King's mutant was apparently by accident, but he regarded it with the interest of a willful creator. Only he and Ted had any emotional feelings about the Phantom. Everyone else was thoroughly immersed in all the cloak-and-dagger except Andy and Lois, the loyal but mostly superfluous daughter. It took the destruction of an entire ship to spur King into eradicating his mistakes, since he lacked any real sense of guilt about the victims of the Phantom who bought the kelp farm.

The patented contours of monstrousness seen in Paul Blaisdell's other creatures were lacking in the Phantom. Photographed in the waters off Catalina, it barely approximated the cross between a white salamander and a sea serpent that was its ad art conception. Underwater cameraman Al Hanson's wife tested the costume and nearly drowned when it got snagged in a kelp bed. Hanson played the Phantom and put rocks where they could keep the feet down. When Ted advised Lois not to go into the water, he cheated the film Phantom of its opportunity to act out the poster pose of the paper one menacing a bikinied girl diver.

All the players were capable except Helene Stanton. Strictly a layabout swim-suited Mata Hari, she was a bomb blondshell — her fake Slavic accent almost as disconcerting as the sight of Kent Taylor minus his trademark mustache.

Nicholson and Arkoff liked *The Phantom From Ten Thousand Leagues* about as much as Joe Levine liked *Beast With a Million Eyes*. Thanks to the top half *Day the World Ended*, AIP's first double bill was a roaring success. Despite the inferiority of their movie, the Milner brothers were able to make one more film. That was the silly but occasionally exciting *From Hell It Came*, which not only had some diverting camp but a sense of deliberate humor, too.

17

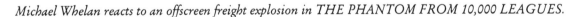

Michael Whelan reacts to an offscreen freight explosion in THE PHANTOM FROM 10,000 LEAGUES.

The Screen's Master of the WEIRD...
IN HIS NEWEST and MOST DARING

BELA LUGOSI

More Horrifying than "DRACULA"
..."FRANKENSTEIN!"

BRIDE OF THE MONSTER

TOR JOHNSON · TONY McCOY

with LORETTA KING · HARVEY DUNN

BRIDE OF THE MONSTER

Banner / Distributors Corp. of America, 1956
Premiered in 1955 as *Bride of the Atom*

Executive Producer	Donald E. McCoy
Producer-Director	Edward D. Wood, Jr
Story-Screenplay	Edward D. Wood, Jr
	Alex Gordon
Associate Producer	Tony McCoy
Cinematography	William C. Thompson
	Ted Allen
Film Editor	Mike Adams
Music	Frank Worth
Assistant Directors	Bob Farfan
	William Nolte
Camera Operator	Bert Shipham
Electrician	Louis Kriger
Makeup	Louis J. Haszillo
	Maurice Seiderman
Key Grip	Thomas Connelly
Special Effects	Pat Dinga
Property Master	George Bahr
Technical Advisor	Igo Kantor
Sound	Dale Knight

Sound Effects	Lyle Willey
	Mike Pollack

A Rolling M. Production
Running time: 68 minutes

Cast: Bela Lugosi (Dr. Eric Vornoff), Tor Johnson (Lobo), Tony McCoy (Lt. Dick Craig), Loretta King (Janet Lawton), Harvey B. Dunn (Capt. Robbins), George Becwar (Prof. Strowski), Paul Marco (Kelton), Don Nagel (Det, Martin), Bud Osborne (Jake), John Warren (Mac), Ann Wilner (Tillie), Delores Fuller (Marge), William Benedict (Newsboy), Ben Frommer (Drunk)

Bela Lugosi's slide into Poverty Row left him poor, elderly and drug-addicted. In Alex Gordon and Edward D. Wood, Jr., he had two loyal friends who tried to keep him working. In 1948, Gordon wrote a story for Lugosi called *The Atomic Monster*. He and Wood first united when Wood was doing script and production work on cowboy actor-producer John

(Above) Dramatic poster art for Ed Wood's BRIDE OF THE MONSTER (1956).

Carpenter's *The Lawless Rider* (1954). Then a lawyer, Samuel Arkoff, was introduced to Wood and Gordon when some legal matters hampered the film.

After Wood directed Lugosi in *Glen — or Glenda?* (1953) and filmed *Jailbait* (1954), co-written by Gordon, he took the *Atomic Monster* story (Gordon claims he authored an entire screenplay of his own) and secured Lugosi and Tor Johnson. William Beaudine the first director, slated the idea and it was taken to Realart Pictures chief Jack Broder, whose sales manager was James Nicholson. Broder rejected Wood's script (which Wood also credited to Alex Gordon), but used its name for the 1953 reissue of *Man-Made Monster* (1941). Wood and Gordon hired Sam Arkoff, who forced Broder to pay them two hundred dollars in restitution.

The name of the script was changed to *Monster of the Marshes*, then *Bride of the Atom*. Wood and Gordon developed several other stories and screenplays. New York distributor Eliot Hyman convinced Steve Broidy (president of Allied Artists when it was still Monogram) that Lugosi and Boris Karloff could do a horror twin bill. Broidy wanted Karloff for *Bride* and intended a project called *Dr. Voodoo* to star Lugosi and Lon Chaney. Lugosi and Karloff agreed to this, but Broidy decided to back the deal only if Ford Beebe wrote and directed two more scripts. One film would be a vampire movie with Lugosi and Chaney, the other a Karloff vehicle. The deal collapsed when Allied wanted a single feature with all three actors. Lou Rusoff wrote a treatment, but at the last minute Allied backed out.

While Gordon was handling an English publicity tour with Gene Autry, Wood went ahead with *Bride*. When actor George Becwar complained to the Screen Actors Guild that Wood underpaid him, even though Becwar had agreed to the specified amount, production was shut down. Spent capital also delayed filming until Arizonian Donald E. McCoy, owner of Packing Service Corps., sponsored the rest under the aegis of Rolling M. Productions. At his insistence, McCoy's son Tony played the hero and became an associate producer — and McCoy wanted the film to end with an atomic explosion.

Lost hunters Jake Long and Lafe McCrea hide under a tree during the latest — and worst — storm to hit Lake Marsh, where a "monster" has taken ten people. Lightning strikes dangerously close. Jake suggests going to the old Willows place, a house supposedly deserted for fifteen years. The idea spooks Mac. They are surprised to see lights on in the house. Jake knocks at the front door and the pair meet ominous, inhospitable Dr. Eric Vornoff. When Jake and Mac refuse to leave, Vornoff calls his brawny slave Lobo. "The monster!" cries Jake before he and Mac run. "Do you hear that, Lobo?" laughs Vornoff, "You are the monster!" To Jake and Mac, he shouts, "Perhaps one day you *will* meet the monster!" Vornoff sends Lobo after them.

Behind a secret fireplace door is Vornoff's lab. He dons a white coat, tests his atomic ray machine and goes to the window of a water tank where he keeps a giant octopus. Exhausted Mac collapses by the lake, where the octopus seizes him in its tentacles. Jake fires his rifle at it until Lobo grabs him from behind.

Jake awakens to find himself strapped under Vorloff's ray and demands that mute Lobo free him. Pseudo-cordial, Vornoff notices a bruise on Jake's neck and slaps Lobo for being too rough. "You will soon be as big as a giant," Vornoff tells Jake as he starts his device, ". . . the strength of twenty men . . . or — like all the others — dead!" Screaming, Jake dies. Lamenting his latest failure, Vornoff finds solace in seeing the octopus swim home.

"Monster Strikes Again" and "Monster Takes Two" shriek the headlines. At Police Headquarters, Officer Kelton tries to question a belligerent drunk found in the swamp who is hauled off to Vagrancy. Kelton hassles a newsboy with late edition papers, taking them to Capt. Tom Robbins of Homicide. Anxious to work on the Monster case, Kelton is turned down. Robbins asks for Lt. Dick Craig, who studies Mac's raincoat and Jake's fired rifle. Twelve have vanished in the past three months. Writer of the monster stories, Dick's intrusive fiancee, reporter Janet Lawton, is peeved at elusive Dick and breaks their engagement. She thinks the police are suppressing news. Convinced there is a monster, Janet plans to visit Lake Marsh over Dick's objections.

In the newspaper real estate office, Janet learns that Vornoff bought the Willows house in December of 1948. On something hot, she asks Tillie, the file clerk, to make up a story for her boss and Dick explaining why she will be gone. Janet runs into a friend, Marge, who warns that the boss wants the monster stories eighty-sixed, but Janet pretends she did not hear her.

In his office, Robbins introduces Dick to Prof. Vladimir Strowski, an enigmatic expert on monsters like the one at the Loch Ness. Discounting Dick's theory that the Loch Ness Monster crossed the ocean and moved to Lake Marsh, Strowski wants to visit the lake. He seems slightly nervous when Robbins offers the assistance of Dick. Dick and Strowski will meet here at ten o'clock tomorrow morning. "Until morning, Lieutenant Craig," says creepy Strowski as he leaves to return to his hotel. Dick finds him strange. "Watch him, Dick," advises distrustful Robbins. Dick expects to go out with Janet tonight, but Robbins relays news of her prepared excuse.

New storm clouds form above Lake Marsh. Negotiating a bumpy dirt road, Janet blows a tire, skids off the road and hits a tree on top of a short embankment. Unhurt, Janet sits on a fender of the car and faints when she sees a snake that Lobo kills. Lobo swipes Janet's hat and takes her to Vornoff. She awakens to meet Vornoff, who hypnotically sedates her. "You will sleep. For the lovely young lady, sleep . . . sleep . . ."

Looking for Strowski, Dick and Det. Martin stop at

19

a forked road and note the unnatural — possibly atomic — atmospheric conditions. Why did Strowski make an appointment to come out here, then fail to show? Up ahead is Janet's car. Strowski arrives at the swamp in a rental vehicle. Guided by a map, he trudges into the marsh. At a coffee joint, Dick calls Robbins, who wants Strowski found. Robbins phones the city desk of the paper to trace Janet's recent activities.

Janet wakes up to meet Vornoff again. He found her press card in her purse. Janet explains she came to see if he knows anything about the Lake Marsh mysteries. She cowers when Lobo enters with a tray of food. Enraptured Lobo tries to touch Janet until Vornoff brutally whips him. Vornoff found Lobo in the mountains of Tibet. Janet becomes defensive until Vornoff hypnotizes her. "Lobo!" he commands. "Take the girl to my quarters!"

Stowski enters the house and in the living room is reunited with Vornoff. Twenty years ago, Vornoff was exiled from Russia for his idea that nuclear power can create super-beings. Strowski later confirmed Vornoff's findings and has traced him all the way from Europe. "Now I am here, sent to bring you home." "Home?" seethes embittered Vornoff. "I have no home. Abandoned, despised, living like an animal. The jungle is my home . . . I'll show the world that I can be its master. I will perfect my own race of people, a race of atomic supermen which will conquer the world." Ordered to bring Vornoff back, Strowski pulls a gun, but Lobo overpowers him. Dragged into the lab, he is thrown to the octopus. "Your country offers fame and fortune for my return," Vornoff says, "but my price is so much more great. You will disappear, Professor Strowski, just as all the others have disappeared."

Dick and Marty locate Strowski's car. Alone, Dick heads for the house. He falls into a pit and shoots at menacing alligators until he works himself free. At the real estate office, Robbins ascertains where Janet is. Ready for Janet, Vornoff telepathically ushers her into the lab. She wears a white gown. Reaching the house, Dick finds Strowski's briefcase with photos of Vornoff, his cap and stumbles across the secret door. Out of her trance, Janet is told by Vornoff, "It hurts . . . only for a moment. And then, you will emerge a woman of superior strength and beauty - the *Bride of the Atom!*" Dick tries to stop the "wedding" until Lobo comes back from getting some equipment and slugs him.

Robbins and some men join Marty. Dick is chained up to watch the experiment. Lobo turns on Vornoff completely, impervious to his fired bullets. Lobo renders Vornoff unconscious and frees Janet, who releases Dick. Lobo turns the ray on Vornoff. Dick orders Lobo at gunpoint to turn it off. He fires a shot grazing Lobo's forehead and Lobo makes a floor mop out of him. Robbins and Marty break into the house. Now superhuman, Vornoff snaps his straps and hurls Lobo into a bank of conflagrating equipment. Robbins and Marty flee smoke as Vornoff kidnaps Janet. Dick leaps across the flames, joining the other cops, who spot Vornoff. When he sets Janet down, they open fire. A bolt of lightning destroys the house.

Inept Kelton stumbles, breaking his leg. To save him, Dick rolls a huge boulder down on advancing Vornoff, who falls into the lake. He and the octopus struggle until another lightning bolt triggers a nuclear reaction — turning them into a mushroom cloud. Robbins intones, "He tampered in God's domain."

Had it gone into production immediately, *Bride of the Monster* might have been the very first film about nuclear creatures. When Ed Wood got hold of Alex Gordon's story, the property became Nostalgia as a tacky but deeply felt recapitulation of every mad doctor cliche pertinent to the work of Bela Lugosi. The Soviet origin of Vornoff afforded a political tone while the Lake Marsh monster — the octopus — was capriciously linked to Nessie (Loch Ness had been one of Vornoff's earlier residences). The story *read* like a Wood original, but it was Gordon's concept down to the presence of Lobo, whom Wood retained in *Night of the Ghouls* and who appeared in Brooke E. Peter's *The Unearthly*.

Whatever troubled mankind in Wood's films evolved from a controlled power that both struck with cold deliberation — as in the intent of Vornoff's experiments — and left eerie earmarks around outwardly normal surroundings . . . such as the ecological disruption of Lake Marsh. The power always went haywire, as in Vornoff's ironic transformation and his reckoning with the octopus, destroying the user or users in a boomerang effect.

Monster of the Marshes aptly described the octopus — the "official" monster. *Bride of the Atom* signified Vornoff's designs on Janet. He himself did not become a monster until the climax and only he would have wanted a bride. Lobo was from Tibet, but Lobo means "wolf" in Spanish.

Flexible substitutions were Wood's forte. In the Alex Gordon Version of *Bride* was a middle-aged desk sergeant name O'Reilley. Paul Marco, a young actor discovered by future Wood player Criswell, did not "look" like an O'Reilley and he was too youthful to play a sergeant.. Marge Usher, the agent who handled Marco, suggested the moniker Kelton from her Kelton Avenue address, and Kelton was developed as a clumsy novice cop to provide some intentional comedy.

The technical compromises in *Bride of the Monster* centered mainly around the lab set and the octopus. An Omega photo-enlarger was the atomic "ray", some of the lab walls had painted masonry patterns and, doubling as a kitchen it would appear, the place had a refrigerator and stove. One of the chemical props was a bottle of Pepto Bismol! The upper ray table straps could not restrain arms, so subjects had to wear handcuffs. Also, they wore a silver bowl with a chin strap and light bulbs. Only on the head of John Warren, who played Jake, was

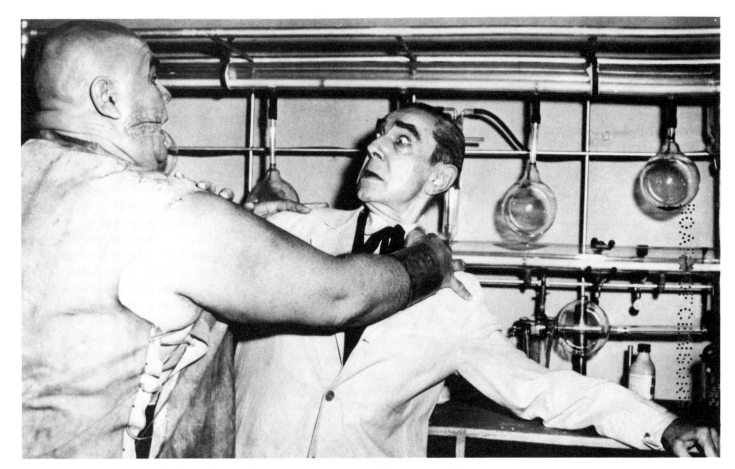

Tor Johnson latches onto the legendary Bela Lugosi in BRIDE OF THE MONSTER.

Bud Osborne is siezed by the obvious rubber tentacles of the giant octopus in BRIDE OF THE MONSTER.

Tor Johnson attacks John Warren in BRIDE OF THE MONSTER.

the bowl a tight fit. The water tank window Vornoff peered into had a fish tank behind it. The live octopus was an aquarium specimen while surface action used the stolen mechanical octopus John Wayne battled in *Wake of the Red Witch* (1948). Lacking a motor and a tentacle that broke off, it forced Lugosi and Bud Osborne to wrap the other tentacles around themselves. The "lake" was an artificially dammed-up stream in Griffith Park. Home for the mechanical octopus was a dry cubicle where an invisible wire was used to give one raised tentacle a semblance of life.

Janet's paper must have paid slave wages since her car was an old 1938 Chevy sedan. Strapped to its roof, Wood poured water from a gardening can onto the windshield to create "rain". The only time Lake Marsh looked swampy was when Wood inserted a panning film clip of jungle flora. The exterior of the coffee ship was a full indoor set with no cars or people around, wasting money and materials that would have been better spent upgrading the fantasy gimmicks.

Atomic bride-to-be Janet's wedding gown was not only a subtle reference to Wood's transvestitism but also a near-literal interpretation of a "planned" marriage. Vornoff had probably never left the house in years — so where did *he* get it? Losing his shirt to Lobo during their fight, Dick wore suspenders over his bare chest. Eddie Parker, Lugosi's double in *Frankenstein Meets the Wolf Man* (1943), was the much taller atomic Vornoff. A bewildered-looking Lugosi wore scar makeup in several close-ups (one of the two makeup artists was the distinguished Maurice Seiderman).

The Griffith Park scenes shot at night, done with firemen present were hell for everybody — particularly addict Lugosi, who felt a sudden need for his "medicine". Usually the man who drove Lugosi to his drug suppliers, Wood was too busy setting up the next scene to take Lugosi to his nearby apartment. Lugosi did not like riding with unfamiliar substitute chauffeurs, but accepted a lift from Paul Marco. At the apartment, Marco was forced to watch as Lugosi prepared his drug injection with methodical ritual. Once "well" he was ready to return to work. When the fire chief at Griffith made a fuss about the blocked stream, a prop man banged a hole in the dam and the water flooded an adjacent golf course.

The Lake Marsh cinematography and dialogue alluding to its primitive conditions afforded some atmosphere. The storm thunder was so loud the many of Jake and Mac's lines were rendered inaudible. The Willows house was a city residence with a canvas tarp erected behind it to look like an isolated country home. Frank Worth's hard-pumping Max Steinerish score was enjoyably anachronistic.

If *Bride of the Monster* showed more of Bela Lugosi the suffering human being than any other film, it was also a vindication of the talent that many outside of the warm, supportive Wood circle no longer took seriously. The dream of one lonely old scientist to rule the world seemed not only antiquated but senile and the Lugosian touch of hammy hypnosis was an expedient recall of *Dracula*. All of this helped establish Vornoff as a broken remnant of Lugosi's earlier test tube megalomaniacs. When Vornoff and Strowski meet, Lugosi communicated some of his personal pain through Vornoff's wounded animal rancor — expressing such details of coincidental misery as loss of professional respect and separation from his family.

Lobo and Kelton "made" the film reputations of Tor Johnson and Paul Marco. Even after he quit movies, Johnson continued the Lobo persona in live performances and a Lobo-like mask of Johnson's face has appeared in at least four films. In subsequent Wood pictures, Kelton became a whiny paranoid malcontent and department scapegoat whose woeful memories of monster encounters gave the films their connecting passages.

Capt. Robbins was played by Harvey B. Dunne, a party clown who entertained kids using a trick bird. As Robbins, Dunne had the opportunity to play with a parakeet. Don Nagel, who played Marty, was another perennial Wood cop. Bud Osborne had worked in Wood's favorite movie genre, westerns, and Ben Frommer, stealing a snatch of dialogue from *Dillinger* (1945) to establish the belligerence of the drunk, came from Vaudeville.

Tony McCoy and Loretta King, who brought much ego but little talent to their roles, visited Lugosi while he was undergoing drug treatment and Lugosi was duped into thinking his next Wood film would be *The Phantom Ghoul* or *The Ghoul Goes West*. Lon Chaney, Tor Johnson and Gene Autry were supposed to co-star. Never progressing beyond a first draft script, the story was a semi-*Bride of the Monster* rehash about a mad undertaker name Prof. Smoke, who used cadaver gland extracts to create a pair of giants named Karl and Tanz. Smoke resided in a castle transplanted from Scotland. The *West* title and the relocation of a Scottish castle came from an actual picture of 1936, *The Ghost Goes West*. Thus the only materialized follow-up to *Bride*, also written for Lugosi, was *Night of the Ghouls*.

THE SCREAM THAT SHOCKS THE SCREEN WITH
300,000 VOLTS OF
INHUMAN!
INVINCIBLE!
INESCAPABLE!
Indestructible
MAN
starring
LON CHANEY
with
MARIAN CARR
Casey Adams • Ross Elliot
An ALLIED ARTISTS Picture
PRODUCED AND DIRECTED BY
JACK POLLEXFEN
SCREENPLAY BY
VY RUSSELL AND SUE BRADFORD

THE INDESTRUCTIBLE MAN

Allied Artists, 1956

Producer-Director	Jack Pollexfen
Screenplay	Vy Russell
	Sue Dwiggins
	(and Jack Pollexfen)
Cinematography	John Russell, Jr.
Film Editor	Fred Fetishans, Jr.
Music Director	Albert Glasser
Art Director	Ted Holsopple
Production Manager	Chris Beute

A CGK Production
Running time: 70 minutes

Cast: Lon Chaney (The Butcher), Casey Adams *aka Max* Showalter (Lt. Chasen), Marian Carr (Eva Martin), Ross Elliott (Paul Lowe), Stuart Randall (Capt. Lauder), Kenneth Terrell (Joe Marcella), Robert Shayne (Dr. Bradshaw), Marvin Ellis (Squeamy Ellis), Robert Foulk, Roy Engel, Peggy Maley, Marhorie Stapp, Madge Cleveland

In *The Walking Dead* (1936), Boris Karloff was John Ellman, an ex-con framed for the mob hit on a prominent judge. Put to death, John was temporarily snatched from the more blissful hereafter by the resurrection experiment of one Dr. Beaumont. John drove his enemies to their deaths by his mere presence, except for two who died by vehicular electrocution. As Dan McCormick in *Man-Made Monster*, Lon Chaney was the lone survivor of a similar accident. Dan's natural immunity to electricity make him the pawn of Dr. Paul Rigas, who turned Dan into a human dynamo and had Dan charged with murder so he could absorb the full wattage of the hot seat.

Dan and John were good men cursed by bad luck. Until his nine lives ran out, the psycho Richard Basehart played in *He Walked By Night* (1947) terrorized Los Angeles with a depraved abandon fully warranting his mad dog dispatch. Neither a scapegoat innocent like John Ellman and Dan McCormick or a thrill killer like Basehart's night walker, Charles "Butcher" Benton lived for revenge, a stolen payroll of six hundred thousand dollars and the affections of a sweet stripper — she the third priority, the money the second and retribution the first. The Butcher was, until his final demise, *The Indestructible Man*. A horror tangent of the late forties police docudramas started by *He Walked By Night*, *Indestructible Man* found Lon Chaney in a combination of all the films mentioned.

Lt. Dick Chasen has spent a year trying to recover the armored car loot stolen by the Butcher, Squeamy Ellis and Joe Marcella. The Butcher killed a guard and was condemned on the testimony of Squeamy and Joe. On San Quentin's Death Row, the Butcher confers with his lawyer, heist mastermind Paul Lowe. His appeal rejected, the Butcher refuses to say where he hid the money, vowing to kill Lowe, Squeamy and Joe.

Dick sees Follies headliner Eva Martin, who knew the Butcher, but still maintains she knows nothing about the whereabouts of the money. Surveilled by Dick, Lowe visits her for the same reason. A radio announces the Butcher's execution. He left Eva an envelope to be opened after his death. When Eva goes on, Lowe finds in it a city sewer map with the money spot marked. He purloins the map and substitutes a fifty dollar bill.

In San Francisco, Dr. Bradshaw, a biochemist, waits for his assistant to bring the Butcher's body to their lab in the basement of a power receiving station so they can experiment with it. With six hundred eighty-seven volts, Bradshaw inadvertently revives the Butcher. The energy has burned out his vocal cords. Bradshaw thinks the revival is just a temporary reaction. He wants to take a blood sample, but the needle of his syringe bends against the Butcher's arm. His whole body is a solid mass of cells. When Bradshaw proposes getting the blood surgically, the Butcher strangles both him and his assistant simultaneously.

Off-duty, Dick shows a personal interest in Eva. The Butcher's real girl had been a former roommate and he took Eva on the rebound. She was unaware of the Butcher's involvement in crime until his arrest. Dick is determined to expose Lowe.

Wandering down a highway, the Butcher sees a sexy brunette posed provocatively by a convertible with a flat tire. Its owner, flamboyant carnival man Carny, was using the girl as bait. To help in fixing the tire, the Butcher raises the front end of the car with enormous strength. Carny sees a profit in the Butcher, who brutally stomps him before the eyes of the stunned girl and steals the car. Police are on the lookout for a maniac. At a roadblock, two Highway Patrol cops stop a driver. The Butcher skids to a sudden halt in the convertible and massacres the officers. The motorist flees into the woods as the Butcher takes his car and continues south to Los Angeles.

In her dressing room at the Follies, Eva is awestruck by the appearance of the Butcher. To let Eva know it is him, he rolls up the sleeve of the arm with his tattoo initials. Eva notices the bullet holes in the Butcher's shirt and no marks on his chest. The Butcher shows his new strength by lunging a pair of scissors against his unharmed hand. He turns to the envelope, finding Lowe's bill instead of the map. Eva innocently thought the Butcher had left the fifty. She mentions that Lowe was here and the Butcher makes a furious exit. Unable to catch him on the street, Eva calls the police, asking for Dick, who is out. She warns that the Butcher is alive

25

Poster art for THE INDESTRUCTIBLE MAN (1956).

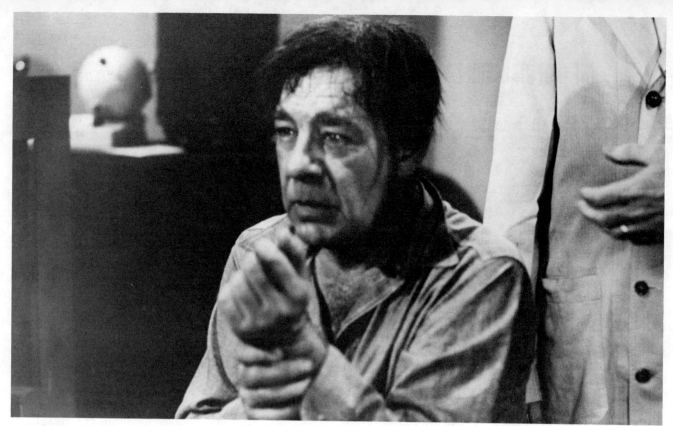

Lon Chaney, Jr. feels his false pulse in THE INDESTRUCTIBLE MAN.

and bullets can't stop him. Eva then phones Squeamy, who doesn't buy her story that the Butcher is back. Rather, he thinks the Butcher hired an assassin.

Dick and Capt. Lauder study the stamped-in fingerprints the Butcher had left on the steering wheel of one car. Only a twin brother, they believe, could have identical prints. A Sergeant informs them of Eva's call. Eva heads for Squeamy's boarding house by tram car. He escapes before the Butcher arrives. Joe is hobbling down the street on his crutches. He sees the Butcher coming and tries to escape, but the Butcher hurls Joe to his death down a steep stone stairway. A cop who confronts the Butcher is immediately killed.

The Butcher goes to Lowe's empty office. Squeamy comes out the elevator and frantically pumps lead into the Butcher. A woman screams as Squeamy is thrown to the ground floor. Descriptions of the killer by witnesses convince Dick and Lauder that the Butcher lives.

San Francisco sends information on the return of the Butcher. A morgue attendant broke down and admitted he sold the Butcher's body for some quick cash to an unidentified man. The corpses of Bradshaw and his assistant were located in the power station. Bradshaw left a notebook indicating he was trying to find a cure for cancer. Dick hopes to contact a Prof. Dwiggins of Cal Tech for more on this. The Butcher has struck again out in the Valley. He killed a man who walked away from his girl after a fight.

Lowe hears a description of the butcher on his car radio. Eva is not at the Follies and Lowe finds her at police headquarters, where Eva tells Lowe what happened to Squeamy and Joe. Dick thinks the Butcher is after the money and wants Lowe to confess to his part in the robbery. Lowe demands protection because the Butcher had threatened him. Refused, Lowe punches the Sergeant so he can be jailed for assault. Dick and Lauder dismiss the charge to make Lowe talk.

Police squads race to all entrances as the Butcher moves through the sewers. Crouched by a drain opening, he overhears Dick say that he contacted Prof. Dwiggins, who thinks fire may kill the Butcher. Dick and Lauder lead separate search teams. Dick has trouble reading his map and his party backtracks. They hear the Butcher rip open the steel box where he put the money. He piles it onto his spread-out jacket when he is surrounded. The Butcher resists and a bazooka blast wounds him in the abdomen. He recoils from a flame thrower that sears his face. Crawling out of a manhole, the Butcher retreats to a power station. He boards and activates an electric scaffold. When a dangling steel hook brushes against an electrode, the intense current fries him.

Case closed. Not completely — Dick has gotten Eva fired from the Follies so he can propose to her. She accepts, of course.

As a film approximating realist conventions, *Indestructible Man* did not do too badly. Effectively, it established milieu with such icons of flatfoot fiction as the seedy Bunker Hill district, the Angel's Flight railway, the Bradbury Building and the local storm drains. A distinct homage to *Man-Made Monster* was when Dick called the Butcher "this monster-made man". Odd description. Dr. Bradshaw was no monster and his restoration of the Butcher was purely a fluke. Supposedly, the Butcher was mute in all scenes but his appearance on Death Row because alcohol had impaired Lon Chaney's dialogue memory and most of the sewer footage came out of *He Walked By Night*. The Butcher had met California's standard of capital punishment in cyanide — only to be raised by another means of execution in electricity — and, in a dual irony, he was killed again by an overdose of the latter.

There was a technical gaffe laugh on Paul Lowe: the holding pen he was put in at the police station was the same set for the Butcher's death cell! In case you thought Lowe got off easy, there was a cut scene where the Butcher crashed station security to kill Lowe, accidentally injuring Eva's arm. In the last scene of the film, Eva wore a sling and the dialogue mentioned her hospitalization.

Indestructible Man was one of the last films where Chaney had top-billing. As he had practically no lines, his emoting consisted mainly of mad bull mayhem, throwing people around like scarecrows and standing up to some pretty graphic gunfire. Otherwise, Chaney's most expressive acting was in his twitching eyes — mostly the same close-up repeated endlessly. Even as an unregenerate killer, Chaney managed to create a little sympathy for the Butcher in his reunion with Eva when Chaney flashed that endearing affectionate pooch smile of his.

Marian Carr had appeared in some of the strangest crime melodramas between 1954, when *The Indestructible Man* was made, and 1956. There was *Ring of Fear* (1954), a circus mystery with Mickey Spillane playing himself. His Mike Hammer thriller *Kiss Me Deadly* (1955) featured Carr as Friday Evello, and in *Nightmare* (1956), she was the enigmatic but nice blonde Kevin McCarthy picked up in a bar. Ever brusque and unctuous Ross Elliott was like an oil-coated Dick Haymes. Functionally passable as a cop, Max Showwalter, under his Casey Adams alias, was inclined to be gooey in Dick's romantic scenes. Robert Shayne took the part of Dr. Bradshaw between his appearances as Insp. Henderson on "Superman" and his assistant was Joe Flynn of "Mc Hale's Navy" and various Disney comedies.

Many of the Allied Artists films sold to TV had their short lengths padded out, starting with video-style teasers. Thus, *Indestructible Man* "began" with the Butcher's resurrection. Between the credits and story proper were inserted crawl prologues and, during them, the theme music was repeated. The theme of *Indestructible Man* had been used before in a Philo Vance film scored by Albert Glasser. Certain bits of action were replayed in jerky slow-motion.

It is interesting that Lon Chaney himself contracted cancer, as had his father, and lost his own voice. When young Lon died in 1973, *his* body wound up in a medical laboratory — but it was willed to science.

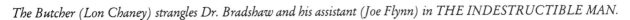

The Butcher (Lon Chaney) strangles Dr. Bradshaw and his assistant (Joe Flynn) in THE INDESTRUCTIBLE MAN.

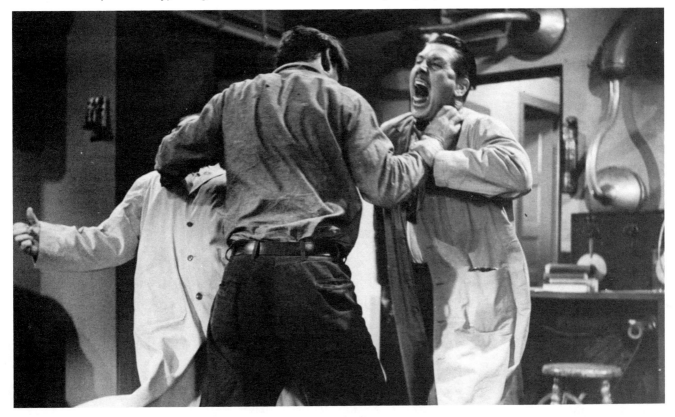

IT CONQUERED THE WORLD

American-International, 1956

Executive Producer	James H. Nicholson
Producer-Director	Roger Corman
Story-Screenplay	Charles B. Griffith
	(credited to Lou Rusoff)
Cinematography	Fred E. West
Film Editor	Charles Gross
Music	Ronald Stein
Production Manager	Lou Place
Music Editor	Jerry Irving
Sound	Jay Ashworth
Properties	Karl Brainard
Makeup	Larry Butterworth

A Sunset Production
Running time: 71 minutes

Cast: Peter Graves (Dr. Paul Nelson), Beverly Garland (Claire Anderson), Lee Van Cleef (Dr. Tom Anderson), Sally Fraser (Joan Nelson), Russ Bender (Gen. Pattick), Jonathan Haze (Pvt. Manuel Ortiz), Richard *aka Dick* Miller (Sgt. Neill), Taggart Casey (Chief Shalet), Paul Harbor (Roy), Karyne *aka Karen* Kadler (Ellen Peters), Charles Griffith (Pete Shelton), Marshall Bradford (Secy. Platt), Tom Jackson (George Haskell), David McMann *aka McMahon* (Gen. Tomlinson), Paul Blaisdell (Venusian Invader)

Charles Griffith was the son of Donna Dameral and grandson of Myrtle Vail, the stars of the hit radio show "Myrt and Marge". Hoping to become a lyricist, he wrote for television through the representation of Myrtle Vail's agent. A meeting with Roger Corman regulars Dick Miller, Jonathan Haze and Mel Welles led to Griffith showing several scripts to Corman. Corman hired him to write the unfilmed Portuguese-set *A Night in Heaven*, then an aborted western, *Girls of Hangtown Mesa*. Griffith's first produced script for Corman was *The Gunslinger* (1956), starring Corman's then-girlfriend Beverly Garland.

Originally called *It Conquered the Earth*, AIP's first sci-fi horror film made after the dissolution of the American Releasing label was more than a coincidental copy of *Invasion of the Body Snatchers* (1956) through its theme of identity-loss courtesy of vegetable-based alien life. Actually, the vegetable part of the Venusian's makeup was developed after the project started. It began because James Nicholson wanted to create an entirely original movie monstrosity. Due to scientific speculation then that Venus was a tropical planet with heavy gravity, Paul Blaisdell designed a thing similar to toadstools — although the creation on screen has often been likened to a cucumber as well as objects like a pointy witch's hat and an upsidedown ice cream cone in terms of blatant ridicule.

Because his brother in Canada was terminally ill, Lou Rusoff was too upset to write a shootable script. Charles Griffith filled in and wrote one in only three days, but in a sympathy gesture Rusoff (Sam Arkoff's brother-in-law) received official credit. Griffith was granted compensation by playing a scientist.

In the control room of a rocket station, radar technician Ellen Peters reports an unidentified object to Dr. Paul Nelson and his other assistants Pete and Roy. They are about to launch an Armed Forces satellite. All planes were supposedly cleared from the area twenty minutes ago. A transcontinental flight is off course. When it safely passes, Roy activates power. "And man is finally ready to move into space," heralds Paul.

Meanwhile, at the Pentagon, Secy. Platt introduces Gen. Tomlinson to eminent physicist Dr. Tom Anderson, who urges cancellation of the launching. He feels the satellite is a menace to the world. Ever since the Manhattan Project and when he ran the Perpetual Missile Program, Tom has warned the government against such a course. The small first satellite mysteriously exploded in orbit — a possible "warning" Tom fully anticipated three years earlier. "You said something about the other planets wanting to keep Earth in its place," remembers Platt. "To keep her out of the skies," elucidates Tom. "Alien intelligence watches us constantly. It will see this satellite of yours and know something must be done. I'm here to ask you — to *beg* you — to save your world!" The satellite is eight seconds from launching. Tom leaves in bitter frustration as takeoff follows.

Paul and wife Joan have dinner with Tom and his wife Claire at the Anderson's secluded country home. The satellite has been up for three months without incident and Paul smugly credits Tom with seeing his dire prophecy as an error. Paul senses that Tom is hiding a big secret. Claire reminds him he promised not to tell, but Tom takes Paul into the living room to undrape a powerful interplanetary radio. He tunes in harmonic signals from Venus. "Listen to it, Paul," urges Tom, referring to another sound. "Listen to the voice". Tom answers the ringing phone. It is for Paul. The installation notifies him that the satellite has suddenly vanished into deep space. Paul summons Joan. "I know what you're thinking, Tom," he says, "and I don't appreciate it".

The installation's chief security officer, Brig. Gen. Pattick, drives past main gate sentries Sgt. Neill and Pvt. Ortiz. He joins Pete, Ellen and Roy as they try to pick up the satellite's faint audio. When Paul arrives, Pete says, "It's back." There is silent tension between Tom and Claire, who weeps because Tom broke his promise. Going home, Paul leaves Pete to head tomorrow's

Lee Van Cleef is attacked by the Venusian creature in IT CONQUERED THE WORLD (1956).

recovery operation.

Tom is called from his bed by a message from his Venusian friend, who drew the satellite to Venus and will arrive soon. "Don't let your imagination bring itself to life," begs disbelieving Claire. "This is no image, darling," insists elated Tom. "It's what I've been predicting for years — and this is good instead of evil. That was my one uncertainty." Signing off, Tom will resume contact at dawn. He stays by the radio for the rest of the night.

From Washington the next day, Platt gives the go-ahead for recovery. The satellite inexplicably refuses to come down. Pattick orders it sent back up, but it abandons orbit and decelerates rapidly. The satellite crashes into the side of a mountain. The Venusian survives and contacts Tom. "You're a sick man," Claire tells him. "The whole world is sick," argues Tom, "— always has been. But that's all over now. At last, every dream of mankind can be realized." Tom asks Claire to phone Paul, but she leaves to go downtown, hoping Tom will be rational when she returns. Tom triangulates the area where the Venusian is, ten miles south of Beechwood.

Paul and Joan are driving down a country road in their convertible. Visible as a moving cone, the Venusian waddles away from the smoking wreckage of the satellite. It raises its clawed arms and wiggles its antennae — releasing impulses that de-energize all local power. A train stops on the tracks. The hands of a tower clock freeze. A record turntable stops spinning. An acetylene welder's torch flames out. Phones are out of order. Newspaper presses grind to a halt. Construction equipment is immobile. Traffic is halted.

Paul's car stalls and he looks under the hood. At the installation, Pattick expresses consternation over the power failure there. He tells his WAC aide to call Washington, but the line is dead. Before the equipment died, the satellite managed to send faint signals. "Sure is quiet out there," remarks Ellen. "It's always quiet in these mountains," Roy tells her. "Not *this* quiet," Ellen feels. Paul finds nothing wrong with his engine and Joan notices her wristwatch has stopped. She winds it up. They hear an overhead drone and see a falling plane explode in the air. Paul wants to time the disaster, but Joan's rewound watch and the car clock are frozen at three past three. "Coincidence?" wonders Paul. "I have a premonition," says Joan. They leave for Tom's house on foot.

Tom gives the Venusian a list of key personnel: Pattick, Mayor Townsend, Police Chief Shalet and Paul. They and their wives make eight the Venusian has prepared special devices for. Raising the broad base of its conical body, the Venusian releases the flying bat-shaped devices.

The citizens in downtown Beechwood feel the shock of their complete isolation. Newspaper editor George Haskell tells Claire that Tom had predicted something like this. Chief Shalet tries to maintain order. Down the street, Tom calls to Claire and is violently accosted by a hysterical man, who Tom fights with until Shalet pulls them apart. Tom ushers Claire to his hidden, still functioning car.

During their hike, Paul and Joan are startled by a fluttering device. Paul throws a rock and it flies away. At home, Tom tells Claire all power has been de-energized at its source — including water. Testing a garden hose, Claire sprays Tom, which works because it belongs to him.

A device swoops down on Shalet as he pushes a stalled car to a curbside. It stings the back of his neck and dies. Now possessed, Shalet deposits it in a trash can. Paul and Joan reach Tom and Claire, who invite them in for drinks. Paul wonders how Tom knew about their car. At Baker's Ridge, Pattick tries to fend off another device that stings him and dies too. Pattick hides his under a rock.

Paul has trouble accepting the existence of the Venusian, asking Tom, "Why aren't you fighting it?" "Because this superior intelligence happens to be a personal friend of mine," Tom answers. "Real chums," coldly interjects Claire. Tom reminds Paul of his dream of building a contained-gravitation spaceship. The idea was thwarted by government red tape — an example of progress-hindering stupidity. With the Venusian, Tom foresees, "the beginning of ultimate freedom. I predicted the possibility. I assist the benefactor." He cannot say how yet, but thinks Paul will be "with us very soon." "I'd have to take a long hard look at anything that could change the whole world — and me — so completely." Since the installation is inoperative, Tom will drive him and Joan home. They wait outside and Tom asks the Venusian to energize his car. Tom feels Paul did not panic because of logic. Claire feels that Paul's logic considers Tom to be insane. The Venusian has overhead everything. Tom tells him that Paul's mind is valuable.

At the installation, Pattick tells Neill and Manuel that there is martial law. This post will be abandoned. The soldiers will go on a reconnaissance march and check the terrain east of Baker's Ridge for sign of enemy activity. So they will know when to move out, Pattick gives Neill his reactivated wristwatch. Ellen, Pete and Roy are told there is a Communist uprising. They are under protective custody confined to their building. As Pattick exits, fine metallic strands can be seen protruding from the back of his neck.

At home, Paul and Joan test their failed power. Paul thinks Tom is trying to attach a pet theory to a natural disaster. "Don't you see? It vindicates him, proves to a laughing world that all his whimsies are accurate." "I see," agrees Joan, "a chance to regain face." Tom advises the Venusian to take refuge in Elephant Hot Springs Cave, where conditions are similar to those on Venus. Tom will stay here until after Beechwood is evacuated. From their front yard, Paul and Joan witness the frenzied

Joan Nelson (Sally Fraser) delivers a "present" to her husband in IT CONQUERED THE WORLD.

stampede of people. Paul forcibly detains one terrified man who says a camp has been set up in the desert.

During the Army march, Manuel sees a passing device. Distractedly, he bumps into Neill and says he saw a "funny-looking bird".

Paul believes the panic is being controlled. Taking a bicycle from his garage, he wants to go to the installation and tells Joan to stay indoors and close all windows. As Paul leaves, Joan turns to the sky as a device descends upon her. Shalet finds Haskell still in town. Haskell refuses to leave, even when Shalet pulls his gun. Paul sees Shalet callously gun Haskell down in cold blood. Shalet wants to arrest Paul. Resisting, Paul is pistol-whipped. Shalet receives a message from the Venusian. "You're to become one of us," he tells Paul, "You're free."

On his terrace, Tom studies a flying device through binoculars. He tells Claire the devices inject electronic receivers into people, then die like bees. "And the people," realizes Claire, ". . . they don't die. Only their minds." They are "the released". "Only the waste is gone," assures Tom, ". . . the hate, the bitterness, the dreams — all of the foolish nonsense." "And the emotions?" asks Claire. "Yes, the emotions," answers Tom. When he tries to embrace her, Claire shrinks away.

"I don't know why you should. It's a waste; an emotion. Tom, you can't rub the tarnish off of men's souls without losing a little of the silver." When Tom declares his undying love for her, Claire shouts, "Don't try and split games with your wife, darling. For a few dollars, you can hire a woman who will match your fetishes to perfection. And if you ever get tired of her, you can go down to the employment agency for another!"

At the closed installation, Paul meets Pattick, who says the others have been moved to the district air base. Paul and Joan are to join them there. Pattick offers Paul a ride back to town in his jeep. When Pattick's jeep starts, Paul expresses dismay. "New experimental model," jokes Pattick, "run by rubber bands." Paul points to a nonexistent rock in the middle of the road to catch Pattick off guard. Slugging him, Paul takes Pattick's gun and the jeep. Down the highway, the device meant for Paul takes several swoops. He scares it away with several shots.

Infuriated Paul confronts Tom, who admits he helped the Venusian. Eight others still inhabit Venus. "They're the last survivors of a race that was born too soon," explains Tom. "It evolved amid the boiling gases and eruptions of Venus — a planet that won't catch up to earth in perhaps a million years in climate." "A dying race," grasps Paul. "Throughout man's career," rationalizes Tom, "every great change, every sudden leap in his station has resulted in torment, chaos and death. The French Revolution brought democracy to Europe. Plagues have brought wondrous cures. War brought about fast planes, atomic power, radiological medicine — our own discoveries!" But those were human changes, argues Paul. The Venusian is not human and such changes have caused as many regressions. "Next to me," reveals Tom, "he wants you." Paul vows to fight the Venusian and Tom. "Your hands are human, but your mind is enemy. You're a traitor, Anderson. The worst traitor of all time! And do you know why? Because you're not betraying a part of mankind, you're betraying *all* of it!" Paul leaves and Tom regrets their rift. Claire mentions the gun she saw in Paul's coat pocket. "A gun?" asks Tom. "That's right, Tom! A gun!" blurts Claire, "You've just had an undeserved stay of execution!" Troubled, Tom wants to see the Venusian, who denies the request.

Paul comes home to Joan, who is in the bathroom, where she has been taking a makeshift shower. Paul is mildly alarmed by a window Joan left open for "fresh air". Smiling, Joan approaches Paul solicitously with her hands behind her back. They stretch out to reveal a "present" — his control device. As it chases Paul around the living room, Joan leaves to take a short walk. "When I come back, you'll feel much better." Paul snatches a fireplace poker and kills the device by impaling it against a wall. Tom calls. He just heard from the Venusian what happened, which means Paul cannot be controlled for a week. Tom wants to see Paul, who has some unfinished business.

Tom tells Claire that Paul must die because he knows what it is he is fighting. Paul removes Pattick's gun from the cabinet where he put it and hides it in his pocket as Joan returns. Feigning possession, Paul asks, "Will we be this way from now on?" "For the rest of our lives," blissfully replies Joan. Paul contemplates for a moment, then shoots Joan and breaks her fall with his arms.

Tom will kill Paul with a rifle when he arrives. When he shuts the curtains of his radio, Claire battles him mercilessly. "Suppose your boss wants you to run downtown and cut out a few hearts? He might get mad when he can't reach you and snaps his fingers. Does he have fingers? The master isn't going to like it when the servant turns off the juice." Claire cajoles Tom into revealing the Venusian's weaknesses and its lair. "Hiding in a cave, afraid of light," exclaims Claire, "then earth must be of no use to him except as a subject of conquest." News of Joan's possession shocks her. The mayor and his wife were killed in the evacuation. One of their devices could have been used on Paul — but they have already been used. "On who?" asks Claire. "I can't tell you," apologizes Tom.

At the installation, Ellen awakens from a rest and is surprised to see the power back on. Roy behaves edgily when she goes to a locker to fix coffee. In it are the expired devices. Roy strangles Ellen while Pete tells the Venusian the installation will be used to further an all-out invasion.

Unable to dissuade Tom from assassinating Paul, Claire radios the Venusian, screaming, "I hate your living guts for what you've done to my husband and my world! I know you for the coward you are and I'm going to kill you!" Claire sneaks away with the rifle as Tom greets Paul. Here to kill him, Paul tells Tom he had to kill Joan. "But she was your wife," gasps Tom. "Kind of makes you think a little, doesn't it," sneers Paul. He wants the names of the Venusian's slaves and where it lives. Camped near the cave, the soldiers hear Claire's car speeding there. Manuel leaves them to rustle up food.

Paul convinces Tom that the Venusian has been using his misplaced idealism for its own nefarious ends. "How could he care anything about you? He doesn't like, he doesn't dislike. He merely reasons, concludes and uses." Tom must either join Paul or die. "I was supposed to kill *you* — *his* orders," confesses Tom, who turns to discover the rifle gone. Deep in the cave, Claire faces the Venusian. "You're ugly! Horrible!" she shouts. "Go ahead! Use your intellect on me! You want to make a slave of the world! I'll see you in hell!" Claire's shots and death screams come over the radio. "Now it's reached you — right down into your heart," Paul tells Tom. Siding with Paul, Tom mentions Pete and Roy. His only weapon is a blowtorch. Manuel sees the Venusian killing Claire and escapes to tell Neill.

Tom leaves Paul at the installation, where Paul discovers Ellen's body lying on the pavement. Pattick will fly to Washington to kill the President and the Cabinet members. Paul kills Pete and Roy, wounding Pattick in the shoulder. One the road to the cave, Shalet tries to ambush Tom with a rifle. Tom sneaks up from behind and blows flames onto Shalet's back. Screaming Shalet runs and drops dead while Paul kills Pattick for his jeep.

In the cave, the Venusian attacks the soldiers, killing Manuel as he charges with a bayonet. The men retreat outside, where the Venusian withstands bazookas and more bullets. Tom arrives in Shalet's squad car and has Neill call a cease-fire. Tom castigates the Venusian. "I made it possible for you to come here! I made you welcome to this earth! You made it a charnel house!" Tom shoves the burning blowtorch into the Venusian's eyes. It wraps its claws around Tom's neck, killing him as it topples over.

Paul arrives, viewing Tom's body. "He acted like he knew it," Neill tells him. Paul tells Neill, "He learned almost too late that man is a feeling creature and because of it, the greatest in the universe. He learned too late for himself that men have to find their own way; make their own mistakes. There can't be any gift of perfection from outsiders. And when man seek such perfection they find only death, fire, loss, disillusionment; the end of everything that's gone forward. Men have always sought an end to toil and misery. It has to be achieved. There is hope. But is has to come from the inside, from man himself."

Career opposites, Tom and Paul were like the classic mad Scientist and his cautious, conservative associate. Well-adjusted to the System, Paul was successful by its standards even when it rejected his most brilliant concept: that of an interstellar craft run by contained gravitation without need of an engine. Tom was a wild dreamer who orgasmed on pure imagination. Paul was a plodding Doer who could leave his work at the lab most days; Tom a schizoid speculator, always adopting and discarding new theories to suit his moods. Where science was Paul's way to legitimate achievement within a government-sponsored group endeavor, it was the psychological refuge of a battered ego for Tom.

The alliance between Tom and the Venusian was a preachment against totalitarianism disguised as positive revolution. When the Venusian contacted Tom, it appealed to his vanity as well as his social conscience. Prisoner of an environmentally-unstable world, one-ninth of its minuscule population, the Venusian had good reason to migrate. Like those other alien flora The Thing and the Pod People, it was amoral rather than evil, but for melodramatic purposes it was interpreted as a foreign devil — draining some minds and deluding Tom, who previously feared alien life. Through his satellite, Paul was an unknowing accessory to the Venusian's journey.

Regionally, the blackout power of the Venusian duplicated Klaatu's greatest feat in *The Day the Earth Stood Still* (1951). Klaatu had been considerate enough to spare hospitals and planes in flight. Here a plane exploded and mention was made of a medical emergency involving a patient in an iron lung. Or *was* the blackout just regional? Budget kept everything in and around Beechwood except for the scenes in Secy. Platt's office, but how would *It Conquered A Town* have sounded? The control devices enabled the Venusian to exercise proxy violence like the *Invaders from Mars* (1953) who implanted their brainwashing gadgets surgically, also in the neck.

"The released" emulated the Pod People by regarding their dehumanization as life on a higher plane. Joan was bland sweetness with Paul. When Roy strangled Ellen, he requested her cooperation like a dentist about to perform root-canal work. To coordinate things better, the Venusian kept Tom's mind free and let Claire indulge her great talent: speaking *her* mind. By expecting Tom's loyalty to wear through thick and thin, the Venusian never anticipated how he would react to new circumstances. Due to this compromise, the Venusian itself was guilty of judgemental fallibility. Had the Venusian died first, "the released" might have returned to normal. Their fates and those of their victims were harsh in order to convey the enormity of what Tom was abetting. This left Paul and a handful of soldiers, the latter not knowing what it was they were combatting, with Tom terminating the Venusian and himself in a

33

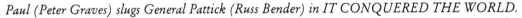

Paul (Peter Graves) slugs General Pattick (Russ Bender) in IT CONQUERED THE WORLD.

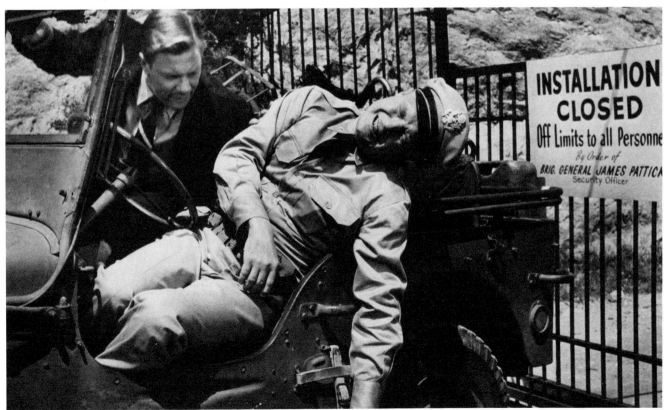

suicidal gesture.

Big Beulah to Blaisdell and Denny Dimwit to Charles Griffith, the Venusian was at first built too small, requiring the head cone that increased its height. Blaisdell had to dismantle Beulah to get her out of his studio and take her to Bronson Canyon, where Beverly Garland struck the first blow of contempt by kicking Beulah over. Originally meant to stay in the cave, the Venusian was left with wobbly arms because grips had carelessly stepped all over them. The attack on Garland got fouled up by missed cues and had to be edited together out of frame patches. Jackie Blaisdell had Blaisdell put on one of the soldier's Army helmets when it was time to shoot the scene where Jonathan Haze lunged his bayonet into the Venusian. Piercing the material that covered crouched Blaisdell, it jabbed the top of his helmet.

Since lighting generators had not been brought along, the rest of the battle had to put the Venusian outside the cave. Duck-walking Blaisdell pushed the Venusian along on its hidden castors while Roger Corman shoved it from behind. An extra kept poking Dick Miller with his bayonet and when it got stuck under the back of Miller's helmet, Miller made a move to get out of the way that caused him to twist his ankle. The blowtorch scene for Lee Van Cleef was hard on him because he had to contain his embarrassment while the crew vigorously cheered him on. The blood that gushed from the Venusian's seared sockets was chocolate syrup shot from a grease gun Blaisdell held. Backfiring, it covered Blaisdell, Corman and everything near with Hershey hemoglobin.

Props on wires attached to flexible poles, the control devices were marvelously lifelike — particularly in their attacks on Paul. The jeep scene was shot around a moving vehicle while the device in the living room cast shadows.

The general production values were typical of the merits and flaws to be found in Corman's black and white work. The installation control room was cheap and Tom's radio was nothing more than a glorified ham set. V-2 rockets came to signify sleazy sci-fi and the satellite takeoff was shown only as the earth rising away from a rocket-mounted camera in an equally familiar but less dated stock shot. The special effects satellite was shaped like a flying saucer rather than a sphere. Beechwood was actually the parts of Woodland Hills where community scenes from *Invasion of the Body Snatchers* had been shot. During the evacuation, one man carried a saxophone!

Static pacing was minimized by Charles Gross' razor-sharp editing. He fashioned a crisp montage of images during the blackout. One image, however, was a freeze-frame shot of a tractor operator who sat immobile as if *he* stopped running. Over Paul's end monologue, bodies of most of the dead were intercut to punctuate each of his points.

Corman was beginning to make films with more colloquial characterizations, but some of the acting was ponderous. In a role meant for Richard Boone, Peter Graves came off best. Lee Van Cleef, replacing John Hudson, essayed Tom's fanaticism passionately, but seeing him express tenderness (in a smoking jacket!) was uncomfortable. The hottest emotional sparks were generated by Beverly Garland, who popped nearly all of her high strings. Until Joan's "release", Sally Fraser was her normal Pollyanna-ish self, improving when Joan became the slave who paralleled Podess Becky Driscoll.

Larry Buchanan's Azalea TV-remake *Zontar, The Thing from Venus* (1966) updated *It Conquered the World* by applying laser technology to its satellite. Playing Peter Graves' role was aging John Agar, who was much more convincing than Anthony Houston, the effete Lee Van Cleef stand-in. For every five or six blunders, the AIP horror remakes by Buchanan had one touch of improvement. *Zontar's* devices were cleverly dubbed ejecto-pods. Instead of gadgets, they injected a growth element linking slaves to Zontar biologically. The *Zontar* Venusians had "released" so many lower life forms on their world that these became sterile and the same threat would have been man's fate. The cave Zontar occupied was a vast cavern. Houston's Tom, Keith Ritchie, was armed with a wand-like laser gun that turned everything negative. A typically humanoid Buchanan beast, Zontar wrapped its body in voluminous wings so as to resemble a cross between a bird and Paul Blaisdell's three-eyed atomic mutant.

THE SHE CREATURE

American-International, 1956

Executive Producer	Samuel Z. Arkoff
Producer	Alex Gordon
Director	Edward L. Cahn
Story-Screenplay	Lou Rusoff
based on an original idea by Jerry Zigmond	
Associate Producer	Isreal M. Berman
Cinematography	Patrick West
Film Editor	Ronald Sinclair
Music	Ronald Stein
Art Director	Don Ament
Production Supervisor-Assistant Director	Bart Carre
Set Decorator	Harry Reif
Property Master	Karl Brainard
Wardrobe	Marjorie Corso
Makeup	Jack Duseck
Sound	Ben Winkler
Script Supervisor	Judith Hart

A Golden State Production
Running time: 77 minutes

Cast: Chester Morris (Dr. Carlo Lombardi), Marla English (Andrea), Tom Conway (Timothy Chappel), Cathy Downs (Dorothy Chappel), Ron Randell (Lt. Ed James), Lance Fuller (Dr. Ted Erickson), Frieda Inescourt (Mrs. Chappel), Frank Jenks (Police Sergeant), El Brendel (Olaf), Paul Dubov (Johnny), Bill *aka William* Hudson (Bob), Flo Bert (Marta), Jeanne Evans (Mrs. Brown), Kenneth MacDonald (Prof. Anderson), Paul Blaisdell (Monster), Jack Mulhall, Edward Earle, Luana Walters

The celebrated Bridey Murphy regression case began in 1952 when businessman Morey Bernstein hypnotized Ruth Simmons, a Pueblo, Colorado housewife. While under a trance, she claimed to be an eighteenth-century Irishwoman living in Belfast. Bernstein wrote a book, "The Search for Bridey Murphey", published in 1956. It became a major film for Paramount that year starring Louis Hayward and Teresa Wright. Several exploitation treatments of the subject had been shown sooner. Universal made one, *I've Lived Before*, about an airline pilot who was the

(Above) THE SHE CREATURE (1956).

Dr. Carlo Lombardi (Chester Morris) keeps a hypnotic control over Andrea (Marla English) in THE SHE CREATURE.

Paul Blaisdell as the impressive She Creature.

reincarnation of a World War I flying ace. Contributing to the suicide of an unstable boy who thought he could come back after killing himself, the Murphy case had been exposed as a hoax by the time the films about it came out.

Bridey Murphy was still hot when Alex Gordon attended one of the annual Christmas parties at the home of AIP West Coast exhibitor Newton P. "Red" Jacobs in 1955. Jacobs left the company to start his own, Favorite Films, the first incarnation of Crown-International, a schlock outfit that got fat off of AIP rejects. Present at the occasion was Jerry Zigmond, a Los Angeles distributor who suggested the title *The She Creature*. That was his only contribution to Gordon's next film, but he was credited with the "idea" — actually created by writer Lou Rusoff. Every horror picture from American-International then required a monster. Such Murphy features more closely aligned to the conventional account as *I've Lived Before* were soft stuff. *The She Creature* would have it both ways, presenting the spirit of an ordinary woman from the seventeenth century and a monster from the beginning of mankind's existence.

On a lonely beach, a dark, mustached man with steely eyes and dressed in black, stares at a distant, twisting sea shape. "Now, on this very night," his voice echoes, "I have called into the unknown depths of time itself. She is here. And with her coming, the world will never be as it was. Neither man nor animal will be the same. This, I, Dr. Carlo Lombardi, have brought into being." Lombardi turns to a strange, oversized footprint pressed into the sand by an invisible leg. His attention is broken by the annoying barks of a dog, King whom Lombardi repels with a hostile glare.

King's mistress is Dorothy Chappel, whose promoter father, Timothy Chappel, is hosting a weekend party at their nearby beach house. Dorothy has invited her boyfriend, psychic expert Dr. Ted Erickson, who was dared by Lombardi to expose him as a fraud and a charlatan. Lombardi had predicted an occult visitation Chappel's wife takes seriously. Lombardi follows more footprints to the violated Jefferson house and passes through the open door. Putting on black gloves he is unsurprised by the damage he sees. There is a moist area in the carpet that means something. Mrs. Jefferson lies in a corner, gazing up with the empty eyes of a murder victim. Lombardi pulls back a couch propped against a wall and Mr. Jefferson's body crashes to the floor.

Ted and Dorothy are walking down the beach when King joins them in a state of extreme agitation. They go to the Jefferson house and see Lombardi calmly departing. King urges Ted to go inside. Viewing the bodies, he asks Dorothy to call the police while he stays there.

Ted is joined by Lt. Ed James and a Sergeant. Both victims have broken necks. A full wallet in Mr. Jefferson's pocket dismisses robbery. There is a piece of seaweed with more trailing to the door. James notices the wet spot on the carpet and has the Sergeant get some flour from the kitchen. The powder defines a footprint a clever man could have forged. James tries to recall a Lombardi remark. "What did he say was coming to roam among us? A creature out of time . . ." "The first life form of someone living today," fills in the Sergeant, ". . . more than a million years old." James and Ted will see Lombardi, leaving the jittery Sergeant, who asks, "What if it comes back?"

Lombardi operates a side show at a seaside carnival closing for the night. Johnny, a nosy concessionaire, tells Lombardi he heard Lombardi's assistant Andrea scream and found her in a deep trance that almost warranted calling the cops. Lombardi resents Johnny's intrusiveness. In Lombardi's showplace, beauteous Andrea lies supine on the couch of a small stage in a pristine white gown. Lombardi goes to a window, glancing the strange shape he saw earlier, and awakens Andrea. She asks how long she was under — over an hour — and becomes upset. "I hate this place . . . ," Andrea complains. "I hate the sound of the ocean . . . I hate you!" As Andrea changes into street clothes behind a screen, Lombardi assuredly declares, "You'll never leave me — you can't." More out of wishfulness, Andrea tells him, "I will — someday . . . soon." "As long as I'm alive," reminds Lombardi, "I'll posses you. It is something beyond yourself that makes you need me." "You've taken my soul away from me," Andrea says.

Anticipating Ted and James, Lombardi tells them the door is open. Andrea catches Ted's admiring eye as she walks by. Once Ted makes his identification of Lombardi, James lets him go. Ted joins Andrea outside. He offers to buy her coffee and she accepts — until a vision of Lombardi's gaze halts her. "I can't go with you . . . ," she whispers. Lombardi tells James he knew the Jeffersons were dead before he entered the house. "She comes out of the beginning of time," Lombardi warns, "huge and indestructible. And I'm the force that gives her life." Thinking him a likelier suspect, James takes Lombardi downtown.

Intrigued by a newspaper item concerning Lombardi's prediction, Chappel tells Ted, "There's a million dollar idea in that. We'll take this two-bit local sideshow man and make him the biggest thing in the country . . . blow him up 'til his name's on everyone's lips. Lombardi books, syndicated columns, lectures, television shows." Asked to endorse Lombardi professionally, Ted adamantly refuses. At the carnival, Chappel is surprised when Lombardi greets him abruptly, claiming he intercepted Chappel's thoughts before Chappel left home. A remarkable guess, presumes Chappel. Chappel offers an even split in profits if he becomes Lombardi's manager. Lombardi will perform for some luminaries at Chappel's home tomorrow night. "Play it up big," exhorts Chappel, "We gotta shake 'em." "We'll shake 'em," Lombardi promises confidently.

Lombardi puts Andrea in another trance. Bursting out of an eruption of churning brine, her primordial self, the She Creature, ethereally materializes and takes on solid shape as she lumbers up some pier steps. Lombardi sends her after Johnny, who hears crunching footsteps as he lies on a cot in his room reading a paperback. The creature breaks through the door. Johnny is paralyzed with fright as the creature flips him and the cot over. James arrests Lombardi for murder. Police close the beaches. Chappel's attorney springs Lombardi on a write.

Present at the Chappel party are the butler, Olaf, his maid wife, Marta, and Bob, an amorous drunk who loves Dorothy and dislikes Ted. Lombardi and Andrea arrive and Ted is again transfixed by Andrea's strange beauty. James also appears. On stage, Lombardi puts Andrea under hypnosis, but she balks momentarily when told to recline on a couch. Lombardi challenges Ted to join them. Ted politely declines until Dorothy urges him and Bob heckles him. Once Ted confirms Andrea's relaxed state, Lombardi sends Andrea far back . . . than forward quickly. Andrea stops when she sees something familiar. She is Elizabeth Ann Wetherby of Oxnam Road, London, in the year 1618. Elizabeth is smiling because Capt. Ernest Blystone has asked her father for her hand in marriage. Ted asks Elizabeth various

historical questions he will verify. Moved to her deathbed, Elizabeth describes where she wants to be interred and the details of an engraved gold medallion to be buried with her.

Lombardi puts Andrea in a deeper state. "Where are you now, Elizabeth?" "In space," she answers. "Floating in space . . ." "Are you alone?" Lombardi inquires. "There are others with me," Elizabeth informs him. Elizabeth's spirit leaves Andrea and those who believe will be able to see her. Mrs. Chappel does. Lombardi has Elizabeth open the window by Olaf and Marta, then close the drapes around Andrea. King pads into the living room from the garden patio, ignoring Dorothy's order to come to her, and faces Lombardi, who throws another hypnotic glare. "You take him away please, Elizabeth?" he requests.

Elizabeth refuses to return to Andrea's body. Something she says shocks Lombardi. "Ladies and gentlemen," he announces, "I regret to say that the creature who has cost so many lives is here among us even now." Mrs. Chappel jumps up from her seat and goes into a faint. The guests immediately clear the room. James asks Lombardi if the creature is coming to this house. Lombardi does not know. She is in the sea preparing to come out. Lombardi has managed to impress Ted to a degree. Behind the drapes, he sends Andrea back further. Ted demands Andrea's release from near-catalepsy and Lombardi refuses since only he

Marla English becomes part of Lombardi's sideshow in THE SHE CREATURE.

can reverse this.

Amid the guests, Lombardi makes a suspicious dash to the beach. Ted tries to catch him. In hiding, Lombardi watches the She Creature creep up behind Ted with raised claws. When Andrea intuitively sits up and screams, the neutralized creature withdraws and vanishes.

Ted wants to study Lombardi under clinical conditions. Lombardi tries to steal what little privacy Andrea has, telling her she is to resist Ted. Even under his power, Andrea turns from Lombardi's longing lips. Woefully, he concedes, "I can make you grovel in the dirt . . . I can turn you into Elizabeth Wetherby . . . but I can't make you love me." "Someday, I'm going to kill you!" Andrea vows. "I should kill *you*, Andrea," Lombardi gently retorts. "But the artist is vain. He can't destroy the beauty that he's created." James wants in on the clinical demonstration so he can record it.

Secretly, Ted fights for Andrea's will. Elizabeth expresses herself in movement by lifting one scientist's glasses off his head and putting them back on. Still, the scientists are skeptical. "You said before that you were giving her substance but not form," James tells Lombardi. "Now what did you mean by that?" "I could have brought her to you in the flesh," answers Lombardi, "— just as she was three centuries ago."

Headlines declare the reality of Elizabeth Ann Wetherby and Lombardi's claim of further murders. A book about Elizabeth passes the million sales mark. Chappel wants Lombardi to find his own house, something Dorothy would welcome, but he prefers to stay. Chappel advises Lombardi to lay off the predictions for now to avert any embarrassing slipups. Lombardi and Andrea embark on a spectacular national tour.

James catches Lombardi alone on the beach "communing with nature". King scampers past a sedan parked by the edge of a cliff. Two kissing teens see the She Creature grab the car's rear bumper before they are pushed to their deaths. James investigates the noise. Lombardi pulled a murder right under his nose.

The car incident disturbs Chappel, who has prepared two bank books worth two hundred and fifty thousand dollars each; Dorothy's dowry and Lombardi's money. Refusing to be stared down, Chappel calls Lombardi a dirty fortune-teller with delusions of grandeur. Lombardi agrees to move out. Some people have been invited for a new demonstration at Chappel's tonight. Andrea has found the will to resist Lombardi, who will soon be going abroad with her. She loves Ted, but Lombardi dictatorially asserts, "You'll never have him! I'll kill him! *YOU'LL kill him!*"

Ted wants Andrea to defy Lombardi publicly. Lurking behind a tall rock formation on the beach, Lombardi wills King to attack Ted. Andrea controls King ordering, "Go away!" "That voice —," declares

39

Ted (Lance Fuller) reveals himself to Marla English in THE SHE CREATURE.

Chappel (Tom Conway) faces the wrath of the She Creature.

perplexed Ted, "it didn't come from you."

At the new demonstration, Chappel offers Ted Dorothy's dowry so he can support her, but Ted turns it down. Dorothy graciously accepts the end of their relationship and swings back to pixilated, faithful Bob. James tells Ted that the footprints of the She Creature always return to the sea in the direction they came. At first, Andrea disobeys Lombardi on stage. In Chappel's study, James runs the demonstration tape and hears what Lombardi said about returning Elizabeth physically. Lombardi announces that the creature is coming to the house. James orders the guests to leave, sending for reinforcements with high-powered rifles. Ted orders Lombardi to free Andrea and Lombardi pretends he will comply if granted privacy. Into Andrea's ear, he whispers, "Deeper — deeper. Time is an endless nothing. You're falling through it . . . deeper . . .," Ted is told that Andrea is in the "recovery process".

James sees the She Creature materialize at the edge of the surf and shoots, but she savagely smites him. Dying, James tells Ted the creature will be heading back this way. "Lombardi was right —," gasps James, "— he did it." "Did it?" Ted asks. "Brought the girl back . . .," answers James in his final breath. Two carloads of police arrive. The Sergeant instructs the men to burn the

creature's footprints with brush, driftwood and gasoline.

The creature chases Chappel into his study, where he attempts to abscond with his and Lombardi's profits. Bullets fail to prevent *his* death. At the stage, Ted faces the creature. "Now do you believe, doctor?" triumphantly asks Lombardi, who tells the creature, "Kill him!" Instead, the creature mauls Lombardi. Crouching, she stares in fascination at Andrea — the woman of her future — and as a ghostly Andrea rises from the corporeal one, the creature turns into departing ectoplasm. "You couldn't kill the man you loved," bleeding, near-dead Lombardi tells Andrea. "I musn't let you die. When I touch you, you will awaken young and beautiful." This done, Lombardi kneels over. The police have set the fire. The only one who can see the creature, Ted tells them where to aim, but their rifle shots fly through empty smoke. The firing ceases. "I was mistaken," says Ted.

Liberated of Lombardi, Andrea wonders if the She Creature will ever come back. Only the sea can answer that.

Even for the fifties design of the creature and its trendy plot, *The She Creature* evoked earlier movie moods with its melancholy noir setting, occult storyline and numerous old-time stars. Even in the mid-fifties, hypnotism still had disreputable voodoo overtones and anyone who displayed mastery of it was considered Svengali. Under his charismatic veneer, Carlo Lombardi was a latterday amalgam of Legendre, the neromancer of *White Zombie* (1932) and Stan Carlysle, the slick but fallible mentalist of *Nightmare Alley* (1947).

Little more than a temporal person between regressions, former carnival groupie Andrea seemed to be a predestined Trilby. Lombardi used Andrea to work a murder forecast scam that was a beautiful idea as homicide: conjure up a hit-monster from the past, be elsewhere at the time of a creature massacre and afterward dematerialize the assassin until encores. The She Creature was a part of Andrea — yet the start of Andrea's evolutionary tether always made grand entrances out of the sea, as if the spirit of Andrea had been sent there to soak up water until it solidified (thereby the seaweed and wet carpet). Lombardi probably did this to suggest the creature was an ocean inhabitant all the time. Stroking a beneficial sponsor in Chappel for as long as he was useful, Lombardi fabricated "futures" by planning them in the present. Killing of innocent strangers helped cover any personal crimes.

The Murphyesque asides concerning Elizabeth Ann Wetherby defined Andrea's other notable incarnation. Along the endless life chain, all people can be all things — poor in one life, royalty in another, good as one person, evil as somebody else. Maybe Lombardi and Chappel were virtuous men once and ethical Ted an erstwhile creep. Was Bob the boozer an ex-teetotaler or would he achieve that phase after his existing liver gave out? If the *She* creature was so powerful and terrifying, what about a *He* counterpart?

Ted Erickson offered lip service to those umbraged by exploiters like Lombardi. Agents of black and white science, Ted and Lombardi drew their opposing powers from Andrea, a more complex heroine than the other women in AIP thrillers of 1956. Usually, they were complete subjugates of a monster's will, such as Sandy of *Beast With a Million Eyes*, Louise Maddison of *Day the World Ended* and Joan Nelson of *It Conquered the World*; or defiant and not long for this world like Ethel Hall of *Phantom From Ten Thousand Leagues* and Claire Anderson of *It Conquered*. Andrea would go from passivity to stirring of independence because she had other lives behind her. Toying with Andrea's spirit like a yo-yo, Lombardi thought neither she nor the creature could assert themselves much beyond the boundaries of his mind until Andrea affected a remote alliance with the creature — her original ancestor — whose monstrousness emancipated Andrea when either Ted or Lombardi had to die.

Cuddles, as Paul Blaisdell call the She Creature, was a garish mosaic of marine animal genes, owning also vague qualities of the cat and distinctly human hooters. Designed from seventy-two sketches of its feline features and thirty-two of its scaly, lobster-clawed body,

the costume was assembled in segments and sundry appliances were added to the face. The chest could endure close-range rifle blanks, the arms were capable of lifting one hundred sixty pounds, the mouth permitting eating and the feet were built around heavy outrigger boots while the foundation of the claws were welding gloves. Several minutes of reserve oxygen enabled Blaisdell to wear the costume around smoke fumes and diagonal "lunch hooks" built into the creature's abdomen afforded ventilation.

Director Edward Cahn suggested the big breasts but impeded the use of the lunch hooks and the creature's draggy, tumescent tail. The hooks were meant to pierce the sides of the victims the creature hugged. Cahn vetoed that idea, calling it "horrible". The tail was fashioned to slap around freely, only Cahn would not give Blaisdell time to set it up.

When Cuddles was supposed to emerge from the ocean Blaisdell was at odds with the creature's natural story element: water. It added over a hundred pounds when it soaked into the costume and pushed Blaisdell out to sea. The first door in Johnny's room was made of balsa wood. Blaisdell smashed through is easily enough, but tripped on a piece of wood and lost his balance. There was no more balsa wood and the new door was a real one made of pine, causing Blaisdell to fall backwards.

Most of the optical effects went into devising the creature's other-worldly conditions. For the materializing sand footprints, the tracks were photographed in reverse and erased for every few feet of film. Through double exposure, the creature appeared as a phosphorescent mass prior to full reconstitution or when semitransparent. Only in the plain light did she lose her ethereality. Her most jarring appearances were when she first catapulted from the pier water and when the lovers saw her through the oval window of their car. Its plunge from the cliff was seen minus the day-for-night effect in Alex Gordon's *Runaway Daughters* (1956).

Frederick West's cinematography, using cloudy milky grays and coal-deep blackness, could be described as Malibu Gothic. Relentlessly cheerless were scenes shot at the carnival, in Chappel's home after dark and in the beach area of Paradise Cove where light and shadow congealed in a moist haze.

Gordon wanted Peter Lorre and Edward Arnold to play Lombardi and Chappel so they could recreate their memorable chemistry in *Crime and Punishment* (1936). Lorre's agency committed him to *The She Creature*, but he refused to act in it changing agents. John Carradine was considered, but in temporary rebellion against schlock horror roles, preferred to do Shakespeare instead. Arnold died a week before production. For Chappel, Gordon considered Chester Morris, whom he met during a New Jersey stage presentation of "The Dark Tower". The ex-star of the Boston Blackie series, Morris was doing the play version of "Advise and Consent" when Gordon approached him. Tom Conway of The Falcon was contacted in London to play Lt. James, but became Chappel. Ron Randall, who played Bulldog Drummond in the last Drummond picture before *Deadlier Than the Male* (1966), assumed the role of James before flying to his homeland Australia the following week to honor a film commitment there.

In the long run, the revised casting worked for the best. A suaver, more commanding Lombardi than the fat, slur-voiced Lorre would have been, Morris would have been too overpowering for the subtler Chappel part. And Conway, with his British accent, would have been miscast as a cynical American cop. Morris and Conway were great to watch as Lombardi and Chappel engaged in the guarded familiarity of partners of convenience, couching imagined insights into one another in acidic repartee. Lombardi was an omniscient spider who hated everything in the world except Andrea. Chappel was a cultivated leech with dollar signs for eye pupils.

Captivating Marla English, born Marleine Gaile English, had been "Miss Science Fiction" at a 1951 sci-fi convention held in her native San Diego when she was fifteen. Pushed into acting by her mother, English's resemblance to young Liz Taylor made her a Paramount New Star and this distinction interested Gordon. Cathy Downs was the second-rank heroine. Mike Connors was to play Ted, but the role went to Lance Fuller, who individualized Ted by his eccentric facial expressions.

Most everyone else was a nostalgia figure, many veterans of Bela Lugosi films. Swedish comic El Brendel appeared in *Women of All Nations* (1931), Luana Walters in the serial *Shadow of Chinatown* (1936) and in *The Corpse Vanishes* (1942), Frieda Inescourt in *Return of the Vampire* (1944) and Frank Jenks in *Zombies on Broadway* (1945).

AIP's first personality monster, the She Creature was scheduled to guest on several Los Angeles TV shows to help publicize the film's opening. In a salary dispute with the company, Paul Blaisdell was replaced by Bob Burns, a video horror host from San Antonio. Burns was helped into the costume by Lionel Comport, son of a famous movie animal-trainer couple. Burns appeared on "Quinn's Corner", hosted by character actor Louis Quinn, and Gene Norman's "Campus Club". On the

latter, he partook in such activities as dunking for apples and chewing marshmallows on the ends of strings. A publicity story claimed that Burns inadvertently frightened a secretary in his costume. When she saw him again, he was drinking Coke out of a bottle through a straw and she thought the bottle was the creature's tongue!

The She Creature ended with a question mark superimposed over the sea, suggesting a possible sequel. Without success, Alex Gordon tried to interest AIP sales manager Leon Blander in one. Like reincarnated souls themselves, the She Creature would return in different forms to be covered in the chapters of *Voodoo Woman* and *Ghost of Dragstrip Hollow*. The head of the creature was only makeup in *How to Make a Monster* while a *She Creature* clip in the ending of *Teenage Caveman* (1958) related her to a product of nuclear war mutation. For his eight-millimeter home digest reel *Filmland Monsters*, Blaisdell shot new footage of the creature. He also sold some thirty-five millimeter frames of it for a slide set called "Hollywood Monsters".

A shabby Gill-Man type monster was the She Creature in *Creatures of Destruction* (1967) from Larry Buchanan. Les Tremayne bravely but unsatisfactorily succeeded Chester Morris as Dr. John Basso, whose slave Dorina found her primordial being rise from the lake near Tanglewood, a lodge owned by Sam Crane, the Timothy Chappel character. Buchanan was filming near an Air Force base. To justify its intrusive jets, he made Ted Erickson into Capt. Ted Dell, a military psychiatrist known for his work in combat psychosis. The movie even added a gratuitous (but timely) Batman song sung by one Scotty McKay, who became a creature casualty when his motorcycle got stuck in beach sand. Instead of releasing Dorina with a tender kiss, Basso killed her with a gun and used it to commit suicide. The creature vanished from this film only to become a giant prehistoric beast in the Larry Buchanan picture titled *It's Alive!* (1968).

Tragedy struck Tom Conway and Chester Morris. Conway slid into drink and poverty, living in seedy Venice, California, where he died in 1967. During a 1970 theater stint in Pennsylvania, Morris took a fatal overdose of barbiturates.

42

MAN BEAST

Associated Producers
Favorite Films of California, 1956

Producer-Director	Jerry Warren
Screenplay	B. Arthur Cassidy
Associate Producer-	
Second Unit Director	Ralph Brooke
Cinematography	Victor Fisher
Film Editor	James Sweeney
Musical Direction	Josef Zimanich
Production Supervisor	Richard George
Art Director	Ralph Tweer
Sound	Jim Donovan
Set Supervisor	Ray Guth
Script Supervisor	Bri *aka Brianne* Murphy
Editing Service	Ashcroft Film Co.

Jerry Warren Productions, Inc.
Running time: 67 minutes

Cast: Rock Maddison (Lon Raynon), Virginia *aka Asa* Maynor (Connie Hayward), George Skaff (Varga), Tom Maruzzi, Lloyd Cameron *aka Nelson* (Trevor Hudson), George Wells Lewis (Dr. Erickson), Jack Haffner (Kheon), Wong Sing (Trader)

The third yeti epic, *Man-Beast* had most things the later Jerry Warren films lacked: an interesting, novel script, challenging, well-photographed locations, mostly able acting and moody (though overly repetitive) music. Like 1957's British *The Abominable Snowman of the Himalayas*, it, too, speculated that, beneath a hairy veneer, the Yeti are our disadvantaged evolutionary cousins.

Connie Hayward and her fiancee, Trevor Hudson, trek to a Himalayan outpost, where they meet fellow American, Steve Cameron. Connie's brother, Dr. Hames Hayward, left ten days ago to ready camp for Dr. Erikson, a yeti-hunting anthropologist, who went up the mountain yesterday. Steve had seen four expeditions brave the mountain and each has lost at least one man. The natives refuse to go there unless they are with

(Above) A closeup of the Yeti creature in MAN BEAST (1956).

Erickson's guide, Varga. It is urgent that Connie find Jim. Steve agrees to help.

Early on in the grueling climb, weakling Hudson voices opposition to the trip. Connie and Steve grow closer to one another. They finally spot Erickson and a native, Kheon, who hear signal shots Steve fires. Erickson views Steve, Connie and Hud through his binoculars. Varga and Jim are at the base camp. Erickson thinks the yeti are primitive men and shows a composite sketch of them. Just before the big climb into snow country, Hud grows increasingly fearful of the yeti. Kheon watches Connie and Steve suspiciously. "What about you?" Steve asks Kheon. "Ever see a yeti?" "No see," answers Kheon. Steve: "Ever meet anybody that did?" Kheon: "See yeti — die!"

The base camp has been ripped apart. During the night, the natives desert the party. Steve and Erickson are searching for Varga and Jim. A yeti watches them. When they return to camp, Varga is with Connie and Hud. Varga says that he and Jim had gotten separated.

Splitting up, Varga and Erickson look for Jim one way while Steve, Connie and Hud take another. Neither Steve nor Hud trust Varga. Connie tells Steve that Jim had taken some experimental injections back in the States. After he left, it was learned that high altitude may kill him. Hud says they need a regular rescue party because Varga never mentioned the dead explorers or the missing natives. Hud knows they are being watched. Varga shows Erickson a view of every locale where yeti signs have been detected. Erickson's friend, Bishop, died in the most recent sighting area.

Hud disappears until he comes back. He followed some tracks to a large fault in a glacier. The group explores its dark cave with flares. A lurking yeti is about to attack, but Varga gives a silent order to wait. On his cue, the yetis ambush the group. Varga sees Steve pull his gun and throws a club to knock it out. A yeti armed with another club knocks Hud to his death in a deep chasm.

Connie revives headachy Steve in one of the tents, saying they should leave. Steve wants to talk to Erickson about Varga. Absorbed in his notes, Erickson is too distracted. Connie looks out for Varga. Steve is sure that Varga slugged him, but Erickson naively thinks Varga acted heroically. Coming back, Varga suggests he and Erickson revisit the cave. Steve wants to come too, after he gets over his headache and Erickson finishes his notes. Since Erickson still respects Varga, Steve must accompany him to the cave and maybe there, finally talk sense into him. Connie will wait for Steve at a predesignated spot with a sack of food. Meaning Varga, Connie swears, "If he comes first, I'll jump!"

Varga gives Steve his dropped gun. As they and Erickson head for the cave, a yeti monitor watches Connie sneak away. Varga speaks of his soldier father and how he preferred living in Sweden to Calcutta as a boy. "I never knew my mother. She died at my birth."

As Steve helps Erickson fix a loose backpack strap, Varga moves ahead and times an avalanche meant to bury Steve. Erickson is forced to accompany Varga up the hill, glimpsing Steve, who survived the avalanche.

In his Spartan lair, Varga changes into an open silk shirt. "Our civilization hasn't caught up with yours," he tells Erickson, who realizes, "You're part yeti!" Steve suspected this. Varga shows a chestful of white hair. "I'll kill anyone who insists upon these expeditions," he declares, "— for if I don't, my people will!" Erickson can make Varga famous. "Put me on exhibition?" he retorts. "No thank you, Doctor. I have other plans for me — for you! I'm going to kill you." Erickson ascertains that the yeti are breeding out their own strain. "I've been fifth generation," explains Varga. "As you can see, it has not been too difficult to obtain the necessary females." Five have been taken this year. "Now, of course, there's —" "Connie!" finishes shocked Ericson. "With her," Varga leers, "I should be able to hedgehop two generations. Our offspring should be most interesting. Don't you think so, Doctor?" Erickson denounces Varga. Cryptically noting, "Perhaps we'll meet again in some other incarnation," Varga shoots Erickson.

The yeti monitor hides behind a rock by where Connie awaits Steve. Varga tells Connie the avalanche killed Steve and hurt Erickson wants her. As she struggles with Varga, Steve reappears and shoots the advancing yeti. Fighting Varga, Steve slugs him. As he and Connie run down the mountain, Varga rigs a slide rope. When the peg snaps, he plummets to his doom. "Take me away from here, Steve," wails Connie, "Take me away."

Unlike the more straightforward yeti films, *Man-Beast* stressed the intrigues of an outwardly normal villain whose origin was biologically gamy for its hint of bestiality. A superior being with the strengths of two races, Varga was loyal to one, but above both. There were some loose ends in his background. Where did he get his worldliness if he was spawned and raised by yeti? Since Tibetan women are Asian and, therefore, should have been the only available mates, why was he part-Occidental with a Castillian-sounding name? Erickson was as much awed by Varga as he was appalled by his revealed intentions, and the usually inept Warren directed well this stimulating encounter between two brilliant but morally diametrical minds. Even when Varga moved onto his next incarnation at the end, wouldn't the yeti's have continued their breeding ritual?

Made in the snowy hills of Bishop California at a ski lodge, *Man-Beast* was technically the best Warren movie because filming conditions seemed to force him to do a diligent job. For the trading post, he sneaked onto a major studio lot to borrow a standing Mongolian set. Most of the spectacular climbing scenes were from an old Allied Artists film. The audio of *Man-Beast* intensified them with the constant sound of wind.

Looking near ten feet tall, the yeti made it hard for us to imagine them engaged in coitus with average sized women. What about the hazards of their child bearing? The yeti were one monster — the albino ape from *White Pongo* (1945) with a new face. The yeti ran past the camera several times so time-exposure would create the effect of a charging horde. One of the men who wore the yeti suit was "star" Rock Maddison. He was cast as another expedition member named Lon Raynon, who was cut completely from the final print. Rock Hudson and Guy Maddison were very big then. Warren could have devised the name of his original leading man to take advantage of their popularity. The pressbook synopsis of *Man-Beast* mentioned Lon Raynon only once, omitting any other reference to him.

Top-billing should have gone to Tom Maruzzi, who resembled a hunkier Ross Martin and gave a spontaneous, decent performance. George Skaff was fascinating as Varga, his face a distinctly odd one but not focused on unduly except in the cave scenes. Where his acting really shined was in Varga's floridly confessed admission of his true parentage. Publicity claimed Skaff's eerie looks so upset the other people in a restaurant near Bishop that he had to eat in a private room. Once wed to Edd Byrnes, Virginia Maynor was leaden at low voice, sloppily shrill at high pitch. Somehow, her career lasted into the seventies, when Skaff was at his busiest.

Script supervisor Brianne Murphy became Mrs. Jerry Warren, working with him in assorted departments. After their split, she became a top-rated cinematographer and sometimes director.

Near sea level, Warren lost the skill that made *Man-Beast* the sturdiest of all his credits. *Man-Beast* may have *encouraged* his sloth as so much of it was composed of stock shots. In the sixties, the Mexi-movie mangler returned to "original" filmmaking only a few times. His reedited Hispanic horrors had most of their American scenes shot in tandem. Rock Maddison was the name given to the star of one of the last, *Creature of the Walking Dead* (1965).

Tom Maruzzi shoots at the advancing Man Beast.

VOODOO WOMAN

American-International, 1957

Executive Producers	Samuel Z. Arkoff
	James H. Nicholson
Producer	Alex Gordon
Director	Edward L. Cahn
Story-Screenplay	Russell *aka Russ* Bender
	V.I. Voss
Cinematography	Fred West
Film Editor	Ronald Sinclair
Music	Darrell Calker
Art Director	Don Ament
Production Supervisor-Assistant Director	Bert Carre
Set Decorator	Harry Reif
Properties	Karl Brainard
	Richard M. Rubin
Wardrobe	Bob Olivas
Makeup	Carlie Taylor
Special Makeup	Harry Thomas
Sound	Bob Post
Script Supervisor	Judith Hart

Song: "Black Voodoo"
Lyrics by John Blackburn, sung by Giselle D'Arc

A Carmel Production
Running time: *77 minutes*

Cast: Marla English (Marilyn Blanchard), Tom Conway (Dr. Roland Gerard), Touch *aka Mike* Connors (Ted Bronson), Mary Ellen Kaye (Susan Gerard), Lance Fuller (Rick Brady), Paul Dubov (Marcel Chateau), Martin Wilkins (Chaka), Norman Willis (Harry West), Paul Blaisdell (Monster), Otis Greene (Hobo), Emmett E. Smith (Gandor), Giselle D'Arc (Singer), Jean Davis (Saranda)

A fter *The She Creature*, Alex Gordon made *Runaway Daughters* (1956) with Marla English and Lance Fuller. Third *She Creature* star, Tom Conway, who was to play English's father, suffered a cerebral

(Above) The Voodoo Woman claims a victim.

hemorrhage and was replaced by John Litel. Meanwhile, Russ Bender and V.I. Voss submitted a script called *Black Voodoo* to an independent outfit. Unable to finance its production, the company turned it over to AIP. Gordon was asked if he could make *Black Voodoo* in six days for sixty thousand dollars.

For the part of mad scientist, Roland Gerard, Gordon thought of using George Zucco. In 1951, Zucco became sick and spent his remaining nine years in a sanitarium.

Ignoring the discouragement of his agent, Gordon asked Zucco to play Dr. Gerard. Zucco thanked Gordon, but was not interested. As scandal gossip had it, Zucco had become a nutcase and died in a padded cell thinking that he *was* a mad doctor. Tom Conway, meanwhile, had returned to passable health and took the role as Gerard. *Black Voodoo* was now titled *Voodoo Woman* in order to sell its She Creature-type monster. Marla English and Lance Fuller appeared as two other heavies. Still Touch, Mike Connors was the hero. After its completion, *Voodoo Woman* would be a deciding factor in Alex Gordon's love life.

Dr. Roland Gerard collaborates with Chaka, the witch doctor of an African tribe, to create a perfect super-being. The guinea pig for their respective powers is innocent young Saranda. Gerard's long-suffering wife Susan is a prisoner in their hut who receives sympathy only from house-boy Bobo while sentry Gandor is always close with a spear. Gerard's mutation drug only has limited effect on Saranda. Chaka insists upon a ritual requiring Gerard to drink a cup of blood.

At the sleazy city cafe of Marcel Chateau, Marilyn Blanchard and her boyfriend Rick Brady feign friendship with crusty Harry West, who plans to locate unspecified treasure. Rick is sponsoring the trip Harry doesn't want Marilyn to be a part of. Marilyn had killed a previous lover back in the States. She and Rick need a map in Harry's room. Marcel provides Marilyn with a gun, as the cafe singer distracts Harry and when Harry senses what Marilyn and Rick are up to, Marcel sells him another gun. Marilyn discovers a clue to the native gold Harry is looking for before Harry surprises her and Rick. Double-crossing Marcel gives Harry an empty weapon. Marilyn unhesitatingly shoots him with hers.

Gerard, meanwhile, turns Saranda into a mutant — but the change works only for as long as Chaka's spell lasts.

Marcel fakes Harry's death as a heart attack. A mail-order guide who never met him, Ted Bronson, is told that Rick is Harry.

Disturbed by Saranda's scream during a new experiment, Susan intrudes upon Gerard, who hints he will develop a new life form to show up the former colleagues who scoffed him. Telepathically, Saranda obeys simple commands from both Gerard and Susan. When she mutates again, Gerard has Saranda destroy another village, but the drug wears off and the monster's

shadow reverts to the shape of Saranda.

The natives monitor Marilyn, Rick and Susan. Bobo tells Susan the whites are coming and she gives him a distress letter. Bob leaves a rifle with Susan, but Gandor spears him before he can deliver the message. Marilyn tries to draw off the native monitor by throwing rocks. Ted becomes difficult and has to be tied up. Gerard shows the sleeping whites to Saranda, but when ordered to kill them, she becomes herself again. Rick discovers a doll with the gold symbol as Gerard sends Saranda back to the village. She runs into Rick, who rapes and murders her. To avenge Saranda, the natives want to kill every white — including Gerard — until he suggests the whites should be made to execute the killer. Marilyn gives Rick away by examining his scratched hand and shoots him.

Marilyn and Ted are taken to Gerard's hut. Gerard claims Susan is mentally ill. Marilyn will learn where the gold is if she agrees to become a priestess. Susan tells Ted what Gerard had done to Saranda. Gerard convinces Chaka that natural killer Marilyn is the right subject for the upcoming Blood Festival. Ted discovers Gerard's lab and wants to go to Bantalaya for help alone, but is caught. Once Marilyn is made a priestess, he will be sacrificed at the festival. Her preliminary mutation unsettles the natives because it happens too fast.

The next night, Ted slips past Gandor, cueing Susan's flight, but monster Marilyn catches her. Gerard has Susan taken to Chaka. Ted stabs Gandor when he sees Susan being taken to the boiling sacrifice crater. Ted is captured and tied to a pole next to her. Gerard summons Marilyn, who incites the terrified natives to throw spears at her and she slays several. Gerard tells Marilyn to kill Chaka, who takes a gold idol with him as he is thrown into the crater. Marilyn shatters a gold pot, discovering all the "gold" is gilded clay — except the idol. Strangling Gerard, she returns to normal as the idol providently wells up from the depths of the crater. As Marilyn stoops to retrieve it, she falls in. Ted uses Gerard's chemicals to make molotov cocktails. One bomb repels the natives, enabling him and Susan to make a run for it.

Ted and Susan turn up at Marcel's cafe. Intuition tells him that Marilyn is still very much alive. As the monster, she rises from the pit.

A gelded memory of *The She Creature*, but not without its moments, *Voodoo Woman* offered up two monsters who were simply Andrea when Carlo Lombardi controlled her and Andrea when she couldn't bring herself to kill Ted Erickson. Since meek Saranda and predatory Marilyn stayed true to their ingrained instincts, all Gerard really endowed them with was an invincibility that came and went like bouts of malaria. Super-race mad doctors aim for the most impossible goal and how do they expect to mass-produce creations if every one requires individual adjustments? We must conclude from Marilyn that only Bad Seeds yield the most permanent Voodoo Monsters and the sacrifice pit

Dr. Gerard (Tom Conway) orders his mutation to attack in VOODOO WOMAN (1957).

Marla English becomes the subject of Gerard's voodooistic ritual in VOODOO WOMAN.

wouldn't hold anyone who could better service evil by remaining topside.

Without time to build a new monster he designed, Paul Blaisdell had to recycle Cuddles. Denuded of her breasts, tail and horns, she wore a burlap sarong to hide the flat front. Harry Thomas made a different head, a plain latex skull mask, and it was given to Blaisdell, who squared the facial contours, added popping eyes and put on a blonde wig. Remembering how showing less of the She Creature made her more awesome, director Edward Cahn repeated that pattern. Gerard, unlike Carlo Lombardi, was granted more extended moments in close company with his monster and "spoke" to the Voodoo Woman directly in echoing mental commands. Then also, Cahn was struggling to finish a jinxed shoot. Sparse presentations of the Voodoo Woman helped cut down on action setups and telepathy let dissipated Tom Conway loop some easy lines.

Voodoo Woman was shot in the chilly Chaplin studio during winter. A severe flu hit most of the personnel. Marla English brought to the set a seven year old niece that only Blaisdell could entertain. The acid test scene used a supposedly "safe" element, Brett Smoke, but it ate through the leg of Blaisdell's costume and burned his own leg. The nearest medicine at hand was bicarbonate of soda.

English looked fetching in her ritual garb, only her character's bravado leaned on too much corny sociopathy ("Those drums are talkin' to me! They're sayin, 'You're rich, Marilyn! You're rich!'"). His upper lip shaved, Tom Conway gave a performance that was all right, but had to wear a silly ceremonial headdress. Paul Dubov was the most entertaining hustler in a film where those who weren't soaked in tarnish were at least flecked by it — unless their names happened to be Susan, Saranda (sound like the name of a certain actress?) or Bobo.

Alex Gordon took his fiance, writer Ruth Alexander, to the Burbank premiere of *Voodoo Woman*. She had never seen any of his films. Gordon liked the picture, but partial to class, Ruth returned his engagement ring. Alex introduced Ruth to brother Richard, who explained to her the handicaps of cinema several grades below her accustomed fare. Ultimately, things worked out. After appearing with Mike Connors in *The Flesh and the Spur* (1957), a Gordon film he helped executive produce, Marla English left Hollywood to marry the young owner of some parking lots in San Diego. Alex Gordon produced two war films for AIP, *Jet Attack* and *Submarine Seahawk* (1958), then left, complaining that AIP's other production units absorbed profits from his.

Having ripped off *The She Creature* with *Creature of Destruction*, Larry Buchanan tore *Curse of the Swamp Creature* (1966) from *Voodoo Woman*. This travesty was a little better in story, its voodooists the poor blacks of a Texas swamp. Its source of treasure was oil. The treasure seekers were a whole gang of hoods led by a girl named Brenda Simmons and the purpose of mad science was the creation of "fish-men". Roland and Susan Gerard were Simon and Laura Trent, and John Agar was an almost entirely sedentary Ted Bronson as geologist and marathon chain-smoker Barry Rogers. The "natives" hated Trent and created an effigy of the doctor to curse him. Trent's failed subject was his own male assistant and the Marilyn "success", Brenda, became a bald, bug-eyed hunk. Taking the role of transformed Brenda was Bill Thurman, who had been cast as Harry West surrogate Driscoll West. Brenda fed Trent to an alligator and committed suicide by jumping into the gator pool after him.

Lance Fuller took some LSD in 1968 and, luckily, didn't jump out of a window or off a roof. His acid madness consisted mainly of smashing car windows in a parking lot. As he was taken into custody, Fuller ranted that he was Christ. Fortunately for Marla English's husband, the lot was not one of his properties. Fuller recovered and became a sparsely employed supporting player while trying to sell scripts.

49

NOT OF THIS EARTH

Allied Artists, 1957
released in Italy as *Il Vampiro Del Planeto Russo*

Producer-Director	Roger Corman
Screenplay	Charles B. Griffith
	Mark Hanna
Cinematography	John Mescall
Film Editor	Charles Gross
Music	Ronald Stein
Production Manager-Assistant Director	Lou Place
Sound	Philip Michell
Key Grip	Charles Hanawalt
Makeup	Curly Batson
Property Master	Karl Brainard
Special Effects	Paul Blaisdell
Titles	Paul Julian

A Los Altos Production
Running time: 67 minutes

Cast: Paul Birch (Paul Johnson), Beverly Garland (Nadine Storey), Morgan Jones (Harry Sherbourne), William Roerick (Dr. Frederick Rochelle), Jonathan Haze (Jeremy Perrin), Richard *aka Dick* Miller (Joe Piper), Anne Carroll (Davanna Woman), Tamar Cooper (Joanne), Gail Ganley (Girl), Ralph Reed (Boy), Roy Engel (Sgt. Walton), Pay Flynn (Simmons), Harold Fong (Specimen), Barbara Bohrer (Waitress)

Roger Corman's early filmmaking was not limited exclusively to AIP. Other companies learned about his efficiency and consistent profit record. Allied Artists hired him to make several films. *Not of This Earth* and *Attack of the Crab Monsters* were especially challenging since Corman had to establish credibility in one story about talking, intelligent mutant land crabs and in another about an alien vampire. These movies furthered the elasticity of his talent.

A quiet residential street. A teenaged girl kisses her date goodnight out of his parked sports car. On her way home, the girl is startled by a hooting owl. She meets an imposing, dark-suited stranger holding a metal

(Above) Alien vampire Paul Johnson (Paul Birch) and Nurse Storey (Beverly Garland) are confronted by Jonathan Haze in NOT OF THIS EARTH (1957).

briefcase. Removing his dark glasses, he casts a fatal stare. From the opened briefcase, the stranger takes two tubes. Puncturing her neck, he drains the girl's blood into a row of vials. His eyes are white blanks.

Known as Paul Johnson, the stranger drives his black Cadillac limousine to a clinic where he has an appointment. Johnson is on the left side of the street and parks by a fire hydrant, a No Parking sign and a red painted curb. He tells genial reception nurse, Nadine Storey, that he wants an immediate blood transfusion without a test. He is type O. "We don't hand out blood like it was gasoline," says Nadine. "We have to find out if you're ethyl or regular." While Johnson sits in a waiting chair, a loud buzzer causes him violent pain. Dr. Rochelle invites Johnson into his office and explains the need for testing. To graphically illustrate his problem, Johnson cuts his write with a scalpel — but there is no bleeding at first. When Rochelle presses the test, Johnson hypnotizes him. "You will test," Johnson commands, "then you will know and you will prescribe. You may study it in all the ways of your kind and you may learn. You may not speak. You will not. You cannot transmit to any other being your knowledge of my tragedy." Rochelle consciously awakens, happy that Johnson has changed his mind about the test.

Rochelle studies a sample of Johnson's blood and is amazed by its structural disintegration. While Nadine administers a transfusion, Johnson solicits her services to preserve his life. "Mr. Johnson," Nadine tells him," no one in this world can guarantee life." "Nor in any other, I fear," he muses. Johnson will pay Nadine two hundred dollars a week and she agrees to take his case when Dr. Rochelle grants permission. "Just what is wrong with him?" Nadine asks. Rochelle is about to reply, but autosuggestion stops him. "I'm — I'm not positive." Nadine walks Johnson to his car, where her motorcycle cop boyfriend Harry Sherbourne tries to ticket Johnson for his multiple traffic violations, but Nadine alibis for Johnson by saying that he is sick.

Harry escorts Johnson to his mansion. Johnson's butler and chauffeur is ex-con Jeremy Perrin. Jeremy is told to stay out of the kitchen so Johnson can open the briefcase and refrigerate the vials. When he exits briefly, meddling Jeremy takes from the case a plastic tube containing a peculiar object. Sneaking back, Johnson mentally freezes Jeremy before he can unscrew the top and returns the tube to the case. Jeremy comes to, startled to see Johnson. If Jeremy continues to spy, he will be "eliminated".

Nadine moves in that night. Johnson startles her

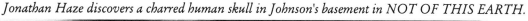

Jonathan Haze discovers a charred human skull in Johnson's basement in NOT OF THIS EARTH.

51

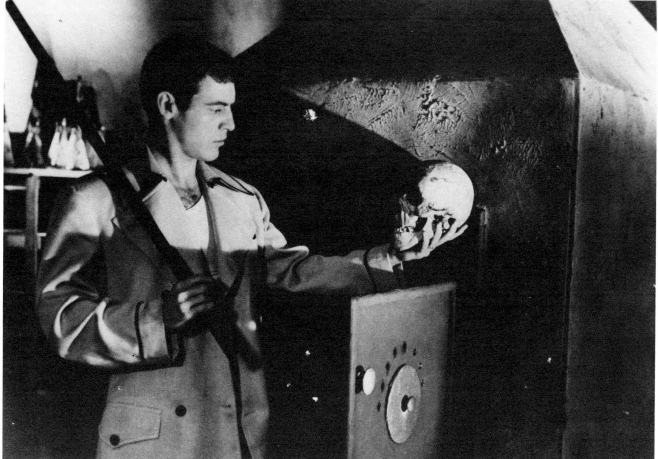

when he locks her bedroom door from the outside. Where he comes from, no one dares to sleep in insecure quarters. "Where do you come from?" asks Nadine. "I believe your expression was . . . 'Good night'?" Johnson says evasively.

In the parlor, Johnson seats himself in a stuffed chair, removes his dark glasses and uses a small transistor to slide back a wall panel concealing a teleporter. A bodiless head, the Courier, reports worsening atomic war on their planet, Davanna. Enemies captured for pasture dwindle. More earth blood is needed. Johnson's mission will consist of five of six Phases, says the Courier. "In the first, you will study all the characteristics of the earth subhumans. In the second Phase, increase the quantity of earth blood for transmission to Davanna. For Phase Three, you must have a live specimen, a subhuman to be used in vivisection research. You are Phase Four: in which earth blood value will be determined by your survival or your death. If earth blood preserves your life, Phase Five will be the conquest, subjugation and pasturing of the earth subhumans. Phase Six will be the utter obliteration of this planet, dependent upon the anticipated failure of your experiment. Phase Six concludes the instructions." The Courier vanishes and the wall panel closes.

Jeremy brings Johnson breakfast, but he does not eat. Johnson wants Jeremy to take him to the Public Library later. For nourishment, Johnson mixes odd pills with water that becomes a dark liquid when he stirs his glass. Nadine is getting dressed behind a screen by her bed. Jeremy pops in. Johnson pays him three hundred dollars a week to guard the cellar and turn gold ingots into money. When Jeremy tries to sneak a peek behind the screen, Nadine slaps him and he whirls out of the room laughing.

While Nadine goes to the backyard pool for a swim, Johnson answers the front door. Aggressive door-to-door vacuum cleaner salesman, Joe Piper, tries to interest Johnson in his product without success until Joe asks Johnson to permit a demonstration in the cellar. "In my . . . cellar?" asks Johnson, who sees Joe as a new victim. "Come right in, young man. I shall be glad to see your machine in operation." In the basement, Joe uses a cleaner attachment to unplug a drain pipe. He turns up to Johnson as Johnson removes his dark glasses. Joe does a goofy double take and dies staring into Johnson's eyes. Taking his blood, Johnson stuffs Joe's body into an incinerator.

At an intersection, Jeremy hits the limousine's brakes when a speeder making a sharp turn cuts him off. The noise bothers Johnson, who glimpses three winos seated at a park bench. Jeremy explains to him what winos are. "Phase Two," mutters Johnson to himself. He gets out at the library and tells Jeremy to invite the winos home for dinner. On his day off, Harry runs into Rochelle, who is waiting at a bus stop because his car is in the shop, and offers him a ride to Johnson's house.

While lounging by the pool, Nadine sees rising chimney smoke. She pokes around the basement and is about to open the incinerator when she hears Harry honk his horn. Nadine goes upstairs, leaving her bathing cap behind. Nadine greets Harry and Rochelle as Johnson and Jeremy come back. Harry remembers Jeremy from his hoodlum days. Harry and Nadine have coffee in the kitchen, while Rochelle informs Johnson that the gluten in his blood is figuratively evaporating. Rochelle is working full time to find a cure. "God forbid if a dreadful new plague should strike the earth." He feels that time is the greatest element. "Time is indeed the *only* element," emphasizes Johnson. Harry and Rochelle leave. Johnson tells Jeremy to collect his "guests". In the basement, Johnson is raking the contents of the incinerator when he spots Nadine's bathing cap.

While Nadine and Harry go out that night, the winos enjoy their banquet in the basement. Johnson zaps two in succession. "They're dead drunk!" exclaims the third. Zap. Johnson has Jeremy lug a heavy steamer trunk with vials of their blood to the parlor. Walking Nadine back to the house, Harry disapproves of her living with a "two-bit crook" and a "creep". Nadine administers a new transfusion to Johnson. The Courier receives the trunk in the teleporter. Within twenty-four hours, Johnson will secure a human.

Sgt. Walton, Harry's precinct chief, tells him about the recent "vampire" murders of the past month. Thirteen are known dead and the missing persons rate is up. The Airways Vacuum Cleaner company reported Joe Piper's disappearance. "They probably don't want the salesman," chuckles Harry, "they want the cleaner." "All I can think of," ponders Walton, "is who will be next."

During his next transfusion, Johnson tells Nadine he has done some medical research. No one knows why uranium is attracted to cancer and Johnson concludes that cancerous tissue is negatively charged. On the street, Johnson hypnotizes a Chinaman. Anarchy reigns on Davanna, where the Chinaman is willed to teleport himself.

Nadine studies a water glass stained with the food supplement's murky residue. Jeremy mentions the odd disappearances of Johnson's "guests". He proposes snooping around. Nadine takes the fluid to Rochelle for analysis. Harry calls while nurse Joanne places a bottle of rabid dog blood in the refrigerator for later testing. Harry has night duty, but enough time to take Nadine to a favorite restaurant. Rochelle will meet them there when he has the test results on the fluid. Before going downtown, Johnson removes the bathing cap from his pocket and hands it to Jeremy as an indication of his lax security.

Downtown, Johnson is followed by and meets a familiar Davanna woman wearing glasses like his. At a newsstand where they pretend to be reading magazines, they telepathically converse. The woman teleported herself to Johnson's dwelling even though unauthorized transmissions are a capital crime. The war is over, but the blood supply diminishes and enemy captives are killed and de-blooded. "I had to escape . . . or perish," says the woman. The Courier was also slain for his blood. Transmissions from earth are now known to be impossible: the Chinaman arrived in a compressed state. The Courier had remained whole only because he never left the dimensional beam. Though he and the woman are doomed to remain on earth, Johnson wants another specimen. When the woman shows emotion, Johnson reproaches her and she tells him that without blood soon, she will have no need of emotion. Johnson sends Jeremy home in a taxi.

At the restaurant, Rochelle tells Nadine and Harry the food supplement contains every known vitamin and more. Johnson breaks into the clinic by shattering a window with his eyes. When Nadine asks if Johnson has managed to combine every vitamin into one primary unit, Rochelle's autosuggestion take over and he asks, "Who's he?" "Mr. Johnson," answers Nadine. Rochelle shows mild irritation at the mere mention of his name and turns to his menu. While the Davanna woman lies down on a table in Rochelle's office, Johnson unknowingly removes the bottle of rabid blood from the refrigerator. The woman rises a few moments later and feels strangely "disturbed", saying, "There is activity within me." Because they look alike, the woman cannot stay with Johnson. She will sleep in a motel and meet Johnson at noon the next day.

On the street, the woman becomes ill. Staggering back to the clinic, she cries, "Davanna!", and collapses by the entrance. Rochelle and Joanne attend to her. Joanne notices that the woman's glasses are similar to Johnson's but Rochelle ignores that. The woman dies. When her glasses are removed, her eyelids blink, revealing blank orbs.

For the new specimen, Johnson hypnotizes a parking lot attendant. A customer's loud horn blasts for service, breaking the spell, and the attendant flees. Harry calls Nadine to mention the dead Davanna woman, linking her to Johnson. Nadine wants to stay at the house and find more evidence despite Harry's protests. Johnson stalks the attendant, who mentally defies him. The attendant runs to the top of a stairway and Johnson zaps him.

Jeremy tells Nadine he saw the woman. He discovers the teleporter transmitter and exposes the device. Nadine feels the teleporter should be smashed, but an invisible barrier protects it. While Jeremy goes to the basement, Johnson secretly returns. Rochelle calls Nadine to discuss the woman, who lived in an immensely radioactive area that affected her blood — an area of all-out nuclear warfare. "But there is no such place," insists Nadine. "There's no doubt in my mind," Rochelle tells her, "that she's something other than human — an alien." Removal from the toxic atmosphere and a change of

blood could have cured the woman. When Nadine questions Johnson's hold, Rochelle hangs up. Over a phone extension, Johnson says, "The doctor is no longer in contact." He hypnotizes Nadine and sends her to her room.

In the basement, Jeremy finds a charred human skull in the incinerator. Upstairs, he sees Johnson on the second floor steps, throws the skull at him and whips out his gun, but Johnson zaps him. Nadine's hypnosis wears off and when Johnson advances, her piercing screams weaken him long enough for her to bolt from the house. "You may conceal your person," Johnson telepathically call out, "but I can find your mind." To kill Rochelle, Johnson removes the object from the briefcase tube. Exposed to a compact ray, it becomes a floating umbrella-like thing that leaves through the kitchen window.

At Rochelle's, Harry tries to call Nadine. "To think she's under the same roof with that monster," he says. "Mr. Johnson is no monster," defends Rochelle. Harry leaves for night duty as Rochelle dials the coroner to report the dead Davanna woman. Through an open window behind him, the umbrella thing enters, plops down on his head and crushes it. Rochelle's body slumps over his desk and blood gushes forth.

From a park phone booth, hysterical Nadine calls Sgt. Walton, telling Harry that Johnson is after her. Harry tells Nadine to stay where she is, but Johnson roars up in the limo. He chases Nadine through the park while Harry and Off. Simmons cycle to the park. Johnson pursues Nadine on foot, ordering her to stop running. Harry and Simmons arrive and split up. Exhaustion overtakes Nadine and Johnson re-hypnotizes her. Since the death of the Chinaman may have been an accident, Johnson will try to send another specimen — Nadine. As they walk to the limo, Johnson anticipates Simmons and zaps him off his bake. Johnson tells Nadine to walk to the house, enter the dimensional beam of the teleporter and slide the power lever. Johnson flees in the limo as Harry turns to Simmons and joins Nadine. Assuming she is safe, Harry chases Johnson.

As Nadine approaches the house, Harry pursues Johnson along a twisting, dangerous mountain highway. Johnson takes off his glasses. "Look into my eyes?" He commands. "My eyes are alien! Look at them! Look at me! Look at me!" Nadine enters the teleporter. When Harry turns on his siren, agonized Johnson clasps his ears. The limo jumps a curve, rolls down a steep embankment and explodes. About to press the lever, Nadine recovers and screams. Flames from the wreckage frame Johnson's face.

Johnson's gravestone reads, "Here Lies A Man Who Was Not Of This Earth." "In a way, I feel sorry for him," Harry tells Nadine. "Why sorry?" she asks. "Buried so far from home, away from everyone he knew," answers Harry. "I can't feel sorry for him," differs Nadine, "he had no emotions as we know them. He was a foreign

53

thing sent to destroy us. Thank God he tried too hard." As Nadine and Harry leave, a distant man with a metal briefcase, black suit and dark glasses walks into the foreground.

Corman's only vampire movie, *Not of This Earth*, written by Charles Griffith and Mark Hanna, inaugurated many future trends, notable teleportation and socially-mobile vampires unafraid of the sun. Intellectually superior but conspicuously unaccustomed to our ways, Johnson was almost mirthful for his naive shortcomings. His scenes of maladjustment were almost like seeing parts of *The Fearless Vampire Killers (Or, Pardon Me, But Your Teeth Are in My Neck)* (1967) grafted into *Horror of Dracula* (1958). Willpower, as Johnson wielded it, was a fine-tuned, free-form gift. He could turn nervous systems on or off like faucets to totally subjugate people or put them on hold long enough to tidy minor messes. Johnson, however, was not psychic (except when dealing with Off. Simmons) and his censoring of Rochelle's mind only applied to matters of his personal health.

The first on-screen meeting between Johnson and the Courier shaped a rough but disturbing impression of Davanna. Blood wasn't an unholy oral pleasure but survival itself. Vampirism as inflicted on other vampires smacks of incest and for all their colder, more clinical attitudes about needing blood (like calling *us* "subhuman"), the Davannians were parasites to the lowest degree. Johnson was lucky to be living here. His homeland was a dying ball of scorched earth where, if contamination didn't kill people, their veins were drained by kinsmen with a shared need. Atomically, Davanna's present was the future we dreaded for ourselves during the Cold War.

Johnson wasn't always an intentional killer. The first such casualty was the Chinaman. The Davanna woman who followed, was a sad being who made us think that a few Davannians may have been worth saving. Where Johnson spoke in rich, brusque tones, the woman related softly and submissively. Telepathy between the two was not just communication without moving lips but an ensurer of intellectual confidence, letting feelings flow. Their dialogue in Rochelle's office brought up the theory of parallel planets to explain why Davannians were humanoid looking, save for their Orphan Annie-Daddy Warbucks eyes. The woman's death by rabies was the first time vampires were ever affected by things the bloodstream absorbs (what about the million-proof blood of the winos?). After Rochelle and Jeremy died, horror depended on whether Nadine would die in the

(Above) Beverly Garland is startled when she sees Johnson approaching in NOT OF THIS EARTH.

unstable teleporter or be vivisected on Davanna. The appearance of a new Johnson at the end was the first of the Vampirism Still Lives endings.

The plot was rather sketchy about Johnson's early arrival. Exactly where did first materialize in the teleporter? The murders he committed in the space of one month were apparent only to the police. How could Davanna expect Johnson alone to keep it supplied with fresh blood? Though shaky in English, not knowing that words like "flip-flops" and "hootch" were slang, Johnson was able to communicate with the Chinaman in fluent Cantonese.

Charles Griffith had been married to a nurse. Her occupation inspired the character of Nadine and the ex-Mrs. Griffith provided much of the medical material. Griffith's organic assassin, for Johnson his version of an *It Conquered the World* control device, was a different entity than the one in the film. In World War II, margarine was white and packaged with yellow food capsules. Griffith had Johnson create a doglike monster with crocodile teeth by mixing capsule liquid in bath water. The idea was to have a Great Dane play the Instant Reptile-Canine. What Paul Blaisdell came up with was the umbrella thing. Its living substance and shape brought to mind the lamp shades of human flesh credited to the Nazis. When Rochelle died, looking like a lamp shade party drunk who couldn't get his off, there was no resolution to what would happen to the thing . . . unless, like the control devices, it had outlived its particular usefulness.

Blaisdell wanted to build a fully-detailed teleporter, but only had time to construct the platform and the framework. The dark glasses worn by Johnson and the Davanna woman were ordinary shades fixed up with black adhesive tape.

The greatest technical achievement of *Not Of This Earth* was the use of white contact lenses. Tor Johnson had worn them in several horror roles, but they were only an incidental detail. The lenses that Paul Birch tried to put up with were such torture that he got into a near-fight with Corman and left the production. A double played Johnson in the clinic reception room scene, the rabid blood sequence and at the top of the stairway of Johnson's mansion when he called Jeremy to help him carry the steamer trunk (Johnson's voice in the last scene sounded like that of Leslie Bradley of *Attack of the Crab Monsters*).

If Paul Birch was a problem (though understandably), Dick Miller and William Roerick exercised much creative initiative. Joe Piper was originally written as a simple kid working his way through college who wore a bow tie and had pencils in his pocket. Dick Miller enacted Joe as a cynical jive-talking pitchman in black suit, black shirt and white tie

who dressed as Miller did when he sold pots and pans in the Bronx. For Rochelle's head-crushing, Hershey's syrup was intended. There wasn't any, so William Roerick put grape juice in his mouth and let it spill all over as Rochelle expired.

Charles Gross' editing used Eisensteinian crosscuts between Nadine's slow walk to the teleporter and Harry chasing Johnson for a fantastic cliff hanger climax. Heard against a Dantesque animated titles sequence by Paul Julian, who did the titles for *Crab Monsters*, Ronald Stein's muted shadowy theme music became the theme for *Queen of Blood* (1966), another space vampire movie that set it to different title graphics.

It was a tribute to Paul Birch's skill that Johnson would be inept and clumsy as well as shrewd and calculating — acting on impulses and expressing sentiments entirely appropriate to what Johnson was. Birch has been something of an enigma. It is known that he died around 1969. Following his Corman career, Birch played Perry Mason creator, Erle Stanley Gardner, in the fact-based TV series "The Court of Last Resort". He also was Mike Malone in the syndicated Canadian trucker show "Cannonball". On "The Fugitive", Birch made recurring appearances as Barry Morse's superior. Beverly Garland was more likeable and emotionally stable in *Not Of This Earth* than she had been in *It Conquered the World*, and Morgan Jones was a pretty convincing cop.

Anne Carroll brought out the wistful recessiveness of the Davanna woman by playing down her part while Birch maintained his dominant tone. Jonathan Haze and Dick Miller — Haze a goon, Miller a buffoon — did what they did best.

In 1988, Corman authorized a color remake of *Not of This Earth* directed by one of his fan proteges, Jim Wynorski. Little better than the AIP film remakes of Larry Buchanan, it cast thin, soft-spoken Arthur Roberts as Johnson and capitalized on the porn notoriety of Traci Lords by starring her as Nadine. Lenny Juliano and Micheal Delano did entertaining impressions of Jeremy and Joe Piper. However, this movie had an aging Flower Child for a full-bodied Courier, a poor woman's Sybil Danning for the female Davannian, a nearsighted Strip-O-Gram girl and hookers in place of winos. Pale as the pic was, it tried to match many props and effects remembered from the original. Robert's Johnson drove a black '56 Caddy — this one a two-door hardtop — in keeping with the nostalgia car vogue and his blank eyes were animated spots (the ghost of Paul Birch must be seething in envy). Permitted to live in the Wynorski film, Dr. Rochelle compared Johnson's disease to a "dreadful new plague" that has *indeed* struck the earth: AIDS.

ATTACK OF THE CRAB MONSTERS

Allied Artists, 1957

Producer-Director	Roger Corman
Screenplay	Charles B. Griffith
Cinematography	Floyd Crosby
Film Editor	Charles Gross
Music	Ronald Stein
Assistant Director	Maurice Vaccarino
Underwater Scenes Director	Maitland Stuart
Props	Karl Brainard
Chief Grip	Charles Hanawalt
Gaffer	Floyd Williams
Makeup	Curly Batson
Titles	Paul Julian
Underwater Equipment	Healthways

Scenes Filmed at Marineland of California
A Los Altos Production
Running time: 62 minutes

Cast: Richard Garland (Dale Drewer), Pamela Duncan (Martha Hunter), Russell Johnson (Hank Chapman),

Leslie Bradley (Dr. Karl Weigand), Mel Welles (Dr. Jules Devereaux), Richard Cutting (Dr. James Carson), Beach Dickerson (Sam Sommers), Tony Miller (Ron Fellows), Ed Nelson (Ensign Quinlan), Charles Griffith (Tate), Maitland Stuart, Robin Reilly, Doug Roberts

Attack of the Crab Monsters was filmed as *Attack of the Giant Crabs*, but the release title made it Roger Corman's top-grossing black and white feature. The size of the crabs was less memorable than their intelligence, an idea he and Charles Griffith developed to lessen predictability. *Day the World Ended* and *It Conquered the World* were both crammed with episodes, but certain stretches of them were tedious and suspense waned when their monsters appeared. For *Crab Monsters*, Griffith had to make every scene shocking or suspenseful, thinking up situations that begged imagination to wonder how the crabs could be connected.

Near a remote South Pacific atoll, the Eugelap atomic test commences. Turbulent tidal water smashes inland, routing inhabitants and destroying buildings.

(Above) The classic crustacean monster of ATTACK OF THE CRAB MONSTERS (1957).

The turbulence subsides. Sent to the atoll to study its radioactive conditions, the McLean expedition vanished.

A small Navy seaplane boat brings Ensign Quinlan and more scientists from McLean's institute. Disembarking on the beach, they are nuclear physicist Dr. Karl Weighand, land biologist Dale Drewer, marine biologist Martha Hunter, botanist Prof. Jules Devereaux, geologist Dr. James Carson and technician Hank Chapman. "Strange," observes Jules, "you can see only a small part of the island from this spot, yet you feel lack of welcome. Lack of abiding life, eh?" "Yeah," concurres Quinlan. "I felt the same when I came here before to rescue your first group. I not only knew they were gone, but that they were lost, completely and forever, body and soul." "Maybe their bodies are gone, but who can tell of their souls, eh?" fantasizes Jules. "Maybe if I call to them, they will answer. Their ghosts will answer." When he calls McLean's name, a flock of seagulls scatter.

While the scientists move on to the prepared shelter beyond a gorge, Quinlan oversees the arrival of another supply raft. The three men on board lose their headway. Quinlan orders Seaman Tate to sit down, but when the boat broaches, he falls overboard. Underwater, a terrifying crustacean shape opens one of its eyes. Tate screams in horror, bubbles gushing from his mouth. Seamen Ron Fellows and Sam Sommers pull him up by his feet, retrieving a headless body. "God help us!" cries Ron. "Cover him," Quinlan murmurs grimly.

Demolition experts assigned to assist Carson in his mountain excavations, Ron and Sam pitch their beach tent near Tate's covered body and several land crabs crawling around in the sand. The scientists move into a renovated house, where Hank bumps into Martha and formally meets her. Karl and Jim are aghast to hear from Quinlan what happened to Tate. All that McLean left was a journal. The Navy believes that he and his party were all at sea in their boat when a sudden typhoon struck. "Lost with all hands is an old story," figures Quinlan. Storm clouds above look threatening.

The scientists are invited to watch the sailors leave. Along the beach path, muffled booms resound and the sailors narrowly dodge a rock landslide. From a cliff top, the scientists, Ron and Sam, watch the departing seaplane gracefully skim across the water. As it rises aloft, it immediately explodes. The Navy may think that Quinlan chose to wait out the storm rather than go back to Eniwetok.

During the storm, Hank attempts to radio the Navy, receiving only music from Manila or Samoa. Karl reads aloud an excerpt from McLean's journal. An unidentified piece of flesh was found, similar in composition to a common earth worm, but measuring twenty-four by eight inches — making the wormlike creature total size about five feet long. The flesh resisted cutting, showing no marks. Fire was applied. The journal ends there. Dale thinks everyone should retire, but Hank wonders about the worm. McLean only meant to imply something similar to a worm, such as the giant sea worm . . . known to grow much longer than five feet. "The journal didn't say anything about the sea," dourly comments Hank. "Just talked about worms." More muffled explosions erupt.

Later that night, Hank notices the agitation of some guinea pigs in the lab. Dale and Karl are debating McLean's worm theory when the hear an odd clicking sound near the front door. There is nothing outside. "Just the wind," muses Karl. Broken wiring taps against the side of the house.

The next morning, Martha goes scuba diving for specimens. Dale joins Martha, startling her. A large "rock" she was using for a landmark vanishes. Back on shore, Dale says he saw a big black shape moving near; but for land crabs and sea gulls, everything appears dead. Jim urgently summons Dale and Martha. The others are gathered around a deep pit in the path Martha had taken to the beach. It has appeared only in the last twenty minutes. Jim wants to explore the bottom, but Karl warns of a possible cave-in. Martha studies a rock that is oddly glazed, as though it was fired in a kiln. Ron and Sam are instructed to put lanterns around the pit.

Asleep, Martha is awakened by a ghostly voice calling to her. "It is McLean," it says. McLean urges Martha to go to the pit, pleading, "Help me, Martha . . . help me . . ." At the pit, Martha encounters Jim, who heard McLean calling only his name. "How could the Navy search this whole island and miss a survivor?" he wonders. "If he *is* a survivor . . .," shudders Martha, who thinks McLean is dead and someone is imitating him. Against Karl's warning, Jim foolhardily ropes up to enter the pit. "You don't know what's down there," protests Martha. "What could be there other than earth, water and a few land crabs?" asks Jim. He tells Martha to hold a light on him until he is out of sight. Martha hears the clicking sound and calls to Jim. Another tremor knocks her out. Jim falls, screaming.

The others revive Martha. Karl calls to Jim, who shouts that his leg is broken. Karl wants to reach Jim through the sea caves because they theorized the pit was created from below. Dale takes Martha back to the house. Ron and Sam appear, describing a massive landslide that nearly destroyed their tent. It seemed to them like the whole island was coming down. "The whole island, yes," apprehensively utters Karl. "We must hurry. There is very little time." "Little time for what?" asks Sam. "That is Dr. Weigand's small secret," answers Jules as the search for Jim begins.

In the house, Martha is reviewing McLean's journal when she hears clicking and she and Dale hear the groaning of torn wood as something tremendous smashes into the lab. Armed with a revolver, Dale cautiously enters. As he clears the door, a huge claw lunges at his gun hand. Dale runs back to the living room and hugs Martha as the intruder breaks things. In the caves, the others hear Jim calling, but find only a

Russel Johnson, Richard Garland and Pamela Duncan are panic stricken in ATTACK OF THE CRAB MONSTERS.

pool of blood. Karl urges Hank not to call. The intruder tries to get into the living room until electricity crackles and the thing howls in pain. The others reach Jim's rope. Karl orders everyone to leave the cave by climbing it rather than going back the way they came. The house electricity is out and the lab is strangely quiet. Dale and Martha find it a complete shambles. There is a gaping hole in the outside wall. Apparently, the intruder wanted food. Dale wants to contact the Navy, but the radio has been scrupulously damaged.

Hank labors on rebuilding the radio while the others attempt to size up what happened. Karl thinks the shorted wiring acted as a barrier against the intruder. "You mean it's afraid of electricity?" asks Dale. Staring through the wall hold, Martha intones, "And once there was a mountain." When the group first arrived, there was a mountain where she is looking. Today, no mountain. Everything that has happened from the death of Seaman Tate to the condition of the radio is somehow related. "We are unquestionably on the brink of a great discovery," proclaims Karl. "It is not likely that that discovery will be of a pleasant nature."

During the resumed search for Jim, a tremor brings down falling cave rock. Everyone else grabs a piece of the wall, but Jules stumbles and a rock severs his right hand. An emergency tourniquet is applied as Ron and Sam appear. They were on the other side of the island when they were called. "We didn't call you," insists Dale.

"It sounded like the other guy," says Sam, "— the one who fell into the pit."

In bed, weakened Jules is sedated by Martha. While playing poker in their tent, Ron and Sam hear the clicking. "Sounds like a kid running a stick across a picket fence," says Ron. Sam pulls back the outer tent flap to investigate and screams. Jules is awakened by the voices of Ron and Sam, who claim they have found Jim. Jules must come to the pit — alone. Painfully, he drags himself there. Ron and Sam are nowhere to be seen. "We're right here, Professor," Ron's voice says as the claw grabs Jules.

Jules' death screams rouse Dale, Martha, Hank and Karl. His disembodied voice says it was only a nightmare. In Jules' empty bedroom, Karl traces the voice to a steel nightstand ash tray. "Congratulations," says Jules. "Where are you?" asks Martha. "Where you all will be," answers Jules. "I will be back tomorrow night." "Is this supposed to be a ghost story?" asks mystified Hank. "We are dealing with a man who is dead," states Karl, "but whose voice and memory live. How this can be, I do not know, but its implications are far more terrible than any ghost could ever be."

The bodies of Ron and Sam are missing from their wrecked tent. So is most of the dynamite. After a long wait that night, Jules speaks through a gun. To be heard, he transmits his voice through metallic objects. He invites everyone to come to the cave. Karl inquires about

Richard Garland and Pamela Duncan are attacked by a crab monster.

Jim. "I am here too," says Jim. "My leg no longer troubles me. It's almost exhilarating. Will you come?" Karl agrees to the appointment.

In the cave, Karl announces Dale, Hank and himself. They hear clicking. A monster land crab attacks. Hank's first grenade is ineffective, but another dislodges a sharp ceiling rock the penetrates the crab's brain. Dale recalls the matter of the worm and how blades passed through it like water. "If a blade passes through it like a finger through mercury," guesses Karl, about to sever a claw with his pick, "then like a river of mercury we should be able to sever a part of it by completely separating it from the rest of the body —," the claw comes off, "— thusly." Dynamite is set to bury the crab when another appears. Karl takes a photograph as he, Dale and Hank throw themselves to the ground before the dynamite blast. In Jules' voice, the angry crab shouts, "You have destroyed my mate and all of McLean's party! You have destroyed them and tried to destroy me? That was a great mistake!"

Composed of free atoms, the crabs are like a liquid with a permanent shape. "Any matter, therefore, that the crab eats will be assimilated in its body of solid energy," espouses Karl, "becoming part of the crab." "Like the bodies of the dead men?" asks Martha. "Yes," answers Karl. "And the brain tissue, which after all is nothing but a storage house for electrical impulses." "This means," adds Dale, "that the crab can eat its victims' brain, absorbing its victim's mind intact and working."

Martha wonders why the minds of Jim and Jules have turned against them. "Preservation of the species," avers Dale, "once they were men — now they're land crabs." To blow up the island, the crabs generate great arcs of heat from their bodies. They melt and fuse parts of the cavern and explode the materials contained, thereby causing the slides. "To get at us, of course," reasons Karl.

"Looks like we're on the verge of a blessed event," remarks Martha, studying the photo Karl took. "What's that? *What's that?!*" he cries. The picture is of the surviving pregnant female crab. Delivery time appears dangerously close. "I, for one," shudders Martha, "should not like to be around to hear the patter of so many tiny feet!" Karl would like to capture the crab alive for study. Hank subjects the crab claw to a mild positive current that disintegrates it. Karl proposes building a positive trap to catch the negatively charged crab.

Hank successfully tests an electric eye. The crab can be de-energized long enough for removal of its claws so it can be caged. A different cave route is needed for installment of the eyes since the old entrance is flooded. The crab can be heard detonating the stolen dynamite.

In scuba gear, Hank and Martha will plant the electric eyes while Dale and Karl will attempt to divert the crab. The oppressive darkness and loneliness of the cave bring Hank and Martha closer together. Hank has started to fall in love with Martha. Before he can say anything, he hears the crab sleeping behind a wall.

Unsheathing his aqua knife, Hank says, "This might be the perfect time to collect some of Dr. Weigand's mercury." But the crab awakens. Dale and Karl see Hank and Martha running toward the sea entrance from above. They escape underwater and surface at the beach, where Dale injures one of the crab's claws with his rifle. "So! You have wounded me!" cries the petulant crab in Jim's voice. "I must grow a new claw. Well, it's good, for I can do it in only a day. But will you grow new lives when I have taken yours from you?"

Hank fixes the radio, but it only receives, picking up a Hawaiian commercial station. With a telegraph key, he can transmit Morse Code. Dale and Karl survey what remains of the island. Near where the pit had been, the blasts have exposed traces of oil coming from two directions. Karl wants to follow the trails separately. "The crab is like a rattlesnake. It can be heard long before it is seen. The crab knows this better than we do. That is why he is trying to reduce this island to a small corner from which there is no escape."

From another part of the cave, Dale sees the crab approaching Karl. At the entrance, he tells Hank and Martha. Told to stay outside, Martha follows Dale and Hank. Recoiling from the crab, Karl stumbles backwards into the field of a paralyzing electric eye. The crab proceeds to devour him. Hank rushes Martha away while Dale hurls his cigarette lighter at the oil, igniting it. But the crab avoids the main stream. "That was quick thinking, Dale," praises the crab in Karl's voice. "The pity is that all fires must one day burn out."

As Hank works the radio again, it dies. "By the time ships and planes arrive," foresees the crab, "this island will have vanished beneath the waves of the sea. But you will not drown. You will be a part of me! And as with McLean, there will be no evidence of how you vanished or of my existence. We will rest in the caves and plan our assault upon the world of men." The fiercest tremors yet force Dale, Hank and Martha out of the collapsing house. Most of the island crumbles away.

Arduously, Dale, Hank and Martha reach a promontory with the radio tower and a tool box. The crab rises up from over rock and lurches their way, withstanding grenades. "Foolish . . . very foolish," it taunts. Dale swings a hatchet at one of its claws. When Hank moves in too close with his last grenade, the crab knocks him down. The dropped grenade explodes, wounding his leg. Hank lures the crab to the tower and scales one side. The crab reacts to its electricity. When the tower topples, Hank and the crab disintegrate. Dale and Martha avert their eyes. "He gave his life —," laments Dale. "I know . . . ," softly moans Martha.

In many respects, *Attack of the Crab Monsters* was a carry over from *Day the World Ended*. Both began with heady anticipation of nuclear spectacle. Aftermaths of the explosions were commented on by similar celestial voices. The characters lived in isolated but comfortable homes. Most sections of their environments looked normal but felt strange. In various ways, the mutants were travesties of people. Audaciously the crabs expressed the dietetic adage "You are what you eat" — their mental attributes meant to balance limited mobility. When they first mutated, their driving force was hunger. Each consumed mind turned the knowledge of its owner to the enforcement of crustacean supremacy. Having eaten the McLean party, the male crab initiated most of the action up to Jim's disappearance. The female caught up by feeding on Weigand's associates.

Suspense was built bilaterally, alternating between the disappearances and the progressive, calculated erosion of the terrain. When someone vanished, the crabs used his voice to play on the emotional attachments of his colleagues. Intellectually, the scientists could not accept these spectral "visitations", yielding to deception out of concern for the safety of their friends. The strategic pit was a lure for the chosen. Once the crabs were exposed, the scientists were wiser, but found themselves painted into a corner by diminishing ground. Electricity was their main defense, but its cumbersome use required exact precision. Karl wound up on the receiving end of the eye and *then* became the newest crab mind (the female seemed to have a special preference for Jules' voice). As in *Day the World Ended*, only romantic leads survived.

Griffith's script and Corman's direction were holeier than thou. To destroy the seaplane with heat, the male crab had to project it across considerable distance without being seen. Details about the big worm helped explain the substance of the crabs, but where did the worm itself go? When Martha and Jim heard their names, it seemed like the male was communicating with two voices simultaneously. The storm had occurred on the first evening, but Dale referred to it on the second night. The crab that wrecked the radio must have consumed a technician in order to know all its intricate facets, possessing incredible dexterity to slash tubes and rip wiring without breaking the cabinet. When Martha pondered the missing mountain, she said the group had arrived the day before, but they had actually come two days earlier.

The crabs were huge, but the female managed to elude Jules around the pit area. There was no clicking and he did not see it until they were inches apart. Real crabs move sideways, not forward. Having the crabs speak through metal was unique, but after exposure they could be heard without it. Normally, they were immune to everything but electricity and dismemberment, but the shot female suffered tissue damage. How could its offspring conquer the world if the crabs only had as much intelligence as they had food? Or could digested minds be passed on natally to the young?

Paul Blaisdell's Venusian could take comfort in the knowledge that the single crab mock-up representing both mammoth mollusks has been painted with scorn too — although not as viciously. The crabs described in

From the depths of the sea...
A TIDAL WAVE OF TERROR!

ATTACK OF THE CRAB MONSTERS

starring
Richard GARLAND · Pamela DUNCAN · Russell JOHNSON
A ROGER CORMAN PRODUCTION · Screenplay by CHARLES B. GRIFFITH
Produced and Directed by ROGER CORMAN · AN ALLIED ARTISTS PICTURE

the script were black with eyestalks. The features on the four hundred dollar Dice Inc. model were roughly humanoid — as if assimilation of people included faces — and the sleepy-looking eyes were thick lidded. The claws were too large for a land crab and the thing even acquired extra feet glimpsed briefly when the crab climbed over the promontory rocks courtesy of Ed Nelson under the crab shell. Or were the sneakers on Nelson's feet actually worn by Jack Nicholson? Beach Dickerson reportedly maneuvered the crab body too. Underwater, the crab looked more frightening, but the aluminum prop was so light that it kept rising to the surface even when weighted down.

Corman began the film with a majestic shot of the globe from the credits of *World Without End* (1956), first seen in color. Now black and white, the image was accompanied by the opening strains of Leith Steven's theme music from the other movie. Most of the mushroom cloud stock shots were cut into at mid-detonation to achieve an apocalyptic effect. Fallout haze blanketing the island was from *Day the World Ended*.

Earth tremor scenes were from *One Million B.C.* (1940).

Pamela Duncan played a heroine who, though more sweetheart than scientist, gave the science some wistful impressionistic slants. A custom-built swimsuit had to be made to keep her size thirty-eight frontal tanks afloat. Russell Johnson was the most agreeable hero as Hank. Stony Richard Garland is remembered mainly as the ex-husband of Beverly. Leslie Bradley and Mel Welles gave the crabs their most distinctive voices. In his first film, Ed Nelson as Quinlan took center stage in the island arrival scene with Quilan's mystical description of the fate of the McLean party.

Welles, Beach Dickerson and Tony Miller were chief laugh getters. Welle's crab voice was the most casual ("Be not shocked that the weapon speaks."). Dickerson and Miller played poker betting with explosives (Sam: "I'll raise you ten." Ron: "If you're not careful, you'll raise us both ten feet."). Dickerson did a turnabout on the crabs in *Creature from the Haunted Sea* (1961) by playing a human gifted in the imitation of animal sounds.

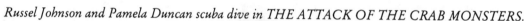

Russel Johnson and Pamela Duncan scuba dive in THE ATTACK OF THE CRAB MONSTERS.

BEGINNING OF THE END

Republic, 1957	
Producer-Director-	
Special Technical Effects	Bert I. Gordon
Screenplay	Fred Freiberger
	Lester Gorn
Cinematography	Jack Marta
Film Editor	Aaron Stell
Music	Albert Glaser
Art Director	Walter Keller
Assistant Director	Melville Shayer
Second Assistant Director	Wilson Shyer
Sound Effect Editors	Douglas J. Stewart
	George J. Eppich
Music Editor	Morris K. McNaughton
Property Master	James Harris
Set Decorator	George Milo
Makeup	Steve Drumm
Sound Mixer	Richard E. Tyler
Optical Effects	Consolidated Film Ind.

Song "Natural, Natural Baby"

Words-Music by Lou Bartel & Harriet Kane
sung by Lou Bartel & Chorus

An AB-PT Production
Running time: 73 minutes

Cast: Peter Graves (Ed Wainwright), Peggie Castle (Audrey Ames), Norris Ankrum (Gen. Hanson), Than Whenn (Frank Johnson), Thomas B. Henry (Col. Sturgeon), Richard Benedict (Cpl. Mathias), James Seay (Capt. Barton), John Close (Maj. Everett), Don C. Harvey, Larry J. Blake (Patrolmen), Frank Wilcox (Gen. Short), Pierre Watkin (Taggart), Steve Warren, Frank Connor, Don Eitner, Rayfor Barnes (Soldiers), Hank Patterson, Eilene Janssen, Hylton Socher, Douglas Evans, Paul Grant, Richard Emory

The initials of Bert Ira Gordon's name show his preference in monster size. Occasionally, Mr. B.I.G. strays from his first love, but he always returns to his specialty. In the low budget field, producer, director,

(Above) An advancing giant locust from BEGINNING OF THE END (1957).

special effects creator and sometimes writer, Gordon was horror's first true autuer. This mad passion was fostered by his boyhood interest in photography. When his aunt gave him a sixteen-millimeter camera, he filmed stories that required elaborate optical tricks. After college, Gordon made TV commercials and industrial films in the Detroit area. Receiving twelve-hundred dollars for a Chevrolet ad, Gordon went to Hollywood with wife (now former Mrs. B.I.G.) Flora, his special effects assistant.

Gordon worked on the TV series "Cowboy G-Men", edited twenty-six British films down to telecast size and was involved in the production of "Racket Squad". Money raised by his prosperous family enabled Gordon to break into features. Gordon's first movie was the 1954 voodoo tale *Serpent Island*. Tom Gries directed, Gordon photographed and edited the film in his garage. Gries wrote *King Dinosaur* (1955), which Gordon co-produced with Al Zimbalist and directed himself. Set on the virgin planet Nova, it was a crude pastiche of lizard footage boasting a giant beetle as its only "creative" creature. The first real Gordon picture, *The Cyclops*, utilized a similar environment on earth, adding a human monster. It did not go into release until after the distribution of Gordon's fourth effort, *Beginning of the End*.

Beginning of the End kicked off AB-PT Pictures Corp., a subsidiary of the American Broadcasting-Paramount Theaters family, which was organized to supply theaters low on new product. Gordon's film and the next AB-PT movie, *The Unearthly*, were bought by Republic Pictures, which had not adapted well to the changing markets of the fifties, even though it had abandoned serials and delved into television production.

A terrible locust invasion in Australia in 1956 covered over four hundred square miles. Damage that locusts caused annually at that time ran up to nearly twenty million dollars. Locusts could do worse in limited numbers if they were much larger, figured Mr. B.I.G., who wouldn't have to deal with rebellious reptials on this particular venture. The screenplay of *Beginning of the End* was a shameless grab-bag of pillaged concepts, its title one letter short of being identical to the Manhattan Project docudrama *Beginning or the End* (1947). The isotope theory of revolutionizing diet in *Beginning Of*, the catalyst for the growth of locusts, was lifted from *Tarantula!* (1955), which, in turn, stole from the "No Food For Thought" episode of "Science Fiction Theater".

Rock music drones from the radio of a convertible parked on a junction cutoff near Ludlow, Illinois. Two young lovers turn up to see something horrible as the girl's screams drown out the music. Near dawn, two Urbana state policemen discover the car all crunched up. Found in the wreckage is the identification of the boy, one William Summerfield of Ludlow. Foul play is suspected. One man will stay and wait for a homicide team while the other goes to the Ludlow address.

The detectives examine the wreck, producing the girl's sweater. The cop who went to Ludlow has not called in. Headquarters summons him over his radio. Breathlessly, the cop runs back to his car and reports, "The whole town's destroyed! Everybody's gone! You gotta do something! You won't believe it! Send help! Lots of help!"

The National Guard throws a cordon around Ludlow, diverting motorists. En route to an assignment, photojournalist Audrey Ames of National Wire Service senses a story. Driving to a hilltop, she sees the horror, but an alert sentry abruptly confiscates her camera and exposes the film. On her demand, Audrey is referred to headquarters in nearby Paxton. She meets Capt. Barton, who will cooperate if Audrey holds her story until the lifting of a news blackout. Last night, over one hundred fifty people vanished from Ludlow without a trace. Barton's superior, Col. Tom Sturgeon, talks to an old man who had left his daughter and son-in-law in Ludlow around eleven p.m. and heard an odd rumble in the air. A switchboard operator reported a bad connection at four forty-five a.m. Sturgeon is about to visit the scene, but forbids Audrey to come. "A town of one hundred fifty people just doesn't vanish," she says. "This one did," insists Barton.

Suspecting radiation, Audrey phones her New York bureau chief to learn if there is any radioactive material being used in the area. The only place with it is a U.S. Department of Agriculture research station outside of Paxton. There, Audrey tries to address botanist Frank Johnson, who ignores her. She meets project director Ed Wainwright, who informs her that a radiation accident rendered Frank deaf and dumb. Audrey is amazed by the giant strawberries and tomatoes that flourish in the lab. "This, we hope," proudly declares Ed, "is the future of the American farmer — and, for that matter, all farmers everywhere." Isotopes cause the growth. "Radiation," Ed explains, "causes photosynthesis. That's the growing process that continues night and day. The radioactive isotopes act as a sort of artificial sun . . . a sun that never sets." Stimulation from the atomic plant food must be limited or the plants would exceed their present size. Frank is cleaning up after snails. Earlier lab intruders have been beetles and locusts. Audrey finds this all very interesting, but Ludlow is her main priority.

Audrey is allowed to photograph the debris of Ludlow until she has had enough. "Around this part of the country," say Capt Barton, "things have a way of vanishing. A couple of months ago, it was a grain elevator. Sort of fell apart overnight . . . just like Ludlow."

Audrey sees a tie-up between Ludlow and the warehouse, whose watchman disappeared, asking Ed and Frank to accompany her there. Ever since the war, Ed has followed Audrey's famous exploits. They "made me realize what a sheltered life we scientists lead." "Sheltered?" asks Audrey critically. "Look what happened to Frank." The walls of the warehouse were pushed out. Over a million bushels of wheat were taken. The grass has been nibbled close to the soil. Ed and Audrey hear high-pitched screeches. A giant locust devours Frank, but Ed and Audrey escape.

One of the soldiers who combed the ruins of Ludlow shows Sturgeon a fired rifle. Most of the other weapons recovered had also been fired. Ed tells Sturgeon what happened to Frank. Sturgeon has seen the giant plants at the lab — proof of mutated locusts. "Are you trying to tell me you bred these things?" he asks Ed incredulously. "In a way, I did," admits Ed. Apparently, the locusts ate some of the radioactive plants and plant food. Growing rapidly, they required more nourishment, consuming the warehouse wheat. That accelerated their growing rate and they killed the watchman. Ed implores Sturgeon to send a company out to the location.

There is only bare ground where Frank died. Sturgeon asks where the body is. "It's gone," answers Ed, "— just like Ludlow." Spreading out to the woods, some of the soldiers joke and others are nervous. "I ate 'em once in Mexico," says a locust connoisseur. "You better watch it," warns Cpl. Mathias. "They might get even." The soldiers hear the screeching and the locusts attack *en masse*. Ed and the surviving soldier hastily retreat.

The screeching indicated countless numbers of locusts. Full artillery is needed, but Sturgeon is unconvinced. Ed fears this is a prelude to "annihilation". "Annihilation?" asks Audrey. "Annihilation!" earnestly replies Ed. "The beginning of the end!" In Washington D.C., Ed briefs the higher authorities on the rapacious nature of the enemy via a filmstrip. Gen. Short trusts the competency of the Illinois guardsmen while Gen. Matt Hanson holds back a feeling of disagreement. The locusts have penetrated the Guard lines. Hanson flies with Ed and Audrey to Paxton, but word reaches them that Paxton has been destroyed. Hanson reroutes the plane to Chicago.

In Chicago, Hanson sets up a line of defense around the city. Ed oversees scientific procedures in an emergency lab high in the Wrigley building. Chlordane is unleashed on the locusts, but fails to even slow them down. Four divisions cover the South and West sides with backup reinforcements. The locusts sound will signal their attack. Forming a spearhead formation, the locusts breach the weak parts of the line, invading the South Side suburbs. That night, they huddle in alleyways and buildings just outside the Loop. At sixty-eight degrees, they stop. At dawn, they will rise.

Hanson is authorized to drop an atom bomb on the evacuated metropolis as a final contingent. Property damage would be in the billions on land too contaminated to rebuild upon. Luring the locusts could

work. Chicago's equivalent of an ocean is Lake Michigan. A high-frequency radio whine fires Ed with a daring idea. He wants to electronically duplicate the locust's mating call. "There's one thing I have to get myself," he says. "Something that will tell me when I've succeeded." "What's that?" asks Hanson. "A giant grasshopper," answers Ed.

Ed and a detail including Maj. Everett capture a small locust in an alley with tear gas. Stored in a makeshift glass cage, it will react to various electronic vibrations measured on a polygraph. Deaf to filtered sound, it may respond to a harmonic pitch. Hanson lets Ed and Audrey stay with Everett and two other men until the bomb deadline. A small observation team will monitor the locusts. Violently irritated by testing, the locust breaks out of the cage, killing Everett. Ed shoots it with a machine-gun, reporting success to Hanson. The bomb plane is immediately recalled. "Get me that equipment on a boat in the lake," Ed tells Hanson, "and I'll be your Pied Piper."

Since the locusts are widely scattered, the lab equipment will draw them to the Wrigley Building. Once they reach the Loop, they will be in the proximity of the boat. At seventy degrees, the locusts will move, going through the suburbs to the South Side. Unless the timing is right, they may leave town. The observer atop the Drayton Hotel is killed by a locusts. When the amplifier starts, some others climb the walls of the Wrigley Building and are machine-gunned. Ed radios Hanson to turn on his equipment. Scrambling madly, the locusts march to the lake in droves and drown. Ed and Audrey clinch in relief as the boat returns to shore.

The first quarter of *Beginning of the End* was almost a straight remake of *Them!* (1954), achieving equal interest in its building of mystery, although the latter had the advantage of being fresh. The deaths of the Ludlow kids was musically novel in their certain doom being counterpointed by the reassuring macho lyrics of the radio rock singer ("Don't ever be afraid . . . Big Lou is here . . ."). Instead of a trailer and a general store, a warehouse and an entire hamlet were decimated. The muteness of Frank was a nod to the traumatized little Ellinson girl of *Them!*.

The giant ants of *Them!*, being mechanical models, operated primarily in tightly shot, claustrophobic surroundings. Budget and technology refused to allow more than several per scene and confining most of their scenes to interiors was cheaper. Bert Gordon wanted straight-ahead action with bolder, more prolific and more single minded insect warriors. When they chose a direction, the locusts stopped for nothing outside of evening cold. Their immunity to chlordane was plausible because of the resistance bugs develop to certain insecticides, but Gordon oversold the locust blight by enabling them to withstand everything from flame throwers to tanks. Adroitly, he turned their sex drive into an instrument of mass suicide while the consideration of the lake was taken from recall that the Massachusetts settlers disposed of their locusts by driving them into the sea.

Unknowingly, the film allowed for two open endings. The other lab insects that followed the locusts could have eaten from the plants and grown too. Mankind then would have been threatened by several species. The review in "The Hollywood Reporter" wondered that if the fish in Lake Michigan ate the dead locusts they, too, would grow. And if people ate the fish before their mutation became pronounced . . .

The locusts were a breed from Waco, Texas, that neither hopped nor flew. Gordon needed permission from the Agricultural Department in Washington and Sacramento to bring them to California and he was refused because state law banned importation of mixed insects. Only males were allowed. Gordon hired a locust expert in Waco to send him two hundred males in bonded crates after each was examined by Agricultural inspectors. To make sure no locusts had escaped during the night, a member of the state Agricultural Department conducted daily head counts. Too tightly caged, the locusts became cannibalistic, and the head counts became body counts. Only a dozen were left when it was time to film the Chicago scenes. Despite overexposed mating, the locusts moved convincingly against Army maneuvers footage, photos of buildings and location shots of empty early morning streets in downtown Chicago. Best of the photo effects was when they were climbing the Wrigley Building — until several locusts crawled onto the sky *around* it.

Gordon took some stark reaction shots when the locusts attacked the kids, Frank and the Illinois Guardsmen. Frank's death was the most grotesque as he lay on his back trying to emit a silent "scream". He was a martyr to radiation, which had not only taken his voice but ultimately created the creature that killed him.

Gordon approached some love interests rather tentatively. The relationship between Ed and Audrey, played by Peter Graves and Peggy Castle, was directly shown as growing intimacy with no time for any hearts-and-flowers. Morris Ankrum had only to show his careworn, haunted-eyed face to telegraph the enormity of the task the Army had cut out for it. Gen. Hanson was almost the apotheosis of all the harried but determined war-horses Ankrum played in dealing with the unknown where he was not a scientist.

Beginning of the End was a critical dart board and of no help was promotion that did not exploit the locusts authentically. In the trailer, they could hardly be seen at all. Some ads used the sloppily designed silhouette of only one locust. Others had toothy big-eyed terrors almost identical to the caricature-like monsters in the posters from *Them!*. This was supposedly the "first" film with "Real-Live Creatures" — a false revelation cleverly described as "Newmendous!" One unperceptive critic thought the locusts were mechanical. Another claimed they were cartoon simulation.

Not long after *Beginning of the End* and *The Unearthly*, AB-PT dissolved. They pulled in some bucks . . . not enough to save their dying distributor Republic . . . and Gordon won a four-picture contract with AIP.

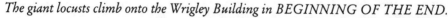

The giant locusts climb onto the Wrigley Building in BEGINNING OF THE END.

THE UNEARTHLY

Republic, 1957	
Producer-Director	Brooke L. Peters
	aka Boris Petroff
Screenplay	Geoffrey Dennis
	Jane Mann
Story	Jane Mann
Associate Producer	Robert A. Terry
Cinematography	W. Merle Connell
Editorial Supervision	Richard Currier
Music	Henry Vars
	Michael Terr
Art Director	Daniel Hall
Sound	Philip Mitchell
Sound Editor	Morton Tubor
Production Manager	Betty Sinclair
Makeup	Harry Thomas
Wardrobe	William Zacha
Set Decorator	Mowbray Berkeley
Chief Electrician	Paul Grancer
Key Grip	Art Manikin
Camera Operator	Ben Wetzler

Property Master	Tony Portoghese

An AB-PT Production
Running time: 73 minutes

Cast: John Carradine (Prof. Charles Conway), Myron Healy (Mark Houston), Allison Hayes (Grace Thomas), Marilyn Buferd (Dr. Sharon Gilchrist), Arthur Batanides (Danny Green), Sally Todd (Natalie Andries), Tor Johnson (Lobo), Roy Gordon (Dr. Loren Wright), Guy Prescott (Capt. Regan), Harry Fleer (Harry Jedrow), Gloria Petroff (Girl), Paul MacWilliams (Police Officer)

With two of its stars, John Carradine and Tor Johnson, *The Unearthly* was a contemporary copy of 1956's *The Black Sleep*. The mad doctor of the latter, Sir Joel Cadman, explored various area of the brain to find a cure for his catatonic young wife. Result: a dungeon full of crazed mutants, plus two kept servants. In *The Unearthly*, Prof. Charles Conway's goal was to

(Above) A mutant from THE UNEARTHLY (1957).

prolong life with an artificial seventeenth gland, achieving before any David Cronenberg scientist New Flesh. Production and direction of the film were credited to Boris Petroff under his alias of Brooke L. Peters and who, in Tor Johnson, secured Johnson's *Bride of the Monster* brute Lobo. Three of the technicians for *Unearthly* were also Ed Week people: makeup artist Harry Thomas, key grip Art Manikin and property master Tony Portoghese.

Though Carradine probably cared less, *The Unearthly* was a consolation for his colorful but demeaning mutant role in *The Black Sleep*, where he had little more to say than, "Kill! Kill!" These films were representative of the Carradine shockers that were sleazy but not *too* disreputable. It was an older, unhappier Carradine who would build Astro-Zombies and develop men with Synthetic Brains.

Conway's endocrinology clinic is in a remote Georgian mansion. An upstairs light snaps on. A girl screams. She is attacked in bed by Lobo. Another doctor, Loren Wright, brings new patient Grace Thomas, who meets Conway and his assistant Dr. Sharon Gilchrist. Sharon takes Grace to her room as Wright says he will have some things sent to her by her father. Upset, Conway shouts in private, "Father?" Their agreement was no patients with families. "Grace Thomas committed suicide," alludes Wright, who will throw her coat and purse into the river. Conway and Wright drink a toast. Wright: "To youth." Conway: "To immortality." Wright is curious about the condition of another patient, Harry Jedrow.

Rigidly occupying a basement chair, Jedrow suffers Thalamic paralysis from an internal radiation burn. Wright has just learned that Jedrow has a sister looking for him. Wright prepares to leave — almost forgetting his suicide props. Showing his suavest bedside manner, Conway promises to relieve Grace's fear-causing malady. In the garden, Lobo subdues an armed prowler dragged to Conway. Claiming to be a lost hitchhiker named Mark Houston, his leather jacket and star tattoo on one hand identify him as wanted killer/thief, Frank Scott. Conway can use Mark, offering him conditional sanctuary.

At breakfast, Mark meets two other patients, Natalie Andres and volatile Danny Green. Deriding Natalie for her tastes in romance novels, Danny becomes so heated up that he needs a calming injection. In private, Conway tells Mark about his immortality gland. On once puny Lobo, it created a dumb giant. Mark is healthy. "Think of it!" enthuses Conway. "To be always exactly as you are now! To see the pages of life go by while you are eternally young and vigorous! Suppose you could wake up every morning and see your face untouched by time!" Mark isn't interested. If he tries to tell anyone about this, it will be his word against Conway's. Wright calls to warn Conway that Jedrow's nosy sister is in his office. Conway tells Wright to make out a false death certificate.

Grace is sunning in the garden, where Mark cordially introduces himself to her. Natalie is pleased to hear she will be leaving soon.

During diner, Lobo prepares to take a food tray up to Natalie's room. Sharon dopes the coffee. After supper, Conway play his organ for Mark, Grace and Danny. Mark and Grace wonder why Natalie isn't there. Lobo drools over unconscious Natalie on the lab surgery table until Sharon has him send the others to bed. Mark finds Natalie's room empty and her clothes in a closet. Conway and Sharon give Natalie the gland. Their radiology equipment makes a loud crackling noise heard throughout the house. Mark tries to tell Grace they are in danger, but she does not believe him.

Eight hours after the surgery, Conway and Sharon go to the basement room where Natalie is recuperating. Groggy and groaning, she has shrivelled into an old woman. Grace tells Conway about Mark's suspicions. Conway says that Mark has a persecution complex and is potentially dangerous during these times. Jealous of Grace, Sharon wants her to become a subject. Conway isn't ready yet.

Mark finds Jedrow, whom Lobo removes from his chair after Mark leaves the basement. Returning with Grace, he discovers the chair empty. They enter Natalie's room. "It's Natalie!" cries Grace and she and Mark see her face. "Yeah —," Mark grimly intones, "—that's Natalie." Mark takes shaken Grace back to her room. Lobo carries a wooden casket with Jedrow in it to the garden for burial. Danny tries to sneak out of the house, but barking guard dogs scare him into going back inside. While Lobo investigates, Mark opens the casket. Jedrow wakes up, startled by where he is. Mark pulls him out.

Mark wants Grace and Danny to leave together while he stays, but Conway, Sharon and Lobo halt them with guns. While Conway and Sharon prepare Grace for surgery, Lobo holds a gun on Mark and Danny in the basement. Danny sees Natalie. Danny distracts Lobo with the story of Ferdinand the Bull, waving his spread jacket like a matador's cape. When Danny throws it over Lobo's head, he shoots Danny. Mark administers a karate blow to the back of Lobo's neck. Urging mark to go on alone, Danny staggers around until he dies. Mark catches Conway in his office, where Conway realizes that Mark is an undercover cop. With a secret alarm button, Conway signals Sharon. As the lights go out, Mark shoots blindly in the dark. He calls headquarters for reinforcements.

Fleeing down a fire escape, Conway reaches his car, but needs the key to unlock it. Mark greets the arriving police, led by Capt. Regan. As Conway fetches his car keys in the living room, he turns to face Jedrow, brandishing a scalpel. "No — you're dead!" cries Conway. "I know you're dead! I had you buried!" Jedrow finally stabs Conway. Lobo kills Jedrow with an arm grip to the neck before he and Sharon are arrested. In the surgery room, Mark revives Grace, helping her away. Regan is glad to see Grace, who had the department dragging the water for two days. An unnerved officer tells Regan there is something he should see down in the basement.

The officer shows Regan Danny's body, taking him to a room where there is a caged menagerie of hideous, shrieking mutants — Conway's worst mistakes. Institutions can take care of them, but Regan wonders, "Good Lord, what if they *do* live forever?" An APB is issued for Dr. Wright. With Mark as her lover, Grace is no longer afraid.

In the matter of immortality, *The Unearthly* used a topic that concerns everyone. Scientists looking for it seem to forget that God created death in order to make room for future generations. As advocates of the Hemlock philosophy know, quality of life means more than quantity. A horror henchman whose own existence had considerable longevity, Lobo was essentially his original self from *Bride of the Monster* with a new origin. His violence and household servitude made him a combination of Mungo and Casimir, two of the less repulsive mutants from *The Black Sleep*. In *The Unearthly*, Lobo could talk a little ("I-found-him-in-the-garden", "Time-to-go-to-bed", "Fer-di-nand?") and wore better clothing, such as sandals for his feet and a white shirt and tie during meals. Feared by Janet Lawton in *Bride*, Lobo even had a friend in Natalie.

Calculatedly the ugliest, the climax mutants (and whatever happened to the girl?) were a horrendous glut of gargoyles reminiscent of Dr. Moreau's handiwork in *The Island of Lost Souls* (1932). The power source of radiology apparatus, they appeared in surroundings not unlike the lab in that film. Conway had achieved success of sorts, but every immortal was better off dead . . . except Harry Jedrow, who was made dead by Lobo. Right out, the cop with Regan asked, "What are we going to do with them?" With Conway gone, the mutants were a burden of the state.

Harry Thomas was in his glory. Noted for working fast with almost nothing, he created the mutants from spare appliances. Each face was distinctly gross, although they assaulted the eyes as a twisted tableau. Several were apelike. One resembled a werewolf. The biggest mutant was Tor Johnson's son Karl, a San Fernando cop who appeared with Tor in *Plan Nine from Outer Space* (1959) and *Night of the Ghouls*. The sounds of the mutants were like feeding time at the zoo in Dolby stereo. Even Lobo's moans were used.

The immortality gland that Sharon put into a surgical tray looked like a dead fish. In Conway's rubber-gloved hand, it resembled a stale prophylactic.

John Carradine made his disdain for the Conway role obvious, but he was still a full-fledged star, not an aging bogeyman written into a paltry part for the use of his name. Luther Burbank's grandson, Myron Healy started at Republic, writing cowboy scripts, playing bit parts in them that helped him get noticed. His hard-bitten acting gave the heroics of Mark some grit. This was the only time that Allison Hayes ever played a passive horror heroine. She wasn't convincing at simulating depression, but was definitely the picture of health. Allison had represented Washington state in the 1948 Miss America contest. Marylyn Buferd, a properly cold helpmate as Sharon, had won the title in 1946. Her acting career began in Italian and Spanish films.

Sally Todd, Miss February 1957, was one of the Playmates who found their way into horror. Arthur Batanides took Danny's manic states on cue to try to out act everyone, flailing spastically in sickness and in death. Tor Johnson's made-over Lobo showed more of his gentle side. He came on like an oversexed big baby when he ogled sedated Natalie, cooing, "Pur-ty gi-rl . . . pur-ty gi-rl . . . "

Those who saw *The Unearthly* as kids will never forget the basement finale. In a few theatres, they even got to see Tor Johnson in person — roaming the isles with his face illuminated by a flashlight he held under his face.

69

PUB-8

#101-188

I WAS A TEENAGE WEREWOLF

American International, 1957

Presenters	James H. Nicholson
	Samuel Z. Arkoff
Producer	Herman Cohen
Director	Gene Fowler, Jr.
Story-Screenplay	Ralph Thornton
	(Herman Cohen, Aben Kandel)
Cinematography	Joseph La Shelle
Editorial Supervisor	George Gitten
Music	Paul Dunlap
Art Director	Leslie Thomas
Production Manager-	
Assistant Director	Jack R. Berne
Script Supervisor	Mary Gibsone
Set Decorator	Morris Hoffman
Property Master	Max Frankel
Wardrobe	Oscar Rodriguez
Hair Stylist	Fae Smith
Makeup	Philip Scheer
Music Editor	Axel Hubert
Sound Effects Editor	Henry Adams
Sound	James S. Thomson
Production Secretary	Donna Heydt

Song: "Eeny, Meeny, Miney, Mo"
Music-Lyrics by Jerry Blaine

A Sunset Production
Running time: 76 minutes

Cast: Michael Landon (Tony Rivers), Yvonne Lime (Arlene Logan), Whit Bissell (Dr. Alfred Brandon), Tony Marshall (Jimmy), Dawn Richard (Theresa), Barney Phillips (Det. Sgt. Donovan), Ken Miller (Vic), Cindy Robbins (Pearl), Michael Rougas (Frank), Robert E. Griffin (Police Chief Baker), Joseph Mell (Dr. Hugo Wagner), Malcolm Atterbury (Charles), Eddie Marr (Doyle), Vladimir Sokoloff (Pepi), Louise Lweis *aka Fitch* (Mrs. Ferguson), John *aka S. John* Launer (Bill), Guy Williams (Chris Stanley), Dorothy Crehan (Mary)

Great monsters are not necessarily originals of their type. Larry Talbot refined and popularized the image of wolfmen, but London werewolf Wilfred Glendon had loped on the scene some six years earlier. Then there is *I Was a Teenage Werewolf — definitely* the first picture about a high school monster, but third place among chemically-created canines. *The Mad Monster* (1942) had been test-tube *loup garou* number one and *The Werewolf* (1956) entry two.

A theater manager in Detroit who rose from usher,

Herman Cohen, ran the local distribution arm of Columbia, handling publicity for the studio in Hollywood. At Real-Art Pictures, Cohen met James Nicholson and associate produced *Bela Lugosi Meets a Brooklyn Gorilla* (1952). For Allied Artists, Cohen produced *Target — Earth!* (1954), based on a short story Nicholson had shown him, Paul W. Fairman's "Deadly City". The movie's score was by Paul Dunlap, who became Cohen's regular composer.

The Werewolf was released during Cohen's Columbia venture. More an achievement of accident than any deliberate excellence on the part of some normally pedestrian talents, this was the tragic tale of Duncan Marsh. Unconscious from an auto accident than caused amnesia, Duncan was brought to Dr. Morgan Chambers and Dr. Emory Forrest, who administered radioactive wolf blood in order to test a fallout immunization serum. Able to transform into a werewolf capriciously, Duncan escaped, rampaged through a mountain town and surrendered to authorities when recognition of his family restored his memory. When Chambers and Forrest tried to silence him in jail, Duncan became a wolf again, killed the doctors and was put away by unblessed lead. Either Cohen had seen the film or read the script — for who was the werewolf that later took shape in his mind but an under-aged Duncan Marsh, afflicted not with memory loss but an easily lost temper. And the scientists who experimented upon the boy, a lean, single-minded pioneer and his pudgy, guilt-ridden assistant, were they not Chambers and Forrest reincarnated?

At United Artists that year, Cohen critically basked in the review plaudits and commercially bathed in the financial failure of his Barbara Stanwyck vehicle *Crimes of Passion*, featuring *Count Yorga* star, Robert Quarry, in a small role. Greeted warmly at AIP, Cohen concluded from instinct and box-office research that horror and juvenile delinquency films could be merged. It wasn't certain how young ticket buyers would take to an unprecedented form of Genre sodomy: would this brash reaming of the senses make them sit up in their seats with interest, or would the minor disappointment of *Crimes of Passion* be followed by Cohen's Folly?

On the AIP lot, Cohen met Aben Kandel, an unsung contributor to the *Werewolf of London* (1935) script, whose novel, "City for Conquest", had been made into a 1940 film. Under the joint pseudonym "Ralph Thornton", he and Cohen wrote *Teenage Werewolf* under its shooting title *Blood of the Werewolf*.

In the schoolyard of Rockdale High, students gather around as notoriously hotheaded Tony Rivers fights another youth, Jimmy. Defiantly refusing to give up, Tony maniacally swings a shovel at Jimmy and tosses a handful of dirt into his eyes. Called by the school, Det. Sgt. Donovan and another cop intervene. Jimmy only touched Tony in a friendly way, but Tony hates any sudden physical contact. Donovan makes them both shake hands, taking Tony aside. Tony has brushed with

I WAS A TEENAGE WEREWOLF (1957).

Dr. Brandon (White Bissell) and his assistant examine defiant, hot-headed Tony Rivers (Michael Landon) in I WAS A TEENAGE WEREWOLF.

the law before. Donovan recommends a noted psychologist, Dr. Alfred Brandon, but Tony smarts at any idea he is crazy. To his girl Arlene Logan, Tony admits, "I say things, do things — I don't know why. I try to control them, but it's too late. I've gone too far. I don't know . . . I — I get certain feelings . . . I don't know . . . I just don't know . . . "

Tony lives with his widower father, Charles, a factory worker who knows he is a good boy. "Sometimes you have to do what people want," says Charles. "You make them happy, they leave you alone." About to begin the night shift, he fixes Tony some lamb chops, telling Tony not to eat them raw like he did some hamburger a few days ago. Still upset, Tony hurls a milk bottle against a kitchen wall. That night, he drives to Arlene's house to take her to a party, meeting her folks. Mr. Logan heard about the fight and lectures Tony on correct dating conduct. Arlene favors Donovan's suggestion about seeing Dr. Brandon, but Tony is dead set against it.

Tony, Arlene, Jimmy, quiet Frank and the other kids hang out at "The Haunted House". Popular Vic supplies music. Vic's girl, Pearl, is made a butt of some macabre jokes. Vic opens a closet and gets soaked by an overhanging bucket of water. When Vic blows a loud horn into his ear, Tony throws Vic across the room and

accidentally knocks Arlene down. Tony feels ashamed.

Tony agrees to see Brandon, who conducts a preliminary physical examination. In their lab, Brandon tells his assistant, Dr. Wagner, to prepare scopolamine, which is combined with a special drug. Wagner fears the consequences of Brandon's secret experiment. After years of searching, Brandon has found a perfect subject. "Through hypnosis," says Brandon, "I'm going to regress this boy back . . . back to the primitive past that lurks within him. I'm going to transform him and unleash the savage instincts he has hidden within." "And then?" asks Wagner. "And then I'll be judged the benefactor," answers Brandon. "Mankind is on the verge of destroying itself. The only hope for the human race is to hurl it back to its primitive dawn . . . to start all over again!"

Giving Tony the drug, Brandon tells him, "You must think of this as a trip . . . a sort of voyage of discovery. On the way we'll find many interesting things about you. And in the end you'll no longer be disturbed or troubled because you will be *you*! I'm the pilot and you're the passenger. But instead of going forward we're going . . . backward in time." Tony is sent back to a beach when he was about twelve. He is playing with some kids when an older child steals one of their toys. Tony attacks him

An enraged Tony questions his doctor in I WAS A TEENAGE WEREWOLF.

with animal ferocity, making the boy cry. Brandon orders Tony to wake up. "Soon," Brandon assures him, "you'll be yourself — your *true* self."

The next trip is more frightening. Tony is trapped in a dark, soul-freezing limbo. "Where are you?" asks Brandon. "You tell me," answers shivering Tony. "You tell me." Brandon evokes the sensation of being a wolf. "Remember how it felt to run over the hills in the moonlight? To hide in silence until . . . " "No! No!" cries Tony. Brandon brutally persists. "Remember how wonderful it was when you sprang suddenly and dug in with your fangs . . . the soft throat . . . the gush of warm blood . . . " "No!" shrieks Tony. "You *must* remember!" orders Brandon. Tony awakens with no conscious recollection.

At a party celebrating a football game, Frank notices moody Tony's disorientation. He has to take Arlene home before midnight. Everyone pairs up except Frank, who takes a wooded shortcut home. Tony drops Arlene off at her place. Whistling as he walks down a forest path, Frank hears running footsteps some distance behind him. No one answers his call. Mild anxiety gives way to open fear. "*Who's there?*" Frank sees something and runs. Stumbling, he cowers against a tree, screaming at the advancing predator to get away.

The kids read about Frank's murder in the morning paper. Police Chief Baker studies photographs of the body but can't discern the slash marks on the throat. "Fangs!" volunteers Donovan. "Whatever it is, we're got to be sure," Baker tells Donovan and officer Chris Stanley. "Just one rumor about fangs and the newspapers will have a field day . . . in Rockdale, we'll have a panic." Pepi, an old janitor, asks Chris to let him see the photos because he knows Frank's father. "That poor boy . . . poor boy," shudders Pepi. Pepi knows the killer is a werewolf. Stories about them were rife in his home village in the Carpathian mountains. " . . . it's a human being possessed by a wolf," elaborates Pepi. "When the evil eye is upon you, the savage beast gets inside and controls you . . . makes you look and act like a wolf . . . makes you hunt down your victims and kill like a wolf." Chris doubts Pepi's sanity and snatches the pictures away. "You just forget I ever showed 'em to you!" "Yes, I'll be glad to forget," murmurs shaken Pepi, ". . . .if I can."

Despite the murder, Brandon feels compelled to experiment further. "You call it progress to hurl the human race back to its primitive beginning?" asks appalled Wagner. "It may be the only road to progress," answers Brandon. Tony is troubled by a vision, but

Brandon tells him he is "adjusting". "And soon, Tony, you'll be your true self again.

In the school gym, Mrs. Ferguson, the principal, lends encouragement to Theresa, a shapely athlete practicing for a competitive event on the parallel bars. Mrs. Ferguson invites Tony into her office to praise him for a new level of conduct equal to his always high grades. Drawn to Theresa, Tony watches her until he is startled by the jangle of a ringing class bell behind him. Becoming the werewolf, Tony approaches Theresa, who sees him from an inverted angle on the bars. She runs to the stage as Tony knocks over a row of collapsible chairs, but the fire exit is blocked. Tony pounces on Theresa in the tangle of a curtain. Her screams bring Mrs. Ferguson and some students. Tony darts past them, runs through the schoolyard and jumps a fence.

Tony disappears into the woods. Mrs. Ferguson and Jimmy tell Donovan they recognized Tony's clothes. Newsmen converge on Rockdale. One reporter, Doyle, criticizes chief Baker for using discretion after Frank's murder. Donovan sees Brandon, wondering why he noticed nothing odd about Tony's behavior. Brandon pretends to believe all this is "mass hysteria" and refers to Tony as " . . . this young man." "Why do you shy away from the word?" queries Donovan. "Everyone else is using it — werewolf!" Brandon talks of the old Carpathian legends. "I amuse myself with fantasy. I live by fact!" At the station, Chris asks Pepi, "In the old country, did they ever catch a werewolf?" "Never . . . " replies Pepi, "never!"

Donovan and Baker lead a torch-armed posse. In stagger fashion, they cover the woods. Lurking Tony is about to attack a deputy who is called away by his partner. A snarling German Shepherd attacks Tony, who kills it. Donovan sees the slaughtered dog. Guards are posted to keep Tony from escaping. An officer staying with Charles advises him to tell Tony to surrender if Tony calls.

In the morning, Tony reverts to himself and sees scratches on his hands. He slips past two guards who found a part of his jacket. Wagner fears Tony may be taken alive but Brandon confidently tells him, "All I have to do is wait. He *must* come here! I'm the only link he has . . . his last hope!"

Downtown, Tony moves freely through the near-empty streets. Across one is a phone booth. A motorcycle cop pulls a driver over and sees jaywalking Tony pass, his back turned. The cop tells Tony to use a crosswalk next time. A man by the booth stares at Tony suspiciously as he dials Arlene's number. The police are at her house, expecting his call. Arlene answers the phone, but Tony hangs up. Tony goes to Brandon, begging for help. "I know what I am . . . what I've become!" Brandon hypnotizes Tony to record his next change on movie film. Donovan hears about Tony being seen and dials Brandon's number.

Maddened by the ringing phone, Tony kills Wagner as Brandon runs for a sedative. Tony kills Brandon, rising to confront Donovan and Chris as they view Wagner's body. Forced to, Donovan and Chris shoot Tony, who dies as the Tony everyone remembers. "What about him?" asks Chris, turning to Brandon's corpse. "I don't know," answers Donovan. "My hunch is, the score was evened." "Boy, the newspapers will eat this up," expects Chris. "Yeah," agrees Donovan, "but after they've had their field day, one thing will be clear: it's not for man to tamper in the ways of God!"

In this and Cohen's subsequent teenage monster melodramas, the real "monster" was always a respected adult authority. A complex personality, Tony was scholastically bright, an obedient son and friendly when relaxed, suffering from a hare-trigger temper that seemed more metabolic than social. Most of his flare-ups were inflicted on kids he liked and usually he was contrite. Apparently, Tony's own dark beginnings were a surplus of "heritage". The idea of wolf genes in homo sapiens was preferred over Darwin teachings because *I Was a Teenage Werewolf* was a film about werewolves and if the ghost of the father of evolution took issue, tough. Yet even if Tony had never met Brandon, his natural primitivism might have escalated to manslaughter. Like many occult werewolves, Tony was hexed with the Sign of the Beast — in this instance multiple traces of congenital origin. "There are certain telltale marks on his body only I could recognize," Brandon told Wagner.

Had Tony's werewolfery been the by-product of an injected compound rather than an exorcism of a monster he always carried deep inside, *Teenage Werewolf* would have been more plausible. Considering himself an altruist, Brandon thought the "true" Tony was the way for everyone to go. Since he wasn't creating a personal slave, Brandon chose to study the werewolf from afar, expecting some independent action on its part. Keeping up with the headlines was his degree of monitorship. After all, in a future world overrun by wolf people, there wouldn't be any doctors around telling *them* what to do. Where *The Werewolf* was aloof to all traditions of their particular monster form, *Teenage Werewolf* fringed its plot with acknowledgments of mythical lycanthropes, partly to educate an audience too young to remember the were-films of the forties. As to the affairs of contemporary Tony, there was nothing about moons, pentagrams, wolfbane or silver bullets. His sensitivity established by Vic's horn prank, Tony was a Pavlovian wolf — one of his major irritations noise and the sudden sound of it a call to kill.

Brandon's rubber-room reasoning didn't look ahead to contingency hurdles far down the road. How could Brandon get people to forsake their God-given being? How could he transform a world population of billions? If man regressed, he could not start over without repeating most of his original mistakes. If the scattered ruins of modern order left still functioning instruments of destruction, an ignorant throwback could press the

Tony becomes a beast in I WAS A TEENAGE WEREWOLF.

wrong button and reduce the planet to a cinder.

Cohen had a fetish for the name of Rivers, using it five other times. There were two other Arlenes in his films and a few key lines from *Teenage Werewolf* were repeated with slight variations.

Son of the famous author, Gene Fowler, Jr. had taken up editing in order to direct. A protege of Fritz Lang, he edited *The Ox-Bow Incident* (1943) and several other Lang pictures. Cohen met Fowler when Fowler started directing for TV. Sherman Rose was the first candidate for *Teenage Werewolf*, then Roger Corman and Edward Bernds, who thought the script was bad. So did Fowler, whose wife persuaded him to film it. Fowler instituted many constructive script changes, assembling several capable technicians. One was Joseph Le Shelle, the Oscar-winning cinematographer of *Laura* (1944). Another was Leslie Thomas, who designed sets appropriate to the dimensional needs of camera setups.

Fowler's editing sense created jarring rhythms of motion in Tony's fight with Jimmy, where rapid shock close-ups drove hard their furious blows. Tony had thrown a milk carton at a bungling supermarket checker and Fowler improvised the milk bottle scene to show his residual anger. The regression sequences in Brandon's office used murky claustrophobia to externalize the abyss-deep inner hell Tony was suffering. When Tony was feeling depressed in the Haunted House, he was sitting next to a gag wall sign that read "Out to Lunch". Free of such synthetic enhancements as full moon, fog and lupine bays, the werewolf track down of Frank raised hackles from its unseen nearness and the gradual disintegration of Frank's composure. Tony's first visible lycanthropy attack was an explosion of release — not the placid paralysis Larry Talbot more comfortably succumbed to. Although seemingly silly for her upsidedown position, Theresa's view of the werewolf was alarming because of her awkward, vulnerable posture. Chase action smoothly connected flows of movement while Tony's death was shot entirely behind his back in one tensely prolonged dolly shot.

Makeup artist Philip Scheer had to change Michael Landon's appearance even *before* he went wolf. Landon had elephantine ears that had to be glued back to improve his looks. After filming, he bought plastic surgery. The werewolf itself was a decadent man-animal thing with its ducktail scalp, phallic fangs and dribbling sperm-like saliva that consisted of toothpaste. Another distinctive feature was Tony's jacket, which not only identified his age but instantly pegged him as the werewolf.

The first German Shepherd was a stand-in for Rin-Tin-Tin. Rainy weather ruined part of one day's shooting in Griffith Park. Fowler brought in his own police dog, who was horrified by Landon's makeup and fled. Once able to smell the human wearing it, the dog grew to like him. Fowler went back to Griffith when he made *I Married a Monster from Outer Space* (1958), which climaxed with two German Shepherds fighting a small

army of aliens.

AIP considered John Ashley and Scott Marlowe for the role of Tony, but Fowler held out for Landon. His own hellish puberty as Eugene Orowitz made it easy for Landon to identify with an outcast. Landon's emaciated-looking features, due to a period of starvation, added to the brittleness of his performance. Everyone knows, of course, the role and the TV show that saved him from the unemployment line forever. Usually a legitimate scientist, Whit Bissell took well enough to the out-of-character Dr. Brandon. Yvonne Lime was an AIP favorite who idealized sweet girls in its delinquency dramas.

Barney Phillips, Robert E. Griffin, who played a Sheriff in the early "Bonanza" shows, and pre-"Zorro" guy Williams were effective as efficient but humane cops. Malcolm Atterbury had some good moments as Charles, especially when defending Tony's character to the muckraking Doyle. Vladimir Sokoloff quivered sincerely as legend-conscious Pepi. Michael Rougas was a convincingly terrified Frank and S. John Launer, who portrayed Dr. Forrest in *The Werewolf*, was Arlene's father.

So many people have been credited with the film's unforgettable title. A classmate of one of the daughters of Jim Nicholson supposedly imagined it and she passed it to her father. Nicholson, Sam Arkoff and Alex Gordon, according to another account, thought it up while remembering lengthy film titles starting with *I Was a . .* Cohen allegedly suggested that part and Nicholson *Teenage Werewolf*. Grammatically, Cohen's part sounded incorrect. It meant that Tony had been a werewolf as described by the first-person. Only his death ended his condition. Still and all, *I Was a Teenage Werewolf* became the tenth top-grossing film of 1957. The blatant exploitation campaign and a title humorists could pick up on (and still do) assured that.

For some time, horror fans were loathe to accept any werewolf movie that did not strictly adhere to Larry Talbot iconography — unaware that most of it had been invented specifically for the first Wolf Man feature. Even in the reactionary early sixties, the Teenage Werewolf had a few fans. During his Chicago youth, fantasy author Don Gout made several amateur films with his version of the Teenage Werewolf (along with the Teenage Frankenstein). He amplified the teen aspect by giving his werewolf a leather jacket. In 1962, "Famous Monsters" held a makeup contest. First prize was a role in some near-future AIP production. The winner, twenty year old Val Warren of Newburgh, New York, cannily disguised himself as the Teenaged Werewolf — canny because Jim Nicholson was an announced judge and Warren may have been trying to influence his vote. It was not until 1964 that Warren went to Hollywood, where he cameoed in *Bikini Beach*. Leather jacketed like the Glut werewolf, Warren appeared in the hangout of the Ratz motorcycle gang as their mascot. Billing identified him as "The Teenage Werewolf".

Scenes from Teenage Werewolf appeared on some of Michael Landon's personal TV appearances and in 1973's ode to the fifties *Let the Good Times Roll*. Near the end of its existence, AIP celebrated its twenty-fifth anniversary with a retrospect of thirty-eight of its films at the New York Museum of Modern Art. *I Was a Teenage Werewolf* was one of the most popular entrants. Obliquely, the werewolf appeared on "Highway to Heaven" in the episode "I Was a Middle-Aged Werewolf". Even if people would remember Little Joe Cartwright, Charles Ingalls and Jonathan Smith first, Tony Rivers had been with Michael Landon longer than any of his television personas.

Tony Rivers (Landon) fights Jimmy (Tony Marshall) at Rockdale High in I WAS A TEENAGE WEREWOLF.

INVASION OF THE SAUCERMEN

American-International, 1957
Released in England as
Invasion of the Hell Creatures

Presenters	James H. Nicholson
	Samuel Z. Arkoff
Producers	James H. Nicholson
	Robert J. Gurney, Jr.
Director	Edward L. Cahn
Screenplay	Al Martin
Additional Dialogue	Robert J. Gurney, Jr.
	based on the short story
	"The Cosmic Frame" by Paul W. Fairman
Cinematography	Fred West
Editorial Supervisor	Ronald Sinclair
Film Editor	Charles Gross, Jr.
Music	Ronald Stein
Art Director	Don Ament
Production Manager	Bart Carre
Property Master	Karl Brainard
Makeup	Carlie Taylor
Wardrobe	Margorie Corso
Sound	Phil Mitchell
Technical Effects	Paul Blaisdell
Special Effects	Howard Anderson
	Alex Weldon
Script Supervisor	Judith Hart

A Malibu Production
Running time: 69 minutes

Cast: Steve Terrell (Johnny Carter), Gloria Castillo (Joan Hayden), Frank Gorshin (Joe Gruen), Lynn Osborne (Art Burns), Raymond Hatton (Larkin), Russ Bender (Doctor), Douglas Henderson (Lt. Wilkins), Sam Buffington (Col. Ambrose), Jason Johnson (Detective), Don Shelton (Hayden), Scott Peters (First Soldier), Bob Einer (Soda Jerk), Patti Lawler (Irene), Calvin Booth (Paul), Ed Nelson (Boy), Roy Darmour (Sgt. Gordon), Audrey Conti (Girl), Buddy Mason (Policeman), Orv Mohler (Boy in Soda Shop), Angelo Rossitto, Floyd Dixon, Dean Neville, Edward Peter Gibbons (Saucermen)

Invasion of the Saucermen was based on "The Cosmic Frame", a 1955 short story by Paul W. Fairman. In it, teenagers Johnny Carter and Joan Haydon ran down a spaceman with their car, telling their fathers, Sam Carter and Lee Hayden. Carter and Hayden intended to exploit the dead alien, keeping its body in a refrigerator, but its comrades took the body, banged up Johnny's car and left him to take the rap for the death

of a farmer named Williams.

James Nicholson thought "The Cosmic Frame" was a natural for filming, what with the teenage angle. Its twist ending became the actual plot of *Saucermen*. The implausibilities of "Cosmic Frame" were the buildup to an irony. For that irony to become a movie plot, *Invasion of the Saucermen* had to dispense with all pretenses to logic and for that to be acceptable it had to be a farce. Sam Carter was written out and Lee Hayden was made a saucerman skeptic. The profit angle of the situation was realized by a small-time hustler named Joe Gruen, whose partner was Art Burns. Williams was turned into another farmer, Larkin. The picture was framed by the covers of a book — Art's account of "the *true* story of a flying saucer"

Lightning flashes across the front of Larkin's house and Art's voice says, "Spooky, ain't it?" The area is Hicksburg. Kids on their way to Lovers' Point pass the home of grumpy old Larkin. Art and Joe have been casing the town for a fast buck without success. After an argument in a diner, Art returns to their boarding house while Joe takes a drive. Johnny is waiting for Joan in front of a soda shop. A friend, Duke, sees a UFO. "Only one?" inquires the soda jerk. "Nobody's got a right to brag these days unless the see six — and in different colors." "This one was blue," claims Duke. Gravely concerned is Lt. Wilkins of the Air Force. When Joan arrives in her clunker "Elvis", she and Johnny leave in his car. They plan to elope.

Driving near Pelham Woods, Joe is bathed in the light of the saucer and sees it land. Larkin's Brahma bull, Walt, visits the kids, sampling some free beer. Johnny announces the elopement plans to everyone. Joe tries to rouse Art from bed, excitedly describing the saucer: "It was big and round and glowed and it made a noise like n-n-n-n-n-n . . . " Apathetic Art returns to sleep. Wilkins mentions the saucer to his immediate superior, Col. Ambrose, who orders a prompt investigation.

Leaving the Point, Johnny and Joan kill their headlights to avoid Larkin and almost hit Wilkins and Ambrose in their jeep. A distorted shape appears in a lightning flash as Johnny and Joan strike what they think is a child. Wedged beneath the front fenders of the car is a little green man. Unseen, one of its hands detaches itself from the wrist. It crawls up to a tire, projecting long needles from the fingers that deflate it. Johnny and Joan leave on foot to call the police. The Air Force discovers the saucer.

In Larkin's empty house, Johnny phones a desk sergeant, describing the saucerman. "Saturday night," the mocking sergeant tells a cop, "that's official!" When Johnny dials the station again, a blackout occurs. Larkin surprises Johnny and Joan with a shotgun. Thinking they killed his prize heifer, he makes them leave. When the power comes back on, he calls the cops to have Johnny and Joan picked up. Joe discovers the saucerman. While Larkin is out, Joe borrows his phone to call Art

INVASION OF THE SAUCERMEN (1957).

and tell him to empty their icebox. "What I'm bringing home is perishable." Absentmindedly, Art climbs out of bed and complies.

Joe needs something to pry the saucerman's body loose from under the car. More saucermen, blaming him for its death, viciously needle Joe — pumping raw alcohol into his veins. Already drunk, Joe dies. Art fully awakens as he cleans out the refrigerator. *What am I doing?* he thinks, and hits the sack again.

Back at the car, Johnny and Joan see the saucermen hammering a fender with a strange drill-shaped device — as if they think the car itself killed their friend. The Air Force is getting nowhere attempting verbal communication with the saucer. After a corporal fires multiple rounds at it, the men assume the saucer is empty. Johnny and Joan meet the police, who see a different body and think they committed a drunken hit and run. A doctor says, "In my day, we were content with pink elephants. Kids these days —." A detective tells him, "They're tough. The girl says to me 'You don't call him human do you?'" The Doctor asks, "Well, what do you expect with all the killings they see in the movies and all?"

At the police station, Johnny is duped into signing a bogus confession. Joan's prejudiced father will help him only for her sake. To the shock of Johnny and Joan, the body they see is Joe's. The police try to call Art, but no answer. As Air Force engineers cut open the hull of the saucer with an acetylene torch, a magnesium fuse suddenly ignites. The saucer explodes, leaving nothing. The police see the blast. Johnny realizes the saucermen were trying to frame him and Joan by substituting the corpse of Joe. To clear themselves, they take advantage of a conveniently open office window and steal a squad car. Hayden, who promised to take responsibility for the actions of Johnny and Joan, is in a spot. The cop sent to investigate the explosion is told that a jet crashed.

In the police car, the living hand menaces Johnny and Joan, who lock it inside. They visit Art, who doubts their story until a call to the police station informs him of Joe's death. A saucerman who wanders onto the Larkin property is gored in the eyes by Walt.. The saucerman needles him as it dies.

Taking "Elvis" ("She shimmies and she shakes", Johnny tells Art), Johnny, Joan and Art go to the police car. Art brings a camera and a gun he lifted off the body of a dead Nazi soldier. When Elvis' spotlight is trained on the hand so Art can photograph it, the hand goes up in a puff of smoke. The remaining saucermen attack. Art's gun does not hurt them. As Elvis' battery dies, the spotlight dies. Johnny and Joan escape, but the saucermen pump alcohol into Art.

Col. Ambrose thinks the saucer cover-up is a success until Wilkins pointedly asks, "Did it ever occur to you that there may be other units covering up other things?" Johnny and Joan call the police to surrender, but because an autopsy showed that Joe died of alcohol-related heart

failure, the vehicular manslaughter charge has been dropped. Thanks to Hayden, the car theft charge is also dropped. Larkin finds Walt drunk, blaming the kids.

Johnny and Joan recruit their friends at Lover's Point to help them. They see the saucermen carrying Joe. On Johnny's car horn signal, the kids fatally illuminate the saucermen in a ring of headlights. Art is safe, but so hung-over that his memory is muddled for now. Larkin fires his shotgun into the air, ordering everyone off his land. "No one will believe us," regrets Joan. "Of course not," says Johnny. "We're crazy mixed-up kids. Let's hope the next person who runs into them is a one hundred percent certified adult." From what Johnny and Joan told him, Art was able to tell his adventure.

The story book closes with "The End" with the living had holding it. The back cover reads "The End — Until the Next Time". Somebody screams.

Invasion of the Saucermen spared nothing to dump creative persecution on Youth. Both the equipment and the biology of the saucermen were made to guard against proof of their existence, pinning a murder rap on two kids whose only crime was wanting to get married. Even the dead Saucerman's hand got into the act — from assisting the frame by disabling Johnny's car to terrorizing him and Joan. This was *The Blob* (1958) Men from Mars style, starting with a disbelieved high school couple and a narrative told entirely in one weekend evening. On all levels there was a complete failure of communication: Art wouldn't listen to Joe about the dead saucermen, Larkin had it in for every Point lover, the police and Hayden made a rash legal equation, the Air Force lied about the saucer blast, the saucermen loathed anything earth-like and Walt the bull reacted in kind to one of them. If Johnny wasn't their leader, the kids at the Point would have kept on drinking and smooching (two back-seat youngsters continued necking all through the climax).

As the first film where teens battled monsters, *Saucermen* credited kids for resourcefulness aided by contrived fortune. Since kids lack the leverage of institutional force, the saucermen had to be killed by something available to them. Kids own cars and cars have lights. With the saucermen gone and Art being thoroughly crocked, only the testimony of a few could back Art's story. It had to be pieced together by him because he was absent from many situations and unconscious during the conclusion.

Paul Blaisdell designed the saucermen after the ones Paul Fairman described. Deliberately stereotypical, their laughability was negated by the gory things that happened to them. The saucer, another Blaisdell effect, hovered like a helicopter and flew like a rocket. Against a stormy sky, it displayed a graceful shape that made it more than just a suspended disc. Blaisdell illustrated the credits like a storybook. Only the blind and deaf could miss the movie's tone. One cartoon page showed images of a kitchen saucer and a flying saucer. Part of

Steve Terrell and Gloria Castillo are menaced by a living hand in INVASION OF THE SAUCERMEN.

81

Joe (Frank Gorshin) cases the town for a fast buck in INVASION OF THE SAUCERMEN.

Ronald Stein's music was derived from "Flight of the Bumblebee".

Steve Terrell and Gloria Castillo were gentle, pleasant leads with Gloria resembling the Joan in "Cosmic Frame". Frank Gorshin had been in a few other AIP films. Although third-billed, he wasn't very funny. Most of the time he performed by himself in isolated surroundings. More amusing was Lynn Osborne, Cadet Happy of "Space Patrol". Homelier than an Edsel grill with his long face, pug ski nose and squarish crewcut, he exhibited low but restrained humor much better than Gorshin's slummy mugging. Gorshin did deliver a realistic death scene. In 1958, Osborne expired after surgery for a brain tumor. Lovely Gloria Castillo also died at a young age from cancer in 1970.

Invasion of the Saucermen was something of an embarrassment to AIP according to a legend that the humor was rationalized. Director Edward Cahn supposedly thought the saucermen were too fakey to be accepted as serious monsters and pushed for laughs. The actual film was a lark, but AIP was insecure about promoting it as a comedy. Ads treated it as an earnest chiller with images of saucermen whose heads were in even larger relation to their bodies. Britain gave Saucermen a more graphic title: *Invasion of the Hell Creatures*.

This was one item for an AIP remake Larry Buchanan shouldn't have botched, but he did. His 1965 *The Eye Creatures* was *Saucermen* without the makeup skill of Paul Blaisdell, the sincerity of Steve Terrell (his ex-delinquency film rival John Ashley was now the star), the warmth of Gloria Castillo or the minimal wit of the script. Dwarves are pretty hard to find in the tall state of Texas, so the Buchanan aliens were played by men of average size suited up in outfits covered with odd globules like condoms full of white paint. In the age of the Fab Four, "Elvis" — now a Falcon convertible instead of a '48 Ford ragtop — should have been called "Ringo" . . . that is if a condition of the car made it justifiable. Someone even asked, "Have you seen this movie before?"

Two hideous, bug-eyed midgets from INVASION OF THE SAUCERMEN.

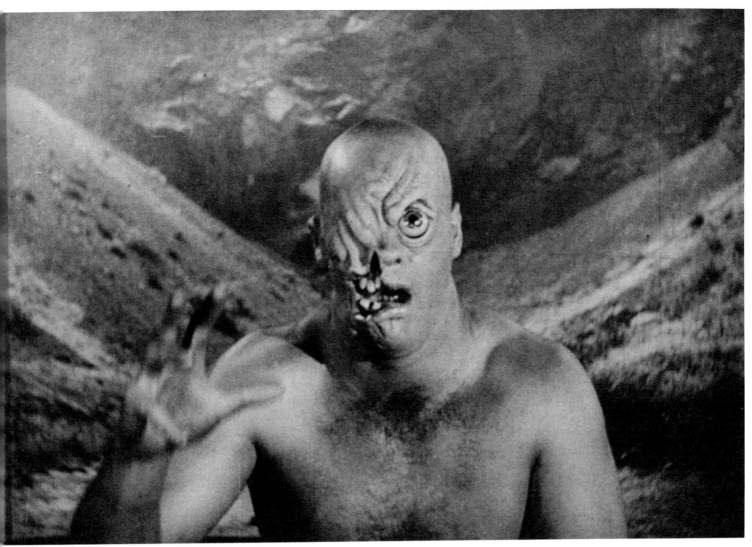

THE CYCLOPS

Allied Artists, 1957

Producer-Director-Screenplay- *Special Technical Effects*	Bert I. Gordon
Associate Producer- *Production Manager*	Henry Schrage
Cinematography	Ira Morgan
	(and Bert I. Gordon)
Film Editor	Carlo Lodato
Music	Albert Glasser
Assistant Producer	Flora M. Gordon
Special Voice Effects	Paul Frees
Special Makeup	Jack H. Young
Animal Sequences	Jim Dannaldson
Properties	James Harris
Makeup	Carlie Taylor
Script Supervisor	Diana Loomis
Aeronautical Supervisor	Henry "Hank" Coffin
Assistant Directors	Harry O. Jones
	Ray Taylor, Jr.
Snake Fight Supervision	Ralph D. Helfer
Sound Effects	Douglas Stewart

Optical Effects	Consolidated Films, Inc.

A B & H Production
Running time: 75 minutes

Cast: James Craig (Russ Bradford), Gloria Talbott (Susan Winter), Lon Chaney (Martin Melville), Tom Drake (Lee Brand), Duncan *aka Dean* Parkin (Bruce Barton / The Cyclops), Vincente Padula (Governor), Marlene Kloss (Salesgirl), Manuel Lopez (Guard)

Atomic mutation in people was at first treated quite tamely. Those who became monsters changed little in appearance or else the state brought temporary powers treated for mirth. Radioactive giantism in a human was created for the first time in *The Cyclops*, which borrowed several parallels from "Ulysses". The only high points of this Bert Gordon film were held off so a routine rescue expedition could pad it out.

Guayjorm, Mexico. Susan Winter pleads with the Governor to let her and her friends go to a remote,

(Above) A closeup of Duncan Parkin as THE CYCLOPS (1957).

forbidden jungle valley where her aviator fiancee Bruce Barton crashed three years ago. For two months, he managed to transmit radio signals. It had taken Susan all this time to form a search party. Officially, the valley is off-limits. The Governor dubiously reviews records of Susan's companions. Bacteriologist Russ Bradford of the New York Institute of Toxicology was Bruce's friend. Martin Melville, the partial backer of the expedition, conducted some shifty stock transactions in Texas and has brought a precision scintillator used for tracing uranium from the air. Hired pilot, Lee Brand, is unemployable in the States. Susan's request is turned down. One of the party must remain in Mexico while a security man escorts the others across the border in their four-seat Cessna.

Russ, Marty and Lee are waiting for Susan at an outdoor restaurant. Russ in particular finds the purpose of Susan's trip morbid. Susan tells them about their obstacle. Marty has a solution. At the airport, he pretends to be the man staying behind so he can slug the guard as Lee starts the plane. The guard fires several shots at the departing craft. Disregarding an official order to return, its occupants are now criminals.

Over the valley, Susan thinks she sees the shape of an animal big as an elephant. Marty's scintillator picks up a positive reading. A strong downdraft seizes the plane. Panicked Marty slugs Lee and seizes the controls, causing a nose-dive until Ross choke holds him and Lee recovers in time. The plane lands in a canyon near where Bruce crashed. Detecting a high-yield of uranium, Marty wants the group to forget Bruce. Russ glimpses a giant lizard that vanishes when he calls to Susan and Lee. Marty tries to talk Lee into leaving Russ and Susan so they can go back to town and file a claim, but Lee is committed to Susan.

Russ loves Susan and is tired of competing with a dead man. He and Susan see a huge rodent and a giant hawk that kills it. Russ suspects a reason for their size. Russ and Susan hear Lee testing the plane's motor. To make sure everyone leaves together, Susan confiscates the ignition key. That night, the group hears strange rumblings from behind the hills.

The next day, the group encounters a giant spider and two battling lizards. Another lies dying. Russ obtains a skin sample from it. The lizard cells divide once every twenty-two seconds. The radiation of the valley affects the pituitary glands of the animals, causing unlimited growth. Russ fears he and the rest of the group may start growing too, unless they leave within the week.

Susan feels something watching them. Wandering off from camp, she finds a wing section from Bruce's plane. She looks up at the staring horror she felt and screams.

Russ, Marty and Lee look for Susan, discovering the wing and another piece of debris near a large cave. Inside, Susan is safe but in shock. There is the plane's engine, a cold campfire, Bruce's flying suit and his wristwatch. A mammoth boulder is pushed in front of the entrance by a hostile, growling twenty-five foot man with one eye and partially mutilated features. For now, the group is stranded. While the others sleep, Marty tries to escape, but his rifle fire only provokes the Cyclops into killing him. Russ urges Susan to attempt to communicate with it. It takes her outside. Russ and Lee follow. When a boa constrictor attacks the Cyclops, Russ, Susan and Lee run away. Russ forces Susan to realize the Cyclops is Bruce — a victim of radiation.

While the Cyclops is resting, Russ, Susan and Lee sneak past him to the plane. The motor balks. The Cyclops awakens, regarding the plane with a vague familiarity. To keep him from wrecking it, Russ lures the Cyclops to a cliffside and hurls a flaming spear into his eye. The agonized Cyclops plucks it out and lumbers towards the plane. He tries to catch it in his outstretched arms, but falls dead as Russ, Susan and Lee wing for home.

Only so much could happen between four people and a giant man in an area otherwise inhabited only by wildlife. This much of *The Cyclops* was *King Dinosaur* again. Because they were not phony prehistoric life, the lizards there had a more legitimate explanation. Gordon couldn't enlarge everything organic in the valley, thinking up the excess stimulation of pituitary glands to rationalize the average-looking vegetation. There had to be some limit to the atomic growth or the animals would have dwarfed Godzilla and found their way to civilization. Had Russ, Susan, Marty and Lee been stranded for good, they too would have eventually shot up to Bruce's present size, while Bruce, who had been in the valley for three years, might have kept dimensional pace ahead of them. In killing Bruce, Russ destroyed the man who kept Susan from loving him.

Gordon had to photograph much of *The Cyclops* himself because his old-time cameraman, Ira Morgan, refused to film into twilight time with Tri-X, a brand new fast-speed film. Strapping stuntman Duncan Parkin made a very good Cyclops, managing even to create a few sensitive expressions behind Jack Young's thickly grotesque makeup. The boa constrictor fight almost killed Parkin when the reptile tried to crush him until snake handler Ralph Helfer repelled it with a stick. For voice effects, Paul Frees copped an easy ten thou.

Albert Glasser had composed the war movie *Huk* (1956) and Gordon asked him to score *Cyclops*. So taken by Glasser's music was Gordon that he put Glasser on retainer.

Susan Winter's identity was the typical Gloria Talbott horror role. In most of her genre films, she was tied to a strong romantic commitment with a man who became a monster. James Craig played Russ as a partial cold fish who was amusingly human when he tried to buy a sports magazine from a salesgirl who did not *comprende*, selling him a copy of "The Ladies' Home Journal" instead. In the showiest human part, Lon

Lon Chaney and James Craig examine the wristwatch of a missing Bruce Barton in THE CYCLOPS.

Chaney was drunk, as usual, but had much dialogue in the outing — most of it gassy diatribes. The magazine gag might have been funnier if it had happened to Marty.

Gordon sold *The Cyclops* to RKO, which planned to release it with *X — The Unknown* (1957), but when the company decided to give up film distribution, most of its final acquisitions were bought by other outfits. Warner Brothers released *X* while Allied Artists paired *Cyclops* with another Gloria Talbott film, *Daughter of* *Dr. Jekyll*. Ads for *The Cyclops*, oddly, billed only James Craig.

The people who stretched Allied films for TV really went berserk on this one. Not only was there an interminable prologue hailing how scary the film was supposed to be, but a grandiose coda suggesting radiation would shape the cause of all future evolution. It certainly shaped the evolution of Bert Gordon's career.

In an attempt to escape, Lon Chaney is destroyed by the Cyclops.

DAUGHTER OF DR. JEKYLL

Allied Artists, 1957

Producer-Screenplay	Jack Pollexfen
Director	Edgar G. Ulmer
Associate Producer	Ilse Lahn
Cinematography	John F. Warren
Film Editor	Holbrook N. Todd
Music Supervision	Melvyn Leonard
Art Director	Theobold Holsopple
Effects Creatures	Jack Rabin
	Louis De Witt
Production Manager	Joseph Boyle
Sound Recorder	Fred Kessler
Set Decorator	Mowbray Barkley
Makeup	Lou Philippi
Property	Irving Sindler
Wardrobe	Robert Martien

A Film Ventures Production
Running time: 71 minutes

Cast: John Agar (George Hastings), Gloria Talbott (Janet Smith), Arthur Shields (Dr. Lomas), John Dierkes (Jacob), Martha Wentworth (Mrs. Merchant), Mollie McCart (Maggie), Margorie Stapp, Rita Greene, Marel Page

Henry Jekyll, as written about by Robert Louis Stevenson, never married or had children. Only as Hyde, the horror hedonist, did he get anything on the side. According to two films, Jekyll left behind a boy child, Edward, and a girl, Janet, both of whom were stigmatized by their father's alter ego. Each plot was a Conspiracy To Attain Wealth By Contrived Insanity number. *Son of Dr. Jekyll*, the male 1951 version, was based on a story coauthored by Jack Pollexfen, the writer-producer of *Daughter*.

Son began with Hyde murdering his mistress. An angry mob chased Jekyll to his London laboratory, which caught fire, and he fell to his death. Edward, Jekyll's bastard son by Hyde, was saved by solicitor John Utterson and Dr. Curtis Lanyon, the trustee of the family estate. Expelled from medical school, grown

(Above) Dr. Lomas (Arthur Shields) orders hypnotized Janet (Gloria Talbott) to accompany him to his lab in DAUGHTER OF DR. JEKYLL (1958).

Edward wanted to prove that the Jekyll formula could cure mental illness. Lanyon tampered with it, adding an ingredient that caused Edward to briefly imagine himself as Hyde. In a public demonstration, the original drug failed. Later, Edward was accused of attacking a young boy and was incarcerated at Lanyon's asylum. Edward escaped, realizing his innocence when he discovered that Lanyon, the actual Hyde, framed Jekyll to get Jekyll's money and recoup his financial losses. When Edward and Lanyon fought, the lab caught fire again. Another mob mistook Lanyon for the Hyde they thought to be Edward and, returning to the lab, Lanyon fell from a ledge.

Daughter of Dr. Jekyll was equally *Son* and two other female twists on male horror, *Devil Bat's Daughter* and *She Wolf of London* (both 1946). Nina McCarron, the progeny of bat breeder Dr. Paul Carruthers, was setup by another medical manipulator, her psychiatrist, and Carruthers, in memory, was absolved of everything he was guilty of in *The Devil Bat* (1941). *She Wolf* was more radical still in that the scheme to make nightmare victim, Phyllis Allenby, think she suffered from a family curse was devised by another woman — a former maid and ex-mistress of Phyllis' father posing as her aunt.

Yet even more radical, *Daughter of Dr. Jekyll* used the Jekyll-Hyde format to present blood-drinking werewolves. What could you call them? Werevamps? Lycanpires? Nos-garous? To make up for its tame, minimal horror, Jack Pollexfen reworked *Son* in a way that deranged three monster traditions. The name Jekyll offered literary certification while vampire-werewolf Hyde was a creature who could arouse more immediate community fear. Killing this werewolf with a wooden stake meant he could be finished by a more graphic weapon than silver bullets. Vampirism created the idea that Hyde could rise from the tomb as any unstaked vampire can. The rest of *Daughter* was the whitewash job of *Son of Dr. Jekyll* except that the Jekyll townhouse was now a remote manor.

In a shadowy, misty prologue, "Jekyll" downs his id-freeing elixir. "When the news of the death of this monster came," says the narrator, "there was a nationwide sigh of relief. No longer would the sound of every strange footstep mean terror. The evil thing would never prowl the night again." The reported "death" is an exaggeration as Hyde turns on us, asking mischievously, "Are you . . . sure? Heh-heh-heh-heh-heh."

Janet Smith and her fiance, George Hastings, drive to the hilltop estate of her unknown father on the eve of Janet's twenty-first birthday. A gangling, ugly servant, Jacob, and Mrs. Merchant, a friendly housekeeper, greet them at the door. Maggie, a shy maid, tends to Janet, who introduces George to her kindly guardian, Dr. Lomas. Janet will learn soon who her father was. Maggie refuses to live in and after work, hurries home past the estate crypt.

While exploring the house the next day, George discovers some hidden wall space. When Janet tips the helmet visor on a suit of armor, she opens a bookcase door. Beyond is a dusty laboratory. Lomas appears and, in private, tell Janet her father's identity. Devastated, she asks George to break their engagement.

In the crypt, Lomas shows Janet and George the sarcophagus of Dr. Jekyll as nosy Jacob watches. Janet reads an inscription on the sarcophagus: "He knoweth not what he did. May his tortured soul rest in peace". "Not *the* Dr. Jekyll?" asks astounded George. "He was my father," ashamedly confesses Janet. Lomas describes Jekyll's attempt to separate the good and evil halves of men. "He wasn't aware that even physically he'd become a monster. Oh, I still shudder when I recall that face . . . like some perverted mask of evil out of a legend of horror." Lomas saw Jekyll as Hyde before the villagers broke into the tomb and drove a wooden stake through his heart. Janet fears her children could inherit her hereditary taint. George thinks this is nonsense. Lomas is noncommittal on the possibilities of the question.

Before bedtime, Lomas puts Janet in a mild, soothing hypnotic trance. Maggie brings in a glass of warm milk and helps Janet into bed. Gazing fearfully at the sky, she tries to outrace the rise of the full moon. In a distorted nightmare, Janet emerges from the crypt and kills Maggie. Janet's screams bring George and Lomas, who comfort her. Alone, she finds blood on the window sill, her hands and her nightgown. Mud stains her shoes. Janet's other face materializes in a mirror.

Maggie is late for breakfast. Jacob enters with her ravaged body — throat torn. "It was no beast that did this," he declares "— least-wise no natural beast. It's a werewolf! We've seen it before! People know what to do about werewolves!" George and Lomas chastise Jacob. Leaving, he turns to Janet, "Good day, Miss Jekyll."

For tonight, Lomas gives Janet a sedative and locks her door. In another dream, Janet spots a young couple in a cozy knoll. The boy plants a sudden kiss on the girl, who slaps him and runs down an incline. Janet moves in for the kill. Shrieking, she awakens with more arm scratches and shoe mud. Lomas insists that no one could have climbed out of her window . . . yet there are marks along the ledge. Jacob reports the new murder, riling George and Lomas, who angrily fires him. Mrs. Merchant up and quits.

While Lomas looks for a new housekeeper, Janet catches George reading a book about werewolves. Over his shoulder, she reads text describing how to kill them. George is surprised to see Janet, who cries, "Then do it! If you love me, please kill me!" Janet needs more sedation. Lomas says that she may be held for an inquest. Janet disappears. George and Lomas find her by the crypt. Jacob sits nearby, whittling a long wooden stake. Again, Lomas tells him to leave.

On this evening, Lomas sits by Janet's bedside, absorbed in a medical journal until moonlight distorts

Janet (Gloria Talbott) is found by Jekyll's tomb by Dr. Lomas and George (Arthur Shields and John Agar) in DAUGHTER OF DR. JEKYLL.

his features into a diabolical expression. Candle in hand, Lomas orders hypnotized Janet to go with him to the lab. George follows them through a secret passage to the crypt. A metal gate slams shut behind him. Handing her a length of cord, Lomas tells Janet she will go to a house and after hang herself as "atonement" for her deeds. In extreme pain, Lomas clutches two iron bars as horrified George sees him become the werewolf. Lomas attacks George, knocks him out and locks the crypt door as he goes.

At the house, a pretty blonde is dressing to go out. She answers the phone and is told by the operator there is a village patrol. Lomas creeps in through an open window and kills the girl while the worried operator keeps asking, "Hello . . .?" Two villagers see Lomas running away and chase him. Coming to, George stops Janet from stringing up a noose and slaps her back to normal. He believes Lomas framed Jekyll to gain the estate and set Janet up for her money. More villagers are after Lomas.

George and Janet try to pass the locked crypt door and see Lomas coming back. A bullet wounds his shoulder. George has Janet lie on top of the sarcophagus as if she is still hypnotized. He hides as Lomas smears more blood on Janet's hands. George attacks him. Lomas proves to be stronger until Jacob leads his men down the crypt stairs. George hurls Lomas backwards into the path of Jacob's stake. It sends Lomas to his

maker. "He'll never prowl the night again," curtly intones Jacob.

The prologue Hyde doesn't agree, repeating his question, "Are you . . . sure?" and laughs.

Pollexfen's script created prejudice toward *Daughter of Dr. Jekyll* from the start by linking the Stevenson's Hyde to werewolfery. On Lomas and Dr. Lanyon, Jekyll juice didn't release evil. Via Hyde, it simply created a murder instrument for two already corrupt men. Because the narrator was discussing Jekyll, the viewer assumes that murkily photographed Lomas is he. In this ostensible flashback, Hyde metaphysically mocks his "death", talking in a high, cackly, wicked witch kind of voice. If we didn't know he was part of the film, we would think Hyde was some "Chiller Theater" host cutting up during one of those customary interruptions of imposed Station Relief humor.

How Jekyll met a Dracula version of lynch justice was without any circumstantial conclusivity. The townies, like the mob that killed Edward Jekyll's father, just went after someone they frightened into fleeing, whose only true guilt, if he had been guilty, would have been the face of Hyde. That face couldn't have been Jekyll's. Or maybe there was something about his appearance, like blood, to create a guilty impression (obviously then, Lomas was lying when he said *he* saw Hyde). Living comfortably off the fat of the Jekylls until Janet came of age, Lomas couldn't rely on mob violence to get rid of her. Her guilt had to be something that would make *her* feel she was a monster. The ways were myriad: The notion of demon genes, the arousal of militant werewolf hater Jacob and the drug-concocted nightmares. Most victims, like Maggie, were chosen ahead of time and the dreams were probably triggered after the real murders so Lomas would have time to plant phony evidence (but why would a werewolf bother to put on shoes?)

The expressionistic look of the dreams was a way of getting around some questions, like the diaphanous low cut white gown Hyde Janet wore. The passage from the crypt to the house explained how she could have left by way of the tomb. The tomb had symbolic significance for it was where Janet finally got to "meet" her father. It was their Special Place.

Lomas' metamorphosis in the crypt showed his wolf being in all too human action as he punched and kicked George like a street fighter. Lomas let unconscious George live for the moment, enabling George to thwart Janet's suicide attempt. Off the top of his head, he figured everything Lomas pulled as much for our enlightenment as Janet's. When Lomas returned, he found nothing odd about Janet lying in her ruse position when she had been ordered to take her own life. The villagers now knew, as surely as Lomas must have been aware, that the monster was male, yet, once again, Lomas ritualistically bloodied Janet. Even if Lomas had been able to change back immediately, there was still that bullet wound to attend to. At the end, when Hyde asked again, "Are you sure?" his voice dropped a few octaves, now sounding like *Jacob*!

The best Edgar Ulmer, picked for having directed Pollexfen and Aubrey Wisberg's *The Man from Planet X* (1951), could do was lay on distractingly potent visuals. Jack Rabin and Louis De Witt furnished the labor. The Jekyll manor, in a long shot, appeared in the 1959 version of *The Bat*. Other angles showed a model of the 1908 Stutz-Bearcat that Janet and George arrived in. *Daughter* didn't settle for paltry patches of fog: it drenched the frames in shifting, drifting, shimmering mist. Was there a big pot party on the set, maybe? Complementing the fog were shots of the full moon, the Jekyll estate and dreamy overlaps of tree branches, skies, hills and dales.

Gloria Talbot left the filming before the nightmare murders were shot and another actress appeared in them. Exteriors were done in ultraviolet in a burned out forest. Ken Terrell stunted for Arthur Shields in most of Shield's werewolf scenes. If there was a bigger mob after Lomas than the few men Jacob actually led, it was because they were from Universal Frankenstein clips.

The manor scenes were done in a house on Sixth Street in the Hancock Park area of Los Angeles. The windows by the breakfast table had curtains, but they failed to hide a procession of fifties cars passing outside. Miscast as a period Britisher, John Agar looked foolish in a striped white jacket, male leisure wear of the time. His best line sounded like a criticism of Gloria Talbott's emoting when George told Janet, "We've got one chance. Lie down. Act like you're still in a trance." Talbott liked her part as much as Agar hated his and did her best. Arthur Shields, the brother of Barry Fitzgerald, used every microinch of his crinkly age lines to give each face of Lomas its contrast to the other. John Dierkes, whose clock-stopping pus was a map of ire, played in Jacob a xenophobic inquisitor who ultimately amounted to a hero. The act that was necessary to save Janet and George was what Jacob had been licking his lips for and, lucky for Janet, Jacob achieved his orgasm by impaling the right heart.

Millie McCart, the meek Maggie, had her last name misspelled in the credits as "McCard". Marjorie Stapp was the girl in the house and the bimbo ambience of her attire and postures may have influenced a B rating from the Catholic Legion of Decency ("A suggestive scene" was the only reason given).

On TV, the nightmare with Maggie was lengthened by the insertion of the opening monster chase from *Frankenstein 1970*. Lomas' flight from the villagers was replayed and the added cast listing spelled correctly the name of Mollie McCarth.

Janet's dream double kills Maggie in DAUGHTER OF DR. JEKYLL.

Frightmare!
BORN OF
JUNGLE WITCHCRAFT!
CREATED BY
A CURSE!
From HELL IT Came
AN ALLIED ARTISTS PICTURE
starring TOD ANDREWS · TINA CARVER with LINDA WATKINS · JOHN McNAMARA

FROM HELL IT CAME

Allied Artists, 1957

Producer-Film Editor	Jack Milner
Director	Dan Milner
Screenplay	Richard Bernstein
Story	Richard Bernstein
	Dan Milner, Jack Milner
Associate Producers	Richard Bernstein
	Byron Roberts
Cinematography	Brydon Baker
Music	Darrell Calker
Production Supervisor	Byron Roberts
Art Director	Rudi Field
Sound Recording	Frank Webster, Sr.
Assistant Director	Johnny Greenwald
Set Decorator	Morrie Hoffman
Script Supervisor	M.E. Fishbone
Property	Ted Mossman
Wardrobe	Frank Delmar
Makeup	Harry Thomas
Hair Stylist	Carla Hadley
Chief Electrician	Wilbur Kinnett
Key Grip	Charles Hanawalt
Special Effects	James J. Donnelly

A Milner Brothers Production
Running time: 73 minutes

Cast: Tod Andrews (Dr. William Arnold), Tina Carver (Dr. Terry Mason), Linda Watkins (Meg Kilgore), John MacNamara (Prof. Howard Clarke), Gregg Palmer (Kimo), Robert Swann (Witch Doctor Tano), Baynes Barron (Chief Maranka), Suzanne Ridgway (Korey), Mark Sheeler (Eddie), Lee Rhodes (Norgu), Grace Matthews (Orchid), Tani Marsh (Naomi), Chester Hayes (Maku), Lenmana Guerin (Dori)

From Hell It Came, the second Milner brothers film, featured another Paul Blaisdell monster. No less illogical and disorganized than *The Phantom from Ten Thousand Leagues*, the movie pretended to both voodoo and science, replacing drab espionage with jungle native menace. Dan Milner's direction was not appreciably better than before, but *From Hell It Came* was a more competently mounted Milner Brothers *production*: decently photographed, energetically scored, weird with a cracked sense of conviction and, in its title monster, had a Blaisdell beast the Billiken company should make a model of.

Kimo, the prince of Kalai Island in the South Seas, lies staked to the ground of his village, where he is accused of killing his father, the old Chief. The Chief was ill with plague, but new chief Maranka blames atomic "devil dust" thought to have been brought by the American doctors Kimo befriended. Kimo says witch doctor, Tano, poisoned the old chief, but Kimo's traitorous wife Korey, who loves Maranka, claims the only thing the Chief drank was the American medicine. "I will come back from the grave to revenge myself!" Kimo swears. "In death, I will be stronger than you in life! Maranka, your days are numbered — and the gods curse you and Tano and Korey!" An execution dagger is pounded through Kimo's heart. Walking near the native cemetery, the only white woman on the island, widowed trading post owner, Meg Kilgore, is a witness.

In their compound, Dr. William Arnold and Prof. Howard Clarke hear ceremonial drums. "How come travel folders never mention the drums?" wonders Bill. "Islands of romance . . . islands of beauty . . . how come they never talk about the malaria or the jungle rot or the stupid blind ignorance of those drums?" Bill tried in vain to save the old Chief. The natives were peaceful until an unexpected typhoon blew bomb fallout from the Nogasa atoll here. When Bill and Clarke came, they found a real problem — the plague. Bill wants to go home and take his old girlfriend, Dr. Terry Mason, who is working for the same foundation that employs him and Clarke, on Boke Island. When Eddie, their Marine aide, joins in a coffee break, the three hear Meg scream as a tribesman tries to kill her. Placed in an upright wooden coffin, Kimo is buried in the cemetery. Meg finds safety in the compound, where she tells what happened to Kimo. Only by curing the plague can Bill and Clarke regain the confidence of the tribe.

The next ship brings a helicopter ferrying Terry, sent to help Bill and Clarke. An eerie force topples a skull pole above Kimo's grave as she is driven by jeep to the compound. Terry meets Meg and Orchid, a pretty half-Dutch outcast. Defying orders not to see the doctors, Kimo's friend Norgu brings his fallout-scarred wife Dori in for treatment. Maranka is preparing poison darts to kill the Americans and Korey is jealous because he now has a new woman, Naomi. Bill still loves Terry, and she him, but her job obsesses her.

At the cemetery, Bill and Terry see an odd stump-like growth breaking the ground around Kimo's grave. Norgu relates a legend about an early chief slain by his enemies who was buried with seeds. The chief became a tree monster. Lightning tore it loose from the ground and it killed many. "They called it — Tabanga!" says Norgu. The Tabanga vanished into the forest. Some say it went into the quicksand. Orchid was just by the cemetery and says the growth has Kimo's death dagger embedded in it. Green ooze emanates from the thing. Highly radioactive, the stump has a human heartbeat and the ooze is akin to blood. Norgu begs the doctors to pull this thing out by the roots and throw it into the quicksand. "Norgu," scoffs Clarke, "what you fear is scientifically impossible." "You know what —," shudders Terry, "I have an eerie feeling this thing knows what

Poster art for the release of FROM HELL IT CAME (1957).

Tod Andrews and Tina Carver examine the Tabanga in FROM HELL IT CAME.

94

we're saying."

A message from Washington tells the doctors to study the Tabanga further. Bill is opposed, but outvoted. "All right, if you people feel like chopping wood, I don't mind a little exercise." Tano is making a drug that will give him control of the Tabanga. For associating with the doctors, he wants Norgu to die too. Maranka also wants Korey dead. Overhearing, she warns the doctors, who let her stay with them.

That night, the doctors uproot the Tabanga. During the operation, Bill brushes the dagger slightly. A circulatory problem is causing heart stoppage. "Why don't we psychoanalyze the monster?" jokes Bill. "Maybe its mother was scared by an oak tree." To save the dying Tabanga, Terry intravenously feeds it experimental formula 447.

The next morning, the Tabanga escapes, wrecking the lab. Clarke thinks the natives took it, then smashed the place. Help is needed from Boku, but the radio is broken. Korey catches Naomi bathing alone and jealously attacks her with a knife. The Tabanga grabs Korey and throws her into the quicksand. Naomi alerts Tano and Maranka, who find the Tabanga missing from the cemetery. After it is killed, the doctors will die next. In the village, the Tabanga murders Maranka. The doctors are informed. "I just wanted it to live," exclaims mortified Terry, "— not to destroy." The radiation and her drug must have built up a chain reaction.

Acting as bait, Tano lures the Tabanga to a brush covered pit. It falls in and the natives burn it with thrown torches. After they leave, the scorched Tabanga climbs out. As Tano strolls down a path, he sees the Tabanga coming and dies. The natives ask the doctors for aid.

During the search for it, Terry straggles a moment and the Tabanga abducts her. The Tabanga is heading for the quicksand. Rifle shots make it turn and the right shot pushes the blade back into the heart. Paralyzed, the Tabanga topples into the mire. The natives now respect white medicine. Glancing at Bill and Terry, Clarke surmises it is a honeymoon and back to the States for them. "By the way, Professor," says horny Meg, "I never asked you — are you married?"

As far as what can be determined in *From Hell it Came*, the Tabanga was Kimo's death curse realized in a form with prior reference. The first monster did not need to be stimulated by radiation, which for Kimo must have been the equivalent of the early chief's enchanted seeds. Being one of wood instead of clay, the Tabanga was sort of a Polynesian Golem. Where the Star of David gave life to the Hebrew Golem, the status of the dagger governed the Tabanga's dormancy and animation. Like the Star, the knife was not part of the basic element of the monster. Initially meant to kill a living man, the dagger acted as a metallic wooden stake. How else could the blade terminate a ghost? Only this ghost was sheathed in a biological body with a heart subject to medical as well as supernatural vulnerabilities.

Bill and Terry were stock lovers, but their chauvinism/feminism clash actually enhanced the plot. He was the voice of caution while she initiated the most daring science. Jointly, they were responsible for the Tabanga's full life — he for accidently upsetting the dagger, she for using the drug. Bill was allowed to undo his error when the Tabanga was stopped by a non-test tube "magic bullet". After Terry was saved, Bill finally got what he wanted from her all along. Down at the bottom of the quicksand, Kimo and Korey were also "together" again. If the first Tabanga was there too, three would have made a crowd.

Since Bill, Terry and Clarke was hellhole healers, the script was full of anxiety-expressing and mocking mirth appropriate to the milieu of "MASH". The wisecracking began with minor discomforts such as the quality of coffee and Bill's romantic frustration ("Why did I ever fall in love with a beautiful, dedicated female scientist?"). A few "earnest" lines were dumb, like when Terry asked, "Can a stump grow from a coffin?", and Orchid said the ooze was like "green blood from a dying man". Funny as overstated awe was Norgu's wide-eyed exclamation of the word "Ta-ban-ga!" Bill liked to "knock wood" at every opportunity, getting Clarke and even Terry to do it. The Tabanga was everything from a "wooden zombie" and a "frozen-faced friend" to an object good for scaring crows and hanging up jackets. Some of this levity was indulged at the expense of the memory of poor Kimo — a fine man who died for trusting an outside culture.

Paul Blaisdell designed, but did not build Tabanga. Exaggerated enough to be parodistic, it was ugly enough to make reasonable fear in who it was supposed to scare.

A doglike face took up most of the frontal upper body. The shoulders were near head-high and the arms extended close to its short legs. Clumsy waddling dampened Tabanga's chill, but its determined movement speeded pace as if the remainder of the story was being pulled with it. Much of the febrile quality in the action was helped by Darrell Calker's rousing music. In a driving din, it pushed the theramin to max audio overload.

The title *From Hell it Came* was more original that *It Came From Hell*, a name that would have been cliche what with "It Came" two overused title words. In a clever play of word reversal, the title's letters appeared in the order of the tentative name.

Tod Andrews had an easy way with Bill's verbal nonchalance, but Tina Carver was a ghastly screamer, the fault being her deep voice. Linda Watkins was a howl as Meg, who could do an about-face from comic opera hysteria to brassy solicitousness in the twitch of a vocal chord. Gregg Palmer was passionate but wasted as Kimo. Baynes Barron's Maranka talked in a hard New York accent and though Lee Rhodes was verbally convincing, he was an awfully pale-skinned native. Suzanne Ridgway was sultry as Korey, but about as South Seas as a hard-boiled showgirl.

The credits and publicity materials of Allied movies must have been prepared by people who flunked a lot of spelling bees. The prologue of *From Hell it Came* misspelled zombie as "zombi" and the pressbook referred to the Tabanga as "Taranga". Proud of one of its weirdest monsters, Allied suggested that theaters display a tree trunk shaped into a replica of Tar — whoops — Ta*ban*ga.

95

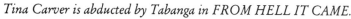
Tina Carver is abducted by Tabanga in FROM HELL IT CAME.

THE AMAZING COLOSSAL MAN

American-International, 1957

Presenters	James H. Nicholson
	Samuel Z. Arkoff
Producer-Director-Story	
Special Technical Effects	Bert I.
	Gordon
Screenplay	Bert I. Gordon
	Mark Hanna
Assistant to the Producer	Henry Schrage
Cinematography	Joe Biroc
Film Editor	Ronald Sinclair
Music	Albert Glasser
Production Supervisor-	
Assistant Director	Jack R. Berne
Assistant Technical Effects	Flora M. Gordon
Second Assistant Director	Nate P. Scott
Property Master	James Harris
Production Design	Bill Glasgow
Sound Editor	Josef von Stroheim
Set Decorator	Glen Daniels
Makeup	Bob Schiffer
Men's Costumer	Bob Richards
Sound Recorder	Jack Soloman
Hairstylist	Joan St. Oegger
Chief Set Electrician	Joe Edessa
Music Editor	Lloyd Young

A Malibu Production
Running time: 81 minutes

Cast: Glenn Langan (Col. Glenn Manning), Cathy Downs (Carol Forest), William Hudson (Dr. Paul Lindstrom), James Seay (Col. Hallach), Larry Thorr (Dr. Eric Coulter), Russ Bender (Richard Kingman), Lynne Osborne (Sgt. Taylor), Diana Darrin (Typist), William Hughes (Control Officer), Jack Kosslyn (Lieutenant in Briefing Room), Jean Moorehead (Girl in Bath), Jimmy Cross (Sergeant at Reception Desk), Hank Patterson (Henry), Frank Jenks (Delivery Man), Harry Raybould (Army Guard at Gate), Scott Peters (Sgt. Lee Carter), Myron Cook (Capt. Thomas), Micheal Harris (Sgt. Lt. Keller), Bill Cassaday (Lt. Peterson), Dick Nelson (Sgt. Hanson), Edmund Cobb (Dr. McDermott), Judd Holdren (Robert Allen), Paul Hahn (Attendant), June Jocelyn (Nurse), Stanley Lachman (Lt. Kline)

(Above) Pensive Manning (Glenn Langan) hogs the highway in THE AMAZING COLOSSAL MAN (1957).

Like it or hate it, *The Amazing Colossal Man* is Bert I. Gordon's most "personal" film — or rather the most emotionally involved. Personal usually means a creative work that springs from the intimate depths of the maker. This was not so . . . certain resemblances to *The Cyclops* notwithstanding. Both the curse and the dignity of *The Amazing Colossal Man* was it being a twist imitation of *The Incredible Shrinking Man* from that year. AIP orginally planned to adapt "The Nth Man", a pulp giant story by Homer Eon Flint published in "Amazing" in 1928. When that didn't work out, Corman author Charles Griffith was hired to write an original script.

Any time Griffith wrote what he wanted to write, creative anarchy took over. His Colossal Man was more Al Bundy than either Scott Carey, the Shrinking Man, or Glenn Manning, the protagonist who evolved later. Roger Corman had found that Dick Miller could be trusted with big roles. Using the screen iconoclasm of Miller as a model, Griffith thought up the tale of a hard-drinking, unhappily married complainer who went to his local Army induction center for a physical. There, he found a vial of an unusual laboratory serum that aroused his curiosity. To hide his snooping, the man took the vial home in his coat. When the man's wife discovered the vial, she mistook the serum for illicit liquor and put it into one of her husband's drinks. The man grew and grew and *grew* into a despotic Amazing Colossal Pain in the Ass of all humanity. Pilfering a few cake crumbs from *The Incredible Shrinking Man*, Griffith's story ended with the man shrinking — which in his circumstances meant his return to his original proportions. Bert Gordon wanted something more conventional . . . a man several miles high was too huge for anyone's budget . . . and when Griffith couldn't abide this, he was replaced by Mark Hanna.

Gordon didn't discard everything Griffith put down on paper. A love relationship had been important in *Shrinking Man*. Glenn Manning was someone engaged to be married. Rather than a potential draftee, he was an established military officer. Atomic energy, of course, was the expedient cause of his growth and laboratory scenes were concerned with finding a way to restore his natural size.

Nevada. A desert highway. Troop personnel are en route to Desert Rock. Two forty-five a.m. Two hours and fifteen minutes before Time Zero. At Time Zero, the Army will detonate the first Plutonium bomb under simulated combat conditions.

Hugging an earthen wall in a safety trench, Lt. Col. Glenn Manning and his men await the end of the countdown — but no explosion occurs. The Control tower reports a delay in the Plutonium chain reaction. The men must remain in the trench, but are permitted to doff their protective dark goggles. The moods range from perplexed impatience to a fearful Sergeant's craven anxiety. "It could go off in a second . . . a minute . . . ten minutes . . . maybe not at all," Glenn says. "We'll just have to wait it out."

The men hear the sputtering engine of a light civilian plane. Control warns the pilot he is in a restricted area, but he attempts a bumpy landing and the craft tips over on its back. Through his binoculars, Glenn can see no signs of life. He alerts Control, believing the pilot may be unconscious, but the bomb cannot be deactivated. Glenn bolts out of the trench, disobeying a General's direct command to stop. Glenn reaches the wreckage of the plane, turns to the bomb and in anticipation throws his arms over his face as the released Plutonium sears his flesh.

Suffering from third degree burns over nearly one hundred percent of his body, Glenn is treated by Dr. Paul Lindstrom and Maj. Eric Coulter. In the hospital waiting room is Glenn's fiance, Carol Forest. She and Glenn were to be married in Las Vegas tonight. "Your name was the only word he spoke," Paul tells Carol. Glenn may not last the night.

Glenn proves his doctors wrong when a nurse who unpeels the bandages on one arm goes running for Paul and Coulter. They and Carol see fully restored skin. "He's going to be all right," rejoices Carol. "What's the answer?" Coulter asks Paul. "When the skin has been burned to the extent that it was on the man's body," claims Paul, "it just doesn't grow back." Paul thinks an unknown element in the Plutonium may possess some regenerative power science could harness. A film of the test shows Glenn before and during the blast. Kingman states, "The fact that Glenn Manning lived after the blast and new skin completely replaced the burned dead tissue in a matter of hours leaves only one conclusion: something out there is beyond the limits of our knowledge."

In her apartment, Carol receives a late-night visit from Lt. Kline of Security, who says she cannot see Glenn for awhile. His hospital room is empty. An orderly and a receptionist deny that Glenn was ever there. Paul is gone too. When the receptionist is distracted, Carol reads a file card. She drives to a former wartime Army hospital. A gate sentry lets her pass, but there is more Reception stonewalling. In a dark hallway, Carol overhears Paul and Coulter discussing Glenn's condition. She enters his new room and faints at the sight of a comatose fifteen foot Glenn.

Carol is told that Washington ordered the cover-up. Glenn is growing from eight to ten feet a day. Tomorrow, he will be twenty-six feet tall. The next day, thirty-five or forty. As Paul explains, "The body is like a factory, continually producing new cells to replace the older cells, damaged cells or destroyed cells. This happens in all the different parts of the body. Bone cells grow new bone cells, skin cells grow new skin cells and so on —." An illustration is two x-ray charts showing a broken bone and a healed bone. "It is this delicately balanced process of new cells replacing dying cells or damaged cells that is causing the growth problem with

Manning contemplates his growing situation in THE AMAZING COLOSSAL MAN.

Glenn," states Coulter. "But how can this make his whole body grow?" Carol asks. "The process is out of balance," continues Coulter. "For some unknown reason, the cells are growing at an accelerated or speeded-up rate while the old cells refuse to die." Should this persist, grimly predicts Paul, "then Glenn Manning will continue to grow until he dies".

Glenn deliriously dreams of his early romance with Carol and his reserve stint in Korea, where he killed an enemy soldier who knifed his buddy Sgt. Lee Carter in the back. War's end is followed by the relived Plutonium explosion. A violently awakening Glenn finds himself sitting in what appears to be a miniature room. He glimpses a normal-sized sentry outside a window. Glenn picks up a tiny telephone and hears a voice over the receiver. Disorientation and claustrophobia cause Glenn to pound at the ceiling and scream at the top of his lungs.

Chief Security officer, Col. Hallach, tells Paul and Coulter that a circus tent has been brought in from winter quarters in Florida to house Glenn — now thirty feet tall. Paul thinks that, psychologically, Carol may do him some good. Despite her presence, Glenn sinks into a bitter depression. "What sin can a man commit in a single lifetime to bring this upon himself?" he asks. A truck driver delivers twenty-five sides of beef and is curious about the tent. "It's for him," a sentry says, hoping to be disbelieved. "The giant. The thirty-five foot one we got livin' here." "Sure ya have," questions the driver.

Outside the tent with Carol, Glenn has difficulty remembering old times . . . they seem to belong in an entirely different world. "You know what they said about me in the college yearbook?" Glenn jokingly muses. "The man most likely to reach the top." Seriously, he articulates his pain. "Do you realize that with every breath I take, every movement, everything reminds me of what happened. Even when I try to sleep at night, I close my eyes so I won't see people and the world getting smaller every minute. The beating of my heart keeps getting louder and louder . . . I never should have lived through that blast." Carol is hopeful that a cure will be found, but not Glenn. He feels a twinge of pain in his chest. "I'm alright . . . I'm alright . . . I don't want to grow any more! *I don't want to grow any more!*" Glenn retires to the tent as Paul joins Carol. "It's not going so well, is it?" he asks. Paul thinks he erred in letting Carol stay and wants to lift her security clearance. "I've got to be here to help him get well," Carol insists. "Suppose that he doesn't get well?" Paul asks pointedly. He has something to show her in the lab. Glenn leafs

Peek-a-boo! Manning violates a young lady's privacy during the climactic rampage scene in
THE AMAZING COLOSSAL MAN.

through a small Bible in his fingers, suffering more pain.

A nervous Sergeant brings Glenn his dinner. Glenn inquires about the headline on the front of the newspaper the Sergeant is holding. It reads "Man Lives Through Atomic Blast." Sardonically, Glenn asks, "This is living?" To play up his surroundings, Glenn rams his fist through the top of the tent and rants, "I *am* a circus freak. Have a tent, will travel. Why don't you make me up a sign reading, 'See the Amazing Colossal Man!'" Then he baits the Sergeant by claiming, "I'm not growing — you're *shrinking!*" Another, more violent cardial pain hits.

Paul shows Carol several anatomical models displaying a step-by-step illustration of Glenn's circulatory system. All of Glenn's parts are enlarging equally except the heart — which is increasing at only half the ratio as the rest of his body. Death could come soon. "A matter of days," estimates Paul. "His mind will go first and then his heart will literally explode."

Carol comes to Glenn that night after hearing him cry out in pain. "How tall do you suppose I'll grow before death releases me from this curse?" Glenn asks. "A hundred feet? Maybe a thousand? Could be a mile. I wouldn't actually have to worry too much about breathing 'till I got three miles up." Glenn feels he is a lost cause and tells Carol to go home. She still clings to

optimism because Paul and Coulter are close to a growth cure. "I stop growing, what then?" wonders Glenn. "Can you imagine what a wonderful life we'd have together? Me up here and you down —." More sharp pain forces Glenn to gulp water out of a barrel. Directly, he tells Carol to get out.

Glenn escapes from the hospital. Coulter believes the growth can be stopped by sulfa hydrol. He and Paul at first thought the problem was some unknown quality in the Plutonium itself. "The secret was in the degree of exposure," fathoms Paul. And the effect of the radiation lies in the bone marrow. Sulfa hydrol can arrest it and stimulation of the pituitary gland will diminish the bulk. Coulter has proved this by miniaturizing a camel and an elephant. He has also prepared a giant medication syringe for Glenn. Paul is a trained helicopter pilot and he and Carol take part in an unsuccessful search.

Dead cattle are found in a desert radius where Glenn is wandering aimlessly back and forth. Hallach must prepare for the possibility of Glenn behaving violently when he is found. Two drunks in a convertible bump into Glenn, sitting in the middle of a highway. As Glenn apathetically gets up and walks away, one swears, "Not another drop as long as I live, so help me." The incident is treated lightly on the TV news. Paul has decided to make Carol's departure an order, but she still stands by Glenn — "a sick man in mind as well as body," insists Paul.

Carol, Paul and Coulter resume the helicopter search the next morning. An observation plane spots Glenn heading for downtown Las Vegas. Paul receives the message. Glenn frightens a woman as he looms over the Sahara casino and lifts the huge crown off its roof with childlike wonder. With Ground Unit Three, Hallach is approaching Boulder Dam from the Arizona side and instructs the observation plane to contact the local police. Glenn peers into the bathroom window of an apartment and scares a girl taking a bubble bath. He breaks the bathroom window, but before he can touch her, sirens announce the arrival of the police. The TV commentator reports, "reality in a king-sized package over sixty feet tall". Carol, Paul and Coulter are about fifteen minutes away from Vegas. Coulter brings up the question of how easily he and Paul can administer the sulfa hydrol to Glenn.

The police have been ordered not to shoot unless absolutely necessary. As Glenn raises the Silver Slipper symbol with an infantile grin, a cop asks the lieutenant in charge, "Are you going to stand around and let him destroy property?" Rashly, the cop fires at Glenn, who angrily uproots a tall palm tree and throws it at the scattering crowd. At the Sands, he flings a car into the air and pounds the neon logo to bits. Glenn turns to the Frontier cowboy sign, crumples it and tosses pieces at people. Sustained gunfire drives him out of town.

Army bazooka men are waiting for Glenn at Boulder Dam. Out in the desert, Carol, Paul and Coulter hover over Glenn — so addled that he cannot recognize them and makes grabbing motions at the cockpit of their copter. On the ground, Paul attempts to reason with Glenn over a bullhorn. With one great lunge, Paul and Coulter ram the large syringe into Glenn's ankle. Howling in pain, Glenn plucks out the needle, studies it and throws the syringe at Coulter, impaling him. Glenn snatches Carol.

Glenn comes in sight of the bazooka men as he crosses the dam. Paul tries again to communicate with Glenn, but it is Carol who saves herself when she reminds Glenn who she is. As Glenn sets Carol down, twin bazooka shots send him plummeting seven hundred feet into the water.

Schmucky as Bert Gordon's tastes can be, he was wise in settling on the final story treatment. Scott Carey was contaminated by fallout rather passively, as befitted the generally placid life of a quiet insurance salesman. The second cause of his lost inches, an insecticide spray, was merely mentioned and wouldn't have been a very photogenic mishap. Glenn Manning, an Army lifer, brought to the Plutonium test a lifetime of experience with danger and faced the bomb putting himself on the line for a stranger who might have been already dead. In retrospect, Glenn's accident, built up to by the shakes

of the Sergeant who wanted to leave, was illustrative of the atomic risks encountered by every veteran of the Nevada tests.

The Incredible Shrinking Man had two "monsters", one a wild housecat that chased Scott Carey, and the giant spider in the basement Scott eventually had to do battle with. Glenn was placed close to the bomb so his burns would provide *The Amazing Colossal Man* with a sensational image of a human being fried to a crisp, seen two more times in this film and *War of the Colossal Beast*. On immediate release, the Plutonium nearly killed Glenn and the compensory healing that would enlarge him was too much of a good thing. As either destruction or therapy, radiation helps or hurts depending on amount and Glenn was subjected to two forms of excess.

Because he was dealing with a Monster monster in *The Cyclops*, Gordon dwelled on the hunt for Bruce Barton, letting in fragmented references to Bruce's past identity. Once again, in *Colossal Man*, a disaster involving a small plane precipitated a person's exposure to radiation and the lover of the man who became gigantic had to buck bureaucratic heads in her Right To Know. Bruce Barton was mostly an enigma; for one thing, we never knew what he did for a living or why he happened to be flying in Mexico. Glenn's background was mapped out according to family (he had no one in *The Amazing Colossal Man* but a sister in *War of the Colossal Beast*), how he and Carol met (at a Chicago intersection over locked bumpers) and his war service (via the dream flashback).

Mutation angst in Glenn was like watching a professional athlete cope with a masculinity-robbing disease or injury. Except for the heart strain and refusal of hair to grow back, Glenn was physically intact, hurting mostly from how giantism placed him at a distance from everyone else. The circus tent, the expandable sarong he wore, the toylike furniture he was surrounded by, all made Glenn feel like a baby and a clown. Scott Carey by contrast, with his improvised clothing and long unkempt hair, took an almost Biblical nobility, living like a primitive but showing resourcefulness in how he used certain large objects. Once trapped in the cellar — a magnification of a corner of his own domain — Scott was forced survival to snap out of self-pity. He was resigned to losing his wife, who thought him dead as the result of the skirmish with the cat. In trying to offer Glenn support, Carol, the person he wanted most to touch, became his whipping girl. Heart trouble can inhibit the sex lives of some men and Glenn's cardial agonies most often occurred when Carol was around.

As Glenn's mental faculties crumbled, the world took on a confusing unfamiliarity. The relentlessness of his growth created a time-limit crisis. By the time a solution *was* found, law enforcement and the military had to exercise their prerogative of protecting the public. No longer did the Army call Glenn by his name, but simply as "the giant".

Since attention was trained so tightly on Glenn, the effects here were among Gordon's most static. Glenn had relatively little activity while under military custody, so Gordon had to insert silly novelties like the big top tent and the exotic choices of the test animals (an excuse to show mini-creatures by our level of perception). Glenn's target because of its geography, Las Vegas is a city that sells cheap dreams and because it was built to monumentalize decadence, there was almost a sense of *constructive* destructiveness when Glenn injured some of the town's tacky tinsel. Not lives, culture or essential services, the police were really defending the gambling interests — without which Vegas would be nothing.

The Vegas scenes in *Colossal Man* would have been better staged if set after dark, when the bright lights would have acted as a diversion from the poor miniatures Paul and Jackie Blaisdell constructed. Gordon could not afford numerous crowd extras, so only a dozen or so people were gathered around in repetitious high-angle street shots or in front of a process screen. Glenn's harassment of the bubble bath girl was reminiscent of the scene in *King Kong* (1933) where Kong went after a substitute girl who also lived in an apartment. Albert Glasser's score during the Vegas footage used the *Kong* effect of thudding footsteps.

The syringe sequence started badly in the air with Glenn reaching out for the helicopter. Not only did the whirlybird have a roof higher than the Sistine Chapel in the over-the-shoulder shot of Carol, Paul and Coulter, but their group cringing from Glenn's fingers made the actors look like they were glued to the backs of their seats. A nice throwaway detail was Glenn's toes restlessly fidgeting as Paul and Coulter readied the syringe. The impalement shot couldn't have offended anyone since it was a goreless two-dimensional effect and the fall of Glenn from Boulder Dam made him resemble a dropping boomerang.

Although *The Amazing Colossal Man* deteriorates once Glenn invades general society, it ran enough footage of Glenn Langan giving the performance that protected him from complete obscurity after the end of his career at Twentieth Fox. Langan was discovered by Darryl Zanuck and was double unfortunate since Zanuck "finds" who flopped were most often women (Irina Demick, Genevieve Gilles, Marayat Andriane and the infamously inept Bella Darvi among others). Maritally, Langan had a very happy life with another forties player who quit the business after working a number of times with AIP Adele Jergens. Cathy Down's performance as Carol was full of bewilderment and anguish, but absent of hysteria or tears. William Hudson was mostly Doctor, letting professional detachment drop at times when the Manning case eroded everyone's morals.

I Was a Teenage Werewolf was AIP's biggest money film of 1957, but *The Amazing Colossal Man* was the first AIP film to play Broadway. *War of the Colossal Beast* was released with Gordon's *Attack of the Puppet People* in 1958 and not only did you get more Colossal Man in *Colossal Beast*, there was also a drive-in scene of the original Glenn in *Puppet People*. No, not the Plutonium scorching . . . Glenn shouting, "I'm not growing! *You're shrinking!*"

Manning reacts to the approaching helicopter in THE AMAZING COLOSSAL MAN.

THE CAT GIRL

Anglo-Amalgamated /
American-International, 1957

Executive Producer   Peter Rogers
Producers   Lou Rusoff
                                Herbert Smith
Director   Alfred Shaugnessy
Screenplay   Lou Rusoff
Cinematography   Peter Hennessey
Film Editor   Jocelyn Jackson
Art Director   Eric Saw
Production Managers   John V. Green
                                Dick Stevens
Production Designer   Dick Stevens
Camera Operator   Paddy A. Hearne
Assistant Director   William Hill
Sound Recordist   Leo Page
Continuity   Olga Brookes
Makeup   Philip Leakey
Wardrobe   Vi Murray

A Malibu Production / Insignia Films
Running time: 69 minutes

Cast: Barbara Shelley (Leonora), Robert Ayers (Dr. Marlowe), Kay Callard (Dorothy), Paddy Webster (Cathy), Ernest Milton (Edmund), Lilly Kahn (Anna), Jack May (Richard), John Leo (Alan), Martin Boddy (Cafferty), John Watson (Roberts), Selma Vas Dias (Nurse), John Baker (Male Nurse), Frank Atkinson (Guard), Geoffrey Tyrell (Caretaker)

AIP expanded its film operations to England by consolidating with Nat Cohen's Anglo-Amalgamated. Each company received profits from its respective territory. In association with Herbert Smith, Lou Rusoff co-produced and wrote AIP-Anglo's *The Cat Girl*, a remake of *Cat People* (1942) that avoided much of AIP's sensational style but captured little of the artistic, understated shock of Val Lewton. It would be lesser known than it is had it not introduced Barbara Shelley, Hazel Court's only challenger for the crown of English Horror Queen.

As it storms, Edmund Brandt anxiously waits for his niece Leonora Johnson to come to his country estate. Edmund keeps a leopard in a cage. At a pub with friends

(Above) Barbara Shelley as Nora in THE CAT GIRL (1957).

Cathy and Allan and her husband, Richard, Nora is reunited with her ex-lover Brian Marlowe. Brian is married to a girl named Dorothy. At the Brandt estate, Nora, Richard, Cathy and Allan are greeted by Edmund's housekeeper, Anna. Nora senses the lurking panther, watched by Edmund. The panther threatens Richard and Cathy until Edmund tells it to leave them alone.

Edmund had asked Nora to come by herself. After Richard, Cathy and Allan have retired, Anna summons Nora from her room. Before Edmund invites Nora into his study, he tells Anna they are about to part. The study is filled with feline statues. For seven hundred years, the Brandts have been cursed. Tonight, Edmund's curse will be passed on to Nora. Shown the leopard, Nora is made to touch it. The leopard will be her servant. Nora's friends must leave by morning. Edmund urges her not to have children. She bolts from the study to the grounds as Edmund frees the panther. When he hurls a cat statue to the ground, the leopard kills him. Richard, Cathy and Allan find the body. Having a sympathetic reaction, Nora faints. Blood is on her hands.

The police are alerted to the panther. Brian wants disturbed Nora to commit herself to his private sanitarium. She describes the bloodlust of the panther. As a sedative takes effect, Nora feels comfort from the presence of Brian and bristles when he mentions Dorothy. Still sensing the leopard, Nora wants to leave Edmund's house, but Richard wants to stay. Brian ascribes Nora's leopard fixation with the occult books Edmund kept and burns them in a fireplace. Brian introduces Nora to Dorothy and Nora makes a cold exit.

Richard and Cathy go for a walk in the garden and make love. Cathy senses the leopard watching them from a tree. Nora sees her and Richard together and wills the leopard to kill Richard. Guilty Nora wants to be arrested for murder. Cathy's story clears her officially and when Nora claws at Cathy, she must be detained. Nora finally consents to institutionalization.

Upset by the conditions of the sanitarium, Nora experiences a change of heart. She is put in a barred room, where she sees the leopard outside. Nora wrecks the room and sees herself as the leopard in a mirror. Brian stays with Nora the next night waiting for her to conjure up the leopard. When a guard shines his flashlight the leopard's way, Nora reacts.

Brian thinks Nora may benefit from outpatient treatment and takes her to the home he shares with Dorothy. During a storm, Nora feels the urge to kill Dorothy until Dorothy needs help with her dress. While Dorothy goes downstairs to get soda for some whisky, Alan phones from his office. He wants Nora to tell Dorothy that the two are to meet him at a tavern. Nora kills a canary in a cage. Dorothy sees the dead bird but manages forced composure. Nora sends Dorothy to go on alone.

Two pedestrians spot the leopard. It stalks Dorothy in the street. The police are called. Two cops see the leopard in their car headlights. Nora meets Dorothy. At the restaurant, Brian learns from his call service where Dorothy went. She leaves Nora to find Brian. Brian hears where the leopard was last seen. Armed officers patrol the area. Nora chases Dorothy into an alley. She tells the leopard to kill. Brian hits it with his car. Nora dies, as if she had been struck, too. A piece of her raincoat is found on the front bumper of Brian's car.

Cat People achieved tragedy by making all of its principals benign personalities who unintentionally hurt each other, in turn harming themselves. Irena Dubrovnik was a desirable girl to be with when allowed to live life from its safe fringes. When her spouse Oliver Queen sought a deeper commitment Irena was not up to, he turned to his friend Alice for solace. She returned his affection because the end of his patience with Irena legitimized Alice's own feelings for him. Irena's psychiatrist Dr. Judd himself became overinvolved with his patient because he thought that his animal magnetism would break the ice he could not penetrate clinically, hoping this would cure Irena and make her a compliant sex partner.

All human interest in *Cat Girl* was soured by people who either cared little about Nora or robbed her of happiness by trying to make her accept unpleasant truths. Edmund was so certain that the curse would continue that he expected Nora to give up on normal life completely. Richard and Cathy felt that Nora's deferential quality would not hinder their romance. Brian believed that he owed Nora concern as a doctor and as someone who had been intimate with her. His attitude was that of cherishing an attachment as long as it is left in mothballs. Dorothy had the most valid reason for wanting to avoid Nora because of her overt jealousy.

The human-animal kinship had some metaphysical gristle. Nora could not get too close to people in their spirits. Wanting them to be part of her was inverted so that the appetite of longing became a physical hunger as felt by the leopard when Nora supposedly possessed it. Her soul had been diminished, but the wants of her psyche were heightened and she got some of her own back via the leopard feeding on accessible bodies.

Cat Girl was certainly one of Lou Rusoff's more intelligent scripts even if he kept notes from *Cat People* by his overused typewriter. Director Alfred Shaugnessy, a respected film and play author, worked up a few chills, but without the palpable sense of stealth that made the *Cat People* panther a terrifying phantom, Nora's spotted friend was just an exotic killing tool no more frightening than if it had been merely trained to obey her.

An ex-model with Italian film experience, Barbara Shelley was forever typecast as a horror star and though she chaffed, she never compromised her talent. Discomfort was her most convincing film emotion, signifying either repression or desired freedom. Hazel Court gave more of herself in a haughty smile and a tempting bosom. Shelley was more introspective but in at least two films, enjoyed immense stature, *Village of the Damned* (1960) and *Five Million Miles to Earth* (1968). During her long stint at Hammer, she did another feline-themed film, *Shadow of the Cat* (1961). Shelley returned to Italy and since has made nothing outside of there.

Jim Nicholson and Sam Arkoff felt that *Cat Girl* needed more fright fibre, so Paul Blaisdell made a cat mask and wore it on a minimal set cut into parts of the British print. The film's trailer dwelled on shots of the leopard with a sexy female voice personifying the beast. The ads substituted a panther, complementing it with a seductive, wildly sprawled, menacing girl. The posters credited cinematographer Peter Hennessy as director — not Alfred Shaugnessy.

Thanks to the Blaisdell images, *The Cat Girl* was a real Monster movie until TV cutting reduced his mask to all that one can see of it now: as one of the creature exhibits in *How to Make a Monster*.

104

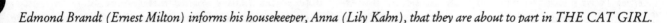

Edmond Brandt (Ernest Milton) informs his housekeeper, Anna (Lily Kahn), that they are about to part in THE CAT GIRL.

I WAS A TEENAGE FRANKENSTEIN

American-International, 1957
Released in England as *Teenage Frankenstein*

Presenters	James H. Nicholson
	Samuel Z. Arkoff
Producer	Herman Cohen
Director	Herbert L. Strock
Story-Screenplay	Kenneth Langrty
	(Aben Kandel)
Cinematography	Lothrop Worth
Editorial Supervisor	Jerry Young
Music	Paul Dunlap
Art Director	Leslie Thomas
Production Manager-	
Assistant Director	Austin Jewell
Script Supervisor	Mary Gibsone
Set Decorator	Tom Oliphant
Property Master	James R. Harris
Wardrobe	Einer Bourman
Production Secretary	Barbara Lee Strite
Sound	Alfred Overton
Makeup	Philip Scheer

Music Editor	George Brand
Sound Effects	Kay Rose

A Sunset Production / Color Sequence
Running time: 72 minutes

Cast: Whit Bissell (Prof. Frankenstein), Phyllis Coates (Margaret), Robert Burton (Dr. Carlton), Gary Conway (Teenage Monster), George Lynn (Sgt. Burns), John Cliff (Sgt. McAfee), Marshall Bradford (Dr. Randolf), Claudia Bryar (Arlene's Mother), Angela Blake (Beautiful Girl), Russ Whiteman (Dr. Eldwood), Charles Seel (Jeweler), Paul Keast (Man at Crash), Gretchen Thomas (Woman in Corridor), Joy Stoner (Arlene), Larry Carr (Young Man), Pay Miller (Police Officer)

T he Universal series had laid the groundwork for the cynicism of most future Frankenstein films. From a brutal man-infant, the monster became an emotionless robot, going from star to bit player. After

(Above) The teenage monster (Gary Conway) meets his demise in I WAS A TEENAGE FRANKENSTEIN (1957).

Son of Frankenstein (1939), he was revived by a succession of nondescript doctors. That changed when the modern American Frankenstein films and the Hammer stories shifted focus to the monster-makers, all of whom were a new version of *the* Frankenstein or sundry descendants. When Universal sold its vintage chillers to TV in the "Shock Theater" package, the Frankenstein name enjoyed renewed currency value. Hammer's first Gothic achievement, *The Curse of Frankenstein* (1957), restored the opulence of period flavor in color, pumping up anatomical grossness and playing up pleasing female anatomies.

Texas theater chain owner R.J. O'Donnell was angry at the major studios because of their costly rental fees. Two sympathetic listeners of his complaint at a luncheon were James Nicholson and Samuel Arkoff, who knew how profitable Thanksgiving week was. Arkoff promised O'Donnell AIP would make two teenage horror films, giving him a low-cost double bill. One film was *Blood of Dracula*, the other *I Was a Teenage Frankenstein*.

Once again, Herman Cohen turned to a director deft in editing skills. The one was Herbert L. Strock, who had produced and directed the TV show "The Cases of Eddie Drake". As the editor of Ivan Tors' *The Magnetic Monster* (1953), Strock convinced the production staff he could direct it better than Curt Siodmak. Automatically inducted into the Directors' Guild, Strock

did over three days of Siodmak footage, but Siodmak won total credit. Strock was the editor and associate producer of Tors' *Raiders to the Stars* (1954), helping third lead Richard Carlson, the star of *Magnetic Monster*, direct it. Strock was finally billed as a director for his third Tors film *Gog* (1954) and worked on his ZIV series "Science Fiction Theater", as well as Carlson's "I Led Three Lives". While visiting the ZIV lot, Herman Cohen met Strock, who had vacation time due. Instead of soaking up Waikiki sun, he directed both *I Was a Teenage Frankenstein* and *Blood of Dracula*. Shown several months after *Curse of Frankenstein*, *Teenage Frankenstein* was a coincidental variation set in 1957 California.

Britain's distinguished Prof. Frankenstein has been lecturing in the United States. At a Los Angeles University seminar, he endorses transplantation of other organs besides eye corneas. One Dr. Randolf labels this theory "preposterous". Dr. Carlton, a physicist, defends Frankenstein, who intends to realize his vision.

In the study of his rented house, Frankenstein requests Carlton's help. He plans to assemble a human being out of choice cadaver parts in an adaptation of selective breeding. Carlton warns there are risks. The experiment will be performed here. "You don't dare," cautions Carlton. "Don't dare?" questions Frankenstein. "'Don't dare.' I'm sure someone said those same words and hurled that same challenge to that great ancestor of

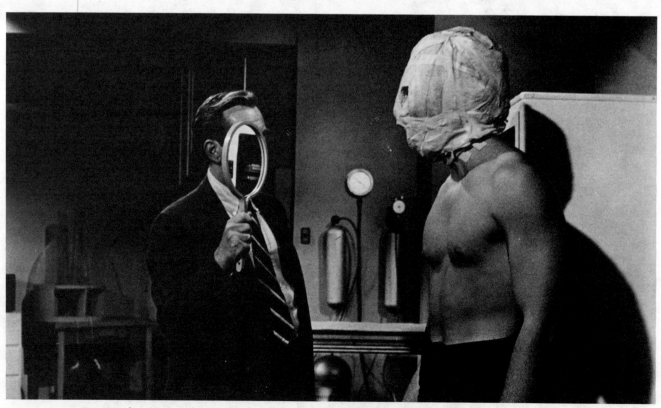

Dr. Frankenstein (Whit Bissell) gives the monster (Gary Conway) the first glimpse of his face in
I WAS A TEENAGE FRANKENSTEIN.

mine whose name I bear." But where Baron Frankenstein created a monster, the Professor will make an inconspicuous normal person. "I'll point the way to perfection in the human race," promises Frankenstein. He will handle surgery, Carlton the electronics. "I shall use only the ingredients of youth," Frankenstein says. "Not the worn out body inhabited by an overtaxed brain. The old are dying, are dead. The whole trend is toward death. If I am successful, if I can create out of different parts a youth I can instruct and control, I'll prove that only in youth is there any hope for the salvation of mankind."

Suddenly, Frankenstein and Carlton hear screeching brakes and crunching metal. They join a throng of people gathered around two burning autos. "Teenagers . . ." gasps a shaken driver who was behind one. "Both cars loaded. Back from a party, I guess. Head-on collision. What a crash!" He saw one boy thrown through a windshield. A woman volunteers to call the police. "I think he's had it," moans the driver. The boy lies in some nearby bushes.

Before the police arrive, Frankenstein and Carlton toss a blanket over the boy and carry him down to Frankenstein's basement lab. The cold lab is a private morgue. Frankenstein asks Carlton to describe the condition of the boy, who is dead. "In this laboratory, there is no death unless I declare it so," Frankenstein mandates. The boy has a crushed head, possible brain injury and an unrecognizable face. In every city where Frankenstein has lectured, he has bought equipment for the endeavor that squeamish Carlton feels needs another assistant. Frankenstein reminds him, "After all, that experiment you assisted me in a month ago made you my ally. I could use another and uglier word — 'accomplice' — but I won't." Carlton was lead to believe that Frankenstein was writing a book. The boy is stored in a vault drawer for the present.

At a farewell party for Frankenstein, his nurse admirer Margaret sadly declines participation in a toast to him. Frankenstein's visa will expire in two months, but assuring her they will not part ways, he asks Margaret to move into his home and take care of all distractions from the secret experiment. Afterwards, they will get married. "I'll be the best watchdog you ever had," promises happy Margaret.

Frankenstein amputates the boy's hands and right leg and has Carlton administer fifty-thousand volts. "I want him to know and feel pain," he explains, "so that when I alleviate it, he'll also know gratitude." Disposal of body parts is no problem. Behind the wall of a false equipment panel is a water pit with a hungry alligator. Members of a college track team die in a plane crash. After their interment, Frankenstein and Carlton steal new limbs from their grave.

Head bandaged, the monster lies on a surgery table fully conscious. He must be taught speech. Frankenstein wants him to say "Good morning".

"Speak!" orders Frankenstein. "You have a civil tongue in your head. I know you have because I sewed it there myself." He instructs the monster to watch his lips, telling him, "You do have vision — at least in the one good eye." A small electrical jolt elicits cooperation. "Good-mor-ning," answers the monster. Frankenstein wants him put back in the vault. "It's . . . dark . . . in . . . here . . ." whimpers the monster. "Yes, it's dark for you," understands Frankenstein, "But you'll have to reconcile yourself to the dark because you'll be in the dark a long, long time." Carlton notices tears streaming from the eye. "Even the tear duct functions!" exclaims Frankenstein. "The whole world will be astounded! It seems we have a very sensitive teenager on our hands."

Neglected Margaret presses busy Frankenstein about the wedding plans he has forgotten. The experiment is still confidential. "If you don't tell," Margaret airily insinuates, "there are ways of finding out myself." "Such as? *What ways?*" cries alarmed Frankenstein. "*Tell me!*" He slaps Margaret, who apologizes for speaking foolishly. Frankenstein blames his behavior on strain. He and Carlton will be leaving for new purchases. "I'll go back to my kennel and be the best watchdog you ever had," says Margaret, still smarting from the episode.

When Frankenstein and Carlton leave the house, Margaret has the lab key duplicated. She sneaks down into the vault. As she opens its drawer, the monster rises up and scares her.

The monster is now taught to say "Yes, sir" and the Biblical quote, "Beware of false prophets which come to you in sheep's clothing but inwardly are ravening wolves". He adapts well to physical therapy for his new hands and leg, but he continually badgers Frankenstein about wanting to meet people. Frankenstein says he is not ready. "Why not?" bleats the monster. "I'll show you why not!" shouts Frankenstein. Unpeeling the bandages, he thrusts a hand mirror in disgust. "Look again, my boy!" Frankenstein commands. "You'll be glad to stay here until I make you fit to go among people!"

Escaping from the lab, the monster explores the dark living room of the house. His hand touches a piano key and he backs away in alarm. On a noisy street, the monster peeks through apartment door windows at a beautiful blonde brushing her hair in front of a window. The blonde sees the monster's reflection before he smashes in. The monster strangles the screaming blonde in an attempt to quiet her, then bursts out the hallway door, frightening the neighbors. Sgt. Burns and Sgt. McAfee talk to them. The monster rejoins furious Frankenstein, explaining, "I wanted to see people." "They saw you," Frankenstein tells him. The monster will need a new face.

Burns and McAfee conduct a house to house query of people in the neighborhood who might know something about the killer and talk to a seemingly innocent Frankenstein. Because invited visitors are forbidden, he explodes at Margaret again when he catches her with a jeweller showing her a ring she wants. After the jeweller is thrown out, Margaret yells at Frankenstein, "I saw your great scientific discovery! I saw your monster!" Feigning forgiveness, Frankenstein gives her money to buy the ring. He convinces the monster that Margaret is their enemy. "We must stop her," the monster urges. "I agree," slyly concurres Frankenstein.

Since Carlton is out of town buying equipment, Frankenstein has Margaret help him give the monster vitamin shots, leaving them alone. Feeling the needle, the monster vents his murderous hostility on Margaret. She flees to the lab door and Frankenstein slams it shut. Margaret's body and her ring are consigned to the alligator pit.

In Frankenstein's car, Frankenstein and the monster go face-shopping. "After I've grafted on your new face," says Frankenstein, "life will really begin." They pull next to a lovers' lane convertible where handsome Bob and his girl and necking. Bob casts a glance at their headlights. He is the perfect face. The monster sneaks up, dragging Bob away. Arlene faints. Burns and McAfee talk to Arlene's mother about Bob and see his picture. Bob's head is taken to the lab in a bird cage.

Carlton returns, told that Margaret has left Frankenstein. The monster is admiring his new face in a mirror as he lies on the surgery table. Carlton wonders how he will pass Customs and Immigration when Frankenstein sets sail for home. All the equipment crates are false-bottomed. "I disassemble him here," explains Frankenstein, "preserve the parts, and then reconstruct him in my London laboratory. I have the facilities, the same equipment and the same assistant — you!" To sedate the monster, Frankenstein will pretend to remove his facial stitches. Terrified of the needle, the monster attacks Frankenstein and throws him to the alligator. Carlton summons a cop. Scared, the monster backs into an equipment panel. When his metal wrist bands connect, he is electrocuted. Carlton bends over the monster, telling the cop, "I'll never forget his face after the accident . . . never!"

Both *Curse Of* and *Teenage Frankenstein* discarded all pretense of civility in their Frankenstein doctors, refusing to let surgery end at implied scalpel-hovering. Whit Bissell's Professor and Peter Cusing's Baron took their medical knowledge to the extreme of expecting results to conform to exact specifications — itemizing everything with an amputation here, a grafting there. Suspense was in how new parts were obtained and the capabilities of their trained monsters. Old-time Frankenstein helpers were deformed idiots who obeyed their masters with twisted glee. The new ones, like Carlton, were coerced or uncertain weaklings who expressed pallid objections to the morality of the experiments. The Professor and the Baron regarded women as mere playthings (Cushing had two — a fiancee

and a mistress). When they tried to take a more active part in the affairs of their men, the monsters became levers for blackmail. The next door they passed through was their coffin lid with nails waiting to be hammered in.

Teenage Werewolf took a boy whose body was changed by tampering with his mind. The anonymous kid in *I Was a Teenage Frankenstein* was an average boy shattered by sudden mishap. He was a mess with nowhere to go but up when Frankenstein found him. Kids saw in the Teenage Werewolf their wildest emotions. The Teenage Frankenstein's preoccupation with his face was like a severe acne problem and even with little working memory of his past self, he wanted to Belong. At the culmination of his existence, the monster evolved into a Greaser God with only the stitches a reminder of where his new face came from. A scalp transplant was evident too — and why didn't Carlton inquire about the donor?

What little credit *Teenage Frankenstein* has received has been due to its Frankenstein witticisms. The only time we saw Frankenstein kiss Margaret was at lovers' lane, what he deemed "a private preserve for teenagers". The "civil tongue" and "tear duct" lines have been quoted *ad infinitum*. Then there was an apartment tenant's description of the monster's face as a mask like those worn by supermarket robbers. The monster's reaction to his Bob visage was an exaggeration of adolescent vanity.

The Universal copyright on Jack Pierce's makeup prompted different ones for the Hammer and Teenage Monsters — both substandard. The worst details of the Teenage one were its obvious putty texture and the swollen eye. In some shadow angles, it looked better than it really was. The phoniness was magnified by the smooth-skinned Muscle Beach physique of Gary Conway. In him, one was a revived corpse that needed only minimal repair below face level. Another shortcut was the cheap, unimposing lab, although medically it was more realistic than the gaudy Ken Strickfaden confections. Only the alligator was a garish fixture — and what was Frankenstein going to do with him once he vacated his American residence?

Apart from the monster, Bob and Arlene, teenagers were hardly seen. This was the least youth-indulgent of Cohen's movies or their rip-offs apart from the non-purebred Teenage Monster. Rock music was incidental sounds from car radios — no songs — and the faintest suggestion of a hot rod (Cohen never showed them in his pics) was the noise of one peeling out on the apartment street.

Cohen could not afford full color, but thought that a little would give the end something "extra". Thus, the Teen Frankenstein met his heavenly father in a color shot of his electrocution.

Whit Bissell managed to retain his sobriety as Frankenstein despite the cheeky lines that made him a more interesting talker than Dr. Brandon. Apart from his fame and British citizenship, Bissell's was one of the more enigmatic Frankensteins. Gary Conway was about as good as anyone could have been under the circumstances as the monster. Deadly when scared or threatened, he was a panty-waist otherwise. Conway achieved his minor fame as Det. Tim Tilson on "Burke's Law" and Capt. Steve Burton on "Land of the Giants". He had one more due to pay before starring with Gene Barry and Amos Burke's Roll-Royce: playing the Teenage Frankenstein again in *How to Make a Monster*.

The teenage monster (Gary Conway) goes berserk at the sight of a needle in I WAS A TEENAGE FRANKENSTEIN.

Dr. Carlton (Robert Burton) summons the police in I WAS A TEENAGE FRANKENSTEIN.

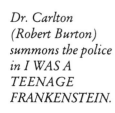

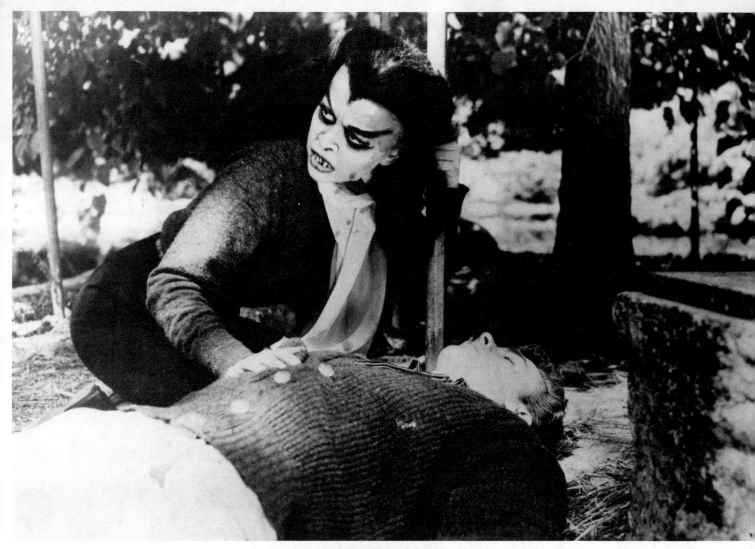

BLOOD OF DRACULA

American-International, 1957
Released in England as *Blood of My Heritage*
Released in Canada *as Blood of the Demon*

Presenters	James H. Nicholson
	Samuel Z. Arkoff
Producer	Herman Cohen
Director	Herbert L. Strock
Screenplay	Ralph Thornton
(Herman Cohen and Aben Kandel)	
Cinematography	Monroe Askins
Film Editor	Robert Moore
Music	Paul Dunlap
Art Director	Leslie Thomas
Production Manager-	
Assistant Director	Austen Jewell
Script Supervisor	Mary Gibsone
Set Decorator	Tom Oliphant
Property Master	James R. Harris
Wardrobe	Florence Hays
Production Secretary	Barbara Lee Strite
Makeup	Philip Scheer

Music Editor	George Brand
Sound Effects Editor	Kay Rose
Sound	Herman Lewis

Song: "Puppy Love"
Music & Lyrics by Jerry Blaine

A Carmel Production
Running time: 68 minutes

Cast: Sandra Harrison (Nancy Perkins), Louise Lewis *aka Fitch* (Miss Branding), Gail Ganley (Myra), Jerry Blaine (Tab), Heather Ames (Nola), Malcolm Atterbury (Lt. Dunlap), Mary Adams (Mrs. Thorndyke), Thomas B. Henry (Perkins), Jeanne Dean (Mrs. Perkins), Don Devlin (Eddie), Richard Devon (Sgt. Stewart), Paul Maxwell (Mike), Shirley De Lancy (Terry), Michael Hall (Glenn), Craig Duncan, Edna Holland, Carlyle MItchell, Voltaire Perkins, Barbara Wilson, Jimmy Hayes, Lynn Alden

(Above) Sandra Harrison is cursed by THE BLOOD OF DRACULA (1957).

Blood of Dracula was Herman Cohen's vampire remake of *I Was a Teenage Werewolf*. What should have been titled *I Was a Teenage Vampire* used the name of Dracula because it, like the name of Frankenstein, was box-office again. Tony Rivers was now the similarly troubled Nancy Perkins, her controller also female and the setting, Sherwood, a girl's prep school.

As Nancy, her father, Paul, and hated stepmother, Doris, drive to Sherwood up a stormy mountain pass, the building tension in Nancy causes her to impulsively grab the steering wheel of their car. Paul hits the brakes in time as the car swerves toward the edge of a cliff and then slaps Nancy. Since her real mother's death six weeks ago and Paul's company transfer to another city, Nancy has been cruelly severed from all the people she holds dear — particularly her boyfriend Glenn. Paul and Doris will be going on their delayed honeymoon once she is placed in Sherwood. The storm lets up and at Sherwood, a more subdued Nancy meets Mrs. Thorndyke, the kindly head mistress.

In her temporary room, Nancy is preparing for bed when she gets hazed by the Birds of Paradise, a sorority led by Myra. Nancy endures the violation of her suitcase belongings until European girl, Nola, holds up a photo of Glenn. Nancy fights back, knocking Myra down. The commotion brings Mrs. Rivers, the strict housemother. The girls scatter and Nancy contrives a story to cover for them.

To reward her discretion, Myra agrees to sponsor Nancy for membership in the sorority. She introduces Nancy to Eddie, a goony caretaker and only available male at the school. Nancy can do without him. Eddie's special girl Terry slaps him because he shows too much interest in Nancy. Eddie and Terry are engaged. Myra assists Miss Branding, the spinsterish chemistry teacher who has written a continually rejected thesis on the possible repercussions of nuclear destruction. Every human, Branding claims, possesses an inner power far greater than the atom. Fear of this unleashed power can deter war. To prove her theory, Branding needs a volatile subject. Myra suggests Nancy.

In class, Branding has Myra switch another chemical bottle for the one she was going to use. Nola rubs its liquid on her hand without harm. When she rubs some on Nancy's, Nancy feels a burning pain and attacks Nola, breaking the bottle. Myra takes over the class while Branding offers Nancy first aid in her quarters. Branding shows Nancy a distinctive cats-eye amulet she bought from an antique dealer who obtained it from a strange woman of Carpathian descent. Securing her trust, Branding hypnotizes Nancy with the amulet. The pain in her hand is gone when she awakens.

During Nancy's initiation party in the dorm rec room that night, Eddie and two pals, Tab and Joe, pay the girls and unexpected window visit by ladder. Terry abetted them. Tab fancies aloof Nancy. From her dark room across the way, Branding hears the loud party music. Putting on the amulet, she sits next to the window facing the dorm and casts a spell over Nancy, who feels odd. Tab and Joe fight over Nola. Mrs. Rivers is coming and the boys split. Nancy turns in early and Nola is sent down to the basement for some school supplies. The closet door behind her closes and a fiend attacks.

The police want to question all the girls who were at the initiation. Myra tries to awaken sleeping Nancy and Branding rouses her. Nancy had a weird dream. Told to forget the dream, Nancy is ordered to feel she had nothing to do with Nola's death. Mike, a junior detective, compared Nola's extreme blood loss to vampire tales he heard from a Carpathian exchange student he roomed with in med school. Mike's ideas are scoffed.

On Halloween, the girls hold a scavenger hunt in a cemetery. The winner gets to keep an expensive compact. In the cemetery with Terry, Eddie finds the place creepy and leaves. While Terry is looking for a treasure clue, Nancy becomes a vampire and kills her. Tab shows up and meets a normal Nancy, attempting another pass. He gets the hint, but Nancy transforms again before his eyes and slays him also. Nancy changes back before the other girls find the bodies.

Every girl has to undergo a police lie detector test. With the amulet, Branding enables Nancy to pass her interrogation. Nancy tells Branding she sees Branding's face in her dreams. To deal with the threat of scandalized Sherwood closing, Mrs. Thorndyke appoints Branding to assume some of the administration duties.

Nancy encounters worried Glenn, who drove three hundred miles to see her and was turned away by Branding. Nancy is at first reluctant to join Glenn in the front seat of his car, where he discusses their planned future. In Glenn's comforting arms, Nancy feels a vampiric twinge and runs to Branding. Knowing fully she is a monster, Nancy begs for release. She turns away as Branding orders her to look at the amulet. Nancy vampirizes and chokes Branding with the chain. In the fray, Branding's dropped cigarette burns the thesis manuscript. A sharp piece of furniture wood upturns and impales Nancy's heart. Myra, Glenn and Mrs. Thorndyke break into the room. Dead Nancy is herself. Myra laments the loss of the charred thesis, but Mrs. Thorndyke perceives the evil it contributed to.

Most of the inversion twists on *Teenage Werewolf* in *Blood of Dracula* worked. Where the rage of Tony Rivers suggested allergic reactions, the anger of Nancy was caused by separation from Glenn and the uncaring attitude of Paul and Doris. Branding's motivation was as mad as Dr. Brandon's, but had an interesting feminist slant cognizant of the macho posture of dominant male politics. She regarded her project as science, yet whatever power the amulet had was occult — who was the mystery lady who once owned the amulet? Why did she relinquish it? *Teenage Werewolf* erred in what kind of animal Tony had regressed to. The greatest implausibility here was the idea that a vampire — something traditionally undead — resides in the bosom of everyone.

The conditions of Nancy's vampirsm were handy for a claustrophobic plot. By reverting to normalcy, she had no fear of sunlight or need for a coffin. None of her victims became vampires. Earlier film vampiresses had either been subservient to male vampires or were assertive in a more humanlike way. In looks, Nancy equalled the ferocity of the Teenage Werewolf with her sharp widow's peak, bushy eyebrows that swept beyond her forehead and snaggly teeth. Each time Nancy transformed, she wore a white scarf around her neck. Although the amulet and not the bite of another vampire was what changed Nancy, this part of her wardrobe has been what a few movie vampire women have used to conceal twin holes in their jugulars.

With Myra, Branding had a helper who was kept in the dark about her real doings. Admiration, not weakness, bound Myra to Branding. Outside of imaginative Mike and concerned Glenn, all men were pretty inferior stuff, from Doris-dominated Paul and riffraff Eddie to the conceited Tab and the overly-cautious coroner. The state school supervisor, however, cut through some hypocrisy by alleging that private schools are an easy way for some parents to avoid their responsibilities, asking strangers to take on every authority role an adolescent needs (Nola was the daughter of circus performers . . . people with a reason to move around).

Quite ably, Herb Strock's direction and Monroe Askins' cinematography copied the atmosphere of *I Was a Teenage Werewolf*. The spacious apartment Branding lived in afforded some brooding shadows and the frivolity of the dorm bash was effectively contrasted by the eerie solemnity of Branding using the amulet. For her visible spells, Nancy transformed in the same kind of ripply, receding shots *Werewolf* used whenever Tony felt lycanthropy bouts coming. Lit for darkness, making them more diffuse, Nancy's scenes had a shivery quietness.

Underplaying Nancy, Sandra Harrison matched the credibility of Michael Landon as a counterpart character beset by a broken home and peer pressure in more cloistered surroundings. The first close-up of her bruised waif-like beauty had good sensitivity value. Even better was Nancy's expression of silent remorse as she turned to the empty chem class seat once occupied by Nola. Perhaps Gloria Castillo might have been a decent replacement, but for some reason, Herman Cohen did not want Harrison and Herbert Strock had to fight to get her cast. Louise Lewis, Mrs. Ferguson in *Teenage Werewolf*, shaped an effective interpretation of Branding by making her insanity unwholesome persuasion rather than raving dementia.

Paul Maxwell could have done something with the role of Mike had Mike been allowed to leave the police station and conduct his own investigation. Jerry Blaine, the song lyricist of *Teenage Werewolf*, did triple threat duty here, writing "Puppy Love", singing it and tepidly trying to play a Joe Cool-type. Michael Hall, in his few moments as Glenn, was wooden but earnest.

Filmmakers were not as comfortable with girl teen fiends as they were with boys. Of the two films that used them (*Frankenstein's Daughter* the other), Herman Cohen could take credit for one — even if *Blood of Dracula* was a warmed over copy of his first and best Teenage horror film.

Nancy Perkins (Sandra Harrison) in full-blown transformation in BLOOD OF DRACULA.

A group of teenagers on a Halloween scavenger hunt discover the victims of Nancys' vampirized hidden personality in BLOOD OF DRACULA.

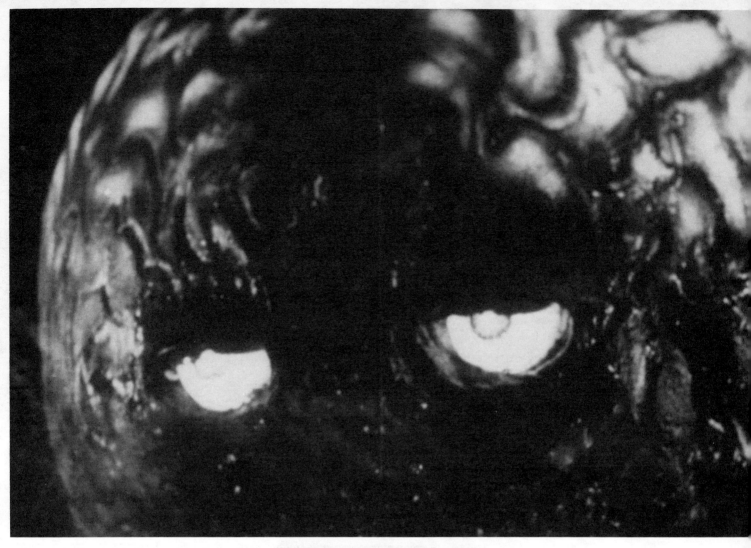

THE BRAIN FROM PLANET AROUS

Howco-International, 1958

Producer-Cinematography	Jacques Marquette
Director	Nathan Hertz *aka Juran*
Screenplay	Ray Buffum
Associate Producer	Dale Tate
Supervising Film Editor	Irving Schoenberg
Music	Walter Greene
Assistant Director	Bert Chervin
Sound	Phil Mitchell
Makeup	Jack Pierce
Technical Advisor	J. L. Cassingham
Props	Richard M. Rubin

A Marquette Production
Running time: 71 minutes

Cast: John Agar (Steve March), Joyce Meadows (Sally Fallon), Robert Fuller (Dan Murphy), Thomas B. Henry (John Fallon), Henry Travis (Col. Froghley), E. Leslie Thomas (Gen. Brown), Kenneth Terrell (Colonel in Conference Room), Dale Tate (Dr. Tate), Tim Graham (Sheriff Paine), Bill Giorgio (Russian)

John Agar's life has been one of notable gains and considerable losses. The ex-World War II Army Signal Corps. sergeant who married Shirley Temple and played to good reception Lt. Mickey O'Rourke in *Fort Apache* (1948) had a celebrity wife, the friendship of John Wayne and an upwardly mobile film career. Then the oyster went bad due to the toxin of alcohol. The first Mrs. Agar charged "Mr. Temple" with extreme mental cruelty and they divorced in 1949, one year after the birth of their daughter Susan. Agar's affair with the bottle led him down the sorry straits of other hellbound hunks like Tom Neal and Lawrence Tierney: several drunk driving charges, county jail time and violated probation. Between the bumps, there were some perks: working with Lucille Ball on *The Magic Carpet* (1951), a successful singing engagement in Miami and a romance that grew into an enduring and happy second marriage, producing two sons.

Agar would rather be remembered for his movies by John Ford and with The Duke, but his exploitation credits will not allow that and the most popular of these

(Above) The face of Gor from THE BRAIN FROM PLANET AROUS (1958).

is *The Brain from Planet Arous*, or *Superbrain* until its release title. To be both a monster and its enemy is quite a feat — especially since alien possession is most always final . . . and fatal.

The cinematographer and co-producer of a low-budget nature documentary, cameraman Jacques Marquette wanted to be a director of photography. Under the major company system, this could only happen if a producer hired him and producers did not usually advance camera operators unless all the Union cinematographers were busy. To create his own work, Marquette formed Marquette Productions. He produced and lensed *Teenage Thunder* (1957), which Allied Artists was willing to pay ninety thousand dollars for. Howco-International president Joy Houck made a better offer. Howco wanted two more Marquette films, agreeing to co-finance them.

To guard his big studio reputation, Nathan Juran directed *The Brain from Planet Arous* using his middle name Hertz as his credited surname. Its second male lead was Robert Fuller, the villain of *Teenage Thunder*, and the latter's hero, Charles Courtney, appeared in *Planet Arous'* companion feature *Teenage Monster*.

Descending upon remote Mystery Mountain, an alien light blasts away part of its face. Nuclear physicists Steve March and Dan Murphy detect intermittent radiation impulses coming from there. Steve's fiancee, Sally Fallon, invites them to lunch with her and her father, John, in the backyard of the Fallon residence. Dan is Steve's friendly rival for Sally. At the mountain, Steve and Dan discover the mouth of an artificial cave created just recently. A high scintillator reading and an eerie glow bedevil them before they are trapped in a dead-end passage by Gor, a floating extraterrestrial brain. Gor overcomes Steve and Dan fires his rifle until a burning light from Gor's eyes kills him. Reducing his size, Gor occupies unconscious Steve.

A week later, Gor impersonating Steve, meets Sally. He claims the trip was wasted and kisses Sally hard. She asks about Dan, who supposedly took off for Las Vegas at the spur of the moment. Sally finds Steve "different". "I don't know how you mean 'different'," says Gor/Steve. "I'm still the same old lovable character I always was." Suddenly, he feels a strange twinge of pain. Sally wants to know what really happened. "It was just a tooth kicking up," says Gor/Steve of the pain. "You acted funny," Sally tells him, " . . .and the way you kissed me. . ." Gor/Steve takes that as permission to make rougher love, tearing Sally's blouse as he pins her down on a lawn sofa. Her dog, George, attacks Gor/Steve, who kicks George away. Apologizing, he runs to Steve's convertible. "You need a doctor," Sally calls. "Don't expert me, Sally," shouts Gor/Steve. "I'm all right!" Next to George, Sally wonders, "What happened to him out there?"

Returning to his lab, agonized Steve writhes in a chair as Gor vacates him. Bent on world conquest, Gor knows of Steve's scientific prominence and entry to confidential places. "I chose your body very carefully, even before I knew about Sally . . . a very exciting female!" "Leave Sally out of this!" demands Steve. "Why?" asks Gor. "She appeals to me. There are some aspects in the life of an earth savage that are exciting and rewarding — things that are missed by the brains of my planet Arous." Steve: "If you so much as touch Sally, I'll —" Gor: "It is *you* who are touching her. Even *I* must have some interest to spur me on." Steve hurls several objects that pass through Gor. "I'm sparing you only because I need you," dictates Gor. "For as long as I wish to be, I *am* you!"

Sally tells John about Steve's strange behavior. John pays a visit to see what is wrong. Reeling in torment, turning his back, Steve fights Gor long enough to scream at John to get out. Sally wants John to go to Mystery Mountain with her.

Steve had taken Sally to the mountain once and she is surprised to see the cave. John discovers footprints inside. Sally spots a fleeting glow. John startles her. They find Steve's scintillator near the burned body of Dan. Vol, a benevolent brain, introduces himself. He says criminal Gor has taken over Steve. Vol will see the Fallons at their home eight o'clock tonight. As Steve, Gor arranges to observe a nuclear test at Indian Springs this Friday. Gor exits Steve, explaining he is indestructible either in Steve's body or his present transitory state. Gor has "the power of pure intellect".

Vol keeps his appointment with John and Sally. George is hostile until Vol pacifies him. Vol was sent to stop power-mad Gor. Unless he is forced out of Steve, Steve must die. "I will need a body that will be inconspicuous and always around Gor," specifies Vol. Sally suggests George. Steve will be picking Sally up tonight, but Gor intends to be her date. "She gives me a very strange, new elation," he says, occupying Steve again.

Driving to Sally's, Gor/Steve pauses to glance at a passing airliner. Gor explodes it with his glowing eyes, laughing malevolently.

Sally and John try to act casual when Gor/Steve arrives to pick Sally up. Vol/George comes along. Parking by a view of the city skyline, Gor/Steve once again comes on strong sexually with Sally. "You see a difference in me," he perceives. "I *am* different, Sally. The whole world is going to know *how* different." He has discovered "a power that will make the atom bomb seem like a firecracker". It will make Steve "the most feared man on earth". "Is that what you want?" asks Sally. "Power? That's what everyone wants," philosophizes Gor/Steve. "That's why the office boy wants to be the boss. That's why the private wants to be a general." Gor/Steve makes still another primitive advance. "I want you, Sally. And what I want, I take." The car radio announces the plane disaster.

Gor/Steve and Sally drive to the disaster scene. All

John and Sally Fallon (Thomas B. Henry and Joyce Meadows) and their dog meet Vol in
THE BRAIN FROM PLANET AROUS.

recovered bodies have radiation burns, yet the only fragment of metal found is contamination-free. Gor/Steve slyly insinuates the work of an alien force demonstrating its power, " . . . the beginning of the end." "If what you say is true," realizes Sally, "we'd be at the mercy of this thing."

Gor/Steve takes Sally home and she rushes into John's arms, thoroughly shook up. Sheriff Wiley Paine drops by the lab to tell Steve that Dan's body was found. Since death occurred a week ago and he loved Sally too, Steve is suspect. Gor/Steve brazenly confesses to the murder and the plane incident. He intends to kill Paine too. Paine draws his gun, but is energy blasted. Gor/Steve hides the body behind a chemical shelf.

At an emergency Pentagon meeting, Gen. Brown concludes from the burned plane component that we are being invaded. A medical report compares the conditions of the plane victims to the death of Dan. A top secret conference will convene at Indian Springs, where the bomb test is still set. There, Gor/Steve will present his "discovery". "It's becoming an obsession," criticizes Sally "— all this power and money. Who needs it?" "I do," answers Gor/Steve. "You will, too. It's habit forming. The more you get, the more you want." After they are married, home will be Washington, D.C. "Love

me?" Gor/Steve asks solicitously. "You know I do," answers Sally with forced composure. "Gonna marry me no matter what?" Gor/Steve asks. Turning away, Sally sobs, "I can't think of anything that could keep me from loving Steve March!"

Gor/Steve is banned from the conference until he professes to Gen. Brown knowledge of what destroyed the plane. All eyes are directed to study a closed-circuit TV monitor showing the test site. Behind the open venetian blinds of a window, Gor/Steve focuses his eyes. The whole room quakes to an explosion a loudspeaker says was not the bomb. "What I did to that small area," boasts Gor/Steve, "I can do to a city, a nation or a continent!" A Colonel rising from the conference table fires a gun point blank at Gor/Steve, who kills him. Gor/Steve orders an assemblage of major world dignitaries within eight hours. Any nation that refuses will have its capital city decimated ten minutes after the time limit. Everyone scrambles to the nearest phone.

At the Fallon home lazy Gor/Steve shows signs of fatigue. Vol tells Sally that Gor can be vanquished only when he leaves Steve to replenish his oxygen. His one weak spot is the brain area known as the Fissure of Rolando. Sally refers to it in an encyclopedia volume.

The dignitaries gather. Last to arrive is the

Gor-possessed Steve (John Agar) wants rough sex from Sally (Joyce Meadows) in THE BRAIN FROM PLANET AROUS.

belligerent Soviet representative. To change some expressions of skepticism he sees, Gor/Steve has everyone join him by the conference room window and makes them look at another plane he explodes. Gor/Steve wants all of the earth's atomic, transportation and industrial facilities, as well as the United Nations building. Engineers will be taught how to build a fleet of spaceships to be armed and manned by the joint military forces, all under Gor's command. "What would you do with all this power?" asks Gen. Brown. "I will return to my planet Arous," explains Gor/Steve, "and through its vast intellect become master of the universe. After I'm gone, earth will be free to live out its miserable span of existence — as one of my satellites. And that's how it's going to be. That'll be all for now, gentlemen. I'll prepare a meeting at the United Nations building tomorrow. You will all be there. After all, you have no other choice — have you?" The delegates sink into collective woe as Gor/Steve emits a burst of triumphant, maniacal laughter.

By the pipe rack next to Steve's cot in the lab, Sally leaves a torn out encyclopedia page illustrating the brain with the Fissure of Rolando carefully marked. She hides when Gor/Steve returns. Gor becomes himself. "You are about to succeed where Caesar, Napoleon and Hitler

failed," he promises Steve. Steve sees the planted information and turns to a fire wood axe. Sally bumps into Paine's body and screams. Gor attacks. Steve axes him as Vol/George watches from a window. "How did you know about the Fissure of Rolando?" Steve asks Sally perplexedly. Quietly, Vol departs. Sally tries to tell Steve about him, turning to George. "Vol . . . George . . . speak to me!" Steve laughs. "You and your imagination!"

Mixing conviction and dopiness, sleazy but not squalid, *Brain from Planet Arous* could almost have been a cinemadaption of one of the marvel Comic space monster tales of the early sixties. The nearest to resemble *Arous* was about an evil Martian named Zetora who switched bodies with an earthman. Zetora was exposed by another George — the dog owned by the man wearing Zetora's gargantuan shape. Zetora was captured, but escaped in a sequel story to do harm in his natural person until earth bacteria — the foe of H.G. Welles' Martians — killed him. Two other Marvel aliens, Goom and Taboo, were stopped by police agents of their worlds. None of the Marvel monsters possessed high testosterone levels, craving nookie from beautiful earth girls. Most movie aliens devise interplanetary miscegenation out of reproductive need. *Planet Arous* gave us a villain as horny as Ro-Man of *Robot Monster*, but a solar satyr with the physical capability of going all the way.

Through the cosmic incubus Gor, it almost seemed as if Steve's released id did most of the talking. Normal Steve was Mr. Average outside of his scientific brilliance until Gor housebroke him. When Gor savored human sensations through Steve — able to find passing diversion in things like the taste of pipe tobacco and romantic drives with the top down — it was as if the part of every man who wants it all was freed from inhibiting restraints. Gor was not that far off in how he articulated his endorsement of power. Instead of ruling the universe, Gor could have achieved more practical clout by, say, becoming the world's most ruthless corporate raider. The positions of Gor occupying Steve, and Vol inhabiting George, resembled the material states of Popeye Doyle and his privileged quarry Frog One; one man living high on the hog, the other slogging through the gutter. The presence of Vol was the only way Sally could help Steve, but once in George, Vol held back and let Steve destroy Gor. Vol's original intent had been to bring Gor back to Arous to face punishment. Passively, he was a vigilante cop!

The Arousian brains were played by a painted balloon on piano wires. An interior light made the upper part and the eye holes glow while air hoses caused the rubber to swell and contract. The laughable "face" did credit to the amusing cartoon ghoulies of Gahan Wilson. Double exposure achieved transparency and the wires were matted out. Nathan Juran asked Dale Tate to read the Gor and Vol voice-overs. Jacques Marquette's neighbor, Tate was an investor in Marquette Productions who worked at Consolidated Film Industries, the company that processed all its movies, and he was the associate producer of *Brain from Planet Arous* and *Teenage Monster*. Tate gave Gor a menacing, lecherous, evilly chuckling voice while humane Vol was polite and soft spoken. The one ill-chosen line was when Vol said to George, "Good dog! Good dog!"

Gor was at his most frightening when Agar and his makeup manifested Gor's evil through Steve. Agar wore silver contact lenses created by optometrist Walter Studt, whose house was the Fallon residence. Each time Gor eyed a target, Agar twisted his round-cheeked countenance into a grinning, obscene mannequin face. The lenses hurt his eyes, since the silver rubbed off each time he blinked.

Marquette, who was happier as a cameraman, showed a fascination for interesting surfaces. When Steve tried to fight Gor in John's presence, Agar was angled behind the distorting glass of a water cooler — as if to visualize the psyche-twisting conflict between him and Gor.

Personifying good and evil in big helpings of friendliness and fiendishness, Agar relished breaking out of his Galahad image for the Gor intervals, except for having to put up with the crude lenses. Joyce Meadows was Agar's best love interest in a sci-fi horror film, sounding distinctly like Cathy Downs, who was not one of them. She was especially convincing in the scenes where Sally had to steel herself in Gor/Steve's company. Robert Fuller was full of animation as Dan and Thomas B. Henry proved he could carry a larger role than those he usually got. Dale Tate was the scientist at the air crash site, wanting his character to be named "Dr. Dale Tate".

Once, when *Brain from Planet Arous* aired on TV, a replica of the original brain (Gor or Vol — take your pick) made a guest appearance, claiming to be unemployed and hard up for money. A few years later, Stephen King wrote "Carrie". It was, he alleged, inspired by *Planet Arous*. But then, how many King stories are *not* based on other people's ideas?

In certain career similarities, John Agar and Richard Burton were brothers. Both had early film promise, both had been married to famous former child stars. Both men were alcoholics. One of the watchable Burton bombs was *The Medusa Touch* (1978). Overendowed with telekinesis, Burton's character, John Morlar, could will small or grand scale death in scenes reminiscent of *Planet Arous*. Morlar caused the crash of a jumbo jet and threatened to blow up a nuclear plant. Under the power of Gor, Steve March destroyed *two* planes and achieved an explosion of atomic proportions by himself.

Burton topped Agar one way when both were nominees for "Worst Actor of All Time" in "The Golden Turkey Awards". Burton won.

118

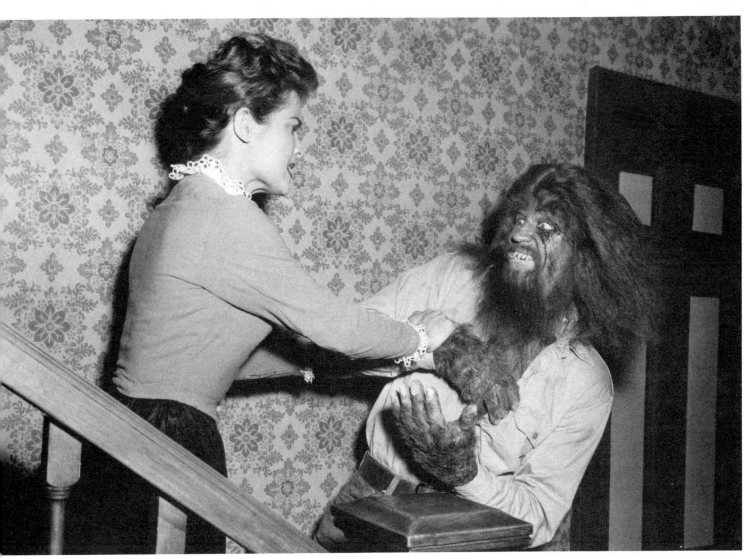

TEENAGE MONSTER

Howco-International, 1958
Television title *Meteor Monster*

Producer-Director	Jacques Marquette
Screenplay	Ray Buffum
Associate Producer	Dale Tate
Cinematography	Taylor Byars
	(and Jacques Marquette)
Supervising Film Editor	Irving Schoenberg
Music	Walter Greene
Sound	George Anderson
	Philip Mitchell
Makeup	Jack Pierce
Wardrobe	Jerry Bos
Assistant Film Editor	Morris Feuer
Properties	Richard M. Rubin
Assistant Director	Ken Walters

A Marquette Production
Running time: 65 minutes

Cast: Anne Gwynne (Ruth Cannon), Stuart Wade (Sheriff Bob), Gloria Castillo (Kathy North), Charles *aka Chuck* Courtney (Marv Howell), Gilbert *aka Gil* Perkins (Charles Cannon), Stephen Parker (Young Charles), Norman Leavitt (Deputy Ed), Jim McCullough (Jim Cannon), Gaybe Mooradian (Fred Fox), Arthur Berkley (Man with Burro), Frank Davis (Man on Street)

Forty-seven year old stuntman Gil Perkins was the *Monster on the Hill* and a *Meteor Monster* before his character in *Teenage Monster* was described by an adjective unheard of in its story's era. None of these title designations were false: the monster *was* an adolescent, he *was* altered by a meteor and the ending *did* take place on top of a hill. Only the world wasn't prepared for Horror Westerns. Still, one of the least of the teen creature features beget a category of its own. Did *Teenage Monster* actor Charles Courtney ever suspect that in 1966 he would play Billy the Kid in a bullet-to-fang showdown with Count Dracula?

Ruth Cannon, her husband Jim and their nine year

(Above) Gloria Castillo gets the upper hand on Charles (Gil Perkins) in TEENAGE MONSTER (1958).

old son, Charles, live in poverty in a shack near Jim's gold mine. After years of sweat, Jim feels that he is getting close to a rich vein. When Jim and Charles go to the mine, a blazing meteor falls out of the sky and explodes. As the smoke clears, Ruth tends to unconscious Charles and throws herself upon the body of Jim in grief. Coming to, Charles asks where Jim is and Ruth sees that his face has mutated horribly.

Seven years go by. Everyone believes Charles and Jim died together. Now a shaggy, imbecilic brute, Charles roams for livestock, killing sheep and cattle. He also slays an old prospector. Ruth discovers the body and sends Charles back to the mine, where he now lives, keeping a rag doll. Ruth keeps trying to convince Charles that his outbursts of violence will put him away. Sheriff Bob Lehman and Deputy Ed discover the dead prospector, Charles' third human victim. Ruth has been working the mine and finally hits pay dirt. She instructs Charles to guard the mine while she goes into town.

Bob is eager to resume his old relationship with Ruth, who has the ore specimen she brought appraised by Fred Fox. Ed reports some new cattle killings. Bob urges Ruth to stay in town. Ruth realizes Charles has been amok again. The gold comes at enough to make Ruth wealthy. She immediately purchases the Fox home.

Charles watches Bob from his bedroom window when Bob comes to take Ruth out that evening. Ruth tells Charles to stay inside, but when she leaves, he throws his doll down and smashes up his room. Charles kills a man in his front yard and scares some kids he wants to play with. On her way to work, waitress Kathy North is abducted by Charles. Kathy awakens from her faint on Charles' bed. Seeing him again, she passes out a second time. Ruth and Bob hear about the murder from Ed, who takes Ruth home while Bob investigates.

Ruth confronts Charles in his bedroom. She senses he is hiding something in the closet and finds Kathy, still unconscious. Ruth revives Kathy and reveals that Charles is her son. Ruth pays Kathy five hundred dollars in hush money. Kathy will earn that sum monthly as a companion. She joins her boyfriend, shiftless pool player Marv Howell, who takes the money from her.

Pretending to be his friend, Kathy tells Charles what Marv did. She leaves a ladder by his window so he can sneak out and go to the place where Kathy arranges a date with Marv in order to have Charles kill him. Back home, Charles sees Bob kissing Ruth and angrily knocks him out. Ruth covers for Charles, realizing he left the house. Bob and Ed find high heel marks around Marv's body. Ruth is forced to alibi for Kathy by backing her story she was in Ruth's library. Kathy tells Charles that if Bob marries Ruth, he will be his new father. Kathy makes Ruth pledge twenty thousand dollars to her in a document signed in Bob's presence.

Expecting the monster to return, Bob waits for it in the barn. Kathy tells Ruth she would have killed Charles if he had been her son. Charles overhears from the stairway. Ruth brings Bob food in the barn while Kathy watches them. Bob wants to go back to ranching and marry Ruth, who would consent of not for Charles. Kathy says Ruth wants him dead, but knowing she lied, Charles kidnaps her. Ed saw Charles around the barn and alerts Ruth and Bob. Out of the barn, Ed takes Charles' broken doll. Bob, Ruth and Ed follow Charles and Kathy to the base of a cliff. As Kathy is thrown from the precipice, Ed shoots Charles, who cries, "Mama!" as he falls.

With slight changes, *Teenage Monster* could have been set in the present. A western backdrop was useful in enabling Ruth to harbor Charles since the dispositions of dead bodies then did not always require such elaborate, mandatory formalities as autopsies, embalming, cemetery burial, etc. This way, Ruth could inter Jim in a real grave next to a fake one for Charles. Had Ruth attempted to hide him by relocating, she could not have extracted all the gold from the mine. No money, no motive for Kathy to pull blackmail.

If real teenage touches were missing, the film composed an interesting tug of war between Ruth and Kathy for control of Charles. Poverty had toughened Ruth but warped Kathy. Ruth's maternal influence on Charles was limited while Kathy had an armory of temptress tricks. Seemingly innocent when Charles first met her, Kathy was the only manipulator of a teen monster who wasn't an adult in an authoritative position. Her sexiness caused Charles to feel like a Man. In yielding to Kathy, Ruth had to come to full terms with the folly of her overprotectiveness. Charles' resentment for Bob was a classic reaction of a child unable to accept a future stepparent. While Bob was the patient ex-lover/suitor waiting to relight an old fire, Marv was a no-good hustler who died for swiping the first installment of Kathy's gains like a pimp fleecing one of his whores.

Cohesive as soap opera, the story's horror was pretty feeble. The meteor was apparently radioactive, but had no theoretical concept behind it. It just fell to bring about Charles' change and kill expendable Jim. Moronic and bestial, Charles looked like an aging hippie with rabies. When he talked, it was in a silly garbled whining. When Charles had something *important* to say — like his denunciation of Kathy — *then* he was slightly audible. Comments of distaste bring up the retardation angle — as if the film was making a mockery of the mentally handicapped and the strain it puts on their parents. The real reason for Charles to look werewolfish was to make him different from any other violent retardate and on the basis of the extremeness of his abnormality, the movie could claim it was based on legend.

Gil Perkins had invested in Marquette Productions and took the role of Charles because Mike Ross lacked agility. The man who was *supposed* to direct backed out the day before shooting. Marquette had to direct and hired an incompetent cameraman who ruined a whole day of day-for-night footage. When that man quit,

Marquette had to photograph as well. Perkins delivered his dialogue legibly, but Marquette and writer Ray Buffum thought it was too coherent and dubbed in the idiot sounds.

Not only was a faded Jack Pierce the makeup artist, but the female lead was Universal's second-string Evelyn Ankers, Anne Gwynne. Near forty, she still looked good and made the amusing scenes of Ruth the Disciplinarian ("You're acting like a baby, Charles!") logical within the context of her burden. Stuart Wade, the man who killed the *Monster from the Ocean Floor* (1954), had an early James Garner kind of presence and Gloria Castillo had a sprightly girlishness to go with her chilly guile as alternately impetuous and calculating Kathy.

In a script whose period was semi-nebulous, the horror catalyst a brushed-aside contrivance and the "monster" a half-wit with long hair, the only true forces to reckon with were motherly devotion and trollopy avarice. What rode on several sets of coattails was a film that should have been called *Two Women and a Monster*.

Jacques Marquette probably wanted an obedient monster of his own to kill the people at Howco-International. Via creative accounting, Howco left Marquette and his investors without a dime. Marquette had a happier relationship with Allied Artists, the company he refused to sell *Teenage Thunder* to, when Marquette made his next film, *Attack of the Fifty Foot Woman*.

Later, Charles has the upper "paw" on Kathy in TEENAGE MONSTER.

THE ASTOUNDING SHE MONSTER

American-International, 1958
Released in England as *The Mysterious Invader*

Producer-Director	Ronnie Ashcroft
Story-Screenplay	Frank Hall
Cinematography	William C. Thompson
Music	Guenther *aka Gene* Kauer
Sound	Dale Knight
Production Manager	John Nelson
Makeup	Nicholas Vehr
Costumes	Maureen
Wardrobe	Norma McClaskey
Chief Electrician	Lee Cannon
Properties	Tony Portughese
Grip Master	Charles Norris

A Hollywood International Production
Running time: 60 minutes

Cast: Robert Clarke (Dick Cutler), Kenne Duncan (Nat Burdell), Marilyn Harvey (Margaret Chaffee), Jeanne Tatum (Esther Malone), Shirley Kilpatrick (She Monster), Ewing Brown (Brad Conley)

122 Ronnie Ashcroft's venture into the sci-fi/horror erotica combined the quasi-nudity of *Phantom from Space* (1953) and the geographical isolation of *Devil Girl from Mars* (1955). It also took the sex of the latter alien, hoping to call its own *The Naked Invader* until censorship mandated that she be *The Astounding She Monster*. Both a stranded visitor and a menace to earth life, the She Monster came to convey yet another extraterrestrial warning about our world's nuclear instability. Instead of the Government, she had to contend with such nonpolitical figures as three low-life kidnappers, a rockhound, a rich girl, a dog, a snake and a bear.

Once, the explosion of a planet threatened to upset the galactic balance. Near Antares live beings who fear that earth science will cause this to happen again. A meteor-like craft bearing their emissary leaves. In Los Angeles, socialite Margaret Chaffee drives past her front gate when another car deliberately blocks her path. Nat Burdell and Brad Conley jump out and snatch Margaret. With them is Nat's alcoholic girl, Esther Malone.

Brad driving, the gang and Margaret head for the San Gabriel mountains. Margaret's disappearance is reported over the radio and the FBI has been contacted. Geologist Dick Cutler and his dog, Egan, are taking a stroll near Dick's lonely cabin when Dick sees the "meteor" crash into the nearby desert. From the smoking crater emerges an incandescent female alien who scares wildlife and kills a snake with one hand. When Brad

sees the alien, he swerves to avoid hitting her and disables the kidnap car. Brad claims he saw "a naked dame".

Nat, Margaret, Esther and Brad walk to Dick's cabin. Dick is testing some rock samples with acids. Egan senses someone outside. Dick thinks he detects a marauding black bear. Nat enters with his gun to "borrow" Dick's jeep, taking the keys. He calls to Brad to bring in the woman. Drunken Esther, at one time, belonged to New York's upper-crust. Brad goes out to fix the defective headlights of the jeep, taking Egan with him. Brad is unable to repair the lights and lets it slip out the cops are after the group. Margaret gets hysterical and Nat slaps her. A fire warden calls Dick in regard to the light in the sky. Margaret tries to scream for help. Dick makes up the story he invited some friends over and one of them has gotten out of hand. Nat slaps Margaret some more and beats up chivalrous Dick. Brad sees the "dame" again and goes looking for her.

Outdoors, Brad drops his hat and Nat hears him shooting at the alien. She kills Brad. Nat investigates while Esther covers Dick and Margaret. Nat picks up Brad's hat, calls for him and sees the alien, who slays Egan. Nat puts several shots into the retreating alien and carries Brad's body away. Esther runs out of booze and develops and itchy trigger finger until Dick gets another bottle for her. Before Esther can take a drink, Nat shoots it. Dick examines Brad's body, noting signs of radium poisoning.

Dick sees a connection between the radium and the color of the meteor. Nat wants to get out of here. He may have contracted secondary contamination from Brad. When the fire warden calls inquiring about gunshots, Dick says his friends were shooting at the bear. The warden mentions the kidnap story on radio. The radio commentator says Margaret's father refuses to pay the ransom. Nat decides everyone will leave in the jeep now, but the alien blocks them. Dick believes she wears a protective metal. He plans to douse her with a bucket of gas and Nat will light the torch. The alien leaps in through a window. The torch drives her away. Outside, the alien swipes the torch from Nat and kills Esther. Backed toward a ravine, Nat sidesteps the alien, who falls to the bottom and appears dead.

Dick and Margaret return to his cabin, where Nat stops them from phoning the highway patrol. Dick insists that Nat needs a doctor. Dick, Nat and Margaret go down the fire road in the jeep. The alien appears. Dick and Margaret run away. Nat tries to start the jeep and the alien fatally squeezes his behind as he turns to jump out. Back in the cabin, Dick and Margaret find the phone useless. The alien's reentry forces them outside again. Dick and Margaret hide as the alien repels the bear.

Aware of the radium content in the alien's body, Dick concocts an acid bomb. He goes outside the cabin as the alien approaches Margaret from the bedroom. Margaret screams and Dick hurls the bomb. The shrieking alien drops to the floor and writhes into nothingness — leaving only her locket. It carries a message announcing that earth is eligible to join the League of Planets. Other worlds have experienced earth's problems and we are invited to consider a meeting with the league to resolve them. The alien was sent to bring the message and relay word of our decision. Exactly how will her world react to her death?

Selling dubious sex appeal and hackneyed crime, Ronnie Ashcroft made a film that was too unreal to be primitive in a docudrama fashion and empty of spirited melodrama save for the conduct of the kidnappers. Existing in perpetual silence, making no effort to communicate, the She Monster was called upon to behave as a deliberately hostile alien would. Her people were worried about *our* effect on the delicate balance of the universe, yet possessed bodies that gave off pure radium — sure death to any earthling who came in contact with their representative. Even the container of the message, the locket, was hot.

By coming up with the ideas of how to combat the She Monster, Dick was her most ruthless opponent. The only scientist in the group, he did not even pause for a second to ascertain the She Monster's motives. Even though Nat and Brad were justifiably afraid of her, she was reacting mostly to their violence. With his acid dispatch of the message bearer, Dick ruined our chance at sealing a pact with the Planet League. Of course, he could not be faulted for the destruction of the She Monster's ship, without which she could not return home in order to relay our acceptance or refusal of the proposed talk. And without the body of the She Monster, how could Dick and Margaret prove the validity of the message unless the locket was composed of an otherworldly metal? From the perspective of the kidnapping, the She Monster did more immediate good by eliminating the captors. When Esther was rich, *she* might have ended up in Margaret's position!

Owner of the editing service that edited *Man-Beast*,

Ashcroft hired William C. Thompson, the ocassionally brilliant cinematographer of *Plan Nine from Outer Space* (1959) to photograph. However, Thompson found little in *The Astounding She Monster* to interest his compositional eye (Thompson only had one eye) other than a few parts of the mountain terrain. As the She Monster, Shirley Kilpatrick wore an outfit that tore in the back on the first day of filming. With no one bothering to fix it, she had to make her exit backwards in many scenes. Ashcroft's wife, Lorraine, doubled for her in a few shots. Kilpatrick was exotic only for her aberrant makeup, hair and costuming, and the optical effect of resonating radiation was unable to make She seem more Monster.

Too cheap to spend money on outdoor synch sound, Ashcroft added narration for scenes that easily explained themselves, taking digs at Margaret for her opulent Brentwood life-style. Radio messages filled in details of the kidnapping and what the police were doing. Ashcroft edited the film in his living room, piecing together sample medium and long shots void of any close-ups.

At least Gene Kauer's music was original. Mostly gloomy, it was used in *The Beast of Yucca Flats* (1961) — an *all* non-synch sound film.

Robert Clarke and Kenne Duncan saved their parts by their particular role associations. Clarke was a hero who knew his limitations around dangerous company. He wasn't always Richard Carlson bright, Kenneth Tobey stolid or John Agar courageous. Clarke hated *The Astounding She Monster*, but received a percent of the profits and used the money to fund his own film *The Hideous Sun Demon*. Having outlasted many of his serial and matinee western peers, Kenne Duncan became a character lead in his old age. Most of his short holiday as a star was spent working for someone Bob Clarke never had to deal with: Edward D. Wood. One of the assistant director's of Wood's *Night of the Ghouls* was Ronnie Achroft!

GIANT FROM THE UNKNOWN

Astor, 1958

Producer	Arthur A. Jacobs
Director-Cinematographer	Richard E. Cunha
Screenplay	Frank Hart Taussig
	Ralph Brooke
Associate Producer	Marc Frederic
Film Editor	Screencraft
Music	Albert Glasser
Camera Operator	William Norton
Special Effects	Harold Banks
Sound Mixer	Robert Post
Makeup	Jack P. Pierce
Wardrobe	Marge Corso
	Grace Kuhn
Script Supervisor	Diana Loomis
Chief Electrician	Lee Dixon
Property Master	Walter Broadfoot

A Screencraft Enterprises Production
Running time: 77 minutes

Cast: Edward Kemmer (Wayne Brooks), Sally Fraser (Janet Cleveland), Morris Ankrum (Prof. Cleveland), Buddy Baer (Vargas), Bob Steele (Sheriff Parker), Joline Brand (Ann Brown), Gary Crutcher (Charlie Brown), Billy Dix (Indian Joe), Whitey Hughes, Oliver Blake, Ned Davenport, Ewing Miles (Townsmen)

When TV producer Toby Anguish retired, his associates Richard Cunha and Arthur A. Jacobs turned his company into Screencraft Enterprises. A service that edited, dubbed and rented out its soundstage, Screencraft did commercials until employee Ralph Brooke urged Cunha and Jacobs to make a horror film. Because of budget, they couldn't develop anything along the lines of giant insects or prehistoric behemoths, so they settled on a human giant for their monster. The right actor was found in Buddy Baer, the brother of boxer Max and uncle of Max, Jr.

The Spanish conquistadors had been a part of old California history, inspiring Brooke and co-writer, Frank

Vargas, the mutinous lieutenant, is discovered in GIANT FROM THE UNKNOWN (1958).

Hart Taussig, to create Baer's character around one. The script was first called *The Giant from Devil's Craig* and *Diablo Giant*. Its tale was a perverse retelling of Rip Van Winkle about a man displaced in time who wakes up in this world. Cunha and Jacobs admired Jack Pierce, hiring him to do the makeup. The right combination of actor and makeup artist, plus Cunha's directorial zeal made *Giant from the Unknown* the best Cunha film.

Since a bad electrical storm, the people of Pine Ridge have been in a state of fear. Citizens have gathered downtown and flock around a pickup truck that arrives with Sheriff Parker and the body of elderly rancher Harold Banks — all torn to pieces like many of the mysteriously slaughtered animals in the area of Devil's Craig. Laughing, crazy Indian Joe asserts, "The spirits of my people return for their revenge." Some locals are inclined to agree. Parker suspects scientist, Wayne Brooks, with whom he has a running feud. Back from three days in the mountains collecting rock samples, Wayne hears about Banks' murder from teenage lodge employee, Charlie Brown, and Charlie's sister, Ann, who is sweet on Wayne. Banks had shot at Wayne for shortcutting across his land last week. Arriving in town are archeologist Frederic Cleveland and his daughter, Janet, who meet Wayne and Parker.

Cleveland is writing the definitive thesis on fourteenth century Spanish explorer, Ptolemy Firello. He is especially interested in finding the remains of Firello's mutinous lieutenant, Vargas, nicknamed "the Diablo" or "Devil Giant". Vargas and his renegade band, the "Diablo Brigade", went inland looking for gold. "As a matter of fact," Cleveland tells Wayne, "very little is known about Vargas. You see, Firello suppressed accounts relating to this officer, but from his name, I'm sure he was a brutal, degenerate and depraved man who disgraced — and almost ruined — the expedition."

Wayne is researching physical antiquity. In his modest field lab, he keeps artifacts from the vicinity of an Indian burial ground and an extinct lizard that came alive when he freed it from a rock. Wayne and Janet go to a movie while Cleveland stays in the lab. Joe creepily peeks in on him from a window. Cleveland assembles fragments of an Indian cross showing European influence. Wayne found it at Devil's Craig.

Wayne, Janet and Cleveland make camp at the craig. Parker drops by to warn them about the killer on the loose. Janet senses someone lurking close. Wayne examines some curiously disturbed rocks and brush before Joe fires his rifle at Wayne — claiming he saw a rabbit. Joe militantly guards his ancestors' resting place. In a charted sector outlined by a grid, Wayne and Cleveland scan for relics with a metal detector. Cleveland has spent over three summers looking for signs of the Firello party and is about to give up. Janet tries the detector. She wanders past the grid area, leaving her compact on the top of a log. When Wayne fetches it for her, the detector loudly registers. Exhumed are possessions and bones of the Diablo Brigade.

Where lightning had struck, is a formation similar to the rock the lizard was trapped in. Finding Vargas' huge battle axe imbedded in a log, Wayne attempts to remove it. As a storm brews, Vargas begins to stir from under a carpet of dry leaves only inches away. When Wayne returns to the spot, the axe is gone. Found are Vargas' gold medallion, breastplate, helmet — all remarkably preserved — and a deep depression. Could he be alive. . . just like the lizard? "That was different!" argues Cleveland. "A lower, less complex form of life perhaps — but a human? No, no! It's just impossible!" Wayne: "I wonder." Strolling through camp with his hunting rifle, Charlie sees the mounted finds. To keep the curious away, Wayne requests secrecy.

Vargas spies on Wayne and Janet during a romantic interlude. Discovering his armor, he dons it. As Janet undresses for bed in the lamp light of her tent, Vargas lustfully advances. His foot knocks over a pail. Startled Janet drops her gun and an accidental shot scares Vargas away. He leaves a massive footprint.

Charlie and Ann live nearby in the cabin of their late parents. Charlie is worried for Ann, but she makes him go to the lodge. Ann carries a bucket to a water well and encounters panting, homicidal Vargas.

Cleveland thinks some element in the earth preserved Vargas. When his men died from a plague, he sank into a deep coma and the Indians prematurely buried him. Someone flashes a blinding light in Wayne and Cleveland's faces, telling them not to move. It is Parker, here to arrest Wayne for murder. Vargas' medallion was found clutched in Ann's hand. Charlie identified it. Parker assumes Wayne wanted silence out of greed. Although Cleveland insists Wayne was in camp the whole time, Parker takes him in. Wayne supposes that Joe took Vargas' belongings.

On the way to town, Wayne and Parker stop at Joe's dark cabin. Parker's flashlight shines on the body of Joe hanging on a wall peg. "There's your alibi," Parker tells Wayne. While Cleveland makes a plaster cast of the footprint, Vargas slugs him. Janet hears Cleveland moan and encounters Vargas. Janet runs to Cleveland's jeep, but the motor will not start. She faints and Vargas takes her. Cleveland comes to, gets the jeep working and heads for town.

Handcuffed Wayne sits in Parker's squad car while Parker investigates lynch talk. Cleveland tells Wayne that Vargas has Janet. Wayne driving, they steal the car. Parker and a posse follow. Back at camp, Cleveland severs the chain of Wayne's cuffs with an axe. Grabbing a rifle, Wayne pursues Vargas, who tries to shove a tall tree trunk down on him. Vargas waits for Wayne with his raised battle axe, but alarmed Janet's scream and a shot from Parker rout him. Parker apologizes to Wayne for reading this all wrong.

The posse chases Vargas to a box ledge. Vargas rolls down a large boulder, wounding a deputy, and throws

125

Vargas goes on a killing rampage in GIANT FROM THE UNKNOWN.

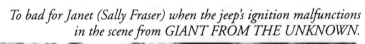

To bad for Janet (Sally Fraser) when the jeep's ignition malfunctions in the scene from GIANT FROM THE UNKNOWN.

rocks. Wayne hurls a lit flare so the deputies can get a bead on him. A would-be hero clubs Vargas in the back with the butt of a rifle and is tossed to his death. Vargas escapes. A sentry stays at the ledge.

Janet and Charlie serve food for the deputies at camp. Charlie is anxious to join in the hunt, but Wayne tells him this is a man's job. Resentfully, Charlie takes a rifle, muttering, "A man's job, huh. I'll show 'em." Going after Vargas alone, Charlie finds the sentry sitting in a stooped position. Charlie touches him and the man falls over dead, The others hear gunshots. Vargas has injured Charlie, who managed to wound him. Parker gets medical help while Charlie tells Wayne that Vargas is heading for a water mill.

Wayne approaches the mill as Vargas spots him from a window. Wayne stoops to examine blood spots as Vargas lunges at him with his axe. Wayne breaks open a boarded-up window to get out as Vargas tries to grab him with one arm. The fighting continues on the bridge above the dam. Losing his balance, Vargas crashes through the brittle railing and plunges into the falls. Cleveland wants to recover the body for science, but Parker tells him the current leads to the depths of a bottomless crater lake. "Well, in that case," says disappointed Cleveland," I guess the world will just have to take our word for it." "You think anyone will ever believe us?" asks Parker. "No," admits Cleveland, who says, "I guess the youngsters are waiting for us." Seeing Wayne and Janet Kiss, Parker tells him, "Wrong again, Professor."

Vargas made for quite a believable "monster". Dangerous in his own age, he was the ultimate verification of Wayne's theories. His inadvertent framing of Wayne for the murders added a minor but useful Wronged Man subplot, though the bad blood between Wayne and Parker was rather hazy. Real suspended animation would never permit human survival without cryogenic support. More potent as a mythical being, Vargas lived off nature and was one with it. Already active at the outset, he symbolically "returned" at the end of his sleep — like some dreadful troll borne up from the bowels of the earth. Repossession of the armor ritualistically completed his definition. The rape fear other monsters generate had the expectation of real-life enactment when Vargas ravaged Ann and took Janet. In the falls, nature took Vargas back, consigning him to where he could never rise again.

Cunha and Jacobs decided to film at Big Bear because a late winter was hurting the ski trade and the locals needed an economy transfusion. All crew members were Unionists, but to cut costs, Cunha and Jacobs shot non-Union and claimed that production would be done at Paradise Cove. Two days into filming, the Union found out where the company had gone. Scenes involving the extras had already been done and the equipment was hidden away in the woods until the Union representative left.

Cunha was also the cinematographer. Each of his films flashed their title over an emblem image; here Vargas' axe striking the side of a log. Sally Fraser's veiled nudity behind the illuminated canvas showed bare breasts with surprising mammalian detail. The water mill was the remnants of the one made for *The Trail of the Lonesome Pine* (1936). The light was so dim around there that a few shots had the crudity of an early outdoor silent. The first staging of the Wayne and Vargas fight had been long and furious, taking until midnight. A closed camera shutter spoiled the film. Briefer, the retake was more spontaneous because it was shot during a sudden snowstorm.

Giant from the Unknown had several names full of in-joke meaning. Knowing Cunha was unaware of the characters in "Peanuts", prankish Ralph Brooke suggested the name "Charlie Brown" for their Charlie. When the preview audience heard it, they laughed. A real Harold Banks did the special effects, making the armor and a human skull out of fiberglass. Joline Brand, who played Ann Brown, later married "Laugh-In" producer George Schlatter and Dick Martin mentioned her name in a skit.

Albert Glasser, between music jobs for Bert Gordon, created a robust, thrilling score — his best since *The Cyclops*.

Kept off screen for a long time, Buddy Baer took center stage when Vargas ended his siesta to visit further grief of Devil's Craig. Required mostly for his size, Baer managed to convey a bestial psyche with glinty, glowery eyes and lips of bated anticipation. He and the man who applied a fake scar, matted hair and grey grease paint received a unique collaborative credit that read "And Buddy Baer in Makeup Created by Jack Pierce",

Cunha and Jacobs only meant to do one horror film. Jacobs once worked for Astor Pictures in New York. *Diablo Giant* was their pick of a release title with Astor preferring *Giant from Diablo Pass*. The final name was a compromise everyone agreed to. Astor, however, wanted a double bill. Cunha and Jacobs filled it with their next film, *She Demons* — with scenes that were actually done in Paradise Cove.

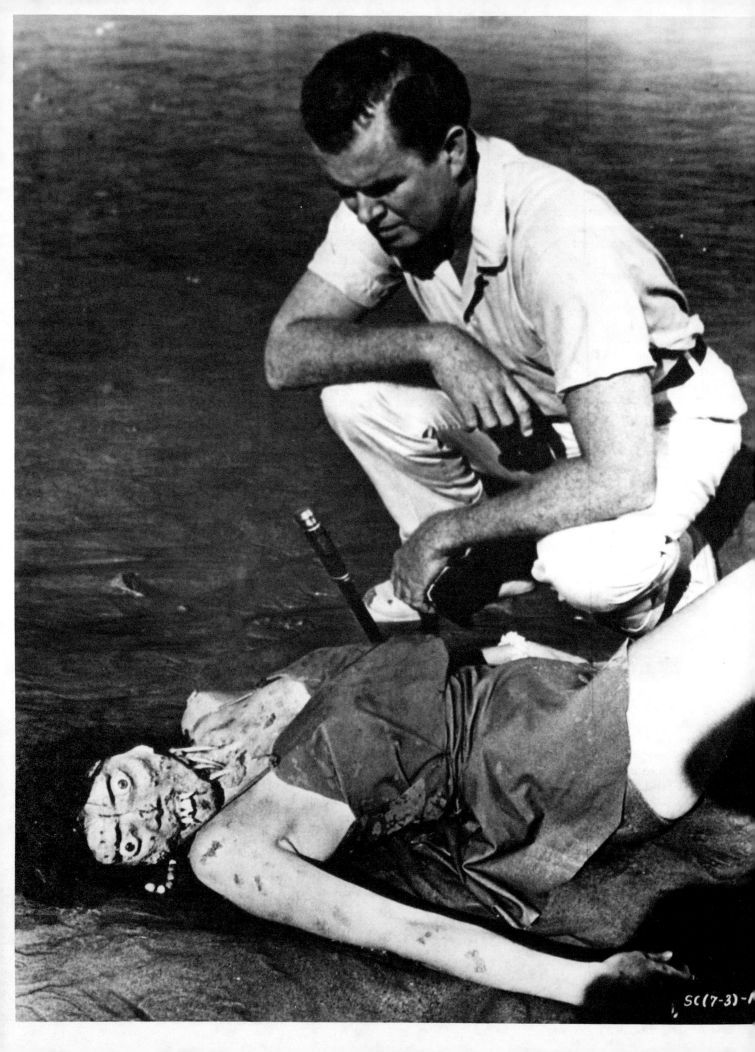

SC(7-3)-

SHE DEMONS

Astor, 1958

Producer	Arthur A. Jocobs
Director	Richard Cunha
Screenplay	Richard Cunha
	H.E. Barrie
Associate Producer	Marc Frederic
Cinematography	Meredith Nicholson
Film Editor	Willaim Shea
Music	Nicholas Carras
Production Design	Harold Banks
Production Manager	Ralph Brooke
Assistant Director	Leonard Shapiro
Sound Mixer	Frank Webster
Camera Operator	Buddy Harris
Makeup	Carlie Taylor
Costumes	Marj Corso
Script Supervisor	Judith Hart
Props	Walter Broadfoot
Chief Electrician	Lee Dixon
Key Grip	Grant Tucker
Special Effects	David Koehler

A Screencraft Enterprises Production
Running time: 77 minutes

Cast: Irish McCalla (Jerrie Turner), Tod Griffin (Fred Maklin), Victor Sen Yung (Sammy Ching), Rudolph Anders (Col. Karl Osler), Gene Roth (Egore), Leni Tana (Mona Osler), Charles Opuni (Kris Kamana), Bill Coontz, Billy Dix, Larry Gelbman, Michael Stoycoff, Whitey Hughes (Storm Troopers), Maureen Janzen, Grace Matthews (She Demons), the Diana Nellis Dancers (Themselves)

Richard Cunha's horror films after *Giant from the Unknown* were unrelieved evil pearls of putrescence but for their happy endings and efforts to make the heroic characters likeable. With the Aster commissioned *She Demons*, Cunha and Arthur A. Jacobs formed a stock company that included H.E. Barrie, who wrote the script with Cunha, cinematographer Meredith Nicholson and music composer Nicholas Carras. As before, Marc Frederic was associate producer.

A work of bad taste bravura, *She Demons* happily trowelled up every uncharted island cliche with the exception of prehistoric life and rare treasure: lost women, fanatical holdout Nazis, horny tyrant rulers, intra-castaway bickering and a climactic disaster that destroyed the whole island. This and Cunha's following films for Astor, *Frankenstein's Daughter* and *Missile to the Moon* used women as both sex objects and figures of horror, giving Cunha his status as a maker of rotgut

Todd Griffin grimaces at a She Demon (1958).

kitsch. In sex, gore and a feeling of general ugliness, these were the fifties' nearest thing to R-rated shock as black and white American-made films went.

A television news reel recaps the havoc Hurricane Emily brought to Surf City, Florida. Its commentator appears live, asking families living along the coast to look out for the motor launch El Paso, which was on an excursion cruise and has been missing for two days. Aboard were skipper Fred Maklin, his mates Sammy Ching and Kris Kamana and heiress Jerrie Turner.

All four were swept to a distant island. Salvaged was a radio Sammy tries to operate. "If it wasn't for your disposition, I might mistake you for a pretty girl," Fred tells spoiled, bitchy Jerrie, more concerned about her wardrobe than practical needs. Some Navy jets fly overhead — too high to see Jerrie desperately waving at them — and the untransmittable radio picks up the pilot's radio conversation. The island is scheduled for target practice. In the sand above tide level are strange female footprints with clawed toes that form a dance circle. Emily had blown the group to their destination — an island of legendary animal women. Kris goes into a ritual chant and declares, "This is an island of evil!" He once spoke to a fisherman who claimed he saw one of the animal women several years ago. Jerrie's obnoxiousness drives Fred to tell her to go jump into the ocean. "And while you're there, give the sharks my regards."

At camp that evening, Fred and Jerrie let their respective barriers drop slightly as she changes clothes. The radio announces that the search for the group is being abandoned because another wrecked boat similar to theirs was found. Fred hears distant drums.

The next morning, Kris guards the camp while Jerrie, Fred and Sammy explore the jungle, walking around in circles until Sammy recovers his lost fraternity key. Coming back, they find the radio smashed. Riddled with spears, Kris is dead. His knife is gone. Some blood is traced to a woman he fatally stabbed lying face down in the surf. Reacting to her hideous features, Jerrie says, "A woman's body, but the face of a demon..." "Demon," mutters Fred, "... she demon." Kris is buried.

Jerrie, Fred and Sammy venture deeper into the jungle, whose steaming water indicates the island is volcanic. Jerrie is menaced by a snake coiled around a tree limb and begins to show vulnerability. More drum music is traced to a small clearing, where a band of native women are performing a ritual dance. "But the faces," notices Fred, "... they're normal." "Even better," smiles leering Sammy. Several men in Nazi storm trooper uniforms led by Egore capture the women and herd them off to a nearby torture camp.

Col. Karl Osler, the leader, is in his lab readying an experimental treatment for a seated woman with bandages over her face, his wife Mona. One of the native girls lies strapped to a table. When Egore reports the roundup of the rest, Mona turns away, begging Osler to

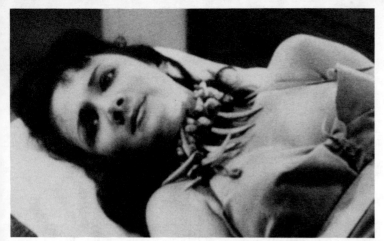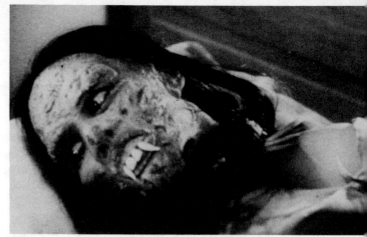

One of Dr. Osler's (Rudolph Anders) little specimens becomes a demon in SHE DEMONS.

130

get him out, and cries. Osler rudely dismisses Egore. The treatment causes Mona no pain, but the girl becomes another she demon. "Always the same reaction," murmurs Osler nonchalantly, ". . . a mindless animal."

To keep the caged women in line, Egore sadistically lashes to death a girl tied to a whipping post. When it is safe to venture into the camp, the demons claw at Sammy's face. Fred cuts the dead girl down. A hillside door leads to the underground lab complex. Examining the dead girl, Egore orders an immediate search for intruders. In the lab, he hears Jerrie upset a flask and finds her hiding in one corner of an alcove. Egore's attempted interrogation is met with flip insults. As he raises his hand to Jerrie, Fred challenges Egore to a fight, sending Jerrie and Fred outside. Exiting before Egore, Fred slams the lab door into Egore's face, then pushes him through the cage door. Clawing Egore to pieces, the demons escape. The effort of Jerrie, Fred and Sammy to do so is thwarted by a trooper who waves his rifle at them, ordering their surrender in German.

Jerrie, Fred and Sammy are brought to Osler, whom Fred recognizes as a wanted war criminal. His subjects are the women who disappeared from the island of Portanais ten years ago. The Feuhrer had delegated to Osler the task of finding a way to heal scarred war veterans. Osler and a colleague gave a woman clear new skin with radiation doses that proved fatal. It was during this experimentation that Osler discovered the power of hot volcanic matter — lava. "What we are doing," he explains, "is extracting heat from the center of the earth and converting it into useful power." "Then what you're saying is, you've accomplished — perpetual motion!" understands Fred. "That is quite correct," says Osler. "You see, although I have succeeded in completing the most sought-after dream since time immemorial, I have to keep it a closed secret between myself and my creatures. I am master of my own isle!" Fred brings up

the impending bomb run, but the Navy has bombed before and the installation is safe.

Mona has heard there are visitors and enters, impressed by Jerrie's beauty. Osler gently sends Mona away. Mona had assisted Osler years ago until some lava badly disfigured her face. From the women, Osler drains Character X — the genetic element that determines appearance — and transfers it to Mona. Temporarily, the women's faces reflect her disfigurements. Since Mona's genes are so void of character, Osler ads animal cells. The women revert to normal — but suffer permanent amnesia; "Do not feel sorry for my little specimens," says Osler, "because in a few days they will be able to regrow their character cells again and be as normal as before. It's very convenient because that way they can be used over and over again." Jerrie is taken to the women's isolation quarters while Fred and Sammy are placed in the custody of the guards and punished for causing the death of Egore.

Abused by the guards, Fred and Sammy are caged alongside the demons. Made to wear Mona's finest dress, Jerrie has to endure the slimy hospitality of Osler. Lonely, despite his professed love for Mona, Osler is willing to make her queen of the island. If Jerrie refuses to submit, warns Osler, "then I have only one alternative — to utilize your beauty to further the experiments on my wife." "A she demon?" asks frightened Jerrie. Mona watches them from behind a door. When Osler loses control, Jerrie crowns him with a champagne bottle. She finds her way out of the complex as Osler summons the guards. Jerrie joins Fred and Sammy. Fred urges her to hide in the jungle.

While evading the guards and one of the stray demons, Jerrie runs into Mona. After the accident, Osler had all mirrors on the island destroyed. Jerrie has a compact one Mona can use. Mona gives Jerrie the key to the cage. On the other side of the island is a rowboat.

Jerrie frees Fred and Sammy, but Osler personally thwarts their escape. "I just remembered. I have some important work tomorrow in the laboratory."

Fred and Sammy are caged in the lab while Jerrie is strapped to the treatment table. "For the last time," Osler tells her, "I give you an opportunity to change your mind on the basis of our discussion last night." Fred and Sammy hear the sound of planes. The bombing run starts, but Osler is unworried. Mona openly rebels, admitting she supplied the key, "Because of what you have done to me!" The volcano threatens to erupt. Panicked Osler wrestles with a valve below a pipe that breaks, spewing lava all over him. Fred and Sammy work loose the cage door and free Sammy. A guard rushes downstairs and is shot by the Luger Mona holds — intended for Osler if necessary. Mona refuses to escape because her place is with her husband. "But why? asks Jerrie. "Why?" asks anguished Mona, reaching for the strip of gauze across her eyes. "Would you go — if you looked like — this?" Ripping the bandage away, Mona bares part of her charred face. Bowing to her tears, Mona returns to the lab amid flames and falling rafters.

A piece of toppling debris pins Sammy until Jerrie and Fred pull him free. A wall behind them collapses and beyond flows a lava stream. "Let's blow this crazy firetrap!" yells Sammy. Jerrie, Fred and Sammy flee through a tunnel, but find one exit blocked by smoke and lava. On the expansive floor of a volcanic crater, they are shot at by guards. Fred shoots one. A sniper atop the rim takes air, but Fred shoots him between the eyes. Another guard is buried under a deluge of lava.

Jerrie, Fred and Sammy finally make it to the beach. Will all this destruction, the entire Naval fleet should be coming. In the rowboat, they set sail for home.

How the castaways of *She Demons* reached the island and the fact it was so close to civilization read like the premise of "Gilligan's Island". Fred was a semi-stolid fusion of the Skipper and the Professor. Jerrie embodied

Egore and Fred engage in battle in SHE DEMONS.

Egore is clawed to death in SHE DEMONS.

Dr. Osler prepares to give Jerrie's face to Mona in SHE DEMONS.

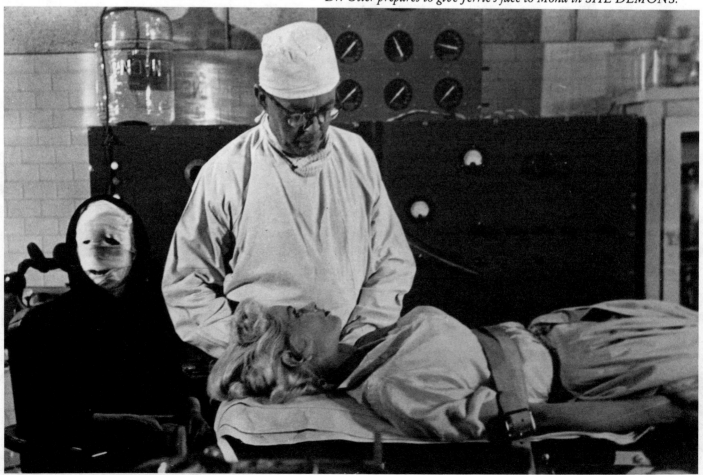

the glamour of movie star Ginger Grant and upper-crust excesses of Mr. and Mrs. Thurston Howell. Sammy was comic relief, only much smarter and more dependable than the most inept survivor of the "S.S. Minnow". Kris Kamana must have been sailing in the wrong ocean — this was the Atlantic but Kris was *Hawaiian*!

She Demons, like *Frankenstein's Daughter*, was morbidly fixated with female deformity. Osler was one of those overly devoted spouse (or father) medics who would do anything to cure an afflicted loved one. Most such stories are about disfigurement. Rather than use surgery, Osler scrambled genes, giving the she demons two kinds of grotesquery. The results were nearly as awful as his obsessive adherence to a practice even *he* knew was limited (we never saw what the gene swaps did to Mona). The she demons were only a lure for monster fans. After killing Egore, they were written out of the plot almost completely. It didn't matter to these Krauts that the war had ended twelve years earlier. Of course, where they were, sadism was their only fun. Osler not only devised exotic cruelties, but developed an amazing advance in the field of energy. The cause of Mona's woe, its backwash was also his retribution.

The post-*Giant* Cunha films gave their characters many unpleasant traits, but some of the lines were funny. After the hurricane, Jerrie petulantly asked, "Where's my powder blue cashmere shortie?" Sammy, a pseudo-hip Chinaman, told a dumb chow mien restaurant joke ("They load the noodles with spaghetti to make 'em stretch"). As to how she reached the island, Jerrie told Egore, "I swooshed in on a dry martini." When Sammy asked if *they* figured in Osler's plans, wincing Fred replied, "Who'd want a wife with our face?"

The she demon makeup was by Carlie Taylor, but had the gloppy style of Harry Thomas, showing Thomas' proclivity for bulging eyes. Genuinely horrific was Mona's death's-head countenance, making the part that showed similar to the skull mask worn by the Crimson Ghost.

Nicholas Carras was one of the true genius composers of exploitation, involving his music so deeply in a situation that the visuals almost appeared to be made to compliment *his* material. Such was not the case, naturally, but Carras scores never slouched even when plain music or none was justified. The *She Demons* theme boomed with brassy nightclub raciness and as it tapered off during the first stock footage wave, introduced the hurricane almost metaphysically. The dance of the She Demons was hilarious because a few of the "native girls" were *blonde*, lending wonder about the mating practices on Portanais, and the only on-screen members of the Diana Nellis Dancers who were musicians were bongo players!

A top pinup girl before playing Sheena, Irish McCalla never had any screen roles as memorable as Jerrie since her other parts were mostly constricted supporting bits. Tod Griffin was like a Fifties version of Herschel Lewis actor William Kerwin. Rudolph Anders and Gene Roth dripped evil like flowers shedding dew, Roth a bellicose bull, Anders a debauched sophisticate. *She Demons* was the last notable credit of ex-Charlie Chan son Victor Sen Yung before settling into the "Bonanza" character of Hop Sing. One of the lesser mysteries of the universe — though its answer may be pleasing since she had a pleasant voice — is what Leni Tana looked like under Mona's bandages) and it wasn't always Tana: Cunha's wife Kathryn did the shock close-up because Tana wouldn't wear the makeup).

Richard Cunha and Arthur Jacobs broke up after *She Demons* with Jacobs becoming Vice President of Production and Distribution for the Wrather Corporation. Several writers have mistaken Jacobs for the late Athur *P.* Jacobs, mogul of the Planet of the Apes series. Rhino Home Video included *She Demons* in its "Midnight Madness" collection of schlockers hosted by Elvira but credited the wrong Tod — saying its hero was Tod Andrews of *From Hell It Came!* (they didn't dare call Irish "English" McCalla).

133

ATTACK OF THE FIFTY FOOT WOMAN

Allied Artists, 1958

Executive Producer-	
Cinematography	Jacques Marquette
Producer	Bernard Woolner
Director	Nathan Hertz *aka Juran*
Screenplay	Mark Hanna
Film Editor	Edward Mann
Music	Ronald Stein
Sound	Phil Mitchell
Assistant Director	Ken Walters
Makeup	Carlie Taylor
Props	Richard M. Rubin

A Woolner Brothers Production
Running time: 66 minutes

Cast: Allison Hayes (Nancy Archer), William Hudson (Harry Archer), Yvette Vickers (Honey Parker), Roy Gordon (Dr. Cushing), Ken Terrell (Jessup Stout), George Douglas (Sheriff Dubbitt), Frank Chase (Charlie), Otto Waldis (Dr. Van Loeb), Mike Ross (Tony), Eileen Stevens (Nurse), Dale Tate (TV commentator), Tom Jackson (Prospector)

If the qualities of a certain type of male monsters are adaptable to both sexes, female counterparts will surely follow. Some of these monsters would make beautiful couples: Count Dracula and Carmilla, the Gill-Man and the She Creature, the Fly and the Wasp Woman, the Colossal Man and the Fifty Foot Woman. Genetically, the only "perfect" children to come from these unions would probably be the offspring of Glenn Manning and Nancy Archer — monsters only because of size.

Produced by Bernard Woolner, whose Roger Corman-directed *Swamp Women* (1956) and *Teenage Doll* (1957) are Genre Switch crime favorites, *Attack of the Fifty Foot Woman* was written by *Amazing Colossal Man* coauthor Mark Hanna for Jacques Marquette, the executive producer of this, and Nathan Juran, directing as Nathan Hertz again. Out of *The Amazing Colossal Man* came another mocking TV commentator, another team of concerned doctors, another scared drunk and another bald male giant, who existed to bring about the dimensions of the first Glenn Manning with tits. She was *The Astounding Giant Woman* until the title sounded too derivative of AIP's *The Astounding She Monster*. But otherwise there was no doubt that Allied Artists was encroaching on Bert I. Gordon brobignania since the writer, producer and director of Allied's earlier release, *The Cyclops*, had decided to make movies for American-International.

Attack of the Fifty Foot Woman and Roger Corman's *War of the Satellites* played their shared engagements during the International Geophysical Year, the heyday of Sputnik. Greater promotion was spent on the Corman film because it was a more concerted capitalization on a subject *Fifty Foot Woman* dealt with only to explain the presence of the giant man heroine Nancy Archer so closely encountered. Sputnikmania in film was almost as short-lived as the Calypso movie fad of 1957, but it ran hot and with *War of the Satellites* and *Attack of the Fifty Foot Woman*, Allied managed to distribute the only Dual Show on this topic, though every ad reference to satellites was drawn from Corman's space adventure.

What *Fifty Foot Woman* was really selling was the first sex monster in the large economy size. *War of the Satellites* is now a hopelessly dated, poor to so-so Roger Corman film. *Fifty Foot Woman* is timelessly unbelievable, enjoyed for that unbelievability, the erotic appeal of Allison Hayes and for a few positive values *other* than its star.

People in the Bering Sea, Cairo and Auckland report a mysterious red object in the sky. A TV commentator referring to a globe estimates it is heading northward. "Judging from the timetable of these reports, the stranger from space should be over our California desert in a matter of minutes." Speeding down Route Sixty-Six, troubled heiress Nancy Archer swerves her convertible as a tremendous alien satellite lands in the middle of the road. Nancy jumps out of the car, clutching her precious Star of India pendant, which the hand of a giant spaceman seems to be reaching for. Nancy runs away, shouting, "Harry!"

In Tony's bar, Nancy's husband, Harry, and mistress Honey Parker, a guest of the local hotel, share a cozy booth. Harry regrets reconciling with Nancy after a brief separation because community property law keeps him from touching her fortune. She had been treated for alcoholism at a private sanitarium. Outside, hysterical Nancy is spotted by Deputy Charlie, who calls for Sheriff Dubbitt, who thinks Nancy is drunk and needs black coffee. Sent to get Harry, Charlie is bribed by Harry into saying Harry took a cab home. To humor Nancy, Dubbitt and Charlie take her back to Sixty-Six, finding only her car. They conduct a token search of the immediate surroundings. Dubbitt believes Nancy ran into some desert tramp who wanted the diamond. Taken aback, Nancy roars off for home.

At her mansion, Nancy is greeted by devoted butler, Jessup Stout. Nancy heads for the bar as Harry gets up from the couch where he has been lounging and tells Jess to leave the room. Nancy sticks up for Jess. "Why don't you marry Jess and hire me as the butler?" Harry acerbically asks. Nancy left the bar because she had seen him fooling around with Honey. "Why did I ever take you back?" cries Nancy. "Why? Why? *Why?*" "Why did you, Nancy?" asks Harry. "Because I love you," Nancy answers. She tells Harry about the giant and he listens

135

William Hudson in ATTACK OF THE FIFTY FOOT WOMAN (1958).

Nancy (Allison Hayes) resist's Harry's (William Hudson) two-timing in ATTACK OF THE FIFTY FOOT WOMAN.

with contained skepticism. Solicitously, Harry tucks Nancy into bed and pockets the diamond.

Back at Tony's, Harry catches Honey dancing with Charlie, who told her the giant story. Harry shows Honey the diamond — which will be hers if she plays her cards right. Already on to Nancy's fragile state, Honey says, "She's on the brink and you know it. All she needs is a little help. Play the husband right up to the end; once she's in the booby hatch, throw the key away. That'll put *you* in the driver's seat." Planting a hot kiss on his lips, Honey tells Harry," You'd make a wild driver, Harry . . . with fifty million bucks!"

Harry summons Nancy's physician, Dr. Cushing, who fears that further stress may kill Nancy. Cushing leaves Jess some pills Nancy is to take and leaves. In an ugly mood because she knows where Harry spent the night, Nancy asks, "What did he say? Does he think I'm crazy?" "Nobody thinks you're crazy, Nancy," answers lying Harry. On TV, the news commentator makes light of her ordeal. "Maybe she's found a man from out of this world, a man who could love her for herself. Come, come, now, Mrs. Archer . . . a man can ignore *one* million dollars — but *fifty!* — that's too much to ask even for the man in the moon!" Nancy shuts him up by hurling a vodka bottle at the screen. She tells Jess to get her car and his revolver. Nancy wants to find the giant and needs Harry along. "I have a strange feeling he's somewhere — waiting for me."

While Harry drives, Nancy scans the back road country for any sign of the giant or the satellite. She spots a flash of light coming from behind a hill, but nothing greets her and Harry except empty space. Suddenly, Nancy sees the satellite. Harry tries to stop her as she joyously touches one side of the sphere. The giant emerges and grabs Nancy. Harry fires the gun at it and races home to pack. Suspicious Jess tries to halt Harry's fast exit in a sprawling fight down the stairs to the foyer. Harry brains Jess with a bottle. Jess crawls to a phone and calls Dubbitt.

Harry wakes up Honey in her fleabag room, rushing her into getting dressed without time to explain what he saw. Charlie and the desk clerk block them at the door. Officiously, Charlie turns down another bribe bill and takes Harry and Honey in. They are kept at Dubbitt's office while Dubbitt conducts a search for Nancy. Over the phone, Charlie hears that Nancy has been found lying unconscious on the roof of her pool hall. Cushing, Dubbitt and a nurse are at the mansion. Cushing keeps Harry from going upstairs because there is a possibility Nancy may be contaminated. Dubbitt is concerned about the missing Star of India and where Harry had taken Nancy. Honey says Harry spent the whole night with her. Only if and when Nancy regains consciousness will she be able to corroborate Jess. Honey overhears Cushing tell the nurse how much medication from a bottle Nancy should receive. Honey passes this on to Harry before returning to town.

While the nurse is asleep, Harry prepares an overdose. The nurse snaps on the bedroom light. Nancy is now a giant. The nurse's screams bring Cushing, who declares, "Astounding growth!"

Cushing consults with a colleague, Dr. Heinrich Von Loeb. The delivery man who brings medical supplies reviews an odd manifest: "Meat hooks — four lengths of chain — twenty gallons of plasma — *and an elephant syringe?*" Van Loeb attributes Nancy's pituitary derangement to radiation from the strange scratches on her throat. Surgery may help. Since Harry's consent is needed and he overhears this, he lays low with Honey. In the garden, Dubbit and Charlie discover a huge footprint. "Whatever it is," opines Dubbit, "it wasn't made by a Japanese gardener." Jess joins Dubbitt and Charlie with a tray of refreshments and they find more prints. Charlie is sent into town to get a riot gun, some flashlights and a box of grenades. Dubbitt and Jess trail the print in Nancy's station wagon.

Near the satellite, Dubbitt and Jess pick up Jess' fire revolver. Warily, they approach the satellite's vapor-spewing entrance. Inside, their distorted faces play across large glass globes. Dubbitt freezes when Jess puts a hand on his shoulder to show him the Star of India draped across one. "Mrs. Archer was right!" exclaims Dubbitt. "The thing *was* after her diamond!" "Diamonds everywhere . . . ," observes Jess. "Different colors. Must

be used to power this thing in some way." Before he and Dubbitt can take Nancy's, they look up to see the giant and carefully back away toward the entrance, fleeing to the station wagon. Its left rear wheel bogs down in the soft dirt. Dubbitt fires his pistol and riot gun at the giant, lobbing the grenade. Only mildly fazed, the giant picks up the wagon with one hand as Dubbitt and Jess hide behind a tree and throws it to the ground. The giant returns to the satellite. Dubbitt and Jess watch it vanish into the far horizon. Dubbitt tries to call Charlie over the wrecked wagon's radio, but communications are out. He and Jess have a long walk.

Cushing and Van Loeb have sedated Nancy and discuss her case in the estate garden. Cushing regrets having talked Nancy into going back to Harry, citing her erratic health. "A very sad case," pontificates Van Loeb. "A case not infrequent in this supersonic age we live in. He adds, "When women reach maturity, mother nature sometimes overworks their frustrations to the point of irrationalism . . . like a middle aged man of our age who finds himself looking longingly at a girl in her early twenties." Suddenly, the echoing voice of Nancy shrieks, "*Ha-a-r-r-r-r-y!*" While Cushing tries to pacify Nancy, the nurse phones Charlie at the Sheriff's office to get Harry. At Tony's, he tell Harry there is an emergency at home, but Harry and Honey are drunkenly indifferent.

Nancy breaks out of her chains. Cushing tries to

137

Nancy is approached by the hand of a giant alien in ATTACK OF THE FIFTY FOOT WOMAN.

call the police in Baker as Nancy bursts through the roof and bellows, "I know where my husband is! He's with that woman! *I'll find him!*" Charlie picks up Dubbitt and Jess on the highway. At the demolished house, they learn what has happened to Nancy. Everyone races for town in the police car. Out in the desert, an old prospector fed up with uranium tells his burro how things used to be better. As he swigs from a bottle, he sees giant Nancy striding by and turns tail.

Approaching a high-tension tower on the edge of town, Nancy grabs it, causing a momentary blackout in the bar. A young couple who exit see Nancy while kissing in the front seat of their car and run away to flag down Dubbitt. People on the street scatter as Nancy heads for the hotel and peers into the window of Honey's room. Her hand breaks through the glass and knocks over the bed as it feels around. "She'll tear up the whole town 'til she finds Harry!" cries Cushing. "Yeah — then she'll tear up Harry!" fears Charlie. Dubbitt sends him into the bar to get Harry so Nancy can be drawn away from town. As Nancy shouts, "*Ha-a-a-r-r-r-ry!*", Honey tells him, "Sounds like somebody's calling your name." Charlie enters as Nancy reaches inside. Charlie is reluctant to shoot. Seizing his gun, Harry opens fire. Nancy rips off the roof as hysterical Honey dives under a table and falling debris crushes her. Nancy lifts Harry aloft.

Dubbitt goes for his spare riot gun. "You're not going to use that?!" protests Cushing. "What'ya want me to do?" retorts Dubbitt, "Put salt on her tail?" As Nancy nears the electrical tower, he shoots a condenser. A blast of showering sparks tumbles Nancy, killing Harry too. Cushing examines Harry's body and intones, "She finally got Harry all to herself."

The plot of *Fifty Foot Woman* seemed like a send-up of aliens and radiation monsters in a nightmare Nancy might have dreamed had all of this not been actually happening. The Star of India evidently was made of some substance from the space giant's world and through some form of ESP, he knew Nancy was decorated by the propulsion element. Considering the proportions of the satellite, this minuscule piece of glass had to be pretty potent. At a mere thirty feet, the giant was smaller than the height Nancy would later attain. The unbelievability of his existence enabled Harry to build an insanity case against Nancy until the Giant became her benefactor. The Star of India fulfilled his want and his incidental contamination brought Nancy size and might commensurate with the rage she would later unleash. To bring Nancy home, the Giant must have had some kind of intuitive knowledge about where.

As if to grant Dubbitt and Jess the privilege of learning what became of the diamond, the Giant left a trail of humongous bread crumbs. Could he alter his size to *become* a giant only when it suited his purposes or did he manage to miniaturize the satellite so Dubbitt and Jess wouldn't be swallowed up by its vastness and miss seeing the jewel collection? Without Jess' faint conjecture, the theft of the Star wouldn't have led anywhere. If the Giant didn't want the diamond, he would've only been interested in Nancy — and once her got her, he wouldn't have relinquished her.

The first thing we saw of giant Nancy was her hand, the prop being the only way "she" could appear in the same shots with live actors. The bedroom was the only place where Cushing and Van Loeb could treat Nancy and since few houses have boudoirs the size of an entire wing, a small room meant a cheap, simple set remarkably free of any damage the expansion of its occupant should have caused. Concealment of the whole Nancy until she couldn't stand her stir craziness any more was well-timed for shock impact. The medical requisition didn't include hair dye or cloth, yet the changed Nancy was blonde and wore a white skirt and matching halter top. In the original script, Harry killed Nancy by shooting her in the face with Charlie's gun. Since the "puny" Space Giant could withstand heavier artillery, the electrical alternative was better.

Fifty Foot Woman's insistence on two giants effectively painted Mark Hanna into a corner. To rationalize the Space Giant, he had to bring in the diamond and to create a catalyst for Nancy's growth, he picked radiation from a living carrier — the Giant being its source. In a plainer mutation story, Harry could have tried to kill Nancy by leaving her in a nuclear testing area or she could have somehow found her way there herself. But without the footage of a secondary monster, how could the running time have been used unless the adultery plot was lengthened or Nancy was allowed to rampage sooner?

Worse than any Bert Gordon illusions was the Mesozoic quality of superimposition. However, since the effects were set mainly at night, the iridescence given off by the Space Giant and Nancy had a ghostly sort of attention pull. It lessened slightly the weak, worn-out appearance of Mike Ross, who played both the Giant and Tony, and showed off Allison Hayes' great body rather lyrically as Nancy appeared from afar. For Nancy's death pose, an enlarged photograph of Hayes lying on one side with her head propped against her outstretched right arm was positioned perpendicular to the street. Never before was a monster mock-up the two-dimensional likeness of an actual person.

With better crafting of surface, the prop hand that was both Nancy's (without hair) and the Space Giant's (with hair) might have worked since the fingers moved believably. They were dexterous enough to slip around the edge of the station wagon's roof, but real lifting would have required leverage. The easiest solution was to pick *everything* up via optical shifting of the frame. The wagon was a new Plymouth — but an old Chevy hit the ground. Substitute autos of inconsistent makes and models are often demolished by cheapie filmmakers so the undamaged originals can only be rented (some of

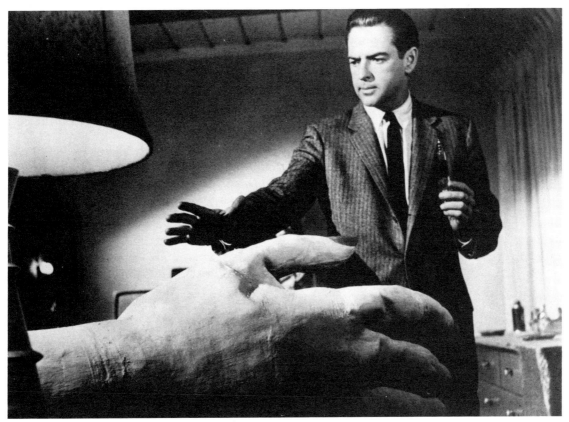

Fifty-foot tall Nancy Archer reaches for her unfaithful, two-timing husband in
ATTACK OF THE FIFTY FOOT WOMAN.

the crummier T.V. action shows that *were* given autos . . . mostly vehicles driven by the bad guys . . . and once you saw and old car, you *knew* what would happen). The car that Dubbitt and Jess returned to was the Plymouth, lying wastefully smashed-up.

An Oscar winner for the art direction of *How Green Was My Valley* (1941), Nathan Juran designed the satellite as a funhouse in Hell with Dubbit and Jess adding to the atmosphere their own distorted faces. The globes and mist were like things in alchemy and a persistent bleeping was taken from the Plutonium apparatus of *The Amazing Colossal Man*.

Nancy Archer must have lived very near Mystery Mountain. The protracted desert shown behind the credits was the *Brain from Planet Arous* scene of John and Sally Fallon driving there in the same station wagon of *this* movie.

Ronald Stein composed a woeful, ethereal theme. Part of it was used in the flooding scene of Roger Corman's *The Terror* (1963). When Corman bought the 1959 Russian space opera *La Planet Bura (The Storm Planet)*, he had Curtis Harrington build a film around it called *Voyage to the Prehistoric Planet* (1966). Peter Bogdanovich was hired to make another film with the footage, *Voyage to the Planet of Prehistoric Women* (1968). Both contained excerpts from the *Fifty Foot Woman* music. The film's sleazy jukebox tune became the theme of *Horrible Honeys* (1988), a compilation of

Female Horror-Girl Gang movie scenes. The trailer for *Attack of the Fifty Foot Woman* was prominently featured.

Fifty Foot Woman left the category of Just Bad when Allison Hayes began to accrue her large following, followed by subsidiary respect for the performances of William Hudson and Yvette Vickers, who managed to make herself a Cult Queen for only two films: *Fifty Foot Woman* and *Attack of the Giant Leeches*. Poignancy was never a common trait in Allison's work, but as Nancy she gave it a good try. At the peak of her beauty, she was so overpoweringly desirable, one wondered why Harry strayed. Vickers was the same person in *Giant Leeches* as she was in *Fifty Foot Woman* — a minxy parcel hot for good times that never stop.

For Allison Hayes, *Attack of the Fifty Foot Woman* was the crest of a career that slid into a succession of minor roles. She found a little distinction on TV. Several times, Hayes appeared on "Bat Masterson" as old flame Ellie Winters. She was the nightclub hostess, Chloe, on "Acapulco" and was an early regular on "General Hospital" as Priscilla Longworth. Throughout the late sixties and early seventies, there were rumors of a proposed *Fifty Foot Woman* sequel.

Hayes kept her good looks, but her career ended tragically from the damage of an incompetent physician's wrongly prescribed drug — a tragedy almost forewarned by Harry's murder attempt on Nancy. Hayes was forced to retire around 1969. In her isolated years as a patient of the Scripps Clinic in La Jolla, California, she became intimate with actor-writer, Barry Brown, who seemed to collect personal misfortune and be associated with others fated for unhappy ends, like his murdered drama coach Laurence Merrick. A horror fan who wrote for various cinema magazines, Brown had received acclaim for his roles in *Bad Company* (1972) and *Daisy Miller* (1974), but alcoholism ruined his rising career. Brown's decline corresponded with the loss of people he respected, such as Bruno Ve Sota. When Allison died of blood poisoning in 1977, his depression intensified. That year, Piper Laurie starred in Curtis Harrington's confused, disjointed fifties nostalgia thriller *Ruby*. Its amusing drive-in footage exhumed some of the livelier moments from *Fifty Foot Woman* and their mention in the closing credits acknowledged Allison Hayes as the star. Though Brown remained active as a performer, he committed suicide in 1978 of a self-inflicted gunshot wound.

Sometime in the early eighties, a *Fifty Foot Woman* follow-up of sorts was produced, *Attack of the Thirty Foot Centerfold*. Its Allison Hayes equivalent was yet another Player who died too soon: Angela Ames. A drug overdose, her 1988 death was also medically related.

WAR OF THE COLOSSAL BEAST

American-International, 1958
Released in England as *The Terror Strikes*

Executive Producers	James H. Nicholson
	Samuel Z. Arkoff
Producer-Director-Story-	
Special Effects	Bert I. Gordon
Screenplay	George Worthing Yates
Assistant Producer	Henry Schrage
Cinematography	Jack Marta
Editorial Supervision	Ronald Sinclair
Music	Albert Glasser
Art Director	Walter Keller
Set Decorator	Maury Hoffman
Assistant Special Effects	Flora Gordon
Assistant Film Editor	Paul Wittenberg
Sound Effects Editor	Josef Von Stroheim
Sound Mixer	Benny Winkler
Special Makeup	Jack J. Young
Script Supervisor	Judy Hart
Production Manager-	
First Assistant Director	H. E. Mendelson
Second Assistant Director	John. W. Rogers
Property Master	Walter Broadfoot
Chief Set Electrician	Babe Stafford

A Carmel Production / Color Sequence
Running time: 68 minutes

Cast: Sally Fraser (Joyce Manning), Roger Pace (Maj. Baird), Dean Parkin (Col. Glenn Manning), Russ Bender (Dr. Carmichael), Charles Stewart (Capt. Harris), George Becwar (John Swanson), Robert Hernandez (Miguel), Rico Alaniz (Sgt. Luis Murillo), George Alexander (Army Officer), George Navarro (Mexican Doctor), John McNamara (Neurologist), Bob Garnett (Pentagon Correspondent), Howard Wright (Medical Corps. Officer), Roy Gordon (Mayor), George Milan (Gen. Nelson), Warren Frost (Switchboard Operator), Bill Giorgio (Bus Driver), Loretta Nicholson (Joan), June Jocelyn (Mrs. Edwards), Jack Kosslyn (Newscaster), Stan Chambers (TV Announcer), Raymond Winston, June Burt, Mary Hennessy, Hal Torey, Rod Dana

(Above) Dean Parkin plays the deformed gargantuan in WAR OF THE COLOSSAL BEAST (1958).

Mark informs Joyce about Glenn's island exile in WAR OF THE COLOSSAL BEAST.

142

War of the Colossal Beast was an excuse to show a fully bestial and degenerated Glenn Manning who, up to the syringe impaling of Dr. Coulter, was more of a dangerous child than a wild animal. Glenn was one monster the *Army* created, first by exposing him to Plutonium, then by pushing him off the Boulder Dam. The Beast Glenn story posed continuity problems. In the absence of Glenn Langan, Bert Gordon needed a stand-in with the same body type. As the Colossal Man had sustained gross mutilations from the dam fall, their facial differences could be disguised. However, flashbacks from *The Amazing Colossal Man* featured Cathy Downs as Carol Forest. With Downs unavailable too, Gordon could either cut Down's shots and redo them with a new actress or he could invent a new heroine for *Colossal Beast*.

Duncan Parkin of *The Cyclops*, now known as Dean, solved the first problem. Glenn Langan was born in 1917 and Parkin in 1930, but with special makeup courtesy of *Cyclops* creator Jack Young, young Parkin could easily get by as a Langan twin. After Glenn Manning's "official" death, Carol presumably married Dr. Paul Lindstrom and settled in his home in Rochester, New York. In *Colossal man*, she told him that Glenn was without kin. *War of the Colossal Beast* contrived as a new worrier for his welfare a previously unknown sister, Joyce. Anyone who paid close attention to the Colossal Man plots would probably wonder where Joyce had been during the early

days of Glenn's giantism. The flashbacks reminded us of Carol. With developments in *Colossal Beast* pointing to the return of her ex-fiancee, wouldn't she be interested in aiding his capture and rehabilitation? And what about Paul, the surviving half of Glenn's previous attending physicians?

A stakebed truck races madly through open Mexican back country. Its terrified young driver, Miguel, keeps looking back to see what it is he is running from. The truck skids into a shallow stream. Miguel jumps out, screaming as he half-runs, half-crawls away. In sleepy Guavos, American gun club owner, John Swanson, reports the missing truck to local police sergeant Luis Murillo. Swanson bought food in Calexico for the season opening of his club. Car trouble delayed him in San Felipe, where he hired Miguel to deliver the groceries. That was yesterday. Lying in the village hospital in deep shock Miguel is identified by Swanson, who roughly demands to know where his truck is. Miguel tries to say something to Luis, but cannot.

In the club station wagon, Swanson and Luis drive to where the truck vanished. Its tire marks just seemed to stop in the mud — as if lifted straight up. "Someone steals, I try to catch the thief and put him in jail, just like it says in the book," Luis tells Swanson. "But about this, *señor*, I don't know. The book doesn't say anything about a thing like this!"

Guesting at the Beverly Hilton Hotel in Los

Angeles, Joyce Manning hears a TV story about the truck. She places a call to Guavos to contact Swanson. In Joyce's suite, he rails at the insurance people for refusing to honor his theft claim. Maj. Mark Baird of the Army calls. Mark asks Swanson if he had seen any "animal" tracks. More to the point, Joyce inquires if Swanson had seen the tracks of "a very big man". Joyce thinks that Glenn survived Boulder Dam and somehow made his way down to the Gulf of California. Possibly, he took the truck. Before leaving, Swanson mentions Miguel. The Army had given up on Glenn some time ago. Mark led the search for his body. "The medical authorities all agree," he tells Joyce. "No man, no matter what his size, could take those two bazooka charges and a drop of over seven hundred feet and come through it alive."

Unconvinced, Joyce sees Miguel and sits vigil by his bedside. Miguel stirs, faintly muttering a word. He sits up abruptly, screaming, "Hombron! Hombron!" "It's a big fellow," Luis translates, "like an ogre in a story. A monster . . . a giant man. He must be dreaming." Mark arrives in Guavos with Dr. Carmichael, a radiologist. Mark is still skeptical of Joyce's ideas until one of one of Glenn's huge footprints is found in the river mud. They trail off in the direction of an uninhabited mountain range. Where the ground is too hard for prints to show, the group finds the wreckage of another truck. A small rockslide occurs.

Joyce wants to find Glenn before the Mexican military does. She and Mark return to the hills and find the strewn debris of other trucks. Mark finds a rifle bent out of shape and a partially empty box of tin cans. Glenn has been raiding trucks for food. Joyce spots Swanson's truck with Glenn's unmistakable thumbprint on one fender. She and Mark hear loud rumbling and see disfigured Glenn, holding a new truck. Disappointed to find no food, he throws it aside.

Joyce write ad copy for a living. She speaks of, ". . . those tired old adjectives: 'Amazing', 'Colossal'. You know what they mean to me mow, don't you? Glenn. A colossal freak, Major, but he's my brother." Mark, Carmichael and Luis load a delivery van with chloral-hydrate drugged bread so they can flush out famished Glenn. He takes the bait and chases them. Mark, Carmichael and Luis hide behind a boulder as Glenn picks up the van and devours the bread loaves. He sees the men and tries to catch them until the drug takes effect.

Once Glenn is placed in U.S. Army custody, authorities are not sure what to do with him. A Washington congressman queried by a correspondent says this is a matter for the Department of Medical Research. That bureau takes it up with Health and Welfare. Congress finds itself re-saddled with the problems until it is dumped in Mark's lap. The transport flying Glenn is circling Los Angeles International Airport. The Mayor will let it land only for fuel and orders it to take off. But to where? Mark notices an unused hangar.

Tied down in the hangar, Glenn fails to recognize anyone. When Carmichael addresses him as "Colonel Manning", Glenn recalls the Plutonium blast, his awakening in the Army hospital, his anguish, the injection of sulfa-hydrol, Las Vegas and Boulder Dam. Glenn struggles against the ropes binding him and breaks free. Distraught Joyce has to be escorted back to her hotel. Fighter jets are alerted. Glenn rampages through the airport until Mark brings him down with tear gas.

Reinforced chains replace the ropes. Glenn undergoes neurological examination. His scars are attributed to the impact of falling on rocks in the river. "The big question now is his mind," states Carmichael. "He may be suffering from amnesia, shell shock, loss of memory — whatever you want to call it. In this case, we have techniques now that will bring him out of it. On the other hand, if his brain has suffered any injury , he'll be a psychopathic case and a menace until he dies." Glenn is hooked up to an ECG machine for an association test. Projected on the hangar ceiling are slides that show the college Glenn graduated from, the ship that brought him back from Korea and his face. "Does this man mean anything to you?" cries Carmichael as Glenn goes into a tortured howling fit. Joyce desperately volunteers questions concerning Glenn's boyhood, but they do not take.

Glenn will be flown to small distant island where food will be parachuted down to him and the Navy will make periodic inspection visits. Mark wants Joyce to believe this is for the best. Glenn possesses an inkling of his fate and feigns sleep until Carmichael shows alarm and flashes a hangar office flashlight upon him. Mark receives a phone call telling him Glenn has escaped. Carmichael is dead.

The hunt for Glenn focuses on Griffith Park. Mark heads up field operations. Searchlights are trained on the Griffith observatory. A cop learns from a bus driver that some kids from Westmont High are in the observatory and the driver is warned about Glenn. All the kids hurry to the bus except for Arthur and Laurie, who chat obliviously where they can see the lights. Laurie's mom, Mrs. Edwards, has come to pick Laurie up herself and brought the coat she had forgotten. Finally heeding their teacher's calls, Arthur and Laurie are chided by her when Glenn appears. He studies some high-tension wires, daring to touch one that sparks. Glenn grabs the bus, holding it above his head in the glare of the searchlights. The trapped kids scream hysterically.

Moved by Mrs. Edward's grief, Joyce hurries to the observatory in a stolen jeep. She begs Glenn to free his hostages. Delayed memory return causes him to mutter, "Joyce", and he complies reaching out to Joyce. Deciding to end his life, Glenn seizes the power lines and disintegrates.

In a rural region full of uneducated and superstitious people, Glenn had the scare impact of some immense ghost to young peon Miguel, whose flight had riveting import. Even when it was established that Glenn was stealing the trucks, there were still curiosity elements to nibble on: the length of time that Glenn had been hijacking and the disappearances of the other drivers. And the timing for Glenn to show his new face could not have been better — Glenn caught with a *new* truck . . . and where did *it's* driver go?

Motor vehicles were a continual motif in *Colossal Beast*. Glenn's capture was accomplished by a food sting employing a van, one of the unwieldiest of escape machines. Then there was the bus at Griffith Park, which could have carried the kids to safety if Glenn hadn't picked it up. To reach Glenn, Joyce had to swipe a jeep, something she was unaccustomed to driving. The wheels of fate moved Glenn and good things seemed to happen to him too late. He received the sulfa-hydrol shot *after* his mind deteriorated, in *Amazing Colossal Man*, and by the time his brain snapped back in the ending of this film, his face was like a Mount Rushmore visage half gone. To rid himself of his unwanted brobdignanity, Glenn turned to electrocution— the death of Nancy Archer — absorbing as the Teenage Frankenstein did a dose of color.

War of the Colossal Beast had better special effects than *Colossal Man*. Glenn was placed in more natural surroundings, Mexico allowing him to menace another country even if he kept to its remotest spots. The graveyard of trucks provided a few moments of disquiet and the interior of the hangar had a more interesting texture than the bland confines of the circus tent. Staging the Griffith Park scenes at night was helpful to erasing technical discrepancies in the matting and model work that would have been more obvious under bright light. The population of Las Vegas mattered less than the school kids, who were put in a position of real danger.

Dean Parkin gave the only true "big" performance with the exception of George Becwar as the bellicose Americano Swanson. Unbelievably, this was the same Becwar who looked and sounded so Russian in *Bride of the Monster*, now looking and sounding like William Conrad. As Joyce and Mark, Sally Fraser and Roger Pace were lightweights against the likes of Parkin, Becwar and Russ Bender. Robert Hernandez's Miguel emitted one of the most alarming male trauma shrieks ever recorded.

Attack of the Fifty Foot Woman, released a few months before, meant that others had beaten Mr. B.I.G. to the creation of a female giant, and the later-seen *The Thirty Foot Bride of Candy Rock* (1959) was not a film of his either. Compensating for these coups, Gordon would show *several* big beautiful women in *Village of the Giants* (1965). One, Joy Harmon, was larger up front than Allison Hayes or Dorothy Provine, but smaller than Anita Ekberg, the billboard behemoth come to life in *Boccaccio 70* (1963).

The Colossal Beast wages war in this scene.

EARTH VS. THE SPIDER

American-International, 1958		Costumes	Marge Corso
Alternate title *The Spider*		Hairstyles	Kay Shea
Released in Belgium as *The Vampire Spider*		Script Supervisor	Elaine Garnet
		Chief Set Electrician	Cal Maehl
Executive Producers	James H. Nicholson	Property Master	Jim Harris
	Samuel Z. Arkoff	Key Grip	Del Nodine
Producer-Director-Story-		Special Designs	Paul Blaisdell
Special Technical Effects	Bert I. Gordon		Jackie Blaisdell
Screenplay	Lazlo Gorog	Spider Handler	Jim Dannaldson
	George Worthing Yates		
Cinematography	Jack Marta	A Santa Rosa Production	
Editorial Supervisor	Ronald Sinclair	Running time: 72 minutes	
Music	Albert Glasser		
Assistant Producer	Henry Schrage	Cast: Ed Kemmer (Mr. Kingman), June Kenney (Carol Flynn), Gene Persson (Mike Simpson), Gene Roth (Sheriff Cagle), Hal Torey (Mr. Simpson), June Jocelyn (Mrs. Flynn), Mickey Finn (Sam Haskell), Sally Fraser (Helen Kingman), Troy Patterson (Joe), Skip Young (Sam), Howard Wright (Jake), Jack Kosslyn (Fraser), Bob Garnett (Pest Control Man), Shirley Falls (Switchboard Operator), Bob Tettrick (Dave), Nancy Kilgas (Dancer), George Stanley (Man in Cave), David Tomack (Line Foreman), Merritt Stone (Pete Flynn)	
Production Supervisor	Marty Moss		
Assistant Directors	Marty Moss		
	John W. Rogers		
Sound Recorder	Al Overton		
Assistant Editor	Bruce Shoengarth		
Set Designer	Walter Keller		
Set Decorator	Bill Calvert		
Assistant Technical Effects	Flora M. Gordon		
Makeup	Alan Snyder		

(Above) The spider rampages through the town of River Falls in EARTH VS. THE SPIDER (1958).

Earth vs. the Spider was Bert Gordon's own Tarantula (1955). Filmed simply as The Spider, it used that name during the release of The Fly (1958) — which it appeared with on an irony title double bill — and the Earth vs. the part of the general title came from Earth vs. the Flying Saucers (1956), another movie George Worthing Yates had been involved in the writing of. From its teenage elements to its banal small-town characters, much in The Spider provided ammunition for Mr. B.I.G.'s detractors. In close confrontation scenes, at least, the suspense outweighed the silliness and the climax sustained tension even better than the one in War of the Colossal Beast.

In his pickup, Jack Flynn drives back to River Falls, admiring a birthday bracelet for his teenaged daughter, Carol. A wirelike object smashes through the windshield and kills him. At school, Carol's boyfriend, Mike Simpson, gives her his present. Carol is worried about the disappearance of Flynn, a former drunk in the town where the Flynns once lived and where he bought the bracelet. Mike upsets Carol by implying Flynn went back to the bottle and she hands him back his gift. In Art Kingman's science class, Mike slips Carol an apology note and she sends one asking Mike to help her to look for Flynn.

Mike and Carol borrow their friend Joe's hot rod. On the road Flynn took is a thick silk strand embedded with shards of broken windshield glass that had been strung across two trees. Carol finds the bracelet box near the wreckage of Flynn's empty truck. A forbidden cave some yards away had been the source of eerie rumors. Mike discovers Flynn's tattered hat and hides it from Carol. She enters the cave with him. Her calls for Flynn loosen a dropping stalactite. Human skeletons lie about. Mike and Carol fall off a short ledge into a sticky large web. They work themselves free when they hear sounds and see a giant spider. Mike and Carol escape to the outside.

Sheriff Cagle receives a call from Mike about the spider and laughs it off. Mike and Carol show the web strand to Kingman, his wife Helen and Mike's father, owner of the local movie theater. Since Flynn is still missing, Kingman has Cagle form an armed search party and sends for a pest control team equipped with DDT. The cave is empty of visible life save a flying bat Cagle shoots down. As Kingman discusses the bloodsucking qualities of spiders, Carol screams. She and Mike have found Flynn's shrivelled, bloodless body. The spider web is in the next chamber. Disregarding Mike's warning that the spider might still be there, Cagle almost falls into the web.

The pest men spray the web before the spider returns and kills Deputy Sanders as he struggles to free himself from the entangling strands. Succumbing to the DDT, the spider falls over on its back. Carol wants to retrieve the bracelet, but the cave is still full of gas. Cagle favors boarding up the cave entrance, but Kingman wants the spider studied out in the open. How it grew is important if other giant spiders deep in the earth are ready to hatch.

Kingman has the spider displayed in the high school gym, where students of Mr. Fraser's camera club are photographing it. It will take awhile for reporters to come and a university will remove the spider for dissection tonight. To Fraser, Kingman again emphasizes the need of learning what made it so big. One of the spider's legs knock Fraser to the floor. A muscle contraction — supposedly. Carol grieves for Flynn, calling Mike at the movie theater and asking him to take her back to the cave so she can get the bracelet. Not wanting her mother to know, Carol sneaks out.

Mike persuades Joe to let him use his hot rod again. Joe and his musician pals pester Hugo the janitor into unlocking the gym door so they can rehearse for a prom up on the music stage. The drama class hears the warm-up music and makes it a real party. Affected by the vibrations of the music, the spider revives and the kids flee. Hugo alerts Kingman at his house by phone before the spider breaks out of the gym and kills him. Helen is about to take their baby to a doctor, but Kingman orders her to stay home with the infant while he hurries downtown. The spider rampages through the streets. It nearly gets Cagle until Kingman rushes him to safety in his car. All long-distance lines to Springdale are cut. Deputy Dave will go there for help on his motorcycle.

Evacuating Jake saw the spider heading for Kingman's street. Helen is feeding the baby in her kitchen when it cries at the sight of the spider looking in through a window. Snatching the baby, Helen finds herself trapped by the spider's legs until Kingman rams the spider with his car and lures it out of town.

At the spider web, Mike and Carol find an opening to another chamber and recover the lost bracelet. Jake sees the spider going back into the cave. Kingman enters Cagle's office with a shrivelled corpse and plops it down on a desk. It is Dave — who never made it to Springdale. Jake tells everyone where the spider is. Road foreman, Sam Haskell has enough dynamite to seal the cave entrance. Simpson stays at the office phone. Joe calls to say Mike and Carol never returned with his hot rod. Simpson contacts Mrs. Flynn.

Mike and Carol realize they are lost. On the wall of a dead end is scrawled in chalk, "George Weston, Lost April 9, 1902". Below that is the skeleton of an explorer who starved to death. Mike and Carol pause for a snack when they hear the spider and find their way back to the web area. Simpson and Mrs. Flynn, en route to the cave, locate Joe's parked hot rod before the cave entrance is blown up. It may take a week to rescue Mike and Carol by removing all the rock. From a flat shelf on top of the hill, a road crew can dig down. Kingman notices some power lines. A cable hooked up to two electrodes may send enough current to destroy the spider.

When Mike and Carol call for help from the blocked entrance, they are heard. They walk along a narrow ledge

Pest exterminators prepare for the spider in EARTH VS. THE SPIDER.

as the diggers penetrate a granite bed and break through. The ledge ends below the wall the spider is climbing down. Kingman throws Mike an electrode with a rubber glove tied to it. Kingman wields the other. Caught in a crackling arc, the spider falls on some impaling stalagmites. After the cave is cleared, Cagle drops lit dynamite down the hole.

No allusions to radiation was a plus for *The Spider*. The specifics of its undetermined growth cause were less important than the fear it was a prototype of any other giant spiders extant or unborn. Kingman wanted to nip speculative danger in the bud by exposing the spider to science, but placed it where Demon Rock 'n Roll could reactivate it. The rockers wanted to play loud enough to "wake the dead". Figuratively, they did. The unease caves create reaches deep into our store of primal fears partly because we associate underground entrapment with live burial. Here, the spider looked bigger, blacker, almost becoming personal in its menace of Mike and Carol — as if knowing they were responsible for its discovery. Their rescue called for more mice to enter the locked crate of a still-dangerous lion. Only when the last inch of accessibility to the surface was sealed did easy rest come.

While Gordon was filming the live spider scenes, Paul Blaisdell built the prop leg and the dummy corpse. To give the tarantula Gordon photographed a pair of disturbing feline eyes, Blaisdell made a light rubber appliance fitted over the bone area behind the spider's eight natural eyes. He and Jim Nicholson tested the appliance successfully, but Gordon thought it was *too* terrifying. For some theater lobby displays, Blaisdell made a number of large fiberglass spiders mounted on red panels with web patterns.

Gordon accomplished the cave scenes by blending set pieces with slides of the Carlsbad Caverns. Fraudulently, the credits claimed that *The Spider* had been shot on location, giving thanks to the U.S. Department of the Interior. *The Spider* was probably the most macabre of Gordon's films, though in spots the cave chills were overdressed. The dead Mr. Weston's bones were a suitable effect, suggesting an alternate doom for Mike and Carol, but the other skeletons were too near the entrance of the cave to imply death from the perils of the cave itself . . . unless these were the remains of spider victims nobody knew about. The web was put to good situational use, only it was rather small and looked like cargo netting. The prop leg was too spindly and not convincingly hairy.

As Mike's father ran a theater, Gordon couldn't help but plug *Attack of the Puppet People* and there was also ad art from *The Amazing Colossal Man* — which was itself recalled in *Puppet People*. In the scene where Joe phoned Simpson, a copy of the first issue of "Famous Monsters" was lying across Joe's lap.

Ed Kemmer should have done more horror films.

With him, fast-acting comprehension was something that raised the tension of a scene, such as when a pest control man — expecting this to be a routine job — recommended a mild dose of DDT and Kingman urged the maximum. *The Spider* was full of reminders of *Giant from the Unknown*. Sally Fraser of *Giant* was now Kemmer's "wife" and the conflicts between Kingman and Cagle were similar to the head bucking of Wayne Brooks and Sheriff Parker. One of the irreverent rockers was Skip Young, Wally of TV's "Ozzie and Harriet".

AIP jazzed up some of *The Spider*'s ad art by putting a large leering skull over the head of the spider. Some foreign art gave it a pair of silly bulging cartoon eyes fixed in the look of surprise.

Like the other Gordon, Alex, Bert became discontented with AIP. In a lawsuit, he charged that Nicholson and Arkoff had used his profits for other companies, collecting fifteen thousand for their status of executive producers. As the manifestation of an alien mind, the spider returned in color-tinted footage for *Journey to the Seventh Planet* (1961). A version of the spider made for the film was gorilly crushed under tons of rock. A regular black and white glimpse of the spider was a hallucination in *Confessions of an Opium Eater* (1962).

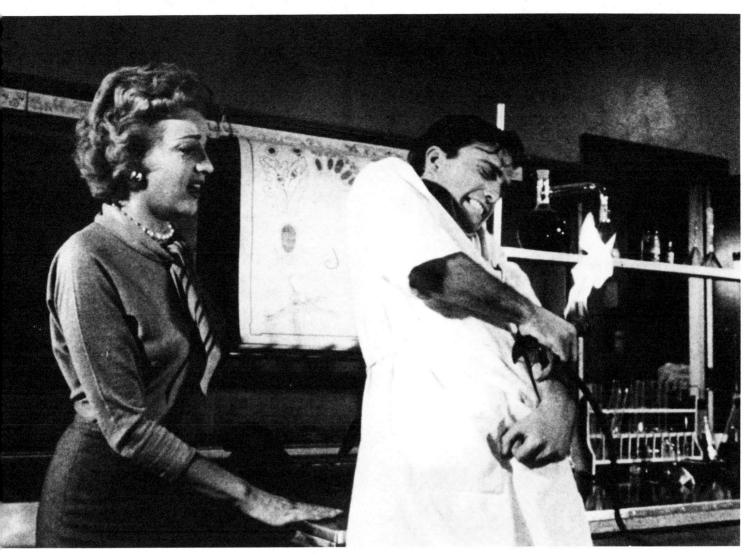

THE BRAIN EATERS

American-International, 1958

Producer	Edwin *aka Ed* Nelson
Director	Bruno Ve Sota
Screenplay	Gordon Urquhart
Associate Producer	Stanley Bickman
Cinematography	Larry Raimond
Film Editor	Carlo Lodato
Music	Tom Jonson
Art Director	Burt Schoenberg
Sound	James Fullerton
Production Manager	Amos Powell
Makeup	Alan Trumble
Wardrobe	Charles Smith
Assistant Director	Mike Murphy
Gaffer	Gene Peterson
Props	Tom Hughes
Title Design	Robert Balser

A Corinthian Production
Running time: 60 minutes

Cast: Edwin *aka Ed* Nelson (Dr. Paul Kettering), Alan Frost *aka Alan Jay Factor* (Glenn Cameron), Jack Hill (Sen. Walter K. Powers), Joanna Lee (Alice Sommers), Jody Fair (Elaine), David Hughes (Dr. Wyler), Robert Ball (Dan Walker), Greigh Phillips (Sheriff), Orville Sherman (Cameron), Leonard Nemoy *aka Nimoy* (Prof. Cole / Protector), Doug Banks (Doctor), Henry Randolph (Telegrapher), Saul Bronson (Prof. Helsington)

Once a stage, radio and television actor in Chicago, Bruno Ve Sota performed in over five hundred TV shows and directed two thousand. Moving west in 1952, Ve Sota anonymously directed much of John Parker's *Dementis* (1953), settling for actor and associate producer credits. When ex-Chicago performer Burt Kaiser produced and acted in *Female Jungle* (1956), he made sure Ve Sota shot some scenes for Roger Corman's *She Gods of Shark Reef* (1958).

Corman asked Ve Sota to make a movie for him and Ve Sota wrote a story called "The Keepers". It resembled

(Above) Paul (Ed Nelson) scares an alien parasite off his arm with a Bunsen burner as Joanna Lee looks on in THE BRAIN EATERS (1958).

Robert A. Heinlein's "The Puppet Masters" except that the intelligent parasites who attached themselves to humans in Ve Sota's tale were subterranean, not from the Saturnian moon Titan. Ve Sota assigned the screenplay job to another actor friend from Chicago, Gordon Urquhart, the star of a Ve Sota series, "Chicagoland Mystery Players". Meanwhile, Ve Sota and Ed Nelson went to Mexico to act in *Code of Silence* (1958), *aka Killer's Cage*, Mel Welles' first try at directing. Welles also wanted to film "The Keepers" — now retitled *The Brain Eaters* by AIP hoping to make it in Mexico for creative use of its locations. This didn't happen because Welles fell out with his partner Berj Hagopain, who later ended up producing the last picture Ve Sota directed, *Invasion of the Star Creatures* (1962).

"Puppet Masters" had a central male character. The hero of *Brain Eaters*, Dr. Paul Kittering, died before the story ended. Narration therefore went to second hero Glenn Cameron, son of the mayor of Riverdale, Illinois. Gordon Urquhart wanted to play Paul, but died of cancer. Roger Corman decided to use Ed Nelson and have him produce *The Brain Eaters*. Nelson lived in Pomona, the site of Riverdale.

A dark Riverdale street. Two pedestrians cross paths in a violent collision. One man drops a breaking jar and strangles the other while a small, slimy creature crawls away from the jar's fragments. Glenn and his fiancee, Elaine, have announced their engagement to her family. Driving back to town, they pause to hear a sound like thunder and see a dead animal lying on the road. Others are found in the woods near a fifty-foot metal cone. A filmed report is sent to Washington D.C. To most people, the cone is extraterrestrial. The report also mentions several murders in Riverdale. Gruff Sen. Walter K. Powers commissions Dr. Kettering and Dr. Wyler to study the cone.

Powers and his aide Dan Walker fly incognito to Riverdale. Glenn meets them at the airport. Mayor Cameron has vanished. His secretary Alice Summers helps Paul and Wyler, who examine the cone from a scaffold. Gunshots Paul fires into its open hatch dramatically ricochet. Tied to a rope, he explores a honeycomb of cyclical tunnels. Cameron is back. In his office, something keeps tormented Cameron from shooting himself. He hides the gun as Paul, Glenn and Powers enter to learn where he has been. Uncooperative, Cameron warns Paul not to open a door. When Paul sees the thing on the back of his neck, Cameron goes berserk and shoots crazily. The police gun him down in the corridor. Cameron was controlled by a parasite with tendrils attached to his nervous system. When removed, they secrete a brain-destroying acid. Cameron was doomed even before he was shot. There may be other parasites.

En route to the cone, the Sheriff sees a man lying on the road. Waylaying him, several parasite hosts make the Sheriff into one. A still-living part of the first latches onto Paul's arm until he sears it with a Bunsen burner. Wyler wants everyone to come to the cone. The guards and the roadblock sign are gone. Wyler thinks the cone is the empty fuel section of a spaceship. The ship itself may be somewhere. When the parasites sought hosts, they ignorantly tried animals.

To look for the ship, the group splits up into three teams. Paul and Alice find a power company truck and find its dead driver, hearing parasites in the woods. Glenn and Elaine enter an old mine shack. Some hosts burn it, but they escape. In a drawer in Cameron's office are parasite jars. Powers calls a telegrapher, telling him to send a crisis wire to the governor. A host, the telegrapher relays a false hoax report. Other hosts plant a parasite in sleeping Alice's bedroom. She becomes one and drives away with them.

Near the cone lies a dying ex-host whose parasite left him because of a weak heart. He is Paul's former teacher, Prof. Helsington. He and Prof. Cole vanished during an expedition five years ago. The Sheriff returns saying the roadblock and guards were unnecessary. In the hospital, Helsington croaks, "Carboniferous" — meaning the parasites are subterranean. Powers tries to call the state capitol, but the phone lines are busy. Paul and Glenn see the telegrapher and a few hosts in his office. Paul and Glenn fight them. Powers sends a distress plea to outside radio listeners. When the group returns to the cone, the host guards shoot at them from atop the scaffolding and are killed.

Inside a chamber of the cone, Paul and Glenn meet a bearded, robed Prof. Cole. "I *was* Prof. Cole," he explains. "Now I hold a position of much higher order." Glass tubes contain other parasites. Paul erroneously believes one of them is on Cole's back. "There is nothing on my back," asserts Cole, a willing protector. "We are in complete harmony. We are inseparable. There is no conflict or purpose here as there is among mankind. We will not engage in combat or violence of any kind. Why should we when we can scatter quietly like seeds." Paul likens the "seeds" to corruption and cancer. "Our social order is pure, innocent," Cole maintains. "It has the exactitude of mathematics. We shall force upon man a life free from strength and turmoil." These parasites are the harbingers of conquest. "It will take time," admits Cole, "but we have learned much patience in two hundred million years." In hiding, the Sheriff aims his gun at Paul and Glenn, but gets shot. A fire erupts as they flee.

With high-voltage wires above, Paul wants to electrify the cone using extra cables. For this, the power truck and a special harpoon gun are needed. When Paul mounts the scaffold, Alice appears. She tries to sway Paul to the parasite's way. His vow to save her only enrages her. When Alice shoots Paul, he frantically urges Glenn to fire the harpoon gun. The current kills Paul, Alice and the parasites. The hosts are still alive and have to be found.

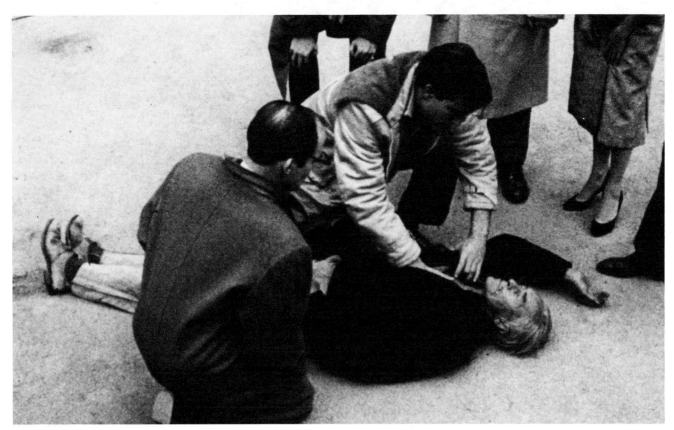

A man laying on the road carries alien parasites in THE BRAIN EATERS.

Brain Eaters improved on "The Puppet Masters" with the more imaginative origin of its parasites. "Puppet Masters" has been likened to *Invasion of the Body Snatchers* for its possession theme and narration by a hero. Though sluggishly paced, *Brain Eaters* was an accelerated retelling of the Jack Finney story. It established its menace quicker, letting its better-equipped heroes take more decisive action. Paul and Alice, though the love interest here was minor, were the Miles and Becky equivalents. Alice, like Becky, became one of "them"; Miles lived, but Paul died. Only wishy-washy Glenn gained any positive experience.

Ve Sota's pacing was a long funeral interrupted by fast, explosive punctuations of violence. There were some tension raising tilt angles used to signify Mayor Cameron's possession. When Alice's parasite invaded her room, the camera assumed its vision, sliding across a rug and snaking up one side of her bed. To help hide bad makeup, Prof. Cole's appearance employed diffuse dream-world lighting, making him resemble a Tibetan holy man seated on the throne of some nirvanic temple.

Created by Ed Nelson, the parasites were pipe cleaner tendrils and patches of cut coat fur placed on top of moving windup lady bug toys. The worst effect, they made it understandable why Ve Sota preferred to dwell on hosts carrying them either in jars or luminous globes. The cone was a weird creation with its deceiving missile shape and myriad passages . . . almost a pyramid with rounded edges which, if Mel Welles had filmed *The Brain Eaters* his way, would have emerged near the pyramids of Yucatan. The art director was Burt Schoenberg, who owned a Laguna Beach coffeehouse called "Cafe Frankenstein" and painted the abstract family portraits for *House of Usher* (1960).

Ed Nelson began his career move to TV soon after *The Brain Eaters* when he won a contract at Universal. Leonard Nimoy, here billed as "Nemoy", was almost a Spockian personage as Cole mouthed the philosophy of the parasites. Joanna Lee, Tanna in *Plan Nine from Outer Space*, had once been a dancer and as the possessed Alice showed off a great pair of legs. Lee realized she had no future as an actress while recuperating from a nasty auto accident. As if to make her break from one life to another complete, she underwent extensive plastic surgery for her face. Started while Lee was on the mend, her writing led to producing and directing for video. The medium that honed Lee's talent and Bruno Ve Sota's was also where Alan Jay Factor, billed "Alan Frost" in *Brain Eaters*, wound up as a director. Jack Hill, who played Powers, was not Jack Hill the exploitation filmmaker.

After *The Brain Eaters* was shown, Robert Heinlein initiated a plagiarism lawsuit — only his ideas had been used so widely that the case had no real legal grounds. It was settled out of court in 1960. AIP promised not to show *The Brain Eaters* again, but sold it to TV. Actor John Payne, for a time, wanted to make a film out of the real "Puppet Masters".

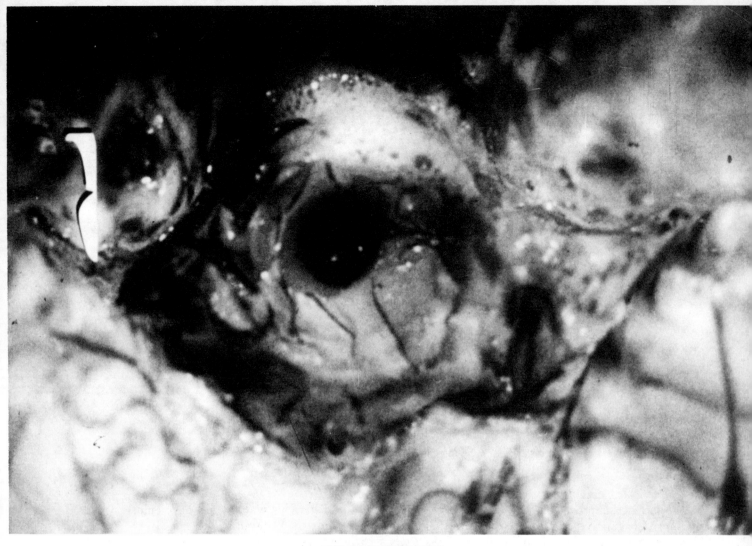

THE CRAWLING EYE

Distributors Corp. of America, 1958
Released in England as *The Trollenberg Terror*

Producers	Robert S. Baker
	Monty Berman
Director	Quentin Lawrence
Screenplay	Jimmy Sangster
	From a story by Jimmy Key
Cinematography	Monty Berman
Film Editor	Henry Richardson
Music	Stanley Black
Production Supervisor	Ronald C. Lisles
Art Director	Duncan Sutherland
Sound Recording	Dick Smith
Special Effects Supervisor	Les Bowie
Production Manager	Charles Perhane
Assistant Director	Norman Harrison
Camera Operator	Desmond Davis
Continuity	Yvonne Richards
Hairdresser	Joy Vigo
Makeup	Elenor Jones

A Tempian Production
Running time: 84 minutes

Cast: Forrest Tucker (Alan Brooks), Laurence Payne (Phillip Truscott), Jennifer Jayne (Sarah Pilgrim), Janet Munro (Anne Pilgrim), Warren Mitchell (Prof. Crevett), Frederick Schiller (Klein), Stewart Saunders (Dewhurst), Andrew Faulds (Brett), Colin Dougles (Hans), Derek Sydney (Wilde), Caroline Glazer (Child), Garard Green (Pilot), Leslie Heritage (Karl), Theodore Wilhelm (Fritz), Richard Golding, George Herbert, Anne Sharp (Villagers), Jeremy Longhurst, Anthony Parker (Climbers)

One of the British sci-fi films adapted from a BBC serial was *The Crawling Eye*, based on Peter Key's "The Trollenberg Terror". Resembling H.G. Welles' concept of "War of the Worlds" in its background of social simplicity and innocence, *Crawling Eye* was a suspenseful but anarchic effigy of Nigel Kneale's first

(Above) The grotesque Trollenburg Terror closeup in THE CRAWLING EYE (1958).

two Quatermass sagas, *The Creeping Unknown* (1956) and *Enemy from Space* (1957). "Trollenberg" was set in a resort in Austria near a mountain peak inhabited by beings later identified as Ixodes. Where the Kneale monsters took organic possession of earthlings, Ixodes exercised telepathic control. Key's heroine was an acutely susceptible clairvoyant named Anne Pilgrim. Quentin Lawrence produced and directed "The Trollenberg Terror" and Laurence Payne starred as the original hero, Philip Truscott. Sarah Lawson, one of the female leads, later appeared in *Island of the Burning Damned* (1967) *aka Island of the Burning Doomed* and *Night of the Big Heat*, a story with "Tollenberg"-like similarities where the characters were gathered at an inn and extreme Fahrenheit — not centigrade — was the alien temperature of choice.

Producers Robert S. Baker and Monty Berman, Berman the cinematographer of most of their films, assigned the cinema adaptation of "The Trollenberg Terror" to Jimmy Sangster, Hammer's chief scenarist during its reputation years. The Trollenberg was moved to Switzerland and the Ixodes rendered nameless. Quentin Lawrence and Laurence Payne were reunited for the film, only with less prestige than before — Lawrence was just the director and Payne's protagonist reduced to a foil for a troubleshooter written to suit the grandstand thesping of Yank name draw Forrest Tucker. Until Distributors Corp. of America settled on *The Crawling Eye*, the proposed U.S. titles made its singular-reference invader everything from *The Creeping Eye* to *The Flying Eye* (*The Flying Eye* was the name of a 1955 British film about a remote controlled model airplane with a TV device).

All solar malefactors who had a tentacle (or comparable appendage) in inspiring "The Trollenberg Terror" had some form of concealment: the Welles Martians their landing projectiles and war machines, the entity that occupied Victor Carewe his mutating shell, the intelligences of Winnerden Flats' tiny hollow meteors, their earth hosts and incubating pressure domes. For the *Crawling Eye* — actually *eyes* — the object of camouflage was a cloud.

The cloud is resting on the south side of the Trollenberg, where it attracts three English student climbers. Inside the cloud, their leader Jim complains of frigid temperatures and says, "Someone's coming." Suddenly, Jim screams and falls. His suspended body is just below the lip of the ledge where his friends are. As they raise Jim's rope, the horrified second climber screams, "No!" and lets go as the third man strains to hang on. The rope frays against the sharp edge of the ledge and Jim falls. "You idiot! We nearly had him!" shouts the third man, grabbing the second, who babbles, "Didn't you see? His head! It was — torn off!"

Bound for Geneva, a speeding train hurtles through a black tunnel. In one compartment, American scientist Alan Brooks reads a newspaper, sitting opposite Sarah

Pilgrim and her sleepy younger sister Anne. Sarah indicates the distant Trollenberg. Gazing at it in a state of transfixion, Anne faints in Alan's lap, crumpling his paper. Coming out of it, Anne accepts a sip of pocket whiskey offered by Alan. When a porter announces Trollenberg, Anne insists, "Sarah, we're getting off at Trollenberg", and mentions the Hotel Europe. That is curious Alan's destination. At the train station, its proprietor, Mayor Klein, agrees to lodge Sarah and Anne on short notice since tourism has been bad this season. During the drive to the hotel, Anne expresses awareness of the recent climbing deaths. The peasants are leaving the mountain because it is bad luck. Climbers vanish into the mist and never come back.

Another hotel guest, Englishman Philip Truscott, cordially introduces himself to Alan, Sarah and Anne. From the window of their room Anne looks at the Trollenberg and tells Sarah, "It's all there . . . the observatory at the foot of the mountain . . . the cablecar. There's a small hut the climbers use. You can see it from the observatory. It's all there. Just like —." Anne is beside herself trying to figure why she wanted to come here instead of continuing on to Geneva. Philip strikes up an acquaintance with Alan, ostensibly here on a holiday, and remembers seeing the Pilgrim sisters when they were conducting their mind-reading act at the London Palladium. Philip notices the gun Alan packed in his open suitcase. Alan overhears as Philip does a phone background check on him.

A geologist, Dewherst, and his Alpine Club guide, Brett, plan to investigate the Trollenberg and see if there is a reasonable explanation for the deaths. Dewherst buys a round of drinks for everyone before they set out. "Keep an eye on your roping, won't you?" ominously cautions Philip, who brings up the student tragedy from last week. Hans, the nervous bartender, is forced by Philip to disclose further information about the condition of Jim. "The guide who found him, also his friends, swear the rope was around his waist. You understand, it was still tied." Almost maliciously, Philip continues to prod. "The villagers have something to say about this too — don't they, Hans?" Hans excuses himself. "What *do* the villagers say?" asks Alan. "They say it happened *before* he fell," answers Philip.

Alan hitches a cablecar ride to the observatory with Dewhurst and Brett. Dewhurst believes that altered rock chemistry may account for the disasters. Stoic, uncomplicated Brett does not feel that way. "To me, a mountain's a mountain. Some people can climb it and some can't. Those who can't shouldn't try."

The director of the observatory is cosmic ray researcher, Prof. Crevett, who summoned Alan and heartily greets his old friend. Proudly, Crevett shows off the television camera mounted on the roof and a fortified shutter for the only window. Crevett asks Alan to think back to an incident in the Andes three years ago. "And then there is the cloud." "What cloud?" Alan

153

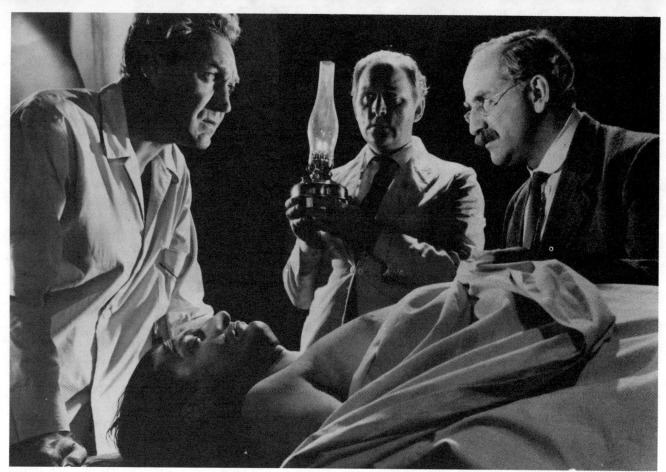

Brooks (Forrest Tucker) and Crevett (Warren Mitchell) examine re-killed Brett (Andrew Faulds) in THE CRAWLING EYE.

Zombied Brett (Andrew Faulds) about to bury the hatchet with unsuspecting Anne (Janet Munro) in THE CRAWLING EYE.

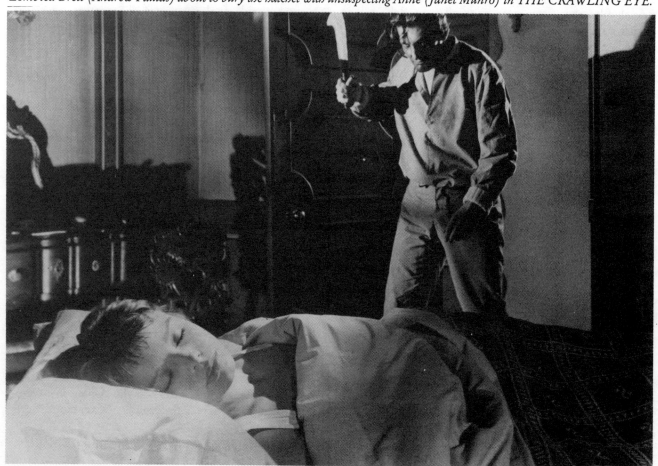

asks evasively. "Come on, Alan," badgers Crevett, "you know what I'm talking about — the cloud where there should be no cloud." The cloud remains static on the side of the Trollenberg, never moving. "Freak of nature," huffs Alan. "A *radioactive* freak of nature?" queries Crevett. Each time the indicator of a radar scanner circles past the cloud, high radiation registers. Everything tallies with the Andes affair — which Alan doesn't want to remember. Unconsciously, he brings up a relevant detail: "mental compulsions". Anne exhibited this on board the train. Crevett's assistant, Wilde, spots two climbers. On radar, they are Brett and Dewhurst trekking to the hut. Crevett wants Alan to tell the authorities about current developments, but all evidence in the Andes disappeared and cast embarrassment upon Alan.

Brett and Dewhurst reach the hut. Brett notices the cloud moving down the peak and phones Klein at the hotel to announce he and Dewhurst arrived safely. Crevett attends a parlor demonstration of Anne's power. Sarah holds objects behind a table screen. One is a French bank note belonging to Philip. Another is a tiny glass ball with a model hut and artificial snow that falls when it is held upsidedown. Anne suddenly goes into a trance. "Snow . . . mountain . . .hut . . . two men in the hut." Sarah tries to break Anne's concentration, but Crevett lets it continue. Anne homes in on the hut and describes what she sees: " . . . the fat one, he is asleep . . . but he is not the one . . . the other one . . . sitting at a table . . . smoking . . . writing in a book . . . he's the one . . .he's getting up . . . he's coming toward the door . . . he's reaching the door. . . . he's coming out . . . up the slope . . . up the slope . . . walking slowly . . . " As Alan rushes to the phone, Anne starts to swoon, whispering, "Paperweight . . . glass paperweight . . ." She collapses on the rug and is carried upstairs to her room. Alan calls Dewhurst, who finds himself alone and calls for Brett. Dewhurst thinks Brett might be hurt, but Alan urges him to stay where he is.

Anne awakens on her bed. Philip goes for some sleeping pills. Crevett notes that Anne experienced the vision as if she had seen it from above on the Trollenberg itself. Sarah and Anne used to work from a code until it was discovered that Anne could guess what Sara was thinking. Crevett wants Sarah to take Anne from here first thing in the morning. "It's not good for her here." Wilde calls. The cloud is moving. Radiation is increasing. The cloud, reports Crevett, "is at the foot of the mountain — where the hut is!"

Over the phone, Dewhurst complains to Alan about the freezing mist outside. He hears a sound from beyond the door. Only a false alarm. When Dewhurst returns to the door to close it, he sees something horrible, barricades the door, turns over his shoulder and screams. The line goes dead. The observatory reports that the cloud is going back up the mountain.

Ringing tower bells alert Trollenberg to the hut

emergency. Alan, Philip and Klein equip themselves to lead a rescue party. The airport will send up a spotter plane in the morning. In another psychic seizure, Anne pleads, "Keep them away from the hut!" Crevett compares her mind to a radio receiver. "But there is a stronger signal . . . a stronger mind jamming the wavelength." He implores Sarah again — this time as an order — to remove Anne from Trollenberg, "before it is too late." "Too late for what, Professor?" Sarah wants to know. "When they reach the hut, then we will know for sure," Crevett answers.

Alan, Philip and Klein reach the outwardly undisturbed hut. The door has been pushed in. The bunk blankets are frozen stiff. Klein sees Dewhurst's' lower body protruding askew from under the bunk. Dewhurst is pulled out — his head gone.

Anne recovers from the seizure. She and Sarah are packing to leave, but when Sarah leaves their room, the cloud takes full possession of Anne. Dewhurst's call was cut off because the hut phone wire snapped. Alan examines a piece and recalls an experiment where intense cold crystallized such wire. Sarah sees Anne taking the cablecar up and phones the observatory. The spotter plane pilot sights the waving figure of Brett below him and radios two searchers, who respond by walkie-talkie. Anne is greeted at the cable stop by Wilde. She has to go up the mountain, but Wilde gently escorts her into the observatory. Anne uses his work distraction to sneak away, but Alan and Philip obstruct her at the door. Alan tells Crevett about Dewhurst's death. Philip candidly compares everything to the Andes.

One of the searchers reaches the summit of a ledge and sees a rock sack. The flap is bloodstained. Inside is Dewhurst's head. Demented Brett murders the searcher with his pick, using it on his partner.

A journalist, Philip had chased the Andes story, but when he got there, the cloud was gone. The United Nations has a special team for investigating phenomenon and Alan should bring them in. Philip wonders if Crevett still holds to his original theory of visitors from outer space. "Perhaps the world that these creatures inhabit is coming to an end," speculates Crevett. "Perhaps they need to find somewhere else to live." As to why they always land on mountaintops: "Its the atmosphere, I think. It gets much thinner higher up, but perhaps these creatures need that. The cloud would seem to indicate this too . . . creating their own atmosphere." "Well, if they can only exist on the tops of mountains," rashly surmises Philip, "they're hardly likely to inherit the earth, are they?" "You see, anyone can get used to anything in time," disputes Crevett. "Now these movements we have recorded. Each time, lower down the mountain. Acclimatization, perhaps." The next move is up to Alan, who must summon the authorities.

Numb, disoriented Brett staggers into the hotel. He claims he got lost and knows nothing about Dewhurst. Turning to Sarah, he asks how Anne is and feels strangely hot. Alan offers Brett a drink from the bar. His spastic bottle hand need steadying and the glass has trouble touching his lips. As Brett tries to light a cigarette, he spills all the matches. Anne comes downstairs in a bathrobe about to ask for something and Brett lunges at her with a knife. Alan throws a punch that sends Brett reeling against a sharp-edged figurine by the couch. Brett's forehead is cut — but there is no blood.

Sedated Brett is locked up in the wine cellar. In the Andes, there was an elderly female clairvoyant the locals considered a witch. A man who went up the mountain there vanished for twenty-four hours and returned with peculiar coordinations — just like Brett. He slaughtered the old woman with a meat axe and both were found dead. "How did the man die?" asks Philip. "The man had been dead already twenty-four hours," Crevett tells him. Before an autopsy could be arranged, the police took the body away. "Are you trying to tell me that Brett's like that?" asks shuddering Philip. "That we've just been fighting a dead man?" "We believe that he was sent down by whatever's up there for the express purpose of killing Anne Pilgrim," states Alan. "They can't afford for Anne to be alive. She's a threat to their security. They tried to entice her up there, now they've tried this. Neither's worked." "So what will they try now?" wonders Philip. "Whatever it is," expects Crevett, "we won't have to wait long to find out."

Brett awakens. Klein goes down to the wine cellar door's window to look at him. Brett throttles Klein for his key and snatches up a meat cleaver from its chopping block. Sarah feels something amiss and gets out of bed. In the corridor, she sees Brett shambling upstairs with the cleaver and desperately bangs on Alan's locked door. Brett turns to Anne, who wakes up, and raises the axe over her before Alan shoots him in the head.

Brett's body is returned to the wine cellar, where Crevett instructs Hans to place a lit lantern on the floor. Crevett studies the crystallized appearance of Brett's flesh, " . . . like meat that has been deep frozen." Hans lets out a gasp as the flesh disintegrates. Philip reports that the observatory is on. The cloud is moving again — toward the village.

In separate groups, the villagers take the cablecar up to the observatory. Panicky Hans tries unsuccessfully to phone the outside and flees in Klein's car. As Alan's group rushes to the cable station, a little girl yanked along by her mother drops her rubber ball. The cloud is nearing the hotel. When the child is missed by her mother, Alan runs back there. Inside the hotel, mist seeps under the twin doors. They collapse to reveal a one-eyed tentacled horror. As the little girl stoops to retrieve her ball, she is ensnared in one of the creature's tentacles until Alan severs it with his ice pick. The creature emits a howl of pain. While the cablecar is ascending, Philip glances at the cables, asking Alan, "Remember the phone wire at the hut?" Frigid cold blasts frost on the cable winch — threatening to break

the jerking lines. Safely, the cablecare reaches the observatory.

The cloud divides. Now there are multiple creatures. There is time to radio NATO. Outside, Hans raps on the door. Wilde admits him. Hans claims the cloud impeded him on the highway and feels, "Zo hot!" Wary of Hans, Anne goes to Crevett's office. Alan and Crevett want to put Anne under hypnosis, hoping she can use her link to the aliens to their advantage. The lowering temperature of a cloud location indicates they need cold. Then there was Brett's reaction to heat. "And Hans, too!" interjects Wilde. "*He* complained of being hot!" Hans is not in the main corridor. In the office, he strangles Anne until Alan and Philip jump all over him. Hans is close to killing Alan when Alan reaches for a pen knife lying on Crevett's desk and thrusts it into his abdomen. Joining Crevett and Sarah, Alan moans, "Poor devil."

Molotov cocktails are prepared. In the corridor, Alan instructs the cablecar operator to close the door behind him and open it only when Alan knocks. Alan scores a direct hit at the nearest creature, who writhes in screaming agony. Philip takes a turn. A creature up on the roof wraps a tentacle around his neck and raises him into the air. Crevett sees it on TV, alerting Alan. He hurls another molotov at the creature, catching Philip as he falls. A NATO bomber arrives. Alan orders the pilot to bomb the cloud. "Sounds crazy to me, bombing a cloud —," he questions. "*Do as you're told!*" bellows Alan. Sarah is ministering to exhausted Anne, who lies on a cot in the office. Deep cracks streak a wedge pattern in one wall and still another creature pushes through. It seizes Alan by the throat, but Philip flings a molotov at it. The bomber commences high and low level runs, dropping napalm. The observatory quakes as the creatures immolate in a chorus of flailing tentacles and screams. The plane wings away.

The window shutter opens on heaps of charred, smoking creatures spread all over. The villagers can return to their homes. "How 'bout a breath of fresh air?" Philip asks Anne romantically. "I'd like a breath of fresh air," she sweetly replies. "For the first time in months, the mountain is clear," Crevett tells Alan, who says, "Let's hope it stays that way."

If *The Crawling Eye* had any sort of practical moral (just ask Jim), never put your head in the clouds . . . especially if they feel cold. Switzerland was an excellent selection of setting with its travel folder images of serenity, cleanliness, leisurely life pace and mostly tranquil diversions. With the trappings of comfort, *Crawling Eye* set up the slow, inexorable violation of a small utopia. The first people in Trollenberg to get bad vibes from the mountain were its superstitious former residents while those in the most immediate danger prior to Anne's coming were outside risk-takers. Almost every current visitor came on account of the cloud and their coincidental gathering put pressure on the aliens, forcing

Brooks (Forrest Tucker) saves a little girl from certain death in THE CRAWLING EYE.

new shows of hand similar to the atrocities of the Andes affair.

Anne might not have brought so much trouble to the creatures or herself if she and Sarah had decided to take a different travel route, or if the creatures had allowed the two women to keep their Geneva booking. One fainting spell couldn't have been that much of a safety breach. Worthier of the alien's paranoia should have been the observatory of Prof. Crevett, even if his cosmic ray program was legitimate and not an investigative cover since the observatory had been built before the aliens moved to Trollenberg. For Alan, the business in the Andes was something he wanted to forget and only a veiled summons from Crevett could bring him here. To Philip, the Andes was a puzzler of a story and he would be the man to make Alan and Crevett own up to their hidden knowledge. Dewhurst, the rock expert, thought he could attach an oddity of nature to the climbing deaths. All that Brett was interested in was the challenge of the peak and, maybe, a generous commission from Dewhurst, who didn't have a drop of mountain goat blood in him (no opportunity was taken to demonstrate what effect the creatures may have had on the intuition qualities of animals).

The film mostly ignored the long-term plans of its invaders, preferring to dwell on the relationship between extraterrestrial activity and ESP — two subjects understood by few and mocked by many. Diligently guarding their front and back doors, the aliens never expected to be tapped in from the sides until the two Clairs — Anne and the Andes woman — became really Voyant. Anne was the more significant and worrisome

subject: educated, able to apply her skill professionally, surrounded by various protectors. Despite the Dead Zonish lapses into unconsciousness that kept her from rationally comprehending, she was the catalyst for everything coming to a (sic) head.

Convoluted in its exposition, *The Crawling Eye*'s attitude toward space beings throbbed with every reactionary Pulp concept of them. Vaguely, the aliens resembled the shapeless, yuckky, potentially-dangerous-if-provoked Xenomorphs of *It Came from Outer Space* (1953). Each time Anne got too close to what they were thinking, she was psychically raped with overtones of physical abuse in her involuntary movements. Unclean, obscene, the aliens were manipulative, hun-like debasers of the small and innocent, bestial in their harm to the decapitated. Intelligence benefited them, but their drives were purely malicious instinct.

Transitional shifts were either sly or jarring. The cloud first appeared as a casual observer might see it — irregular but hardly black smoke on a forest horizon. From the discovery of Jim's beheading, the film sharply forwarded to the train tunnel scene, which signified the start of a dark adventure for the plot principles on board. The model hut in the parlor act was a prophetic visualizer of the next place where the aliens would strike. The broken phone wires were an advance example of what deliberately inflicted cold could do to the aerial life lines between the village and the observatory. The ball belonging to the little girl lay in the proximity of where the first exposed creature revealed itself, taking on the seductiveness of a pedophile's bait.

Entirely successful as horror, the fiction was pretty

sloppy as science. Did the cloud simply provide the aliens with their atmosphere or did it transport them from home to earth too like a cumulus flying saucer? How were they able to create the cloud since they had nothing technological with them that we could see? It was unclear how much the aliens and the zombies were involved in several killings unless they acted together. Jim claimed he saw "someone", not a something, although the density of the cloud probably obscured his sight. Dewhurst had to have been killed by an alien, but why did he react as if it was inches behind him unless he was looking at a window? Only Brett could have stolen Dewhurst's head and placed it in the rock sack. But why? Was he *expecting* to run into rescuers? All this did was scare one of the rescuers. Perhaps the aliens were testing Brett's ability to kill. The only reason for the scene itself was to show how much he changed. If Brett could be willed into going up the mountain, why was it necessary to kill him before making him a slave? And how was it done? Induced heart attack? Stroke? Wasn't it dangerous to send Brett back among the living instead of making a sneak return?

The zombies were too animated to be convincing as walking corpses unless they were directed to feign normal habits like smoking and drinking. Blood settles in the lowest body cavities after death — that would explain Brett's dry head cut — but it would most noticeably pale his complexion. Only live people can be sedated or knocked unconscious and Brett lost his initial awkwardness when he became violent. Was the lantern heat what disintegrated his flesh or prolonged exposure to natural warmth? Hans was not uncoordinated at all. Though he and Brett were dead, they could feel heat (a handy tip-off device) and guns and knives were able to finish them for good.

Meager budget money hurt the special effects of Les Bowie, although the crawling eyes shot through the top of most Disgust-O-Meters as horrendous sacs of encephalopodic tissue with orbs of unnervingly fine optical detail. They could even be ascertained as some kind of mobile testicles with their tight scrotal-like skin. When subdued, the aliens emitted a low, reverberant shudder or a dinging staccato beep. Injured, they released a mewing, high-pitched whine. Most attention was on individual creatures, who were at their most frightening when they charged head-on at low angles. Even at distances, the often-twitching eyes were able to communicate conscious impulses. Process shots of the aliens were uneven and the far ends of their tentacles were made slim so they could move between the screens and the actors. A very good setup was where Philip tossed a molotov at the alien that invaded the office and the gas explosion on the process reel was perfectly timed to approximate the result of Laurence Payne's arm throw.

Bowie hated the cloud — a piece of cotton wool nailed to a photograph of the mountain. Optically blurred to look cloudier, it took on an eerie luminescence in a night shot.

Although the crawling eyes were commercially revolting, promotion excluded their actual appearance. The poster art eye was an illustration of a magnified human eye with swirling tentacles holding a girl. Action stills where people confronted the eyes replaced Bowie's bogeys with indistinct substitute images.

Forrest Tucker's histrionics in British sci-fi were too rich, too broad, too overbearingly American for some. Salvation in the post-BBC version of "The Trollenberg Terror" needed a strong, take-charge hero who could whip people into fighting shape, although Alan was initially unenthusiastic about getting involved in a sequel to the Andes case. Tucker let Alan know doubt, hesitation and revulsion and Alan had to be a regular guy if he kept a fifth in his pocket and his favorite part of the paper was sports. Laurence Payne played this Philip Truscott as a well-meaning but impotent fop. Warren Mitchell was affable as Crevett, although his over-accented German was pure Ludwig Von Drake. Jennifer Jayne made some horror films in the sixties and wrote the 1974 Amicus anthology thriller *Tales That Witness Madness* as "Jay Fairbank".

Janet Munro as Anne was completely believable as a sheltered child-woman with little control over her extra sense. Anne's psychic spell during the takeover of Brett was like watching a fragile musical instrument on the verge of breaking at its highest note. Several things factor into why Munro became a Walt Disney celebrity. Disney wasn't adverse to making stars out of people with sci-fi-horror credits, such as Fess Parker of *Them!* and Tom Tryon of *I Married a Monster from Outer Space*. Disney acquired a taste for the Swiss culture. That plus Munro's wholesomeness probably made these aspects of *The Crawling Eye* enjoyable to him if he had seen it. Munro was signed to play Katie O'Gill in *Darby O'Gill and the Little People* (1959) along with Sean Connery. Her next Disney film, *Third Man on the Mountain* (1960) returned her to a Swiss setting and after that came — yes — *The Swiss Family Robinson* (1960). Munro, regrettably, committed suicide in 1972.

Actors who can shock facially with makeup or through natural deformity are rare and future Parliamentarian, Andrew Faulds, belonged to this unique clique.

Jimmy Sangster wrote two other Baker-Berman films, *Blood of the Vampire* (1958) and the controversial 1959 *Jack the Ripper*. Baker and Berman also made *Mania* (1960) *aka The Flesh and the Fiends*, and *The Hellfire Club* (1962). Then they concentrated on TV, producing their crowning success, "The Saint", followed by "The Baron", "The Champions" and "My Partner, the Ghost". Baker also devised and produced that little appreciated gem, "The Persuaders", starring Tony Curtis and The Saint himself, Roger Moore.

THE COSMIC MONSTERS

Distributors Corp. of America, 1958
Released in England as *The Strange World of Planet X*

A John Bash Production
Running time: 75 minutes

Producer	George Maynard
Director	Gilbert Gunn
Screenplay	Paul Ryder
	based on the novel by Gene Ray
Cinematography	Joe Ambor
Film Editor	Francis Bieber
Music	Robert Sharples
Art Director	Bernard Sarron
Producer Manager	John Dark
Special Effects	Anglo-Scottish Ltd.
Sound Recordist	Cecil Mason
Camera Operator	Gus Drisse
Continuity	Kay Mander
Assistant Director	Frank Ernst
Makeup	Charles Nash
Hairdresser	Daphnie Martin
Wardrobe Supervisor	Irma Birch

Cast: Forrest Tucker (Gil Graham), Gay Andre (Michelle Dupont), Martin Benson (Smith), Wyndham Goldie (Birg. Cartwright), Alec Mango (Dr. Laird), Hugh Latimer (Jimmy Murray), Geoffrey Chater (Gerald Wilson), Patricia Sinclair (Helen Forsythe), Catherine Lancaster (Gillian Betts), Richard Wagner (Insp. Burns), Hilda Pennemore (Mrs. Hale), Susan Redway (Jane Hale), Neil Wilson (P.C. Tidy)

Actress Rene Ray's "The Strange World of Planet X" was a novel, a BBC serial and a motion picture America called *The Cosmic Monsters* for its giant insect attraction. Another Forrest Tucker vehicle from the people who made *The Crawling Eye*, this film was made first but runs a very poor second in reputation. Rather than scaling hazardous peaks, *The Cosmic*

(Above) A victim of THE COSMIC MONSTERS (1958).

Monsters was nestled in flat English county terrain. Instead of hurling molotovs, killing zombies and saving little girls, Forrest Tucker wasn't much more than an alarmed observer, leaving the real heroics to the British Army and a stranger from the Strange world. The nearest equivalent of a zombie was a deranged tramp and every horror that crawled can be found in most back yards. As to which film had greater coherency — this or *The Crawling Eye* — Brand "X" had it.

Briley Bay, England. Expatriate Canadian scientist Gil Graham assists Dr. Laird, who is experimenting with altered magnetic fields to produce molecular change in metals. When the computer operator carelessly works the GF-2 circuit of Laird's apparatus, the energy arcs. The assistant burns his hand and a resonance of power causes the telly at the village to blow its tube. Government official Gerald Wilson must find a new computer operator. His superior, Brig. Cartwright, fears the risk of dangerous side-effects.

The new operator, Frenchwoman Michelle Dupont, solves the problem of power distribution and gets along nicely with Gil. In the woods lives a friendly tramp, fond of bugs like little Jane Hale, the daughter of a landlady. While a piece of special aircraft alloy is being tested in the lab, there is a loud screech. As a briefcase and the hook it is on fly toward Michelle, Gil tackles her to the floor. The pub TV's new picture goes bust and a chain of sudden atmospheric disturbances follow. The tramp suffers burn scars on his face. The accident happened because Cartwright left his keys in the lab.

A meteoric object crashes to earth and explodes. To capitalize on related saucer sightings, a London paper suggests there is an invader from "Planet X". What the briefcase contained was the metal that reacted — not the alloy.

Security requires the services of agent Jimmy Murray. Gil had cut the power before the briefcase flew, but the circuits still operated. Steps are taken to make the equipment's force directional. On a bug hunt in the woods, Jane encounters a benevolent stranger with odd whiskers named Smith. He is interested in Laid's work. Shaving his face, he removes a communicator from his coat pocket and stakes out the lab. Gil tells Gerald the machine is building a dangerously excessive magnetic field. A recording of the briefcase mishap disappears. Jimmy will meet Gil, Michelle and Gerald at the pub tonight.

That night, new schoolteacher, Helen Forsythe, arrives at the train station and will be staying at the Hale house. On a dark lane, Helen glances at a newspaper with a saucer headline when the mad tramp attacks her. Jimmy's car scares him away and Jimmy takes Helen to the police station. Insp. Burns mentions reports of the tramp and the condition of his face makes him wonder if Laird is using atomic material.

Gil, Michelle and Gerald are at the pub, where a dance is being held. Smith enters before Jimmy does and over his first earth drink intently listens in on the group. Art Deverson, an acquaintance of Gil's, is waiting for his date, Gillian Betts. Along the lane path, the tramp strangles Gillian as an awful screech emanates from the pub's loudspeaker. Gil realizes that Laird's machine is creating a magnetic syndrome through ever-accumulating power. Gil tries to warn unruffled Laird — who learned this over a week ago, but kept quiet.

Art finds Gillian's body. In his shock, he stumbles across the dead tramp and is killed by a giant insect.

Michelle and Gerald hear about Gillian's murder. Smith requests a meeting with Michelle and Gil at the pub tomorrow night. He warns that Laird's machine may be upsetting the magnetic balance of the earth. This could bring a large concentration of cosmic rays. If the heavy-set layer of the ionosphere is bent or fractured, people exposed to the rays may go insane and kill many before they themselves die. Mutation would be more radical, and faster, in insects.

Jane discovers a colossal insect egg in the woods. She wants to show it to Helen, who is at the schoolhouse, but disappears into another room when Jane approaches a window. Jane takes the egg home. Mrs. Hale tells Michelle about the egg. She urges Mrs. Hale to boil it. Michelle learns that Helen is at the school and senses danger. Jimmy and Gerald are skeptical of the cosmic peril, but Cartwright wants Laird's experiment postponed. Art's mutilated, bloodless body has been found. Gil blames the voracious insects. The nearest Army depot is contacted.

In the schoolhouse, Helen sees the insects swarming outside. Gil hears about the insect egg and where Michelle has gone. When she nears the schoolhouse, Helen tries to warn her away. A beetle larvae chases Michelle. Gil, Jimmy, Smith and the Army arrive. Michelle runs into the web of a giant spider. Smith kills it with a ray gun. Gerald tries to stop Laird from activating the machine. Threatening Gerald, Laird shoots him. While the woods are being cleared of insects, Smith admits he is the legendary spaceman. Dying, Gerald phones Cartwright, urging him to get to the lab. The early magnetic disturbances had destroyed a spaceship. Laird's machine threatens to reverse global polarity. Briley Woods was the only land area affected — although certain oceanic spots have felt radiation. Mutation there could be worse since conditions would be the same as they were on earth during the creation of life before the ionosphere existed.

The group learns that Gerald is dead and Laird intends to resume the experiment. He has barred the lab door. Asked to help, Smith stipulates that another machine must never be built. A saucer he directs hovers above the lab. As Laird starts the machine, it fires a beam that explodes the building. Smith bids everyone farewell, leaving earth.

Trying to touch many bases on caterpillar feet, *The Cosmic Monsters* took the expediency of talking things out, but did so with a fine ear to the importance of dialogue. If prompt action was wanting, involvement went far in the supposing of and reactions to disaster. Enormity was in enormity itself — amassed in a vicious circle of self-perpetuated syndrome. Laird's machine required detailed explanation to make any sense and every probable concern of the plot was selective with Laird becoming personally dangerous only after the accidental harm of the insect situation was pretty well resolved.

Nominally, Smith was only a conduit character put into the plot so the earth people could fully understand the trouble Laird's experiment was causing. Smith was more laconic than most alien saints. Like the best, he could relate to kids on their own wavelength. When Smith jokingly told Jane he came on the wings of a giant dragonfly, she said, "There are no giant dragonflies anywhere." "What about the one on the moon?" Smith asked. "Oh. If you come from the moon," Jane answered, "that's different." Several times suppositions hit upon the truth. The Planet X invader that the newspaper contrived was Smith. To Smith's race, *earth* — distant and alien to *them* — was "Planet X"! *Man*, the X people believed was the true cosmic monster!

Macrophoto insects, the Briley bugs contributed more than slightly to audience dislike of *The Cosmic Monsters*. Kept mainly to shadow and thick foliage, the insects were often difficult to notice when they were shot from ill-chosen angles. One danger opportunity was passed up when the egg Jane found failed to hatch a new monster, presumably because Mrs. Hale heeded Michelle's advice in time. Some other film would have probably shown the baby insect bursting from its shell just before or during the boiling ritual to either terrorize the Hales or show them disposing of the thing in a messy manner. Helen's predicament and the entrapment of Michelle in the web made the most of female helplessness. In these shots, the insects were unseen, glimpsed in silhouette or photographed to one side. The web sequence had a singular nightmare effect because the surrounding patterns of silk made the web almost a self-contained environment. Then there was a truly ghastly scene where a bug nibbled part of a dead soldier's head like it was a juicy pear, its ravenous chewing sickeningly lifelike.

The acting was mostly starchy but professional. Alec Mango put some dictive sting into Laird's arrogant, impatient demeanor. Stiffly vivacious Gaby Andre was stilted but nice as a lady scientist who felled male chauvinism (winning even over Laird) with grace instead of abrasive know-it-all-ism. Lout at times, but less forceful than usual, Forrest Tucker had to defer to the quirky charisma of Martin Benson who, in other films, has been comparable to things found under rocks.

HOW TO MAKE A MONSTER

American-International, 1958

Executive Producers	James J. Nicholson
	Samuel Z. Arkoff
Producer	Herman Cohen
Director	Herbert L. Strock
Story-Screenplay	Kenneth Langry
	(Abel Kandel, Herman Cohen)
Cinematography	Maury Gertsman
Editorial Supervisor	Jerry Young
Music	Paul Dunlap
Art Director	Leslie Thomas
Production Manager-	
Assistant Director	Herb Mendelson
Music Editor	George Brand
Sound Recorder	Herman Lewis
Sound Effects Editor	Verna Fields
Set Decorator	Morris Hoffman
Script Supervisor	Mary Gibsone
Property Master	Sam Gordon
Wardrobe	Oscar Rodriguez
Production Secretary	Barbara Lee Strite
Dance Choreographer	Lee Scott
Makeup	Phillip Scheer

Song: "You've Got to Have Ee-ooo"
Lyrics by Skip Redwine

A Sunset Production / Color Sequence
Running time: 73 minutes

Cast: Robert H. Harris (Pete Drummond), Paul Brinegar (Rivero), Gary Conway (Tony Mantell), Gary Clarke (Larry Drake), Malcolm Atterbury (Richards), Dennis Cross (Monahan), Morris Ankrum (Capt. Hancock), Walter Reed (Det. Thompson), Paul Maxwell (Jeff Clayton), Eddie Marr (John Nixon), Heather Ames (Arlene Dow), Robert Shayne (Gary Droz), Rod Dana (Lab Technician), Jacqueline Ebeier (Jane), Joan Chandler (Marilyn), Thomas B. Henry (Martin Brace), John Phillips (Det. Jones), Pauline Myers (Millie), John Ashley (Himself)

(Above) Two teenage monsters from Herman Cohen's HOW TO MAKE A MONSTER (1958).

Real and reel horror blend well because the environment of manufactured fantasy can either camouflage a killer or allow genuine macabre forces to pass as illusion. Another benefit of shooting a thriller in a film studio setting is economy. Moviemakers have only to use spare props lying around or film scenes on bare soundstages. By 1958, AIP had become a mini-Universal. Like Universal, it was not hesitant to spoof its own horror heritage and even in its serious pictures, AIP threw in occasional references to some other films.

Except for the *Gill-Man*, Universal produced no sequel monsters of the fifties. AIP had four recurring menaces: The She Creature, the Colossal Man, the Teenage Werewolf and the Teenage Frankenstein. AIP wanted to bring the "kids" back in its own answer to *Frankenstein Meets the Wolfman* (1943). The movie that did that, *How to Make a Monster*, was Herman Cohen's self-mocking conclusion of the teen terror films he produced. It was also a showcase salute to most of the AIP monsters from 1956 to then — a goodly percentage Paul Blaisdell creations — and a tongue-in-cheek study of AIP as a more prestigious company than it really was. This was the year when most of AIP's house producers of the period were either leaving home altogether or, in Cohen's case, moving from domestic production to foreign. Cohen made his transition a festival affair.

Pete Drummond is American-International's monster makeup maestro. Assisted by Rivero, he turns youthful actor Larry Drake into the Teenage Werewolf for "Werewolf Meets Frankenstein". Larry is scared by the mirror reflection of his own made-up face. "Just remember that an artist must have no fear," coaches Pete. "Why, a creation is almost a sacred thing — all creations. The Good Lord created saints and he also created sinners. He created the lamb and the fawn and He also created the wolf and the jackal. Well, who can say which is the most praiseworthy?" "For twenty-five years, he's been the master," beams Rivero. "He created them all." "And if I may say so in all due modesty," touts Pete, "each one is a creation — no more important than this."

All eyes on the back lot turn as Pete escorts Larry to the "Werewolf Meets Frankenstein" set. Director Martin Brace is most certainly pleased. "All I can say," he tells Pete," is you've given birth to a fine pair of sons. Tony Mantell appears as the other "boy" — the Teenage Frankenstein. "Werewolf, meet Frankenstein," introduces Brace. "Shake hands and come out snarling." Pete returns to the makeup room while Brace instructs Larry and Tony in the moves for the big climactic fight scene between the monsters.

Two men enter Pete's workshop without knocking. They are Jeffrey Clayton and John Nixon, the Eastern executives who now run AIP. Pete's services, they tell him, are no longer needed. "Monsters are finished," explains Nixon. "They're coming out of your ears." "Saturation," interjects Clayton. "The horror cycle is over," Nixon decrees. "People want to hear music. They

want to laugh. They want to see pretty girls." Pete tries to reason with Clayton and Nixon, but they are unmoved. After "Werewolf Meets Frankenstein", he must go. Bitterly, Pete rejects severance pay. "You turn down money. Maybe you've been living too long with monsters," ridicules Clayton. "Sometimes I find them better company the humans!" huffs Pete.

Devastated Pete talks to the poster images of the monsters in the corridor to the workshop. "Werewolf . . . Frankenstein . . . they want to put an end to us. They say we're through. That's gratitude. Don't they realize that the monsters I've created, from my fist prehistoric man to the spacemen of the future . . . why, all these paid for this studio, made the owners rich and famous. And now, they say it's over . . . but it isn't over. I'll destroy this studio! See it go up on flames before I—" A different idea takes seed. "No. No, I'll destroy them first . . . and I'll use the very monsters they mock!" Rivero joins Pete. "I heard voices." "Just mine," Pete tells him. "You were talking to yourself?" asks Rivero. "Not entirely—" replies Pete, "I was reassuring my children that I won't let them perish — that I'm going to stop these men from destroying us." Pete ushers Rivero into the workshop to show his solution.

Pete prepares some foundation cream cooking in a hot plate pan. "Those fools," he says. "They think a monster is just put together with glue, hair, putty, foam rubber. They don't realize that a monster, even on the screen , is human. It must be infused with a spirit by its creator. " Pete adds a new ingredient to the cream. By accidentally mixing novocaine with greasepaint, he was able to hypnotize James Duncan, the actor who played the Prehistoric Man, into remembering his lines. The new element enters the pores, acting like a prefrontal lobotomy. "I'll do the same with these young men," Pete tells Rivero. "As I see fit, I'll order them what to remember — and what to forget."

Studio guard Monahan has finished his night rounds and joins his lazy senior partner Richards at the gate booth. Go-getter Monahan itches for some action.

When Larry reports for work the next morning, Peter primes him by playing on the grim news about the job shake-ups. "Don't forget, Larry, the people who've seen you — your fans — they don't know your real face. The only hope you have for a future is here." Pete applies the hypnotic makeup. "If you place yourself in my hands, we can change their minds . . . " Larry receives whispered orders on what to do after today's shooting.

In the screening room, Clayton and Nixon view the dailies of a promising new musical with its proud director. Nixon stays to watch yesterday's rushes from "Werewolf Meets Frankenstein". As the monsters fight on-screen, werewolf Larry — acting like a real one — creeps up from behind Nixon's seat and strangles him. In the workshop, Pete deprograms Larry while Rivero washes his bloody mitts. Pete and Rivero check out with the rest of the night crew. Det. Thompson and Det.

Jones investigate the murder. The Coroner notices animal-like wounds on Nixon's throat. "So what do we have to do?" asks Jones. "Look for a monster?"

Thompson and Jones talk to Clayton to see if Nixon had any old enemies. During a dance with his girl Arlene, Larry feels faint. He recalls the scene he did where the werewolf had to escape the police. " — I still feel as if I'm running. I don't know what it is, but I'm running away . . ."

Ambitious Monahan visits Pete and Rivero that evening. Unsatisfied with the handling of the big brass, he has written down some things in his little black book. He thinks the murder was an inside job. Pete and Rivero did not leave the studio until after the time of the murder. Monahan wants Pete to go to Capt. Hancock of Homicide. "The security of this lot means a great deal to me," he declares. "This studio'll be around a long time and someday, I expect to be its chief of police." After Monahan leaves, desperate Pete hurries to his makeup.

Richards plays his radio loud while Monahan goes on his rounds. In the commissary, trench-coated, Neanderthal looking Pete clubs Monahan to death and steals the notebook. Calmly, Pete and Rivero pass Richards as they check out. Richards looks for Monahan and finds his body. Thompson and Jones learn about Pete and Rivero from Richards.

Pete watches John Ashley perform a rock number for the musical being shot. Clayton is adamant on the view he shared with Nixon that horror is dead, seeing this as an example of the wheels of progress. "No matter who they run over," pouts Pete. "That's the way the footage cuts!" tersely affirms Clayton. While Tony is being readied for his Frankenstein makeup, two girl reporters for a high school paper drop in. "How does it feel to be the last of the Frankensteins?" one asks. When the girls leave, Pete says to Tony, "I told you I was right when I said they were cutting the ground from under us." Tony is put under.

Driving home that night, Clayton is attacked in his garage by Frankenstein Tony. Some of his makeup rubs off on Clayton's hand during their struggle. As Clayton's body falls on the blasting car horn, the noise is heard by Millie, a maid walking down the street. Fleeing Tony knocks her over. Pete and Rivero wait for Tony at Rivero's house, where Tony is deprogrammed.

Officials consider closing the studio. En route to the police station for questioning, Pete and Rivero encounter Larry's angry agent Gary Droz, who considers Pete a negative character for putting fear of unemployability in Larry's head. Millie describes the monster she saw to Capt. Hancock, Thompson and Jones. They get to Richards, then ask Pete if the killer could be a crackpot influenced by his movies. Wondering why Rivero is so quiet, Thompson bullies him, inferring that Rivero may be trying to frame Pete to show who is a better makeup artist. "I only do what

Pete tells me!" tells Rivero. "I'm a good assistant!" As they leave the station, Pete berates Rivero for nearly cracking. Rivero fears what may happen if Larry and Tony are interrogated. They are still under his power, insists Pete. The police chemist has determined that the makeup found under Clayton's fingernails was a homemade concoction. Hancock went to check Pete's workshop for a spot analysis.

Pete and Rivero return to the workshop, where Pete's belongings have already been packed for him. Larry and Tony are there. Pete invites them to his home for a farewell party. They have dates, but reluctantly accept. Pete throws a used greasepaint jar into a wastebasket as they go. The police enter the workshop and find it. The chemist makes his analysis.

Passing through the front door of Pete's residence, Larry and Tony are shown his cathedral-like monster museum. Pete and Rivero go into the next room for refreshments. "Pete's got ways about him," uneasy Tony tells Larry, " . . . strange ways." Larry agrees. They compare notes on their strange memory lapses. Rivero wants to leave town and visit his brother's ranch. Although he professes loyalty, distrustful Pete picks up a knife from a table, whirls around and stabs Rivero in the abdomen.

Larry and Tony try to leave, but find the museum's doors locked. Pete brings a tray of soft drinks. He wants to add their real heads to his collection. "My new additions will be lifelike. Just think, in the years to come, you'll both be up here. A refuge . . . a permanent home." Larry and Tony are openly frightened and admit they tried to leave. "Three murders," reveals Pete, "and we're all involved. Each one of us must take credit for one." Tony: "You're crazy, Pete!" Pete grabs a knife from the wall. "Not crazy enough to let you escape!" he threatens, advancing toward the boys. Larry knocks over a candelabra, setting the curtains ablaze. The police break in. "My children!" shrieks Pete. "I must save my children!" Larry and Tony are helped to safety as the inferno consumes Pete. As layers of burning mask material peel away, human skulls appear.

The character of Pete Drummond was analogous to Universal's pink-slipped Jack Pierce. Pete was the most identifiable Cohen villain because the power he discovered was put to use only when he received his walking papers. Around people who actually made films, Pete was a pleasant eccentric and a respected employee. Any laid-off worker — particularly a dedicated craftsman — could understand Pete's gut-eating rage and his vendetta made more sense than the control of the youngsters in *I Was a Teenage Werewolf* and *Blood of Dracula*.

Pete's particular mode of subjugation began with a long-ago blunder that became a constructive boost to the performance of the Prehistoric Man. Larry Drake and Tony Mantell were quite the opposite of other Cohen youth pawns. New members of the work force

Larry (Gary Clarke) wonders if he will become a werewolf after union hours in HOW TO MAKE A MONSTER.

165

Another mysterious death occurs during the making of the "Werewolf Meets Frankenstein" film in HOW TO MAKE A MONSTER.

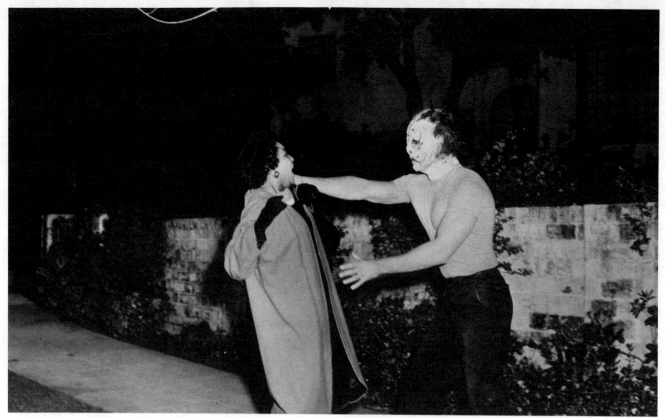

Tony (Gary Conway), in his costume, frightens a poor maid named Millie (Pauline Meyers)
in HOW TO MAKE A MONSTER.

free of any personality kinks, they were merely gullible — babes of the industry set to kill when Pete made them think they were protecting their livelihoods. The necessity of triple homicides was part of the morbid Hollywood tradition of deaths in threes. To dispose of spur-of-the-moment target Monahan, Pete found it necessary to bloody his own hands, assuming the identity of the monster that launched him over a quarter-century ago. No one was supposed to see Larry, Tony and Pete commit the murders, so their alter ego appliances were strictly Pete's vanity. This time, because they were skin-deep monsters, the teen fiends turned against their Parent unscathed, though coming close to getting burned as Pete died in the flames of his inanimate monument to pride.

Monster movies of the fifties were almost over only in the sense their founding decade was on the wane. Into the sixties spilled a few delayed fifties films and, occasionally, a picture imitating them turned up. Hammer's gory, low-cleavage makeovers of period shock and a rash of psycho cinema didn't nudge out completely the atomic mutant, the alien or the dinosaur. *Teenage* monsters faded because they were a derivation of Delinquency drama and only certain monsters were adaptable to youth personalities. The immortal pair Herman Cohen invented were obliquely mentioned in generalizations because "teenage" would have sounded self-conscious.

AIP had done most of its soundstage scenes at the Kling Studios, once owned by Charles Chaplin, but relinquished it due to high overhead. *How to Make a Monster* was shot at Herb Strock's old home ZIV Productions. Fronting as a venerable Major, AIP put on the dog for all purposes, but couldn't lose true identity. Werewolf Larry elicited all kinds of amused reactions on the AIP lot ("Boy, when Pete makes 'em up, it's for real") and a tour bus guide said the *Horrors of the Black Museum* (1959), the first Cohen picture made in London, was being done there. Even the technical shortcuts of AIP were shown in jest. Martin Brace, the director of "Werewolf Meets Frankenstein", was an example of the Edward Cahn speed course who told Larry and Tony that the monster battle had to be shot in one take. Clayton and Nixon were only two agents of a New York conglomerate, but as intimate partners were near-counterpoints of Nicholson and Arkoff.

In the story of *How to Make a Monster*, "Werewolf" and "Frankenstein" were treated as Pete's newest laurels, yet advertising for *I Was a Teenage Werewolf* and *I Was a Teenage Frankenstein* inserted proof of their preceding solo vehicles (Michael Landon was no longer the Teenage Werewolf, but the *Teenage Frankenstein* poster acknowledged Gary Conway, continuing the Frankenstein role as Tony Mantell). "Footage" of the epic Werewolf-Frankenstein fight consisted of only one shot of lurking Larry and violent sound effects heard moments before Nixon's death. As Larry slaughtered Nixon, he inexplicably dribbled animal saliva just like the actual Teenage Werewolf. Then there were the skulls beneath the heads of the trophy Children. Pete acted like his plan to mount Larry and Tony's heads was a startling innovation — but where did he get the skulls? If he had killed every actor who ever played a "child", wouldn't there have been a history of decapitations?

How to Make a Monster eased viewers into accepting its milieu with an imaginative titles sequence. On a white-surfaced makeup mirror, an artist's hand drew the letters of the main title. The following credits appeared to the left. In a blank area on the lower right, the hand quickly sketched in the face of the Teenage Werewolf. The illustration dissolved into a matching close-up of Larry seated in the makeup chair undergoing final touch-ups.

Paul Blaisdell must have been thrilled to see most of *his* "kids" (plus a few new faces made for this movie) in one film *until* the fiery finale. The second Larry and Tony entered the proverbial spider's parlor, the film went to color for its most prolonged use in a black and white AIP picture. The Fire Department stood by ready to extinguish a staged blaze, but the effects man — drunk according to one report — prematurely tested the gas jets and the conflagration props ignited early. Herbert Strock and cinematographer Maury Gertsman used separate cameras to record the scene. A few of the masks did survive, albeit toasted for the wear.

Robert J. Harris was the most unreservedly unbalanced of all of Cohen's evil adults. Neither suave like future Cohen mainstay Michael Gough or clinically detached like Whit Bissell, Harris was a rotund, balding gnome who looked through glazed eyes, letting his mouth drop like a gulping fish, and everything he had to do quickly he lurched to in gangway zips. Paul Brinegar's Rivero (there's that Rivers name again) was about as gutless as the Bissell stooges, but played his role with more heart. The Teenage Frankenstein Gary Conway enacted in this film was more comfortably performed because he was merely an extension of another character. Of Larry and Tony, Larry was the actor the film seemed to like the most, probably because Gary Clarke had a gentler demeanor than Conway. Clarke played nice guys very satisfactorily, but such roles only took him a limited way. He was Dick Hamilton on "Michael Shayne" and Steve Hill on "The Virginian". After that, Clarke faded into small parts.

Millie was the only useful female character. The cast was strictly a Man's World of Character veterans: Morris Ankrum, Walter Reed, Thomas B. Henry and Malcolm Atterbury. In his guest appearance, John Ashley let loose a set of competent but non Elvis-threatening pipes.

With *How to Make a Monster* in the can, Herman Cohen took off for England, where he made *Horrors of the Black Museum*. Cohen never forgot his teenage films and found excuses to inject their elements into his new scripts (as late as 1968's *Berserk*, he was still using the name Rivers and the killer was an adolescent but completely independent girl). Sound business sense kept Cohen from making his 1960 *Konga* into its original conception: *I Was a Teenage Gorilla*.

Tony thinks his looks will improve by brushing his "Frankenstein" hair in HOW TO MAKE A MONSTER.

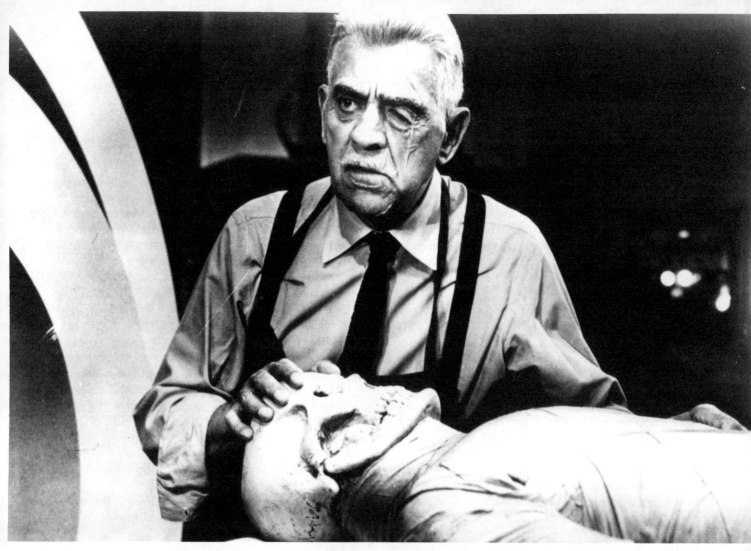

FRANKENSTEIN 1970

Allied Artists, 1958

Producer	Aubrey Schenck
Director	Howard W. Koch
Screenplay	Richard Landau
	George Worthing Yates
Story	Aubrey Schenck
	Charles A. Moses
Cinematography	Carl E. Guthrie
Film Editor	John A. Bushelman
Music	Paul Dunlap
Production Design	Jack T. Collis
Sound	Francis C. Stahl
Set Decorator	Jerry Welch
Assistant Director	George Vieria
Makeup Supervision	Gordon Bau
Makeup	George Bau
Electrical Supervisor	Ralph Owens
Key Grip	Chuck Harris
Property Master	George Sweeney

Cinemascope / An A-Z Production
Running time: 83 minutes

Cast: Boris Karloff (Baron Victor von Frankenstein), Tom Duggan (Mike Shaw), Jana Lund (Carolyn Hayes), Donald Barry (Douglas Row), Charlotte Austin (Judy Stevens), Irwin Berke (Insp. Raab), Rudolph Anders (Wilhelm Gottfried), John Dennis (Morgan Haley), Norbert Schiller (Shuter), Mike *aka Michael* Lane (Hans / Monster)

As Dr. Gustav Niemann in *House of Frankenstein* (1945), Boris Karloff had experimented with the monster he once enacted. He got the chance to do it again as an actual Frankenstein family member in *Frankenstein 1970*, which was first dated 1960 in its title. Producer Aubrey Schenck and Charles A. Moses wrote a story about a German Frankenstein descendant who exploited exploiters of the family's notoriety for an experiment that would have been the ultimate achievement in "bringing together" creator and creation. It was Edwin Zabel who interested Allied Artists President Steve Broidy in the Richard Landau-George Worthing Yates script. To give it a classy look, Broidy wanted the film done in Cinemascope.

(Above) The great Boris Karloff is seen with his creation in FRANKENSTEIN 1970 (1958).

Schenk, Zable and Howard Koch had done some work at Warner Brothers following their exit from United Artists. Koch had impressed Jack Warner with his direction of *Untamed Youth* (1957) and Warner allowed him to film *Frankenstein 1970* on the more spacious Warner lot. At Koch's disposal was an expensive standing set built for the Errol Flynn movie *Too Much Too Soon* (1958). The Cinemascope lenses were borrowed from Twentieth Century Fox because Aubrey Schenck was related to Joseph Schenck. The cast would even include two personalities from local Los Angeles radio and TV, Tom Duggan and Irwin Berke. Without Boris Karloff and his historic association with the Frankenstein film that started it all, none of these extravagances would have mattered much.

Frankenstein 1970 sounded misleading, but the futuristic date was a bid to sci-fi, as was the idea of using atomic energy to give the new monster life. In infamy, this was Karloff's *Bride of the Monster* — but a *Bride* with budget and talent.

Dressed in eighteenth century clothes, Carolyn Hayes flees through a dark, foggy forest to escape a shambling, faceless monster clad in a grey suit with a bent leg and animalistic claws. Carolyn wades into a steamy lake where the thing shoves her head into the water. Director Douglas Row yells, "Cut!", but the "monster", local man Hans, keeps Carolyn's face submerged until a butler named Shuter yells at him in German to stop. Row, Carolyn, press-agent Mike Shaw, script girl Judy Stevens, Row's latest ex-wife, and cameraman Morgan Haley are filming a TV show about the two hundred thirtieth anniversary of the Frankenstein legend at the family castle. Row is famous for getting realism at any cost. Carolyn complains a bit while drying off, but is willing to roll with the hardships of the shoot.

Shuter's master is Baron Victor von Frankenstein, who chides his lawyer friend, Wilhelm Gottfried, for persuading him to let the bothersome Row troupe film here. Frankenstein has been selling off the family's art treasures and spending money for a secret endeavor. Part of it entails an atomic reactor he has ordered. The conversation turns to Frankenstein's interment in Belson, where the Nazis tortured him. "But you won, they didn't, " Gottfried reminds Frankenstein, whose surgical hands were spared so he could be made to assist in unholy operations. "But look what they did to the rest of me!" shouts bitter, scarred Frankenstein. *My body!*" "But you didn't give them what they wanted," insists Gottfried. "You didn't go over to their side. They didn't take your mind, Victor." "Would anyone believe that you and I are the same age?" asks Frankenstein. "That I'm still a . . . man?" Offered a scientific government post, the last of the Frankensteins is not interested in politically-controlled employment. "How much time do you think that I have left? Every hour is a day out of my life. Every day a month, every month a

year. A month can see the end of my life!"

Gottfried is about to inquire about the intended use to the reactor when the Row troupe enters the living room from tonight's shooting. Row gives Gottfried television releasing forms for Frankenstein to sign. Row has decided to revise the start of the show, wanting Frankenstein to narrate it from the vault. Carolyn thinks the success of the program could lead to a possible series made from here. "That would be my pleasure," charmed Frankenstein tells Carolyn, taking her hand, "with you as my leading lady, Miss Hayes." He tells Row, "I'm becoming reconciled to your presence here. Your presence here could be the answer to all my problems." Emitting a raucously cryptic laugh, Frankenstein hobbles to his organ and plays music. "What did I say?" asks puzzled Row.

In the vault, Frankenstein relates the story of his great, great-grandfather, Richard Freiherr von Frankenstein I who, in 1740, began work to create a living being. "First, he had to learn how flesh was made. He had to discover the art of transplanting vital organs from human beings into his creature and knitting them together until they had all the attributes of God-inspired birth. I must admit he was not too scrupulous about where he got his — raw material. But after seventeen years, his labors were at last rewarded — he created a living man. But, to his horror, what did he discover but that his creature was a monster — hideous, foul, its evil brain with one thought: that of survival. In order to survive, it killed and killed and killed again until it became the very image of the devil incarnate. But because he was the creator, he could not bring himself to destroy it utterly." Frankenstein walks over to a sarcophagus with a covered body lying on top. "In this stone sarcophagus, deep in the bowels of the earth, he buried his creature, his creation, in the passage of an ancient vault of the family burial place. He sealed it away for all time, without vital organs or soul, so that nevermore it could bring terror to mortal man or challenge God — the only true creator for whose forgiveness he prayed."

As Frankenstein raises a knife over the body, Carolyn gets carried away from the rehearsal sidelines and screams. Under the sheet, horrified Hans sits up in alarm. Row is elated by the performance. Asked his opinion, Mike unenthusiatically comments, "A real gasser." Shuter says that Hans is afraid to work here because the place gives him nightmares. Row remedies that with a few bills. Frankenstein lingers for a few moments in the vault as the others exit.

In the living room, Mike is setting up a promotion deal over the phone. Following the TV show, a Frankenstein party will be thrown and an international horror contest will pick Best Goblin. Gottfried is disturbed by the macabre tone of Frankenstein's organ music. Shuter offers Carolyn some coffee. She was in town and bought him a plaid scarf to keep him warm

Frankenstein (Karloff) in the castle vault in FRANKENSTEIN 1970.

when he works in the cold vault. A nice kiss in the cheek from Carolyn raises his temperature. Frankenstein observes with repressed jealousy. Row has worked on the altered version of the script and would like to go over the new scene with Carolyn as a pretext to a seduction she politely wards off. Mike suggests that Judy join him for a walk, but she still carries a torch for Row. Gottfried is troubled by Frankenstein's dealings with a morgue director and what the reactor is for.

When the others have retired, Frankenstein lights a candle, switches off the living room lights and, with the candle, returns to the vault. Frankenstein twists the head of a cherub statue and the sacophogus lid opens to expose a flight of stone steps. Down in his hidden lab, Frankenstein uncovers a clay bust of a face, adding a small detail as he refers to a photograph of himself. Bugging devices linked to an intercom monitor the sounds of the guests in their rooms. Judy pats cold cream onto her face. Row is busily typing. Carolyn hums prettily as she files her nails. Mike is silent until he drops ice cubes into a glass and pours himself a drink. Everything Frankenstein does is recorded. Out of a circular storage space — the "target" of a bull's-eye patterned wall — slides a gurney with a bandaged body topped by a skull. Frankenstein tests the flexibility of a stitched-on hand and comments on the reshaping of the skull.

Shuter is dousing the candle lights in the vault. His arm accidentally upsets the cherub head and he sees the sarcophagus lid open. Dropping his scarf, Shuter descends into the lab, where he faces Frankenstein. "I do not understand what is happening here," trembling Shuter tells Frankenstein, who explains, "A miracle, Shuter." Unnerved by the body, Shuter gasps, "You have opened the grave. You have brought the thing back." "*Will* bring it back," explains Frankenstein. Using his surgical scissors, he hypnotizes Shuter, who begs for mercy. "You will live again, Shuter," reassures Frankenstein. "You will live again. You will hear me and your brain will obey. Think what glory it will bring to the house of Frankenstein. No more pain, no more suffering. I'm doing you a favor, Shuter. I'm saving you the pain and misery and discomfort of old age." Frankenstein transplants Shuter's heart into the monster.

In Shuter's absence, Carolyn fixes breakfast. Frankenstein says Shuter has gone to Nurenburg to visit relatives. Hans will replace him. "We've already met," says Carolyn — alluding to their water scene. Frankenstein is happy to learn the reactor has just arrived. He gives the monster Shuter's brain. From a refrigerator, Frankenstein removes a jar containing eyes. When the door bumps against his arm, he drops the jar, ruining them.

While playing his organ, Frankenstein notices Carolyn with Shuter's scarf, which she found in the vault. "I was saving it for Shuter," says Carolyn, "when he . . .

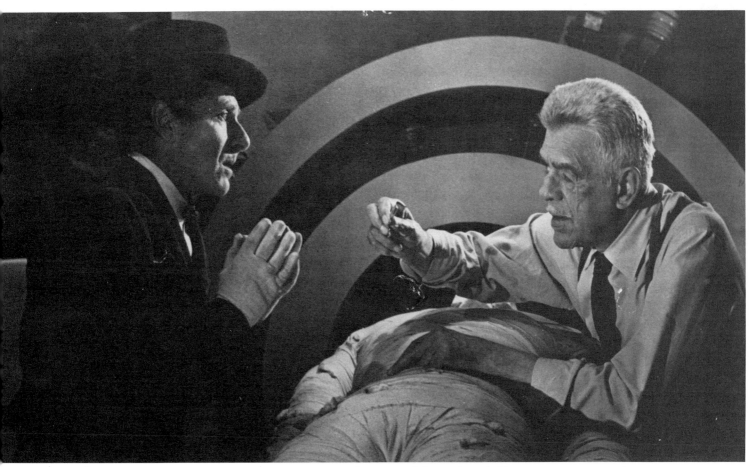

Shuter doesn't know it, but Frankenstein is saving him the pain and discomfort of old age in FRANKENSTEIN 1970.

comes back." "That may be some time," softly remarks Frankenstein. Saying he will send the scarf to Shuter, Frankenstein wraps it around his neck. Gottfried knows Shuter has no relatives anywhere. His clothes are still in his room. Frankenstein has been meaning to tell Gottfried the story of an overly-inquisitive commandant at Belsen who disappeared. "And then, one bright, lovely day, they found the fellow. He had no tongue. Oh, I know. I was called in to examine the poor wretch. A beautiful job of surgery if I say so myself . . . beautiful."

With the reactor, Frankenstein brings the monster to life. Dimming of the castle lights is noticed by Morgan in the kitchen and Row while he is at his typewriter. As the monster rests against the vertical table it is strapped to, Frankenstein tests Shuter's mental reactions to his words with an ECG unit. The monster obeys orders to raise each of its arms. "Yours is not the brain I would have chosen," confesses Frankenstein, "but at least you are obedient. And now we must get eyes for you."

Row still has a yen for Carolyn, who refuses him admittance to her locked room. Judy is in her room typing notes and she invites in sociable Mike, who brings a bottle of wine. Mike steals a kiss from Judy and gets the taste of toothpaste. Judy might go for Mike if — and when — she finally gets Row out of her hair. Judy is about to retire and when Mike gets too amorous, she ejects him from the room. Mike begs for reentry on the

corridor side of the locked door as Judy changes into her nightgown until he finally gives up. Judy hears a sound at the door, flinging it open, expecting to see Mike, and faints when the monster enters. "I sent you for Row!" angry Frankenstein tells the monster when he brings the wrong corpse to the lab. "Now you have no eyes, this poor girl is dead and we're both in great danger!" Judy's remains are dumped into a gurgling disposal device.

Believing Judy's disappearance may have been foul play, Row shows Mike an alimony check sent to her by her New York attorney. Mike thinks Judy left the castle to escape both of them. Inspired by the reactor, Row wants to shoot in the lab. The lab is not included in the filming contract and Frankenstein emphatically declares his unpatented equipment off-limits. Morgan and Carolyn are sent to the vault to line up shots down there. While Carolyn rehearses an entrance from a dark corner, the shadowy monster makes several attempts to grab her. After Carolyn goes, Morgan sees the monster in his viewfinder and dies. He had rare A-type blood — so his eyes are useless.

After this disappearance, Row summons Insp. Raab, who arrives with two uniformed policemen. To throw off suspicion, Frankenstein insinuates that Judy was upset by her relationship with Row and claims Morgan said he was going to Hamburg to pick up a special lens. Frankenstein takes Row, Mike, Raab and his men into the vault for an inspection. The monster opens the sacophagus lid from below, but Frankenstein manages to close it up. There have been wild rumors of a monster taking people. Raab accuses Row. Mike admits he spread them. Frankenstein wants to press charges against Mike. Gottfried accuses Frankenstein of conducting illicit experiments. "What a wonderful commandant you would have made," Frankenstein tells him.

Frankenstein takes Gottfried to the vault, where the sarcophagus lid opens and Gottfried is transfixed with fear as the monster comes toward him up the steps. *His eyes occupy the monster's sockets*. "Gottfried, Gottfried . . .," moans remorseful Frankenstein as he disposes of Gottfried's clothes.

Row and Mike decide to examine the vault on their own while Frankenstein listens in over the intercom. Row discovers Morgan's viewfinder. He drives to the police while Mike guards Carolyn, who will feel safer in her room. Mike tells Frankenstein that Row is in his room working. Frankenstein notes Mike's fascination with the castle library, particularly an old anatomy book. Frankenstein shows Mike an album collection of Rare coins. Holding a gold one insured at ten thousand dollars, Frankenstein hypnotizes Mike into divulging where Row has gone. When the clock strikes the quarter, Mike will tell Carolyn that Row is back and wants to see her in the living room. As his conscious perception of time returns, Mike stares at the coin in awe. In Raab's office, Row shows pictures of Judy and Morgan to a cab driver who denies ever having taken them to the train station. A porter there saw the pair only when they arrived. Raab agrees to investigate.

As Row and Raab speed to the castle, Mike carries out Frankenstein's command. Carolyn faints when she sees the monster. In the vault, he hears Frankenstein order him over the intercom to take Carolyn downstairs. As the monster approaches the open sarcophagus, Carolyn comes to and hears Frankenstein call the monster Shuter. Appealing to his dormant mind, she frantically begs, "Upstairs, Shuter, upstairs." Row and Raab rush into the living room. Hearing Row call, Carolyn shouts she is in the vault. The monster frees her. To destroy the incriminating lab, Frankenstein starts the reactor. Manifesting the rage of Shuter, the monster knocks over some equipment and lumbers toward him. Frankenstein tries to warn Shuter about the radiation, but atomic steam billows from the reactor and both he and the monster perish.

When the contamination clears, a Geiger counter man in a radiation suit tells Row, Mike and Raab it is safe to enter the lab. The monster's loose face bandages are pulled back — revealing the features Frankenstein had before the war. Row plays back a recorder tape. The voice of Frankenstein says, "I made you in my image so the name of Frankenstein could survive. I gave you eyes, ears, a heart, a brain . . ."

What should have been *Frankenstein 1958* was set in a modern Germany still mending from the turmoil visited it by the Third Reich. After the Holocaust, the gory details of the Frankenstein experiments seemed almost minuscule. In his ambition to improve upon God's handiwork, Richard von Frankenstein had practiced a master race theory with a nobler aim. At Belsen, Victor Frankenstein had felt the receiving end of surgery, his interment a contrivance to give the film its only horrible face. Using Richard's idea solely for personal rehabilitation, Frankenstein's dream of bodily renewal — remindful of Ygor's similar goal in *The Ghost of Frankenstein* (1942) — was meant to replace the years blasted by political madness. Frankenstein was rightly embittered — yet the creative doctor in him appreciated the black humor of a nosy Nazi paying for his loose lips by the amputation of something else. At least the Commandant was not parted from the organs that could make his third leg go, "Seig heil."

An aristocrat with little more than title, Frankenstein prostituted his family's name by selling out to the story version of a tabloid "reality" show. With a recouped bank account came the heavy debt of having to play host to the TV troupe, who demonstrated how condescendingly some show folk treat "civilians". Hyper, irreverent, womanizing Row perceived everything about the castle as a compliment to Transylvania. Docile Shuter was "perfect typecasting" and big but timid Hans "Horrible Herman". Carolyn brought grief to Frankenstein only by being a beautiful woman. She was unresponsive to Row's passes, so Frankenstein could find a little consolation in knowing the American he truly hated could not touch base with her. One did not have to have tattooed arm numbers to pick up Judy's tasteless innuendo when she told Carolyn, "You'll never know who you'll find dead in an oven." While these vidiots were making their mundane tribute to the past, Frankenstein was busy writing a new horror chapter in their blood, achieving actual fulfillment through the flesh of a loyal servant and a lifelong friend . . . two people who worked for and cared about him.

Medical concerns were not all logical. How could the eyeless monster be expected to get around? Shuter undoubtedly knew the castle well, but blindness requires adjustment even at home. If not for dramatic symmetry decreeing those of an intimate who saw too much, Frankenstein could have used *Judy's* eyes. And who was going to replace Shuter's brain with Frankenstein's?

Since everything else was castle-bound Frankenstein 1970 made its first and scariest shock scene a Big Gun loaded with pure Gothic grain. Except for the one man who lensed in color, Whale, Kenton and Fisher wouldn't have changed a thing — except maybe pass over Jana Lund or redub her asthmatic screams. But Lund looked good, ran to beat the devil and didn't trip outside out of her key light. Presumably the Richard Frankenstein monster, Carolyn was fleeing from a thing made up of donors who were Quasimodo for his hunched back, a werewolf for his clawed fingers and Kharis for his draggy leg. The Victor creation was all mummy-looking except for its skinless skull introduction and the cylindrical shape of its bandaged head. Only when seen in a technical perspective by Morgan Haley was it terrifying. The "young" Frankenstein face was a 1932 photo of Karloff's and the fact Willhelm Gottfried was played by Rudolph Anders of *She Demons* gave the materialization of Gottfried's eyes in the monster's head an image reminiscent of the unmasking of Mona Osler.

There was much to look at in the lab and a lot done with it. They should have eliminated the clay bust because it was a tip-off to the surprise ending (the photo of Karloff was another insertion of a star's publicity art into a film like the redundant Bela Lugosi stills Prof. Strowski carried in his briefcase in *Bride of the Monster*). The bugging devices didn't pick up any sounds of interest except Carolyn's humming, bringing to Frankenstein's face an appreciative smile. Closed-circuit TV would have probably shown her in a state of partial undress. The atomic reactor was to indicate that raising monsters by electricity had become passe, but its noise was the same electric razor that passed for the exhaust sound of Flash Gordon's rocket.

The monster making scenes created some ripe ballyhoo. Several technicians allegedly fainted when they saw the grisly prop eyeballs. They and a massaged heart were animal organs. Peter Cushing's Frankenstein got rid of his "garbage" with acid, Whit Bissell's an alligator

and Karloff's a trash compactor — or that was what it was *supposed* to be. The censors objected to the noise of crunching bone and the new sound was a toilet flushing.

Probably wishing that was where he could toss the script, Karloff did not hide his distaste for the film, making it work in Frankenstein's Holocaust recollections and in the scenes where Frankenstein had to put up with the boorish antics of Douglas Row. Row was one of the few big part characters Donald Barry was able to play after the end of his Red Ryder series. Coming on as a bush-league Mike Todd, Barry was no more of a real hero than the dorky Tom Duggan. Shuter, in his revenge on Frankenstein, was the only "hero" and the actor under the bandages was former wrestler Mike Lane, seen earlier as Hans. Lane was thus the only actor in a Frankenstein film with several monsters to play both of them. He was later cast as a more standard-looking but good Frankenstein monster in the kidvid show "Monster Squad".

Schenck, Zabel and Koch wanted to use Karloff one more time for the unmade King of the Monsters, dissolving their contract with the intended third film still owed, Karloff took the termination of the agreement hard. This may be why he was more vocal about criticizing *Frankenstein 1970* than any other film he made. The year following Karloff's death was the real 1970 — when *Frankenstein 1970* was reissued.

173

Shuter returns as Frankenstein's future body in FRANKENSTEIN 1970.

THE SCREAMING SKULL

American-International, 1958

Executive Producer	T. Frank Woods
Producer-Screenplay	John Knuebuhl
Director	Alex Nicol
Associate Producer	John Coots
Cinematography	Floyd Crosby
Film Editor	Betty Jane Lane
Music	Ernest Gold
Assistant Director	Maurice Vacarro
Second Unit Cinematography	Kenny Peach
Sound	Al Overton
Script Supervisor	Betty Fancher
Makeup	Don Roberson
Lighting Supervisor	John Millman
Chief Grip	Charles Hanawalt
Sound Editor	Nadine Rogne
Assistant Editor	Florence Williams

A Madera Production
Running time: 70 minutes

Cast: John Hudson (Eric Whitlock), Peggy Webber (Jenni Whitlock), Alex Nicol (Mickey), Russ Conway (Rev. Mr. Snow), Tony Johnson (Mrs. Snow)

Gaslight heroines are usually rich, fragile young things with a past history of trauma. Someone they marry or who is natural kin fabricates memories or devises scares symbolic of their ordeal. Justice or fate upsets the fortune-hunter's carefully-laid plans. A slight but atmospheric study in How To Drive A Woman Mad was *The Screaming Skull*.

The estate of Marion Whitlock has been empty since her death two years ago. Marion's widower, Eric, returns with his new bride Jenni. She is taken on a tour of the gardens, where peacocks roam. As Eric carries Jenni over the threshold of the front door, they are watched by Mickey, an idiot gardener. Eric's old friends, Rev. and Mrs. Snow, pay a surprise visit, meeting Jenni. She is introduced to shy Mickey who has never really accepted Marion's death. Mr. Snow tells Jenni that Marion drowned in the garden lily pond when she

(Above) Mickey (Alex Nicol) spies on Eric (John Hudson) and Jenni (Peggy Weber) in THE SCREAMING SKULL (1958).

smashed the base of her skull against its cement wall. In psychic contact with Marion, Mickey talks to her self-portrait, asking her to make the others leave. Coexecutor of the estate, Eric has little more than the house. Jenni is rich. Her parents died in a boating mishap and she was institutionalized

That night, a noisy shutter awakens Jenni. Eric is gone. She hears screams from the portrait. Eric surprises her. A wet lily pad lies on the floor. Jenni heard screams while in the hospital. These apparently were peacock screeches. The next afternoon, Eric goes into town on business, expecting to be gone a long time. Jenni tries to befriend Mickey, who claims he hears Marion.

That evening, Jenni stirs from a nightmare to hear more screams. In a corridor cabinet, she finds a screaming skull. Scratches mark her hand. Jenni throws the skull out of a window onto the lawn. There is loud rapping at the front door. Jenni opens it to see the skull again and faints. Eric revives Jenni. He suspects Mickey of trying to scare her out of supposed resentment Mickey has for Eric, but Jenni doesn't think Mickey is clever or quick enough. Mr. Snow thinks Jenni scratched herself on the rough texture of the cabinet wood. Eric cannot find the skull. Jenni feels guilty about her parent's death because she hated her mother.

To end her nightmares, Eric wants Jenni to burn Marion's portrait on an outdoor pyre. As it burns, there is a faint scream. When Jenni rakes up the cooling ashes, the skull reappears. Eric does not see it. Jenni faints. Eric — who planned all this — hides the skull in a corner of the pond. Mickey watches from the bushes and removes it. Jenni wants to return to the hospital. Eric tells Mr. Snow she tried suicide there. When Eric goes back to the pond, he cannot find the skull. Eric chases Mickey, trying violently to make him admit he took it, but Mickey will not confess. Mickey hides it in a basket, taking it to the Snows. Because Eric said he did not see it, this means he is plotting to collect Jenni's fortune .

Jenni goes to the greenhouse to say good-bye to Mickey. A full-bodied apparition, Marion's real ghost, scares her away. Upstairs in the mansion, Eric knocks Jenni out so he can fake a suicide hanging. He hears rapping at the door and opens it to confront Marion. Panicky Eric pushes her down. As a storm rages, he tries to escape, but the skull haunts him everywhere. Eric flees to the pond, where the skull sinks its teeth into his throat. Waking up, Jenni finds Marion's dress on the floor. The Snows appear. Mr. Snow discovers Eric's body in the pond. He and Mrs. Snow leave with Jenni. At the pond, Mickey tells Marion they are gone.

Screaming Skull made the most of an empty house, its manicured grounds, some interesting dime-store fright effects and five actors, including the director, actor Alex Nicol, in an uncharacteristic Dwight Frye-type role as the gimpy, slovenly, childlike Mickey. The film was made skillfully enough so that its cheapness looked like creative austerity. More spare and intimate than most Gaslighters, it thrust its shocks farther and more jarringly into the foreground. The added twist of a genuine ghost present covered Eric with false innocence that held up almost to the climax.

Nicol drew heavily on the extant details of the estate to create dread, importing only a few outside props that looked like they belonged there. The lack of furniture (explained as a condition of Eric's lengthy departure) enhanced Jenni's vulnerability and made the rooms and halls more omnipresent. Appearances by the skull made imaginative use of its sundry hiding places. Optical effects were also clever, like double-printing that made the skull roll across the grass like a phantom boulder. Subjectively, it straightened up in a tilted lawn-level view of the house. When the skull assaulted Eric's senses, there was one shot of it lying in a seat of Eric's car and the skull appeared to be *laughing*. Over a full view of the front of the house, it was magnified to enormous proportions. At the pond, the struggle between Eric and the skull was caught in blinding flashes of lightning that whited out most of the screen.

The choral and xylophone-flavored score was an early work of Ernest Gold, who went on to such contrastively weighty films as *Exodus* (1960) and *It's a Mad, Mad, Mad, Mad World* (1963).

Writer-producer John Knuebuhl let Nicol direct by having him play Mickey so Knuebuhl could economize. A rather primitive role for one of Elia Kazan's first students, but Nicol did not condescend. John Hudson, cast as another louse spouse, was the twin brother of *Attack of the Fifty Foot Woman*'s William Hudson. Peggy Webber had been a radio writer, producer, director and actress in Tuscon before moving to Los Angeles. Profiled in "Time" in 1944 for her career in that medium, Webber became part of Jack Webb's acting repertoire on TV. Two years before Janet Leigh did it to much fanfare in *Psycho* (1960), Webber had a scene in *Skull* that showed off a large bust line supported by a heavy-duty bra.

Screaming Skull emulated *Macabre* (1958) by offering free burial to anyone who died of fright. *Skull*'s gimmick was part of the film in a teaser that focused on an empty coffin and moved to a close-up of a certificate on the pillow stating the casket was reserved for this purpose. Another promo idea was the notion of having patrons utter taped screams and the winner would partake in a radio campaign.

Unrelated to this film was 1973's videotaped TV-movie *The Screaming Skull*, which aired on "ABC Wide World of Entertainment". David McCallum's villain killed his wife by pouring molten wax into her ear. Her skull then killed him and her brother.

TERROR FROM THE YEAR 5,000

American-International, 1958
Released in England as *Cage of Doom*

Executive Producers	James H. Nicholson
	Samuel Z. Arkoff
Producer-Director-Screenplay	Robert J. Gurney, Jr.
Cinematography	Arthur Florman
Editorial Supervisor	Dede Allen
Art Director	Beatrice Gurney
Assistant Producer	Gene Searchinger
Production Coordinator	Mark Hanna
Scenic Designer	William Hoffman
Assistant Director	Jack Diamond
Makeup	Rudolph Liszt
Sound	Robert Hathaway
Script Clerk	Anita Hathaway
Key Grip	Jack Wallace
Gaffer	Richard Gable
Properties	Gus Brockway

A La Holla Production
Running time: 74 minutes

Cast: Ward Costello (Robert Hodges), Joyce Holden (Claire Erling), Frederic Downs (Prof. Howard Erling), John Stratton (Victor), Salome Jens (Future Woman), Fred Herrick (Angelo), Beatrice Furdeaux *aka Gurney* (Miss Blake), Jack Diamond, Fred Taylor (Lab Technicians), Fred Downs, William Cost

Time travel on film was largely untapped when Robert Gurney, Jr. wrote, produced and directed *Terror from the Year 5,000*. The few occasions when the theme had been seen before, it was pure fantasy, a perfected science or a dimensional accident. Without crediting its author, Gurney based his much different plot on Henry Slesar's short story "Bottle Baby". *Year 5,000* tried to pretend time travel was entirely new, starting the premise from scratch and building from there. This created some very turgid exposition, but many incidental details were interesting.

In his island lab off the coast of Central Florida, Prof. Howard Erling operates a time vault. An abstract statuette materializes and Erling's assistant-sponsor Victor sees a grotesque female face. Erling thinks it was

(Above) The future woman with her "Salome Jens" mask on in TERROR FROM THE YEAR 5,000 (1958).

an optical illusion caused by a refracted image. The power alarm prompts an immediate shutdown of all systems. Erling wants to delay further tests until outside verification. "I never pretended to be a scientist," grumbles impatient Victor. "My old man didn't get rich waiting for outside verification. He plowed ahead and got results." Erling: "If you want to withdraw your help —." Victor reminds him, "You know I wouldn't walk out — and why."

Erling sends the statuette to his former pupil, Dr. Robert Hedges, an archeologist at the New York Museum of Natural History. A carbon-14 test measures the age of the gift in minus, not plus. Grabbing the statuette, stymied Bob yells at it, "Listen you she-devil. I don't know why Erling sent you to me, but this I do know — you don't exist! Not now! Not for another three thousand years!" Two lab technicians find the object to be highly radioactive. One man asks Bob if Erling would want to see him dead. Radiation would have made Bob the victim of a near-perfect murder.

Bob flies to Spooner Beach, Florida. As he leaves the airport, a mysterious motorist races to catch up with him. Could the person be after the statuette, wrapped in a package on Bob's car seat? Overtaken, Bob meets a blonde, who says, "Dr. Hedges, I presume." Erling's daughter, Claire, she was sent to pick Bob up and just missed him at the airport. Bob never received any of Erling's letters. He and Claire go to the island in a motorboat steered by Angelo, a handyman. Erling had to relocate because his work was messing up mainland TV reception. Victor's secret experiment with the time vault kills the boat motor. He turns off the machine and something alive he conjured up cracks the view plate. Victor replaces the pane.

Bob is greeted by Erling and surly Victor, who is engaged to Claire. The radiation problem, Erling says, forced suspension of his work. Victor has Angelo put Bob's luggage in his own room, not the locked guest quarters. Victor resents Bob for sharing the caution of Erling. "Just think of it," Victor contemplates, "the first man to unlock the future would really be on top of the world."

When Bob falls asleep, Victor sneaks off to the locked room, taking from it two boxes. Bob awakens and follows Victor to the lake, where Victor dumps the boxes.

Bob and Claire go to the lake the next day for a swim. Bob dives in while Claire puts on her suit in view of voyeuristic Angelo. Bob opens one box, containing a dead four-eyed cat. He keeps this from frolicsome Claire. Angelo says Bob is wanted in the lab. Bob watches Erling transmit a bottle replaced by a second piece of statuary. Via barter, Erling has communicated with future beings. Bob submits an unprepared object, his Phi Beta Kappa key. A small disc materializes. There are Greek words on it which Bob translates. "It reads .. . 'Save us'."

Using the time vault again without permission, Victor is clutched by a female arm protruding through the partially opened door. Claire sees someone at her bedroom window and screams. Victor beats the arm off with large pliers and sends the woman back to the future. She has scratched his arm. Bob tackles the other intruder, Angelo, who won't admit he was peeking. Bob looks in on Claire and their embrace is interrupted by disapproving Erling. Victor tends his arm.

Bloodstains traced to the guest room alert Bob of Victor's doings. He returns to the lake to retrieve the box with the cat. Panicky Victor sees him from the lab window. Victor races to the lake and throws the salvaged box at Bob. In a rowboat, Victor attacks Bob with an oar. Angelo tells Claire and Erling that Bob is beating up Victor. Erling thinks the fight was about Claire until Bob exposes radiation burns on Victor's body. Against his will, Victor is taken to the town hospital for radiological tests. Bob, Erling and Claire will wait for the results. Victor sneaks away.

Victor gets drunk at a bar, steals an outboard motor boat and hurries back to the lab. At the bar, Bob, Claire and Erling learn that Victor had been there. Victor runs the vault at full power. Erling realizes this when he notices a distinctive pattern of interference on the bar TV set. Bob, Claire and Erling take off in their boat. The motor stalls again as house lights flicker erratically. The vault generator explodes. The Future Woman strides forth, attacking Victor. Bob, Claire and Erling find Victor lying on the floor, mumbling, "Don't come near me . . . keep away . . ." Angelo is sent for a doctor. Too sick to be moved, Victor is kept in bed. The doctor will send a nurse over from the mainland. In the swamp, Angelo spots the lurking Future Woman with her back turned to him. Hypnotically, she draws Angelo close and charges head-on, slashing him with her nails.

Bob recovers the box with the cat, showing it to Claire. She sees a half-hidden form lying in the edge of the water — Angelo. Victor reveals the existence of the woman. He thought he had contacted savages and the cat was something made by their witch doctor.

When the nurse comes, she hears the concealed Future Woman calling to her in Greek. When the nurse calls, "Who's there?", the surprised woman exclaims, "You speak English!" She begs, "You must help me!" "Your face!" cries the horrified nurse. The Future Woman sprints after the fleeing nurse and kills her. From a cylinder, the woman removes a robbery cast and puts it over the nurse's face. It becomes a mask. The nurse now has no face. In radiation suits, Bob and Erling are about to hunt the woman, taking a shotgun. Posing as the nurse, the uniformed beautiful-looking Future Woman arrives. "You were expecting me," she announces.

Victor tells the Future Woman about his encounters with her real self. Enchanted by her serenity and beauty, he tells her, "You're a very remarkable woman . . . very

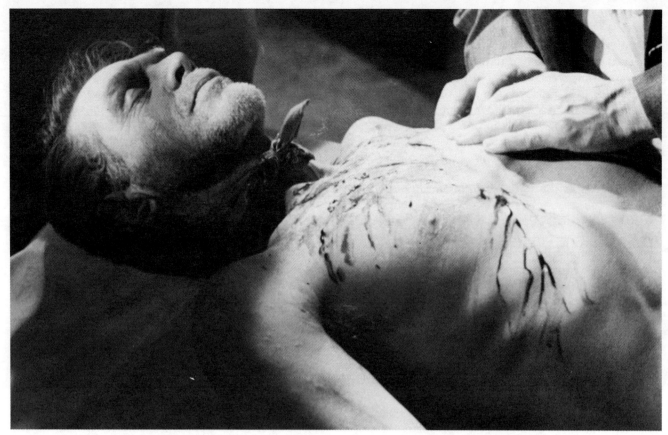

The slashed and bloody remains of Angelo in TERROR FROM THE YEAR 5,000.

unusual . . ." "Perhaps more unusual than you realize," responds the woman, removing her black gloves. Seeing her glitter fingernails, Victor is startled. "You . . . you must come with me," the Future Woman entreats. "We need you." In her age, contamination has turned every fifth child into a mutant. Victor saw one of them in the vault earlier. The machine probed one of the mutant colonies. Only with undamaged pre-atomic genes can the hereditary chain be broken. Hypnotized Victor will provide them. Claire enters, offering to relieve the woman. When she knocks over a water pitcher, Claire glimpses the Future Woman's odd shoes. Victor snaps out of it briefly. "I must have been dreaming." Brusquely, the Future Woman orders Claire to leave.

Put under once more, Victor dons a radiation suit to accompany the Future Woman. Claire confronts them. "I'm going into the future," Victor tells her. Bob and Erling stumble across the faceless body of the real nurse, knowing from one of her shoes who she is. The Future Woman tells Claire she killed Angelo to protect herself. "Did you hear that, Victor," shouts Claire. "Now what do you think of your angel of mercy?" Victor: "They need help." Claire: "You're all confused." "It is *you* who are confused!" accuses the Future Woman. "Our history clearly records that the women of the twentieth century stood idly by while the atmosphere was contaminated and the children of the future doomed." "If she's so right," Claire tells Victor, "why

did she hypnotize you?" The woman spits in Claire's face. Claire rips off her mask. Victor regains his mind. "You! You're one of those freaks!" Victor fights the Future Woman to save Claire until Bob and Erling appear. Shot, the woman staggers into the time vault. Victor tries to open the door. Both he and the woman are electrocuted when his body short-circuits the machine.

Looking at the dead Future Woman, Claire laments. "She said every fifth child was being born this way. Is this what the future holds?" Bob wants the time vault fixed so the Future people can get our genes. Claire is afraid millions of them will come here. "After all," Bob feels "they're human beings." "You're right, Bob," smiles Erling. "There's another way. The future is what we make of it — whether there will be creatures like her depends on us, all of us — on all mankind — on what we do today . . . in the present."

Erling's work was not the usual stuff of people plunging blindly into a limitless void. Like most prototype devices, the time vault was full of defects. The script conceded how fragile is the continuum between planes of duration, their joining courtesy of the vault, a shaky, transient passage. Even the design of the vault, which resembled a crude gas chamber, had an interesting primitiveness. The barter system of mind meeting had a historical precedent in the careers of Marco Polo, Columbus and Byrd and Perry. Erling and Victor had no control over what they received and the Future Woman needed apt timing to extend her stay.

Year five thousand as a world in decline was old tomorrow, but Gurney worked around that by defining the future as unholy earmarks made dangerous by their residual roentegens. Lepers of their age, the mutants could only better themselves by sapping the vitality of the past. Since it was our age that threatened to despoil the quality of later life, the plan could almost be called a form of Victim's Compensation. Victor, an intended human sperm bank, was a male counterpart of the women in other horror films (such as *Man-Beast*, music from which was heard in this movie) who are essential to the parenthood plans of a monster race.

Some of the time vault scenes were rather hokey. Transmissions were heralded by superimposed sparkler flashes. Only a second after Bob's key was sent, the Greek disc appeared. How could a message be inscribed on metal so quickly? Didn't the Future people know that Florida — the supposed site of this particular mutant colony — is on American soil? If the colony was situated on the island, it had to be pretty small. The Future Woman was a credibility-breaker too. When Angelo first saw her, she was surrounded by pulsating animated bubbles. The Woman's face was nothing to have screaming nightmares about, but it had the believability of what some women look like after disfiguring cosmetic surgery. Cosmetically outrageous were the trance-inducing fingernails. So was the Future Woman's face-lifting technique — as if she knew such an occasion would arise.

The giveaway of the Future Woman's high heels clashing with the nurses uniform was an amusing use of one of the most common gaffes in filmed drama: incongruous footwear. In many western dance halls, girls wear shoes of the current style. In hospital stories, nurses wear white dress pumps (and not always pumps of *that* color!) instead of regulation type shoes. Gurney was clever in making this chronic error a device of incrimination for his Florence Nightingale.

Unlike most AIP films where Bronson Canyon or Griffith park were "exotic" settings, *Terror from the Year 5,000* was shot in Dade County, Florida. A little of "California" crept in when Bob, Claire and Erling left a theater showing *I Was a Teenage Frankenstein* and Bob imitated the standard monster's stiff walk.

Introduced in another Florida-made film, *Angel Baby* (1961) — which also marked the screen debut of Burt Reynolds — Salome Jens preferred to be remembered as an Evangelical sexpot rather than a rubber-visaged vaulter through time. With her pensive, quavery, foreign-sounding voice, peculiar face and massively cantilevered bust, Jens resembled a beautiful version of the ugly nurse from the "Eye of the Beholder" episode of "Twilight Zone" . . . a story where deformed people were normal and the attractive were sent to their own isolation centers. Jens made the Future Woman sympathetic and sensual when she traded her spangled black tights for the nurse's uniform. Victor's concession into future sex might have been easier had the woman kept her Salome Jens mask on.

179

The future woman sneaks about in TERROR FROM THE YEAR 5,000.

No girl was safe
as long as this
HEAD HUNTING THING
roamed the land!

NIGHT OF THE BLOOD BEAST

MICHAEL EMMET · ANGELA GREENE · JOHN BAER · Executive Producer ROGER CORMAN · Produced by GENE CORMAN · Directed by BERNARD L. KOWALSKI · Screenplay by MARTIN VARNO · AN AMERICAN-INTERNATIONAL PICTURE

NIGHT OF THE BLOOD BEAST

American-International, 1958

Presenters	James H. Nicholson
	Samuel Z. Arkoff
Executive Producer	Roger Corman
Producer-Story	Gene Corman
Director	Bernard L. Kowalski
Screenplay	Martin Varno
Cinematography	John M. Nickolaus, Jr.
Editorial Supervision	Richard Currier
Music	Alexander Laszlo
Art Director	Daniel Haller
Production Coordinator	Jack Bohrer
Sound	Herman Lewis
Assitant Director	Robert White
Property Master	Karl Brainard

A Balboa Production
Running time: 71 minutes

Cast: Michael Emmet (Maj. John Corcoran), Angela Greene (Dr. Julie Benson), John Baer (Dr. Steve Dunlan), Ed Nelson (Dave Randall), Georgianna Carter (Donna Bixby), Tyler McVey (Dr. Alex Wyman), Ross Sturlin (Alien)

In Roger Corman's *Teenage Caveman*, a rebellious prehistoric youth challenged tribal law by daring to explore the domain of a legendary creature known as the God That Gives Death With A Touch. When killed, the creature — or "God" if you prefer — was unmasked as the last man of pre-World War III society and the tribesmen were actually our descendants. Why the Methusalisic survivor had the appearance of a monster was because of his radiation suit, which gave death due to its own contamination. Only what did the designer of the suit have in mind by making it resemble a crud-covered parrot without wings?

Under Roger's executive guidance, brother Gene Corman made *Night of the Blood Beast* out of hand-me-down material. The film, making the God an extraterrestrial, combined the Nuclear Warning of

(Above) Poster art for NIGHT OF THE BLOOD BEAST (1958).

Teenage Caveman with the Sputnik mania of *War of the Satellites* — using the Possessed Astronaut theme to lead up to the Atomic Threat. Gene's story was called *The Creature from Galaxy 27* and the script was written by Martin Varno, who gained attention by being only twenty years old.

The X-100 rocket, piloted by Maj. John Corcoran, takes off from Cape Canaveral. Above the earth's atmosphere, it suddenly loses altitude. John opens the drag chute, but he is falling too fast. The hull blows open and the ship is five hundred pounds heavier. John records the crisis before blacking out. Communications man Dave Randall and photographer Donna Bixby race to the crash site by jeep. Dave extinguishes the burning capsule and reaches through the jagged hole in one side to feel lifeless John's pulse. Donna takes the photos while Dave radios Dr. Alex Wyman, Dr. Steve Dunlap, and John's fiancée, Dr. Julie Benson, in their truck. Donna hands Dave a sample of strange mud clinging to one part of the capsule. Most of the mass slides away, creeping into the bushes.

When Wyman, Steve and Julie arrive, Dave notes the increased size of the hole. Wyman and Julie examine John. Though dead for three hours, he shows no signs of physical decay. The body is taken to a deserted radar tracking station.

Dave tries to radio Canaveral, but all electronic gear is dead. An odd triangular puncture is on John's arm — as if something had been forced through the skin. His heart has stopped, yet he has the blood pressure of 120 / 80. Steve mans the radio while Dave checks the outside tower. The lights go out before something attacks Dave, who shoots it three times. Sounds of breaking glass come from the lab. On part of a shattered window, Dave finds an odd leathery fragment.

Julie studies a sample of blood taken from John and she and Wyman are surprised to see foreign cell-devouring organisms. Steve and Dave must go to Desert City for help, but both the jeep and truck engines are burned out. All wristwatches have stopped too. The source of the trouble is magnetic — perhaps emanating from the space capsule since some early missiles came back heavily magnetized. Donna has developed the capsule photos. The first shows all the mud. The second, taken ten minutes later, reveals the bigger hole and the mud's disappearance.

Steve and Dave wake up to hear a strange noise. Investigating, they see Wyman's body hanging from a rafter — his head partially gone. John's body has disappeared from the examination table. He reappears alive behind the plate glass window of the surgery room, scaring Julie and Donna. John can barely remember what happened after the X-100 lost control. His head and neck fool sore and as he rubs the back of his neck, another triangle puncture is seen. John notices the one on his arm. When told he was dead, John claims he was in a state of suspended animation brought on by the pressure change of landing. He speaks in terminology Wyman would have used and feels a part of Wyman is influencing him. Defending Wyman's killer, John says it didn't come to destroy.

John's blood sample is normal now that the foreign cells are gone. On his own suggestion, John submits to an examination under a fluoroscope powered by a radium cathode tube. The cells are now eight embryos growing in John's chest cavity. If they die, fears John, he could. The creature from the capsule breaks in, recoiling from the lit kerosene lamp Steve waves in its face. Dave lets rip with a rifle, but when Steve hurls the lamp, it explodes against the side of a wall and the fleeing alien shows a greater fear of fire. The alien only came to nourish its young. When Steve and Dave decide to use very pistols against the alien, hysterical John must be calmed down with sodium amatol. Steve tells Julie this is not the same man she was engaged to.

The alien's trail leads Steve, Dave and Donna back to the capsule. Their watches work again, as though the magnetic field has been broken. While Donna stands by a bridge, Steve and Dave approach the capsule from two sides. Steve fires a very shot inside, but the alien wasn't there. The watches stop again. The alien grabs Donna. When shots are fired over its head, it drops Donna and jumps into the brush.

John tries to convince Julie the creature came for a purpose. He can lead the others to the alien. Dave concludes that the magnetism comes from both the alien and John. John will take the group to the alien in the morning so they can let it justify itself. Steve and Dave anticipate the worst and make molotov cocktails. They are hidden away as John enters the lab and raises the sheet covering Wyman's body to see how he was killed. John stays with the corpse.

Steve and Dave bring the cocktails and very pistols in secret as John takes the group to a cave. Afraid of trouble, John grabs a knife and runs into the cave, where he meets the alien. In Wyman's voice, the alien explains it had to kill him in order to assimilate his speech processes and be able to communicate. John and the alien emerge from the cave. Wyman, the alien claims, has "immortality". The alien's race discovered and fatally misused the Ultimate Power. For centuries, they have circled the earth waiting for a retractable satellite to bring this one here. The aliens want to unite their intellects and ours into one body. Within the hour, John will give birth to the first new hybrid generation. Realizing the aliens want to dominate, John urges the others to kill him. The alien tries to take John hostage, but he stabs himself. Steve and Dave burn the alien, who warns that when we send up more satellites, the rest will come to save us.

Night of the Blood Beast took the life force of *The Creeping Unknown* and made it a pseudo-benevolent emissary rather than a rampant all-devouring appetite. Food was also why *The Thing from Another World* (1951)

181

Dr. Wyman, Steve, Julie and Dave examine the crashed rocket capsule that contains the body of Major John Corcoran in NIGHT OF THE BLOOD BEAST.

cared anything about earth. John Corcoran's master was somewhere between the physical extremes of The Thing and The Unknown. As much a reproductive threat as either, the Blood Beast needed surrogate aid, finding it in John, the Unlucky Lindy of this space flight opus. If Lazarus had returned from the dead in a state of ectopic (or non-uterine) pregnancy, *he* would have been the original John Corcoran — the only "raped" male prior to Kane of *Alien* (1979) to become a Mr. Mom. Carrying a fetus to full term can endanger unhealthy women. The maternal cross of John was that his restored life couldn't get along without the little beasties his torso was incubating. Once they spontaneously delivered, John would only be head and limbs.

Isolated like the soldiers and scientists of *The Thing*, John's friends were in their own quandary: whether to regard him as an unwilling host or a dangerous apologist for his impregnator. John was the only military man present, but acted like overprotective *Thing* groupie Dr. Harrington while Steve and Dave adopted the hard line of the Capt. Hendry camp. Even though the alien held a mortgage over John, it couldn't afford to harm the oven of its "buns". In his martyristic act of prenatal genocide, John cleared the way for the type of righteous immolation that cooked Joan of Arc and the witches of Salem. If everything else fails against an embodiment of blasphemy, there's fire.

With Bernard Kowalski, Gene Corman had a director who did about as much as Roger Corman would

have to put tricky moves into possibly static scenes. The attack on Dave had a steady, zooming rush and the condition of Dr. Wyman's body approximated two acts of similar slaughter cut from the final print of *The Thing*. Donna's fright at the resurrection of John and the sudden entrance of the alien were photographed at perfect pan speeds. When the alien made off with Donna, rescuers Steve and Dave and the fleeing alien took to bold flying leaps.

Thanks to the widest-angle launch pad shot from *War of the Satellites*, it looked like Canaveral was readying *three* rockets. The animated titles sequence of the X-100's ascent worked as an expressionistic depiction of the takeoff, but the fall of the capsule was a cartoon clip, not a three-dimensional model. The organisms in John's blood were a drawn effect too.

A cadaver throughout much of his role, Michael Emmet made up for lost activity time in his scenes of John's schizoid reactions to his possession. At much length he was bare-chested, setting him further apart from the rest of the cast. It would have been a bit much if John had swelled up like real mothers big with child do. *Night of the Blood Beast* wouldn't do anything for Emmet's film career what *Rabbit Test* (1978) did for Billy Crystal, but if it holds any satisfaction for Emmet, he was the first fertile fella (as was Marcello Mastroianni in one of his comedies) and his predicament was bravely played straight.

Represented by the Forrest J. Ackerman agency,

Martin Varno had to make script alterations for the Corman brothers and was denied an extra six hundred dollars to go with the original nine hundred he received. Gene and Roger were reported to the Writers' Guild. Gene was temporarily and Roger permanently blacklisted. Varno finally got his money and let it be put on record that he wanted to buy and burn the negative of *Blood Beast*. Its *Creature from Galaxy 27* title was scotched when Gene and Roger felt it sounded too sedate. A group of Los Angeles high schoolers were asked to chose which name for a movie was worth their money. *Night of* won the Bad Taste test by a bloodslide.

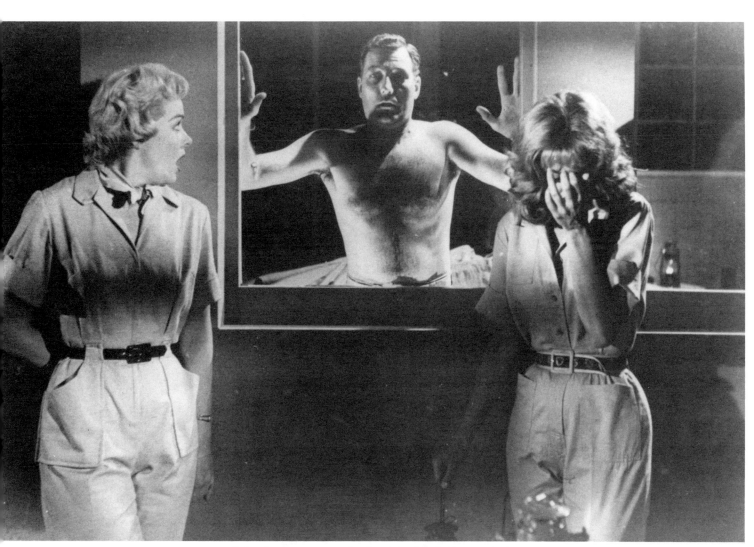

John Corcoran, once dead, miraculously lives again in
NIGHT OF THE BLOOD BEAST.

MONSTER FROM GREEN HELL

Distributors Corp. of America, 1958	
Executive Producers	Jack J. Gross
	Philip N. Krasne
Producer	Al Zimbalist
Director-Film Editor	Kenneth G. Crane
Screenplay	Louis Vittes
	Endre Boehmn
Associate Producer	Sol Dolgin
Cinematography	Ray Flin
Music	Albert Glasser
Production Design	Ernst Fegte
Art Director	John Greenwald
Special Photographic Effects	Jack Rabin
	Louis De Witt
	Irving Block
Special Effects	Jess Davison
Sound	Stanley Cooley
Set Decorator	G.W. Gertsen
Makeup	Louis J. Haszillo
Wardrobe	Joe Dimmit
Sound Editor	Charles Diltz

Music Editor	Robert Post
Script Supervisor	Doris Moody
Property Master	Robert Benton
Production Manager	Byron Roberts

A Gross-Kane Production
Running time: 71 minutes

Cast: Jim Davis (Quent Brady), Robert E. Griffin (Dan Margon), Barbara Turner (Lorna Lorentz), Eduardo Cianelli (Mahri), Vladimir Sokoloff (Dr. Lorentz), Joel Fluellen (Arobi), Tim Huntley (Territorial Agent), Frederic Potler (Radar Operator), La Verne Jones (Kuana)

I n 1957, producer Al Zimbalist bought a copy of *Stanley and Livingstone* (1939), feeling its footage could exploitably augment a horror plot. The Big Bug fad was a suitable rationale. Safari tales usually concern a search, containing much incidental danger. *Stanley and*

(Above) A giant insect claims a victim in MONSTER FROM GREEN HELL (1958).

Livingstone had lots of it. *Monster from Green Hell*, therefore, was only a little horror with lots of Incidental. Its notion of suspense — and conductor of what little there was — was the idea of people facing giant mutant wasps in an isolated area with meager weapons.

At a Southwestern rocket station, scientists Quent Brady and Dan Morgan launch three missiles to determine the effects of cosmic rays on lower life forms. The second rocket, containing wasps, goes out of radar range. A computer estimates it will crash somewhere in Equatorial Africa.

Six months later, a native slain by a "monster" is brought to Dr. Lorentz, who runs a missionary hospital in the village of Mongwe with his daughter, Lorna. Lorentz's native aide, Arobi, says the dead man followed a trail into the dreaded Green Hell area. A toxic element found in his blood shows he died from paralysis of the nerve centers. Animals have been fleeing in droves from Green Hell the past few weeks and an entire native tribe was routed by a monstrous queen wasp.

Quent and Dan read about the monster disturbances. Quent suspects a mutation factor because no previous specimens have been exposed to cosmic rays for more than forty seconds. Animals from the recent rocket flights have changed: A brown guinea pig has turned white, alligators are in a trance and a baby spider crab dwarfs its mother. The wasps were bombarded by rays for over forty hours. Travelling to Libreville, Quent and Dan meet a Territorial Agent who says the wasps are concentrated in the area of Mt. Virunga volcano. Mongwe is nearby.

Lorentz and Arobi decide to explore Green Hell. They hear a wasp sound that stampedes an elephant herd. The two bearers with Lorentz and Arobi turn back, only to be killed in the claws of a wasp. Lorentz and Arobi discover gaping wasp footprints near one bearer's good luck charm. They follow the prints to smoking, unstable Virunga, where they hear the wasp sounds again. Instructing Arobi to stay behind, Lorentz ventures down into the volcano.

Quent and Dan have been waiting for a week to get a safari started. Among their supplies is a crate of grenades. With Arabian Mahri guiding, the journey starts. The group is ambushed by hostile natives that Quent repels by setting a forest fire. When heat and thirst set in, the party loses a native who drinks from a poisoned water hole. Dan becomes sick before rain alleviates the water problem to stormy excess. Lightning hits a tree and Quent is struck by a falling branch. Quent succumbs to strain . . .

. . . and wakes up in Dr. Lorentz's mission to meet Lorna. Arobi returns with the grim news that Lorentz was killed by one of the monsters. A piece of stinger found imbedded in his shoulder is wasp tissue. Taking her father's death hard, Lorna expresses her disapproval of reckless pioneer science. The bearers who accompanied Quent and Dan have deserted. Lorna

recruits new men from the village by shame when she tells them that she — a woman — is not afraid to enter Green Hell. Quent is initially reluctant to let Lorna come along.

The safari happens upon a village destroyed by a stampeding herd of water buffalo. Wasp tracks lead in the direction of the group's destination. At their next camp site, Quent impresses on everyone the importance of killing the queen wasp and her colony before the wasps overrun all Africa — and eventually the world. The wasps can be sensed surrounding the camp. Believing they fear fire, Quent fans the flames of the campfire with gasoline to drive them off.

Wasp sounds are traced to the colony, located in a fissure under a rumbling volcano. Grenades thrown at the wasps fail to kill them. The queen chases the group into a cave and tries to seize Quent with one claw. He throws one grenade at their box, burying the entrance under rubble. The group follows some dark passages to an opening near a ridge. Virunga erupts, loosing rivers of lava that destroy the wasps.

The story and visual concepts came out of resolved differences of committee. One writer, Louis Vittes, wanted the wasps to be cattle-sized. Special effects man, Jack Rabin, thought they should have been bigger. Al Zimbalist — with typical mogul modesty — demanded stupendous. For additional location scenes, he formed an association with Gross-Krasne Productions. Executive producers Jack Gross, the brother of *Green Hell* publicist Mickey Gross, and Phil Krasne specialized in jungle dramas. Publicity boasted how associate producer Sol Dolgin led a safari of location scouts who spent over five months covering twenty-five thousand miles of perilous African terrain. The human cast was to include members of the Nasai, Watusi, Bahuta and Wared tribes — but not the vicious North Ugandan Karamojos, who were practically nude.

En toto, *Monster from Green Hell* could not overcome the hell of Al Zimbalist's mercenary, tasteless thought processes — fixated on a different kind of green. His types of shortcuts often created a ruinous kind of ineptitude, not the sort that brings laughs or surreal interest. The singular title, given their multiplicity, should have been *Monsters from Green Hell* and the earlier wasp adjectives made the "monster" the *Beast from Green Hell* and the *Creature from Green Hell*. The *Green Hell* part of the title sounded like *Green Hell* of 1940 (several horror cheapies of the late fifties described their jungle environs as "green hell" in trailer announcements).

The guinea pig rockets were V-2's and, in order to match the appearance of Spencer Tracy in *Stanley and Livingstone*, Jim Davis had to wear a nineteenth-century pith helmet. This move was reminiscent of how actors in the last Republic serials were dressed in order to pass for *their* stock shot others. Davis was also obligated to narrate the film and his headwear was ludicrously emphasized: once when Quent used the helmet to collect rainwater and when he handed it to Dan before tossing the first grenade at the wasps.

Designed by Paul Blaisdell, the wasps had exotically fearsome faces that helped to offset the inconsistency of their stop-motion animation. Made of simple casing, the wasp bodies lacked armatures and without special wiring for flight, they were grounded by the *Beginning of the End* excuse of underdeveloped wings. Wah Chang sculpted an impressive wasp head and pincers operated to one side off-camera for process shots or from behind prop brush. More than *Beginning of the End*, *Monster from Green Hell* resembled the atmospheric coal mine scenes from *Rodan* (1957), whose most frightening moments involved the underground man-killing Meganeurons. The first Rodan to hatch devoured these insects and the same force of nature that dispatched the Rodans — volcanic energy — would cause the demise of the *Green Hell* wasps. Distributors Corp. of America released *Rodan* as well as *Monster from Green Hell*.

The original wasps killed by Mt. Virunga were puppets in a model cavern with two cameras photographing the lava. A technician added dry ice to create more steam, only to fog up one camera that recorded practically nothing. The second camera, with maximum clarity, photographed the technician's hands at work. A montage of earlier wasp scenes and volcano footage had to suffice with pink tinting to hide the fact the volcano shots were color.

Prior to "Dallas", Jim Davis was known for his earlier TV shows "Stories of the Century" and "Rescue Eight". Barbara Turner had been married to the late Vic Morrow and, with Morrow, wrote *Deathwatch* (1966), a Morrow-Leonard Nimoy production based on Jean Genet's play. Turner and Morrow produced actress Jennifer Jason Leigh.

When *Monster from Green Hell* aired on a New York kiddie show, host Claude Kirchner was told not to use the H-word — so he discreetly called it *The Green Monsters of Africa*. The film's title, however, was screened as originally shown!

186

Man vs. the giant wasps in MONSTER FROM GREEN HELL.

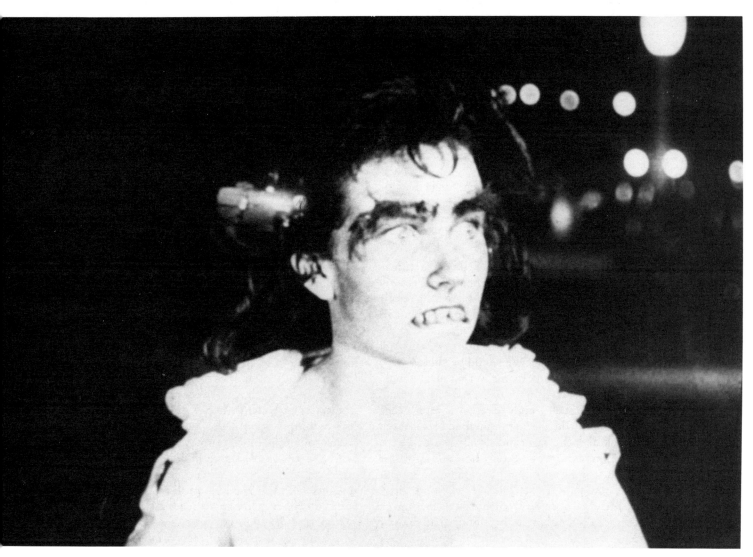

FRANKENSTEIN'S DAUGHTER

Astor, 1958
Eight Millimeter title *She Monster of the Night*

Producer	Marc Frederic
Director	Richard Cunha
Screenplay	H.E. Barrie
Cinematography	Meredith Nicholson
Film Editor	Everett Dodd
Music	Nicholas Carras
Art Direction	Sham Unlimited
Production Manager	Ralph Brooke
Sound	Robert Post
Assitant Director	Leonard J. Shapiro
Set Director	Harry Reif
Special Effects	Ira Anderson
Camera Operator	Robert Wyckoff
Sound Effects Editor	Harold E. Wooley
Makeup	Harry Thomas
Script Supervisor	Diana Loomis
Props	Walter Bradfoot
Electrician	Frank Leonetti
Grip	Grant Tucker

Songs: "Daddy Bird" & "Special Date"
by Page Cavanaugh & Jack Smalley

A Marc Frederic-George Smalley Production
Layton Films
Running time: 85 minutes

Cast: John Ashley (Johnny Bruder), Sandra Knight (Trudy Morton), Donald Murphy (Oliver Frank *aka* Frankenstein), Sally Todd (Suzie Lawlor), Harold Lloyd, Jr. (Don), Felix Locher (Carter Morton), Wolfe Barzell (Elsu), John Zaremba (Lt. Boyle), Robert Dix (Det. Dillon), Harry Wilson (Monster), Voltaire Perkins (Mr. Rockwell), Bill Koontz, George Barrows (Warehousemen), Charlotte Portnoy (Woman), Page Cavanaugh and his Trio (Themselves)

A stor did so well with *Giant from the Unknown* and *She Demons* that Richard Cunha was hired to make another twin bill. Marc Frederic, now his partner, called Layton Drive home and named their new company

(Above) Digenerol-degenerated Trudy (Sandra Knight) of FRANKENSTEIN'S DAUGHTER (1958).

Layton Films, co-presenting *Frankenstein's Daughter* and *Missile to the Moon* with Astor employee George Foley. The remake of Astor's own *Cat Women of the Moon* (1953) played with a rip-off of *I Was a Teenage Frankenstein* that was the only Frankenstein film with two female fiends (although one certainly didn't look it).

On a street corner, teenaged tease Suzie Lawlor wards off a last kiss from her date Don. Miffed, he jumps into his car and drives away. Suzie turns to see a brunette girl in a blue negligee running down the sidewalk and screams. She has the face of a monster.

Also wearing a blue negligee, Trudy Morton is gently awakened the next morning by her loving, elderly uncle, chemist Carter Morton. Trudy is late for a tennis date with Suzie, Don and her boyfriend, Johnny Bruder. Carter's assistant is surly Oliver Frank. Carter is trying to perfect a miracle drug. "It will be a boon to mankind. Think what it would be like. We would be able to wipe out all destructive cells and organisms that plague man. No disease. No destructive tissue or growth. Man would be ageless!" To hold the formula together, Carter needs Digenerol, a violently disfiguring compound. He is irked by Oliver's lack of enthusiasm and closely guarded past.

At the tennis court, Suzie tells her wild monster tale to amused Johnny and Don. Forbidden to go out last night, she could not tell her folks. Trudy joins them, asking Suzie to describe the woman exactly. Begging off from tennis, Trudy confides in Johnny that she saw the monster as herself. Carter had left the house. Oliver fixed her a glass of fruit punch. She felt sleepy. Then she dreamed. "I'm going with a grown-up girl who decided to believe in dreams!" scolds skeptical Johnny.

Without Digenerol, Carter cannot function. He can get some at the Rockwell labs, but Oliver paranoically fears police trouble for both of them. Carter is paranoid about the intrusive gardener Elsu, who knocks on the lab door to say he has finished a chore. Trudy is curled up on a couch in the parlor reading a magazine when she feels chills up her spine caused by perversely fond Elsu, who offers her a rose. Carter brusquely dismisses him and goes out. In the foyer, Oliver and Elsu share a conspiratorial exchange. Oliver: "Tonight?" Elsu: "Tonight. There will be an automobile accident." Oliver: "Good. You know what we need." Elsu: "I'll get it. Don't you worry. I'll get it." Oliver makes a lurid pass at Trudy, who slaps him. She goes for a swim in the backyard, suggesting he take a cold shower. Oliver furtively unlocks the lab door.

In the lab, Oliver reviews scientific notes next to a gurney with a headless, bandaged body. A hidden door disguised as a bookcase swings open and Elsu emerges from an unused wine cellar with a gauze-wrapped object in his hands. Oliver dramatically pulls back the gauze to reveal a useless body part. Another car came before Elsu could get everything. What peeved Oliver needs is a head. "Did anybody see you?" he asks. "I swear, no

one, Mister Frankenstein," answers Elsu. "The name is *Frank!*" reminds Oliver, who prefers anonymity for now. "I was only a boy when your grandfather first created life from the dead," reminisces Elsu, "but I helped your father. I surely did. Father to son . . . that's the way it should be." Oliver had Elsu return the body to the storage room.

It troubles Elsu that Oliver has been putting Digenerol in Trudy's punch for test purposes so he can preserve the cells of his creation. As Trudy towels off from her swim, Oliver gives her the drugged punch as a fake peace offering. It tastes sour. "A toast doesn't mean anything unless you drain your glass," coaxes Oliver. "I'll say one thing for you, Oliver," remarks Trudy, "you sure make a lousy fruit punch. The one last night was just as bad." Feeling woozy, Trudy staggers to her room. Oliver watches her collapse face down on the bed. In her second monster state, Trudy gets up, goes to the mirror, reacts to her ghastly reflection and turns on Oliver. Trudy escapes as Oliver shouts for Elsu.

Lt. Boyle of the police receives a phone call from a gas station attendant who says he was attacked by a girl in a bathing suit with the head of a monster. A lady from around the block reports her, too. Boyle and Det. Dillon leave to investigate. Oliver frantically mixes an antidote. At a cross street, Boyle and Dillon hear screams and meet the hysterical woman. The monster tried to kill her in her apartment. In an alley, Boyle and Dillon spot Trudy in the glare of a flashlight. She flees and stumbles into some trash cans as she is shot at. Sneaking up from behind, Oliver subdues Trudy with chloroform.

Carter reads about the incident, thinking the story is only trick to sell newspapers. "If it isn't flying saucers, they're seeing monsters . . . I wouldn't be surprised if they dragged in the Frankenstein creation." Reacting to a touched nerve, Oliver vocally defends his ancestor. "Oliver, you're a strange boy," muses Carter, who shows him a bottle of stolen Digenerol. Still terrified of the law, Oliver explodes. Carter loudly reminds him of who is conducting the experiment. Disoriented Trudy wakes up normal in her bathing suit.

Boyle and Dillon talk to Mr. Rockwell about the Digenerol theft and the danger of the drug. While he and Carter are working, Oliver sees Elsu opening the secret door. To distract Carter, he knocks the Digenerol out of his hand. None of it can be saved.

Suzie calls, meeting Oliver at the front door. She shows Trudy a copy of the paper with the monster woman story. Trudy is more certain than ever the woman was her. Suzie accuses Trudy of looking for glory after having taken Johnny from her. Johnny enters as Suzie goes. Oliver sets up a date with Suzie. Johnny still doubts Trudy, but sympathetically proposes marriage. Oliver reprimands Elsu for what happened this morning. When Carter unlocks the lab door, Oliver shoves Elsu out the secret way. Carter is surprised to see Oliver, who claims he left his cigarette lighter and that Carter absentmindedly opened the lab door before he thought he did. Despite further admonishment, Carter is determined to procure more Digenerol. Oliver makes him promise not to use the lab tonight. "By the way," asks Carter, "are you spending the evening at home?" "No, I'm not," lecherously replies Oliver. "I have a most interesting engagement."

On Mulholland Drive, Oliver roughly seduces Suzie in his parked convertible. Fighting him off, she taunts his virility and retrieves a missing shoe. Suzie calms down as Oliver wonders why she met him on a corner instead of at her house. Suzie sneaked out. "And no one knows you're with me," realizes Oliver, who hears a voice in his head: "Where can we get the brain? I need a brain, I need a brain." Frightened by his predatory stare, Suzie flees in her bare feet. Oliver's car sharply whips around a turn and runs Suzie down. Oliver takes Suzie's covered corpse back to the lab so he can graft her head onto the male body. "A female?" cries Elsu. "It's never been done!" Oliver tells Suzie, "Tonight, you'll live again, you vixen!"

Before he can get his eight hours sleep, exhausted Boyle learns from Dillon that the Rockwell Labs watchman took a shot at an old man who stole more Digenerol.

Trudy comes home from a date with Johnny and thinks she hears someone in the lab, calling Carter's name as she knocks on the door. When Trudy is gone, Elsu tells Oliver, "Your father and grandfather never used a female brain." "Well, now we know that the female brain is conditioned to a man's world," informs Oliver, "and therefore takes orders where the other one didn't." As Oliver is about to infuse his creature with electricity, Elsu softly proclaims, "Frankenstein's daughter." "Frankenstein's daughter!" declares Oliver more intensely as he throws the switch. Awakened by the steady hum of the current, uneasy Trudy calls Johnny. The noise stops.

Even with more electricity, the monster fails to respond. Staggering into the foyer clutching his weak heart, Carter collapses at the foot of the stairs. Oliver detects a faint heartbeat in the monster before he and Trudy hear Carter moaning their names. Elsu leaves the lab while Oliver and Trudy attend to Carter. Carter vetoes Trudy's wish to call a doctor. "I got this," he whispers to Oliver, pulling the new bottle of Digenerol out of his pocket. In a delayed reaction, the monster comes to life. Trudy brings Carter some pills. She and Oliver help Carter upstairs as the monster rises. It lumbers into the foyer, smashes the window of the front door and leaves. Oliver sees the breakage and finds the monster gone. "Someone must have broken in," thinks Trudy. "Then she's alive," mutters awestruck Oliver.

At Associated Storage, two loaders are working overtime. One goes into the warehouse while the other hears a noise and investigates, armed with a bailing hook.

The worker recoils from the monster and slams the hook against its chest. The monster pummels the worker, who shouts for his partner. He tries to get past a heavy door the monster crushes him with. The other worker opens the door causing the body to slump to the ground, and calls the police. Dillon has compiled a list of former Rockwell employees. Now he and Boyle have a homicide.

Oliver and Elsu have combed the neighborhood for the monster. Elsu steps into the kitchen for a bite to eat. Oliver and Trudy hear someone at the front door. Expecting Johnny, Trudy opens it and faints when she sees the monster. Oliver summons Elsu, who leads the monster upstairs. She needs revitalization. Johnny rushes in. Oliver says Trudy only imagined her fright, citing stress from concern about Carter's health. This monster, she claims, is different. Johnny thinks vanished Suzie contrived the monster stuff and left town when it got too much.

Carter's spirits begin to improve. For three days, the monster is chained to a chair in the attic. Oliver plans to eliminate Carter. "He's a sick man and I need the freedom of the lab. I have an idea he's going to have an attack — a fatal one!" Trudy is throwing a pool party. She looks for Don, who scares Trudy by jumping at her in an ape mask. "I'm a monster," he says. For penance, Trudy makes Don sing.

Carter is now optimistic about the experiment, but Oliver derides him. Oliver tries to choke Carter when Boyle visits. The Digenerol thefts have been narrowed down to Carter, once a Rockwell researcher. To deflect his own guilt, Oliver deliberately incriminates Carter, who is arrested.

Oliver gives the monster a new injection to make it fierce. Elsu is disturbed that Oliver wants to give it a controlled killing instinct. "Why this conscience all of a sudden?" Oliver asks. "I don't know," answers tired Elsu, "I just feel that I've had enough. Two times before, I've seen this experiment end in disaster." We've proved a point. We've made a female being. She's more responsive to command. We have succeeded. Now it's over." In the parlor, Trudy shows Oliver the engagement ring Johnny has given her. Oliver mentions Carter's arrest. His father an attorney, Johnny agrees with Oliver that he should go to the police station by himself.

Once they are alone, Oliver showers Trudy with passion. "I'm not just Oliver Frank!" he raves. "I'm Oliver Frankenstein! And while your uncle was wasting his time on a trivial experiment, I was completing a masterful one!" Trudy tries to resist, but Oliver drags her into the lab, where the monster makes her faint again. "You've always treated me as a monster," threatens Oliver, "Now you're going to be one!" Elsu rebels completely. Oliver unleashes the monster in him. Elsu reminds the monster he is its friend and it stops until Oliver shouts, "Kill! Kill!" Conscious Trudy sees Elsu die and flees the house.

Already at the station, Johnny is told by Boyle that Carter suffered a relapse and is at the hospital prison ward. Hysterical Trudy rushes in, describing everything she saw and reveals Oliver's real name. Dillon learns over the phone that Carter has just died. Boyle and Dillon see Oliver, who refutes Trudy's story. Upstairs, the monster makes noise. Oliver claims it is Elsu. He scoots upstairs, ostensibly to fetch him. Boyle knows Oliver was in the lab because of a distinct odor of chemicals in the foyer and Carter had been taken downtown several hours ago. Oliver says he saw Elsu go out the back. While Boyle returns to the station for Carter's lab key, Dillon decides to go upstairs. Oliver lets Dillon see him as he goes to the lab.

Dillon is lured up to the attic, where Oliver fiendishly presents the monster. "You used a human to make that!" blurts Dillon. "Of course I used a human," Oliver tells him, "don't you recognize her? *Suzie Lawlor*. Or course, she's not as pretty as she once was." Dillon orders Oliver to stop as he unchains the monster. "I've surpassed the abilities of my forbearers," Oliver boasts. "I've created a female!" He sics the monster on Dillon, who shoots as the monster chokes the life out of him.

Parked outside, Johnny and Trudy hear the phone ringing. It is Boyle, asking for Dillon. Looking for him, Johnny and Trudy see the lab door open, discovering the wine cellar one ajar. Snapping its chains, the monster comes down the attic steps and chases Johnny and Trudy into Oliver's path. Trudy calls him insane. Turning to the monster, he says, "So that's insanity, eh? We'll see. We'll show them. *Kill them!*"" Johnny slides the gurney between the monster and himself for protection. Hearing Boyle's siren, Oliver runs to the foyer. As Boyle breaks in, he locks the lab door from the inside. Smashing a window, Boyle shoots at the monster. Pressed against a chemical shelf, Johnny throws an acid bottle at the monster — hitting Oliver by mistake. Doubled over in pain, Oliver throws his melting face back from the fingers clutching his head and screams as he drops dead. The monster gazes at Oliver, brushing its sleeve against a lit Bunsen burner. As the monster goes up in flames, Boyle joins sickened Johnny and Trudy. "It's all over," he says. "I'll call the department."

At poolside the next day, Don pays an unwelcome visit to Johnny and Trudy with a newspaper carrying the Frankenstein story. Neither of them wants to be reminded of it, even though Johnny is the hero. "You can leave any time," he tells Don, who says, "You're all wet." Johnny shoves Don into the pool. Still holding the soaked paper, he gasps, "All I wanted you to do was read this." "Like I said," grins Johnny, about to kiss Trudy, "you can leave any time."

Sharing the sexual decadence of Peter Cushing's Frankenstein, Oliver had none of his class, detachment or charm. He came from nowhere, as did Elsu, who somehow managed to secure employment with Carter too. Oliver had reason to be desperate: forced to adopt an alias, deprived of his own personal lab, catered to by an occasionally inhibited oaf and fatally attracted to Trudy. As Carter's drug had some bearing on Oliver's work, *Frankenstein's Daughter* was deeper into chemistry than surgery. Digenerol was not an Oliver invention but a deformity-causing agent of a reputable pharmaceutical firm.

The moral characters of Trudy and Suzie helped determine which girl would be a temporary monster and who would die a permanent one. Suzie had been first to see the monster Trudy and was ridiculed by Johnny and Don, but when Trudy told Suzie it was her, Suzie took that as an upstage lie. A nice girl, Trudy killed no one as the first monster. Her condition wore off. Helping to finish Oliver's creation, Suzie lost her looks while gaining a new gender. The sexist notion that female brains are meant to obey men was disproved by Trudy's brief rampage and the only reason that the Suzie monster lacked will, apart from leaving the house, killing the warehouse worker, hesitating when Oliver told it to kill Elsu and breaking out of the attic, had to be cell deterioration. Oliver accomplished one thing — his was a Frankenstein monster that did not kill its master. And in regard to his fetish for defacing faces, Oliver's accidental acid demise was tit for tat.

Though there was less of it than in *She Demons*, more Cunha whimsy lightened the dialogue. Describing monster Trudy, overwrought Suzie said, "Don, the minute you drove your car away, this monster came flying right at me." Despite her reluctance to tell her family, Don chided, "It's the duty of every good citizen to report monsters." Seeing the humor of Trudy running amok in a bathing suit, Dillon cracked, "Can hardly get enough of those bathing beauty monsters any more." Referring to the news headline, Carter told Oliver, "Some sort of a monster was seen around town last night." When Oliver prepared to give the Suzie monster a Digenerol fix, he warned Elsu, "She may react violently to this." Oliver meant the *drug*, but Cunha cut abruptly to the party. The music of Page Cavanaugh and his Trio could have been interpreted as "this".

The Trudy monster came off pretty much as planned. High-key street lighting in the horrific opening accented the ferocity of her bushy brows, wild eyes and buck teeth. Harry Thomas wanted to make Sally Todd up as the Suzie monster, but Cunha and Marc Frederic thought she lacked physical menace. Naturally ugly Harry Wilson, Wallace Beery's stand-in, took over. Wilson was the mug in *Abbott and Costello Meet Dr. Jeckyll and Mr. Hyde* (1953) who asked for a match and the wino in *Them!* who wined at singing Jensen, "Please, my nerves!" In some scenes, Wilson's makeup was only slight scar tissue and blackened lips while in others his face had a burnt puffiness. The black suit of the monster had thick white stripes running down the front of the jacket to and below a silver waist band. Black rubber gloves covered the hands. Suzie's costume not only had leather fetish appeal but the top half resembled a high school jacket. Obviously, the script of *Frankenstein's Daughter* created Digenerol so its disfiguring effects would not only conceal the identity of Suzie but also whoever took the monster's role.

For Oliver's death, Thomas gave Donald Murphy's face wrinkled, perforated strips of lens paper, hair gel and chocolate for the holes. The mouth and lower chin were untouched, giving the burned flesh a shape like the Phantom of the Opera mask worn by Claude Rains. Overlighting and a blast of music timed to Murphy's scream completed the effect.

John Ashley, who had left AIP, was desired by independent producers for AIP-type roles. Once wed to Jack Nicholson and mother of their daughter Jennifer, Sandra Knight had been introduced that year in *Thunder Road* and acted with Nicholson in *The Terror*. Donald Murphy, with his rusty voice, glazed gaze and crinkly grin, was hammy but excellent as Oliver. An Ivy Leaguer, he was the only real "swinger" of the male Frankensteins — guiltless and proud of it. Wolfe Barzell as Elsu gained sympathy as Elsu progressively became more human.

Felix Locher, who did not begin acting until he was seventy-three, was the father of Jon Hall. Many consider his performance the worst due to his strained enunciation of certain words. Manly Robert Dix, once a fledgling actor at MGM, was Richard Dix's surviving identical twin son. Medical student Richard, Jr. died in a 1953 skiing accident. John Ashley had quit singing and Harold Lloyd, Jr. took care of that, becoming a popular nitery vocalist. He suffered a brain hemorrhage in 1965 and spent his last years as a sanitarium patient. Exactly four years after father Harold Sr. passed on, Lloyd died in 1971. Sally Todd must have seen a lot of Mamie Van Doren movies, pushing to the point of parody the overstated sexiness of Suzie. Wiggle-walking in a too-tight dress, she must have received an ass transplant from Vikki Dougan, the duchess of derrieres.

The final Layton film, also released by Astor, was the Brazilian-set murder mystery *Girl in Room 13* (1961). After that, Richard Cunha gave up directing except for commercials. Since the career of Oliver Frank, there has been *Jesse James Meets Frankenstein's Daughter* (1966) — actually having to do with a *grand*daughter — and 1971 produced two actual daughters with *Lady Frankenstein* and *Santo Contra La Hija de Frankenstein* (*Santo vs. the Daughter of Frankenstein*).

Elsu (Wolfe Barzell) and Oliver Frankenstein (Donald Murphy) conspire to eliminate Carter in
FRANKENSTEIN'S DAUGHTER.

THE MAN WITHOUT A BODY

Budd Rogers, 1959
Released in England in 1957

Producer	Guido Coen
Directors	W. Lee Wilder
	Charles Saunders
Screenplay	William Grote
Cinematography	Brendan Stafford
Film Editor	Tom Simpson
Music	Albert Elms
Art Director	Harry White
Sound Recordist	Cyril Collick
Production Manager	John "Pinky" Green
Assistant Director	William Lang
Camera Operator	Tony Heller
Makeup	Jim Hydes
Hairstyles	Ivy Emerton
Continuity	Splinters Deason

A Filmplays Ltd. Picture
Running time: 80 minutes

Cast: Robert Hutton (Dr. Phil Merritt), George Colouris (Karl Brussard), Julia Arnall (Jean Kramer), Nadja Regin (Odette Vernet), Sheldon Lawrence (Dr. Lew Waldenhaus), Peter Copley (Leslie), Michael Golden (Nostradamus), Norman Shelley (Dr. Alexander), Stanley Van Beers (Mme. Tussaud's Guide), Tony Quinn (Dr. Brandon), Maurice Kaufmann (Chauffer), William Sherwood (Dr. Charot), Edwin Ellis (Publican), Donald Moreley (Stock Broker), Frank Forsythe (Detective), Kim Parker (Maid), Ernest Bale (Customs Officer)

It takes more than slight suspension of disbelief to accept a factual person's role in a fantasy story, but the famous French seer Michel De Nortedame, better known as Nostradamus, had been gifted with foreseeing everything from the French Revolution to the atomic age according to the enigmatically written prophecies published in his book "Centuries". Nostradamus, however, never mentioned that someday his memory would be exploited by so bizarre a film as *The Man Without a Body*. Of the two directors who worked on it, one was British Charles Saunders, the other was the

(Above) Full-bodied Nostradamus attacks a curious canine in THE MAN WITHOUT A BODY (1959).

American director W. Lee Wilder. Wilder attained some small reputation with *Phantom from Space* and its 1954 follow-ups *Killers from Space* and *The Snow Creature*, all filmed in an ascetic, resolutely deadpan style. Unless Saunders, who also directed *The Womaneater* (1959) for *Man Without a Body*'s producer, Guido Coen, had been the principal helmsman, *Body* was strictly a Wilder anomaly.

Karl Brussard is a ruthless New York financier living with his spoiled French mistress Odette Vernet. Lately, Brussard has been ill with temper tantrums, memory lapses and delusions. For a moment, he fails to recognize his own physician, Dr. Charot, who presents an x-ray of his brain. "I've built an empire out of nothing and this is the brain that did it," self-congratulates Brussard. "I shined shoes and now bankers lick my boots." The dark spot on the x-ray indicates that Brussard has an inoperable brain tumor. Reaching for a cigarette in a box, he displays another symptom: double vision. Charot knows of an American doctor in London, Phil Merritt, who has been doing work in brain transplantation.

Brussard arranges an appointment to see Phil, assisted by Jean Kramer and Dr. Lew Waldenhaus. Brussard sees a monkey in a crib and the artificially sustained head of another. While Brussard has his brain charted, Phil transplants the head of the bodiless monkey onto the other. The brains graph only confirms Charot's findings. "All you would need for me," Brussard tells Merritt, "would be a brain. Find one, steal one —." The two go to a restaurant in Brussard's limousine. Left abandoned on the street, Odette is taken by Lew to the restaurant where Brussard and Phil are. The monkey's head had been preserved for six years in a crypt. Its brain was normal, but in the body of a circuit-trained monkey, it can learn new tricks. A superior mind would be most adaptable. The daughter of Brussard's late business partner, Odette coquettishly tells infatuated Lew, "I know *too well* what I want in a man."

At Mme. Tussaud's Wax Museum, Brussard sees a figure of whom the tour guide describes as "the sphinx of France — the oracle, the prophet, the physician, the astronomer — Nostradamus." In a pub, Brussard finds an alcoholic ex-doctor, Brandon, and pays Brandon to accompany him and Odette to France. In Nostradamus' crypt, Brandon surgically severs his head. Brussard smuggles it past Customs in a plaster bust made to resemble Odette. "A present for Mademoiselle," he declares.

Once he breaks the plaster, Brussard delivers the bandage-wrapped head to Phil, who knows it was stolen. The head, Brussard claims, belonged to "someone unknown — unknown, unmourned." For twenty-two days, the head shows no signs of revitalization in its elevated solution tank. Lew falls asleep while minding the head on the next night and when she and Phil show up for work the next day, Jean sees air bubbles emanating from the head's mouth. Brussard's chauffeur knocks, holding Brussard, who suffered a mild stroke while en route to the lab. Brussard is placed in an upstairs room and sedated for eight hours. Phil does not want to tell Brussard about the progress of the head, fearing his intentions. "He didn't bring this here in the interest of pure science. It's obvious he's only thinking about when that brain will be alive again. He'll appraise its thinking power; its intelligence. He'll try to make it Brussard . . . then he'll insist."

While Lew goes out with Odette, Phil and Jean administer shocks to the head. Odette wants Brussard dead with Lew's help, but Lew is a doctor first. Brussard comes out of medication and barges into the lab. He sees the head of Nostrodamus hooked up to life support tubes on a table, telling him, "To them you're just an experiment. To me, you're life." Paranoid, Brussard rips out a cable and is felled by shock. Nostrodamus shows signs of awakening as he mutters his name. Phil realizes who he is. Told this is the twentieth century, Nostradamus asserts, "I have always lived in the future."

Brussard wakes up in his room, angry at being locked in. Immediately, he attempts to indoctrinate Nostrodamus with his personality, but Nostrodamus stubbornly insists, "I am Nostrodamus!" "*Karl Brussard!*" screams Brussard. Brussard receives an urgent business cable from New York. Secretly visiting Nostrodamus, he says he must either sell or keep his considerable oil holdings. Nostrodamus tells him to sell. Lew has sneaked in and after Brussard leaves, intends to placate Odette by disconnecting Nostrodamus' life support. "You want to destroy Brussard — not me," says Nostrodamus. "I know his purpose. Think . . . he can get another brain. There is one way to destroy Brussard — and I'm doing it!"

Instead of reaping success in the stock market, Brussard hears he is ruined. Odette picks up the news over another phone and packs her bags to leave Brussard, taking all his expensive gift jewelry. Raging at deceitful Nostrodamus, Brussard tries to kill him and Phil throws Brussard out of the lab. Brussard follows Odette to Lew's flat to reclaim the jewels and chokes her with a necklace. When Lew enters, he finds Odette lying dead on a couch and Brussard threatens him with a gun. Brussard chases Lew back to the entrance of the lab, where Lew is shot. Phil and Jean rush to fallen Lew, whose cranial nerves are severed.

The police are called in and Brussard becomes a fugitive. While Lew lies at death's door, Brussard returns to complete his vengeance on Nostrodamus. Seeing double, he shoots the life support device. To save Nostrodamus, Phil and Jean graft his head onto dead Lew's body. Again, Brussard attempts to kill Nostrodamus and behind a screen sees him in a chair hooked up to feeding tubes with his head in a massive plaster cast. Deranged, voiceless Nostrodamus lunges at Brussard, who escapes. Phil tries to catch Brussard while Jean checks the loose feeding tubes. With his clammy hands, Nostrodamus menaces fainting Jean and flees.

Men with police dogs chase Nostrodamus into an empty schoolhouse. Brussard runs inside, confronting him on a staircase. As his vision fails, Brussard falls to his death over the railing. Nostrodamus' casing gets entangled in the bell tower rope, which tears away the falling body of Lew while the head dangles from its noose.

A horror recap of *Citizen Kane* (1941) in its study of tycoon tyranny, *The Man Without a Body* also drew from the evil of that original Citizen Brain, W. H. Donovan. More credibly, Donovan had been saved from immediate death, not resurrected after four centuries. Donovan was willing to live on as an immobile cerebrum, transferring his personality to Dr. Corey only to have his plans carried out by an Arm, Leg and Torso man. The Donovan of *Man Without a Body*, Karl Brussard thought he could will relocation of his consciousness to another memory bank — bad childhood memories and all — then have Nostrodamus' brain inserted into his noggin thinking as Brussard. Regarded as a madman, Brussard was only acting on the results of the monkey experiment, which inspired his notion. And by giving the Merritt team the human head they were able to revive, Brussard helped Nostrodamus fulfill the prediction of his return.

Had Brussard and Nostrodamus *shared* their attributes — Brussard's body and Nostrodamus' intellect — the symbiosis could have increased their respective endowments. With the ESP of Nostrodamus, Brussard could have made Wall Street killings indefinitely. In Brussard's frame, Nostrodamus could experience worldly pleasure. On second thought, Nostrodamus would have been better off if he was wearing the body of Lew Waldenhaus or even stuffy Phil Merritt, not the long-in-the-tooth physique of an aging Sugar Daddy. As Odette proved, diamonds are a girl's best friend, but cold rocks are no substitute for a hunky stud on chilly nights.

With Brussard's Dow Jones dethronement, the grotesquery was more darkly colored. Reviving Nostrodamus was a moral mistake — yet to uphold the Hippocratic oath, Phil compounded it by giving him Lew's body as a lifesaving measure. This done, Nostrodamus degenerated into a Frankenstein monster emitting canine-like sounds. Now Brussard and Nostrodamus were *both* crazy. As merged men, Nostrodamus and slain Lew achieved revenge for each other. Terminally ill, a pauper and wanted for murder, Brussard, at this dismal juncture, had nothing to lose by dying. After Brussard died, there was no reason for Nostrodamus and Lew to stay integrated and the bell rope granted their "parting".

George Colouris, who happened to be one of the players in *Citizen Kane*, performed his own resurrection experiments in that other Cohen-Saunders movie *Womaneater*. Both it and *Man Without a Body* were melancholy, fatalistic and morbid. *Body* was the more entertaining of the two because of ample laughability. Phil's lab was more of a Community Center than a tight-ship workshop with people coming in whenever they felt like it and mundane tasks juggled with revolutionary endeavors. Among the organs gracing the walls like pathology trophies was an eye that gave Brussard the willies, as if showing disapproval of him. Phil Merritt was a real piece of work too. Except for practical irritation, nothing fazed him much and, like Brussard, he took the woman in his life too much for granted. Jean had to be very much in love with Phil to keep lighting his cigarettes while Phil kept ignoring the burning flame of Jean's adoration. Everything melodramatic in the film read of Charles Saunders' handling of *Womaneater*. Everything blase, or where side matters were dwelt upon interminably like the wax museum tour, was W. Lee Wilder. The name of the production company that made *Man Without a Body*, Filmplays Ltd., was a shortened version of Wilder's old outfit Planet Filmplays.

Donovan's brain was a demon; therefore it didn't care that Donovan wasn't a complete man anymore. Nostrodamus was of high moral character, yet should have felt deep anguish or initial trauma over his bodiless state. Instead of yelling the George Gipp question, "Where's the rest of me?" he inquired, "Have they burned my books?" Transcendental would be the word to describe Nostrodamus' adjustment, except in one moment when he said the experiment was against nature. Other risible scenes were the clash of wills between Brussard and Nostrodamus in the, "You are . . .", "I am . . ." sequence, Brussard's constant breaking and entering to kill Nostrodamus and the head casing (composed of the same material that got the head past customs), which made it appear that Lew's neck had grown a mammoth molar while that dark face of Nostrodamus seemed like a big cavity.

Colouris, simply because Brussard was the most vital character, towered above every other player except Nadja Regin, who was competition for very Over-acting. Regin was one of the rare Bond girls with more than one 007 credit. Hers were *From Russia with Love* (1964) and *Goldfinger* (1965). Honor Blackman, Pussy Galore, had been married to Maurice Kaufmann, the actor who played Brussard's chauffer. Robert Hutton, past his young leading man days at Warner Brothers, acted in England for twelve years, there becoming Britain's John Agar.

The Man Without a Body was the first Living Head picture, the most notorious of these, *They Saved Hitler's Brain* (1964), but it was *Body* that showed Hitler first as a wax dummy in Mme. Tussaud's (the prop head of *Hitler's Brain* was wax, too). There was also a series of Mexican horror films about a vampire named Nostrodamus, who claimed to be his descendant.

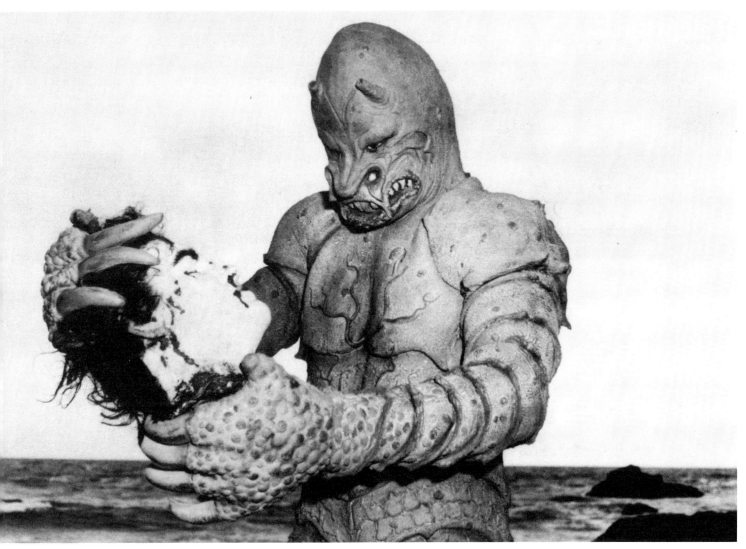

THE MONSTER OF PIEDRAS BLANCAS

Filmservice Distributors Corp., 1959

Producer	Jack Kevan
Director	Irvin Berwick
Screenplay	C. Haile Chace
Cinematography	Philip Lathrop
Film Editor	George Gittens
Sound	Joe Lapis
	James V. Swartz
Set Operation	Walter Woodworth
Lighting	Tom Oulette
Property Master	Eddie Keys
Script Supervisor	Luanna Sherman

A Vanwyck Production
Running time: 71 minutes

Cast: Les Tremayne (The Doctor), Forrest Lewis (The Constable), John Harmon (The Lighthouse Keeper), Frank Arvidson (The Storekeeper), Jeanne Carmen (The Girl), Don Sullivan (The Boy), Wayne Berwick (Little Jimmy), Pete Dunn (Eddie), Joseph la Cava (Mike)

Learning his craft at MGM, Jack Kevan created many of the fantasy figures in *The Wizard of Oz* (1939), making up Spencer Tracy for his version of *Dr. Jekyll and Mr. Hyde* (1941) and creating the decomposed face of Hurd Hatfield in *The Picture of Dorian Gray* (1945). Kevan was a rising star in his field, but when he joined Universal, it was department head Bud Westmore who took all the greasepaint glory. Stills of Kevan and Westmore show a harmonious looking team, and maybe they did actually like each other. There was also a monster designer Millicent Patrick, whose own anonymity was compensated for by a lush Latin beauty that won her a few acting roles. At least in the case of the Gill-Man, creativity was not all in the makeup. This monster demanded a real performance, carried out underwater by Ricou Browning and Ben Chapman on dry land. Where billing of creature contributors was concerned, Bud Westmore was the whole show. Makeup was in his family and Westmore artists shared a last name that enhanced Bud's administrative status.

At Universal, Kevan befriended Irvin Berwick, the dialogue director for such contract stars as Rock

(Above) The beastly creature carries a victim's head in THE MONSTER OF PIEDRAS BLANCAS (1959).

 Sturges (John Harmon), the lighthouse keeper, goes up against the creature only to meet his demise when he is tossed onto the cliffs below in THE MONSTER OF PIEDRAS BLANCAS.

Hudson, Tony Curtis, Sandra Dee and John Saxon. An associate of theirs, C. Haile Chace, was a technical advisor on auto racing films. When Universal instituted a massive lay off program in early 1958, Keving and Berwick started Vanwyck Productions. It was slated to make five films, starting with a *Gill-Man* type shocker. The locale and title of *The Monster of Piedras Blancas* came from Point Piedras Blancas, but the real filming was done in the town of Cayucos and at Point Conception (Piedras Blancas is white rocks in Spanish, white from gull droppings on the seaward side).

Morning sets on the Point Piedras Blancas lighthouse as the beacon is turned off. Looming over a cliff rock, a tusky claw grabs an empty enamel pan, pulls it out of sight and throws it back. About to go into town, lightkeeper Sturges warns away two fishermen trespassing near the rocks. His worry is more than just property.

Sturges bicycles into the village, where people view a squall-battered rowboat on the beach with the pale, headless bodies of the Rinaldi brothers. Garage owner Jake openly holds Sturges up to suspicion. Constable George Matson has the bodies taken to Kochek's general store. Kochek tells Sturges he saw the boat drifting in the water while tending to his lobster traps. He thinks the "accident' was caused by the Monster of Piedras Blancas — a local legend for over thirty years. When Sturges wants his weekly supply of meat scraps added to his regular groceries, Kochek says he sold them to a hog farmer who paid for them. Sturges blows up, saying Kochek will be sorry. The bodies are put in Kochek's ice room, where Dr. Sam Jorgensen will do autopsies. Matson owns the Wings Cafe, where Sturges' daughter, Lucy, is waitressing between college semesters. Her steadiest customer is her marine biologist boyfriend, Fred. Matson questions cantankerous Sturges about whether he saw anything unusual during the squall

Fred and Lucy take a picnic lunch to a romantic cove where Fred wants to collect some specimens. Jorgensen has finished the autopsies on the Rinaldi brothers, who were decapitated as if put to death by the guillotine. Kochek, naturally, blames the Piedras Blancas Monster. Officially, Jorgensen tells Matson all blood from the dead men was drained as if pumped out by a powerful suction. Either a monster is loose or a very clever lunatic.

Fred and Lucy make love in the surf and Sturges frets about Lucy having to work nights. Kochek's monster talk irks both Sturges and Matson, who threatens to jail Kochek for inciting a riot.

Fred drives Lucy back to the light. Years ago, Sturges was a lovable father until his wife took ill during a storm. He phoned a doctor who refused to brave the weather and had to stay in the tower to help a ship in trouble. Mrs. Sturges died. Embittered Sturges transferred here. Most of Lucy's years since were spent in boarding school. After Fred leaves, Lucy impetuously

decides to take a nude moonlight swim. The monster's outstretched arm reaches for her clothes as Sturges calls for Lucy. As she dresses, she hears heavy breathing. Lucy returns to the lighthouse. Sturges is willing to dismiss the swim until Lucy casually mentions the breathing sound. Alarmed Sturges suddenly reprimands Lucy, sends her to bed and goes out.

In town, Kochek works late at his office desk. The monster's prowling shadow enters through the open front door. Kochek looks up from his ledger and recoils as a claw lunges at his face.

During the funeral for the Rinaldi brothers, a crippled boy, Jimmy, whittles wood on a curbside and finds a loose quarter. He enters Kochek's store to buy candy and sees Kochek's body lying on the floor. Jorgensen is conducting the funeral eulogy. Jimmy hobbles to the cemetery crying murder. Jorgensen keeps the service going while Matson, his cafe helper, Eddie, and Fred rush to the store. Jorgensen joins them and discovers a curious gill. Eddie will put the body in the ice room and wait for a relief. Jorgensen and Fred analyze the gill at Jorgensen's home until hysterical Lucy runs in, saying Sturges has fallen from the cliff.

Matson, Jorgensen and Fred help Sturges into the lighthouse. His dog Ring is missing and Lucy calls for him. Patched-up Sturges is taken to Lucy's bedroom. Fred stays, questioning Sturges about the legend and the nearby cave. Sturges forbids any exploration of it. Back in town, Jorgensen and Matson see a traumatized man carrying the covered body of his little girl, whose mother sent her to the store. Lucy tells Fred that when Sturges caught her playing in a cave he became angry and immediately sent her away to school, refusing to let her come home even during vacations. This means going against his possible future father-in-law, but Fred is determined to visit the cave.

In the ice room of the store, Matson calls for missing Eddie. A loud animal roar is followed by his scream. Injured Matson staggers out as the monster scares spectators — clutching Eddie's head. A man who swipes at the monster's arm with a meat cleaver is felled as it escapes. On the blade is another gill. Matson warns Lucy to stay inside the lighthouse and joins Fred at the mouth of the cave.

Matson and Fred organize a posse. They trace the monster's footprints back to the cave. Matson's flashlight picks up a crab crawling around the head of Eddie. Fred shoots the crab. Three signal shots are heard. The monster kills one deputy, wounding another.

Lucy confronts Sturges with her own suspicions about why he guards the cave. Soon after arriving here, Sturges found the cave at low tide and discovered a narrow opening at the top. As the tide rushed in, he heard the same heavy breathing and swam out through a fissure. Sensing something alive was there, Sturges left some fish that disappeared. He knew Lucy would eventually find the opening and had her sent off for her own safety. The monster tired of fish and Sturges gave it meat scraps until Kochek sold the last batch. Lonely, Sturges adopted the monster.

The monster is a mutation of a prehistoric reptile known as the diplovertebron. His actions indicate awesome animal intelligence — like knowing that if he remained in the ice room of the store he would be fed. Fred proposes luring the monster with a side of meat so he can be netted and shipped to a university. Concerned with public welfare, Matson is forced to agree with Fred and Jorgensen that this is the safest way. Sturges has to fix the light, emotionally begging Lucy to help him up the tower steps. At Jake's garage, a large net is secured.

Creeping up to the lighthouse, the monster watches Lucy undressing for bed and breaks in. Lucy thinks Sturges came downstairs and opens her door, facing the monster. Sturges hears Lucy scream and collapses on the balcony. Matson tells Fred the light is off. Fred tries to call the lighthouse. He and Jorgensen go there while Matson gets help. From the tower, Sturges sees the monster carrying fainted Lucy toward the cliffs. Throwing an oil can, Sturges goads the monster to drop Lucy and climb the tower stairs. Lucy revives, tripping over dead Ring. On the stairs, Sturges battles the monster with a rifle. Lucy runs away, meeting up with Fred and Jorgensen.

Matson and some men arrive. Fred tosses a clothesline up to Sturges, but the monster smashes through the barricaded balcony doors. Sturges tries to circle around as the monster scales some beacon windows and jumps down, hurling Sturges to his death. Fred fights the monster, armed with a shotgun. Jake shines a flashlight into its eyes. Fred orders Lucy to turn on the beacon. With the butt of the shotgun, he shoves the blinded monster over the railing and it plunges head first into the sea. Fred and Lucy passionately embrace.

The Monster of Piedras Blancas was a slow-paced but fascinating study of accumulated repressions breaking loose. The plight of Sturges was like that of the Little Dutch Boy plugging the dike hole with his finger. For Sturges, the water was a living thing he could coexist with because both were isolated. The monster exploited their union just to keep its belly full until its palate grew jaded and, after having tasted human blood, savored Lucy's charms. Spoiled for different food, having discovered sex, the monster grew more independent as Sturges' rigidly enforced routine fell apart. When Sturges became incapacitated, the monster finally decided to "paint" the town; and what better person to kill in town first than Kochek, who long believed in the monster, didn't get along with Sturges and whose store afforded a reasonable hiding place.

With the monster amok, all of Sturges' psychological barriers fell down. He started to live again, becoming more of the father he used to be. When the monster wanted something belonging to Sturges it

couldn't have before — Lucy — Sturges had to face his dubious "friend" for what it really was. Until the monster broke in, the lighthouse represented a bastion of protection. It couldn't save Sturges, but a critical application of the light helped take care of the monster in an ending with sequel hopes attached to it. The monster fell, but there was no actual confirmation of death . . . just as the bullets fired into the Gill-Man in the endings of his first two films showed he was down but not necessarily out.

Kevan and Berwick were not interested in creating a sympathetic beast, working instead to make the Piedras Blancas monster a cold, pitiless butcher. Given Gill-Man limbs, Mole People claws and Metaluna Mutant feet, the monster beat all the aforementioned for a ghastly face, which the film saved for last. Medical speculations of the murders conjured hideous visions of the thing lopping off heads and sucking blood through the neck stumps like soda through a straw.

Some loose end questions were apparent, like how did the early settlers suspect the existence of a monster if no one had seen it? Why didn't the previous lightkeepers have any contact with the monster? Why didn't it kill before slaying the Rinaldi brothers? Why was a creature spawned in the sea so dependent on land food?

Financing the film on money contributions obtained at Universal, Kevan and Berwick hired many studio people. On a budget of thirty thousand dollars, the movie required a documentary style and Cayocos and Point Conception were ideal backdrops. Irv Berwick directed the film while recovering from surgery from a broken back and Les Tremayne suffered an accident that cracked several ribs. The Coast Guard refused to let any scenes be shot inside the beacon to protect its delicate equipment. To get the closing shot of Fred and Lucy, Jake Kevan took supervising Guard commander Bob Cannon to a bar, distracting him with drink and conversation while Berwick, hampered by strong winds, finished the scene.

The opening images of the picture — a stark, unsettling hilltop view of the lighthouse followed by the claw and the dish — vividly condensed the relationship between the monster and Sturges. Emphasis on the monster's claws was a device taken from early scenes of the Gill-Man, especially the first glimpse of one of his own. Shots of the monster's magnified silhouette was a forced flourish, but scary for being cast against white building walls. The death of the little girl, an homage to Maria's fate in *Frankenstein* (1931) and the of the child in *The Leopard Man* (1943) who was also sent on a store errand, implied unspeakable violation. The naked grief of the girl's father was a delayed trauma mercifully cut away from as if to honor the sanctity of his bereavement. In censored footage, Matson saw the body of Eddie hanging on a meat hook. More like a bloodied mannequin part, Eddie's head was a good shock

Poor, frightened Lucy (Jeanne Carmen) comes face to face with the Monster of Piedras Blancas.

substitute for the hidden upper half of the monster and the cave insert with the crab provided an extra fill up of disgust.

Auspicious radio veterans Les Tremayne and Forrest Lewis and John Harmon, the godfather of Berwick's eight year old bit player son, Wayne, gave the best performances. Harmon brought to Sturges a fidgety, bottled-up desperation and he was excellent in the monologue scene where Sturges came clean with Lucy about why he harbored the monster. As Lucy, languidly inviting, outdoorsy Jeanne Carmen was a trick golfer who modelled for cheesecake photos. An affair with Frank Sinatra led to Carmen aborting a love child by him. Diana Darrin, an actress in *The Amazing Colossal Man*, helped arrange the abortion while Carmen's best-known friend was Marilyn Monroe, who phoned Carmen on the night of her death. Likeable Don Sullivan would prove his capabilities further in *The Giant Gila Monster*. Frank Arvidson was a merchant in Cayucos whose corny performance as Kochek gave the character its needed color.

Publicity of *The Monster of Piedras Blancas* was augmented by a fake "Famous Monsters" Shock Award in the shape of a plaque with a clawed hand in the middle. The magazine was referred to simply as "Monsters of Filmland" and *Piedras Blancas* won First Place in a "contest" with no actual competition. Forrest J. Ackerman was ignorant of this publicity stunt thought up by FM publisher James Warren until he saw the poster in Brooklyn. Several people who thought Ackerman had endorsed the movie wrote letters of indignation after seeing it.

Kevan and Berwick made *The Seventh Commandment* in 1961. Kevan went into the cosmetics business and Berwick made more exploitation films, many with John Harmon. The head of the Piedras Blancas monster adorned a new creature body in an episode of "Flipper" that had to do with the making of a horror film. Berwick went back to Universal as a dialogue director and in later years has taught cinema at USC. Wayne Berwick broke into professional film making with *Microwave Massacre* (1979) and later featured John Harmon in the nostalgia horror comedy *Attack of the B-Movie Monster* (1989), made in 1984, the year Harmon died. Wayne Berwick would love to do a sequel to *The Monster of Piedras Blancas* if he can cut the copyright red tape imposed by National Telefilm Associates, owner of the film's TV syndication rights. A new *Piedras Blancas* film would have a ready-made audience, in Cayucos, where the movie has been screened every Fourth of July and Halloween for a number years now.

THE GHOST OF DRAGSTRIP HOLLOW

American-International, 1959

Executive Producers	James Nicholson
	Samuel Z. Arkoff
Producer-Screenplay	Lou Rusoff
Director	William Hole, Jr.
Associate Producer- Production Manager	Bart Carre
Cinematography	Gil Warrenton
Film Editors	Frank Keller
	Ted Sampson
Music	Ronald Stein
Art Director	Dan Haller
Set Decorator	Harry Reif
Assistant Director	Lou Germonprez
Properties	Karl Brainard
Sound Editor	Joseph Von Stroheim
Musical Editor	Albert Shaff
Music Coordinator	Jimmie Madden
Wardrobe	Marjorie Corso
Hairstylist	Scotty Rakin
Makeup	Bob Marks
Sound	Jimmy Thompson
Script Supervisor	Judy Hart

Songs
"Charge", "Geronimo", "Ghost Train" by Nick Venet
"Tongue Tied" by Jimmie Madden
"He's My Guy" by Charlotte Braser
"I Promise You" by Bruce Johnston, Judy Harriet

An Alta Vista Production
Running time: 65 minutes

Cast: Jody Fair (Lois), Martin Braddock (Stan), Russ Bender (Tom), Henry McCann (Dave), Elaine Dupont (Rhoda), Leon Tyler (Bonzo), Jack Ging (Tony), Nancy Anderson (Nita), Dorothy Neumann (Anastasia), Sanita Pelkey (Amelia), Kirby Smith (Wesley), Jean Tatum (Alice), Beverly Scott (Hazel), Bill St. Johns (Ed), Tommy Ivo (Alan), Judy Howard (Sandra), Roy Wright, Harrison Lewis, Paul Blaisdell (Monster)

The end came for both AIP's earliest youth and horror films when Lou Rusoff wrote and produced this even sillier sequel to his comedic 1958 Hot Rod Gang. Like a skeleton plan for the fanciful and more buoyantly energetic Beach films of AIP, Ghost of Dragstrip Hollow was designed to sell records of its every song. Now that the company was lengthening its britches, it decided to dabble in the making of sound track albums. Filmically, Dragstrip Hollow was very hollow, much of it a real drag and the palest ghost of anything directed by Edward L.

Cahn. The director's name might have inspired more confidence if it had been William *Hale* and not William *Hole*, Jr.

Lois Cavendish of the Zenith hot rod club and her enemy Nita conduct a grudge race in the city storm drain basin. An alert motorcycle cop gives chase and Nita wrecks her roadster against a cement wall as Lois escapes. At the Zenith hangout, reporter Tom Henry fraternizes with the club to do a story on legal drag-racing. In three weeks, the club will face eviction for lack of money. Nita's rival crowd pays a menacing visit. Nita wants to take on Lois again and her ringleader boyfriend wants to take Lois from her cleancut guy, Stan.

A business client of Lois' dad, Wesley, is eccentric Anastasia Abernathy, who brings her unusual pet parrot, Alphonso, to the Cavendish home for a stay. Implicated in Nita's accident by the press, Lois is grounded, but allowed to host a house party. Tony's gang crashes and Lois defuses real trouble by permitting him one dance. Anastasia offers to let the kids use the haunted house where she and her late husband, John, lived. Some kids spend the night and a "ghost" spooks them.

Charging admission, the kids throw a Halloween costume bash. Unknowingly, Lois dances with the "ghost". When the rivals come back, Lois sneaks off to accept Nita's rematch challenge and wins. Stan and Tom look for a secret room. Egghead Dave unveils his talking car, Amelia, named after his statuesque girl. Amelia opens the fireplace door to the ghost's hideaway. The only person unwilling to unmask, the captured "ghost" is an unhappy, jobless horror film actor. Out of his wall portrait emerges the real spector of John Abernathy. "The Endest, man".

"Going Out of Business" was stamped over most everything in *The Ghost of Dragstrip Hollow*. The hot rod milieu was more technical jargon than action, the club jester had only one bad in-joke line to be remembered by ("I Was A Teenage Carburetor"), the fussy Wesley was more wimp than tyrant, Tony's villainy was mere bluff and the rematch between Lois and Nita was off screen. Amelia the wondermobile and the chassis of her human namesake were the only visual diversions outside of two dancers in skeleton costumes and Paul Blaisdell's mastectomized She Creature suit — bereft also of its original feet with Blaisdell wearing sneakers.

The major players were among the lowest-billed. Ex-child actor, Tom Ivo, was a dragster champ and Jack Ging went on the play ass-pain authoritarians on "The A-Team" and "Riptide". With his smoky voice and slow-burn expressions, Ging does malice so well there should have been a summons for wasting him.

Hard jail time should have gone to every party involved in Paul Blaisdell's mistreatment. Forced to make do by resuscitating the stripped down She Creature, Blaisdell was put in a degrading cameo that farcially trivialized his own incipient dismissal from AIP. Adding further humiliation was the squeaky dubbed in

THE GHOST OF DRAGSTRIP HOLLOW (1959).

voice of his overly autobiographical character (AIP must have been pretty excited about *Horrors of the Black Museum*; not only was it mentioned in *How to Make a Monster*, but Blaisdell complained in *Dragstrip Hollow* that he wasn't used in that film). *Ghost of Dragstrip Hollow* was made as *The Haunted Hot Rod*, but they should have named it *I Was a Has-Been Monster Maker*. Occasionally, Blaisdell came down with foot-in-mouth-itis. He contributed to his own anonymity by loudly criticizing an article about him in the first issue of "Famous Monsters". Its petulant publisher, James Warren, retaliated by having Blaisdell's name banned from all future editions. Hypocritically, the magazine continued to run pictures of Blaisdell's work.

Dogged by bad luck into his final years, Blaisdell relived his past triumphs in a publication he helped found, "Fantastic Monsters of the Films". Serving its model right, it was edited by FM defector Ron Haydock. "FanMo" went under, or rather went up, when the corrupt printer set an insurance fire and ran off with the money. Ron Haydock enjoyed a short spell in films working for Ray Dennis Steckler, edited another horror magazine Blaisdell contributed to, "Monsters of the Movies", and was killed by a reckless driver in 1977.

Turned embittered recluse, Paul Blaisdell died of cancer in 1983. He had outlived both "Famous Monsters", which expired that year, and AIP, which died in 1979.

202

A creepy scene from the shoddy "old-dark-house" programmer THE GHOST OF DRAGSTRIP HOLLOW.

ATTACK OF THE GIANT LEECHES

American-International, 1959
Alternate title *The Giant Leeches*
Released in England as *Demons from the Swamp*

Executive Producer	Roger Corman
Producer	Gene Corman
Director	Bernard Kowalski
Screenplay	Leo Gordon
Cinematography	John M. Nickolaus, Jr.
Film Editor	Carlo Lodato
Music	Alexander Laszlo
Art Director	Daniel Haller
Production Manager	Jack Bohrer
Sound	Al Overton
Associate Editor	Tony Magro
Assitant Director	John Chulay
Props	Richard M. Rubin

A Balboa Production

Cast: Ken Clark (Steve Benton), Yvette Vickers (Liz Walker), Jan Shepard (Nan Grayson), Michael Emmett (Cal Moulton), Bruno Ve Sota (Dave Walker), Tyler McVey (Doc Grayson), Gene Roth (Sheriff Kovis), Daniel White (Slim Reed), George Cisar (Lem Sawyer)

Another Gene Corman production directed by Bernard Kowalski, *Attack of the Giant Leeches* broke away from such Big Bug movie truisms as verified theory, the superiority of authority over local folk and conclusive extermination of a monster breed. In their place were sweaty redneck passion and scenes of the messiest bloodletting on black and white film. Better known as a tough guy actor (he has done time), author Leo Gordon didn't sugarcoat humanity as he wrote it. Look at his cast of characters: a brazen hussy, her obese lovesick spouse, a slimy rake, a shirker sheriff and a slow-to-act hero.

Everglades poacher Lem Sawyer fires five rifle slugs into a giant leech that sinks beneath the water. At Dave Walker's general store, Lem tells his tale to Dave, Cal Moulton, Sam Peters, Porky Reed and Bill Evans. Dave

(Above) A closeup of a giant leech from ATTACK OF THE GIANT LEECHES *(1959).*

complains to his restless young wife, Liz, that the record music she is playing in their bedroom is too loud. Sassy Liz appears dressed in revealing boudoir clothes for the boys to look at her. Lem leaves to clean his otter lines. Dave tries to make Liz show respect and she entices him just to push him away. Liz goes out for a walk.

An avowed enemy of the poachers, game warden Steve Benton is forced to kill a young animal caught in the newest illegal trap he confiscates. As Steve and his girl, Nan Grayton are about to kiss, they hear a male cry followed by a female shriek. Steve rushes to the area of the sounds and sees Liz screaming hysterically at Lem, who drops dead from blood loss.

Sheriff Kovis thinks Lem was felled by a freak alligator. Steve says that Nan's father, Doc Grayson, found wounds like those made by an octopus or large squid. Kovis resents Steve for throwing his weight around. Steve decides to search the swamp for any unnatural signs of life with Nan. Still shaken by her encounter with Lem, Liz would feel safer living in town, but Dave refuses to sell the store. While Dave goes on an errand, casanova Cal drops in and puts the make on obliging Liz.

Liz and Cal make love on a bank on the swamp. Liz was married before to a drunken wife-beater who was sent up for armed robbery. Feeling down, Liz met sympathetic Dave and became his wife. Dave catches Liz and Cal together, hearing Cal denigrate his manhood. Dave turns a loaded shotgun on Liz and Cal, prodding them into fleeing through the swamp. Exhausted Liz and Cal flee to the edge of the water. Whimpering Cal tries to save his hide by claiming Liz led him on. Dave forces them into the water up to their waists, making Cal promise not to see Liz again. Two giant leeches rise up behind them. Horrified Dave shouts a warning, but Liz and Cal are dragged away.

No bodies are found. Kovis does not accept Dave's story and arrests him for murder. Sam and Porky decide to look for Liz and Cal and collect a reward. Despondent Dave hangs himself in his cell. Doc Grayson took his trauma seriously, theorizing the leeches are nocturnal creatures and shun daylight. Dynamite should raise them, but Steve cites ecological damage. Nan takes Grayson's position, calling Steve pig-headed. At the swamp lake where gators normally thrive, Sam and Porky see none. The leeches capsize their canoe, taking Sam and Porky to an underwater alligator cave with air, where Liz and Cal lie in state of partial consciousness. The leeches gorge on their victims.

Kovis refuses to investigate the disappearances of Sam and Porky. Steve forms his own search party and the absence of wildlife is noticed. Aided by Nan, Grayson dynamites the lake as Steve appears. Cal, Sam and Porky fall into the cave pool when a ledge crumbles and their floating bodies surface. Steve has to arrest Grayson. Autopsies show inconsistencies about how and when the men died. Steve believes they were taken

to a lair with oxygen since the sea carved out caves around here. Grayson feels that Liz is still in the cave — alive.

Steve and his Navy pal, Mike, go to the lake with scuba gear. Tied to a safety line, Steve spear guns one leech. Grayson thinks they were mutated by radiation from one of the first-stage launchings at Cape Canaveral. Steve and Mike fight the second leech. Dying Liz falls into to cave pool and her corpse floats to the top. Steve and Mike recover the body and the carcass of the dead leech emerges. Steve has the honor of igniting more dynamite. The sound of other leeches can be heard.

Treating the origin of the leeches perfunctorily, *Giant Leeches* revelled in the ritual of having the victims set in motion the causes of their deaths. Each was some kind of sinner polluting the swamp. Sin had an arousing personifier in Liz. From boogey-woogey music tastes to her pouty gyration in trash undies, her aura was a ripe harbinger of trouble for anyone whose appreciation of her went beyond lustful gawks. When Dave's double-barreled indignation petered out, the leeches were the ones to "punish" Liz and Cal — incidentally getting Dave in water of a hot legal kind for what he only threatened to do.

Since the leeches were water bound, letting people come to them, Bernard Kowalski had to direct for the visceral. Rarely did giant insects do worse than approach someone and maybe for a moment or two hold them in their claws or mandibles. Scenes of consummated death were quick or there were cuts away from the agonies. The leeches were constantly being compared to gators — in their size, dwelling and feeding habits. Non-carnivorous, they drained the life fluid from their prey, taking their sweet time just as alligators are wont to see their victims soften up before chowing down. Interminably, the cave scenes lingered on the leeches slurping all over captured riffraff. Liz was obviously Special Stock. Even after their deaths, she, Cal, Sam and Porky were contributory props when their return to the surface was photographed in incongruously serene underwater close-ups.

Behind the seams, er, scenes, *Giant Leeches* was as botch-plagued as any film Roger Corman directed. Ed Nelson, who had to give up the role of Cal when another job beckoned, was the man who was supposed to create the leech outfits. Ross Sturlin of *Night of the Blood Beast* and UCLA basketball star, Guy Buccola, applied for the leech parts, but had to make the costumes. Formed out of raincoat fabric, the suits collected air pockets and torn material had to be pinned together. The flippers and bulging scuba tanks Sturlin and Buccola wore were sometimes visible. Whenever the leeches held or grabbed people, their elbows protruded (in describing the leech he saw, Lem mentioned that it had arms).

Exteriors were shot at the Pasadena Arboretum. Thanks to too many Bomba films, that place is the jungle answer to Bronson Canyon. A brother to Roger in more

Poster art from ATTACK OF THE GIANT LEECHES.

CRAWLING HORROR...
RISING FROM THE
DEPTHS OF HELL...
TO KILL AND CONQUER!

THE GIANT LEECHES

STARRING KEN CLARK · YVETTE VICKERS · JAN SHEPARD · MICHAEL EMMET · WRITTEN BY LEO GORDON

PRODUCED BY GENE CORMAN · DIRECTED BY BERNARD L. KOWALSKI · AN AMERICAN INTERNATIONAL PICTURE ways than blood, Gene Corman wouldn't pay the grips to push the water raft the camera was mounted on. Kowalski and his script clerk brother had to do it themselves. Gene took over the task the next day. After nearly twenty-four hours of continual exposure to water, he had to recuperate in a hospital.

Underwater scenes were done in the windowed swimming pool of a Studio City resident. At the Chaplin Studio, Dan Haller designed the cave set around a large canvas tank supported by pieces of wood. Sturlin, Buccola and the victim players emerged from three feet of water. In the middle of the scene where Sam and Porky were hoisted up, the weight of everyone caused the tank to burst. The set was flooded and death from electrocution was averted when power was cut in time.

Sympathetic roles were rare for Bruno Ve Sota and Yvette Vickers was Honey Parker in the Dirty Daisy Mae idiom of female Southern promiscuity. Part of her

Baby Doll getup included the Oriental robe she wore in her July 1959 "Playboy" spread. The seamy marital life of Liz and Dave was replayed in *The Giant Spider Invasion* (1975) in the characters of farm couple Ben and Ev Kester. Ev was the rejected mate, Ben the cruel adulterer.

Hyper schlock grinder Fred Olen Ray, formerly based in Florida, made a combined homage to *The Brain Eaters* and *Attack of the Giant Leeches* called *The Brain Leeches* (1977). In further tribute to *Giant Leeches*, Ray planned to make *Swamp of the Blood Leeches* until he altered the plot, turning the monsters into a group of people on a houseboat who became flesh-eating zombies from meteor radiation. The film was shot in 1978 as *It Fell from the Sky* and released in 1982 as *The Alien Dead*. Buster Crabbe played a sheriff named Kowalski in reference to the director Bernard.

206

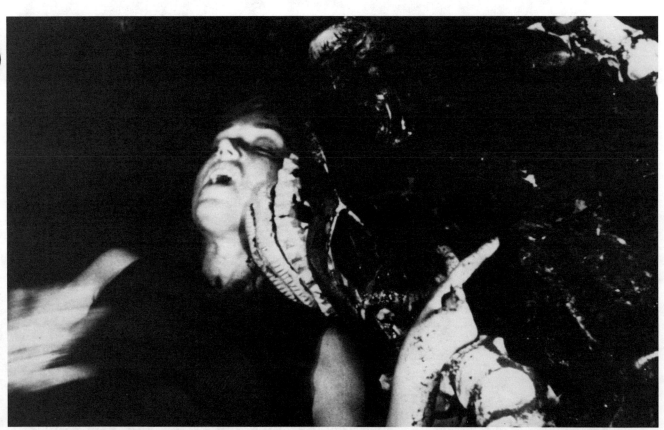

Liz (Yvette Vickers) makes a tasty leech-lunch in ATTACK OF THE GIANT LEECHES.

THE WASP WOMAN

Filmgroup / Allied Artists, 1959

Producer-Director	Roger Corman
Screenplay	Leo Gordon
Story	Kinta Zertuche
Cinematography	Harry Newman
Film Editor	Carlo Lodato
Music	Fred Katz
Art Director	Daniel Haller
Sound	Philip N. Mitchell
Production Manager	Jack Bohrer
Property Master	Karl Brainard
Makeup	Grant R. Keats

A Santa Clara Production
Running time: 73 minutes

Cast: Susan Cabot (Janice Starlin), Fred *aka* Anthony Eisley (Bill Lane), Barboura Morris (Mary Dennison), William Roerick (Arthur Cooper), Michael Mark (Eric Zinthrop), Frank Gerstle (Les Hellman), Bruno Ve Sota (Night Watchman), Roy Gordon (Paul Thompson), Carolyn Hughes (Jean Carson), Lynn Cartwright (Maureen Readron), Frank Wolff (Delivery man), Lani Mars (Nurse Warren), Philip Barry

The acquisition of beauty, the restoration of same, and the fear of losing it have long been motivation staples for some varieties of monster women. After *The Fly* (1958), Roger Corman read about women's cosmetics that used bee jelly. The first film he was going to produce and direct for his new company, Filmgroup, was tentatively conceived as *The Bee Girl* until it was decided that a female humanoid wasp made better Scare sense. Loosing his premise in the corridors of the cosmetics trade, Corman wedded the sexual supremacy of certain female insects with the out-of-control career ambition of stereotyped movie businesswomen. *The Wasp Woman*, then, unlike Andre Delambre, was to be pitied as someone who was only intermittently "buggy".

A research chemist for Holiday Honey, Eric Zinthrop collects — and talks to — wasps. Barker, the

(Above) Mary (Barbara Morris) becomes frightened when Janice (Susan Cabot) begins to transform into the Wasp Woman (1959).

visiting field supervisor, has not received any new reports on Zinthrop's assigned task of extracting royal bee jelly. Barker is nettled by wasps infesting the work area. Outside his small workshop, Zinthrop shows Barker two Dobermans. The small dog is the same age as the big one because Zinthrop has slowed the aging process with royal queen wasp jelly. Skeptical, Barker has to let Zinthrop go.

Manhattan. Janice Starlin, founder and president of Janice Starlin Enterprises, calls a conference to determine why sales of her beauty products have dropped in the last fiscal quarter. Present are Janice's private secretary, Mary Dennison, Arthur Cooper of Research, and advertising manager, Bill Lane, who knows the reasons. "Where would you place the responsibility for this decline?" asks Janice. "On you, Miss Starlin," boldly answers Bill. Until last February, only Janice's face adorned the company ads. The public does not trust a new face — and Janice's is getting older. The problem started earlier. Janice tells Cooper about a letter Zinthrop sent concerning his rejuvenation work with wasp enzymes. "Socially, the queen wasp is on a level with the black widow spider," warns Cooper. "They're both carnivorous, they paralyze their victims and take their time devouring them alive . . . they kill their mates the same way, too. Strictly a one-sided romance."

Zinthrop sees Janice, who grants limited appointment time. "It is time I give *you*," he promises, "— ten, maybe fifteen, years I give you." Zinthrop has a calico cat and a guinea pig in a portable cage. An injection of his formula turns the guinea pig young before Janice's astonished eyes. Then the cat is injected. Zinthrop is unsure about human effect, but Janice stipulates, "Janice Starlin will be your guinea pig." The cat is transformed into a kitten. Early treatment on Janice over the next three weeks is limited. She wants it stepped up. Zinthrop has a concentrated enzyme compound he feels is best for emollient purposes.

Bill is dubious of Zinthrop and has Mary purloin Zinthrop's letter from Janice's desk. Cooper deciphers its contents. Bill and Mary see Zinthrop as a con man. Cooper thinks he is after more than money. "A quack can be fatal." Surreptitiously, Janice takes the concentrated enzyme. The kitten, meanwhile, has become a cat again. Janice stuns everyone by showing up at work aglow with youth. "How old do I look?" she elatedly asks Mary. "Tell me!" "Twenty-three, twenty-two," guesses Mary. "I'm back where I started," realizes Janice, "eighteen years ago — with what it took eighteen years to accomplish. It's like a dream!" Janice plans to market the enzyme with a gala Return To Youth campaign.

In his lab, Zinthrop is checking the animal cages when he sees the one that was holding the cat empty. The mutated feline leaps from the top of a refrigerator onto Zinthrop, who throttles it. Cooper tells Bill and Mary about the monkey gland fad of the twenties and

how deterioration set in. This could happen to Janice. Zinthrop cremates the cat, exiting the building in a daze. Cooper breaks into the lab to get his notebook. Feeling strange headaches, Janice knocks on the door calling for Zinthrop, and unlocks it. Cooper hides until she leaves. Zinthrop steps off a curb into the path of a car.

To find Zinthrop, Janice hires private eye, Les Hellman, who needs background data. Janice recalls the missing letter. Since only she could have taken it, Mary is questioned. A comatose John Doe at Central Emergency is Zinthrop. Cooper returns to the lab to make a qualitative enzyme analysis. He hears loud buzzing from the next room and wasp-headed Janice darts out to grab him with her claws and sink her mandibles into his face.

Janice continues her Youth campaign, although her public relations man cautions, "Cosmetics are one thing. Medication is another." Janice's headaches are getting worse. Now conscious but memory-impaired, Zinthrop is moved to a room of Janice's suite under the care of a nurse. "I must . . . tell you . . . something . . . important," he mumbles as he is placed in a collapsible bed. Cooper is missed.

That night, a watchman hears buzzing from the lab and goes in. Zinthrop and the nurse hear him scream. The nurse convinces Zinthrop it was only a dream. The watchman's raincoat and lunch pail are found. Janice is unconcerned about his disappearance. Bill and Mary hear about the "dream".

Bill and Mary find Zinthrop's notebook in Cooper's desk. Cooper's indispensable pipe sits in an ashtray — meaning he never left the building. Distraught Janice tells Zinthrop something is happening to her. She only has enough enzyme for one more injection. The nurse is eavesdropping. In front of overwhelmed Zinthrop, Janice becomes the wasp woman and kills the nurse. Swiftly, she drags the body away. Janice takes the last enzyme dose. Bill and Mary join Zinthrop and see the nurse's bloody sweater lying on the couch. Mary phones Janice's office and no one answers until Janice picks up the receiver, hearing the frightened, incoherent raving of Zinthrop on the other end. Mary goes to the office to call the police but Janice violently restrains her. "Miss Starlin is not a human being any longer," Zinthrop tells Bill. "She'll destroy the girl, as any wasp will destroy its enemy, and devour the remains."

While Mary tells her about the discoveries in the lab, Janice re-metamorphoses into the wasp woman. Terrified Mary tries to escape. Bill sees a fleeting corner image of fainted Mary being dragged to the elevator. While it descends to the lab, he and Zinthrop take the stairs. Bill kicks open the locked door by kicking in the glass. Janice attacks Zinthrop and throws him to the floor. Bill defends himself with a stool. Faltering Zinthrop hurls a bottle of carbolic acid into Janice's face and drops dead. Bill pushes her through a window to her death on the street below.

People react to *The Wasp Woman* as either a Corman strike-out or a worthy entry in his feminist canon. More reserved and sedentary than Corman's jail-broads, Viking women and gang girls, Janice Starlin made it in the male universe professionally. Long on top when we meet her, Janice sold merchandise used by women to make men want them, yet the ordinary goods of Janice's firm seemed absent on the drawn, somber image of a woman who looked so inhospitably Old Maid. All-business and asexual, how could *this* Janice merit distinction as a beauty icon? And since she was in her early forties, would Janice's beauty photographers have had such a hard time glamourizing her visage artificially?

Her office structurally akin to a hive, Janice was a queen benevolent to her female drones and occasionally very waspy to the men. Until new subject Zinthrop worked his backfire-prone Miracle on Janice, her Lair didn't take on the dangerous connotation of that word. Prior to the cat turning on Zinthrop, *The Wasp Woman* was free of horror, except in something rare to horror films of that time: a movie reference. It involved a pair of secretaries discussing the nebbish boyfriend of one. Almost providentially named Irving, his favorite picture was *Dr. Cyclops* (1940), which the girlfriend secretary had already seen twice (the other one called Zinthrop a "two-eyed cyclops"). The channel that *Dr. Cyclops* was scheduled to appear on, Nine, happened to be the number of one of New York's principal horror movie stations (home of "Million Dollar Movie").

The motto for everyone at Starlin Enterprises seemed to be Cover Your Ass. This even went for Bill and Mary, the people most eager to protect Janice. Zinthrop's particular kind of glandular "monkeying" brought out in gorilla size the creature whose secretions were a youth boon demanding payment in the flesh of anyone unlucky enough to be in the building way past happy hour time.

Most of Corman's earlier horror films had extensive outdoor scenes. The claustrophobic *Wasp Woman* tried to be extremely urban in everything from decor to talk, but didn't convince anyone that it really took place in the Big Apple. An insert shot of traffic at a Manhattan intersection featured a classic automobile. Weeks later in the story, there it was again in the repeated shot. And then there were the bees. Yes, *Wasp Woman* began on a honey ranch — but only in tacked on footage shot years later for TV. Credits were superimposed over a packed cluster of bees and the shot was used in a montage of Zinthrop's activities. Aesthetically, the bees were more appealing, but Corman thought that scouting for wasps would have been useless (to say nothing of expensive). Wasn't the *main* wasp what the audience came to see?

And that main wasp was hardly a patch on the shudder power of *The Fly*, except that she killed people and moved like greased lightning. When Michael Mark, playing Zinthrop, threw the acid bottle at Susan Cabot,

209

Bill (Fred Eisley) learns from Zinthrop (Michael Mark) that Janice is no longer human in THE WASP WOMAN.

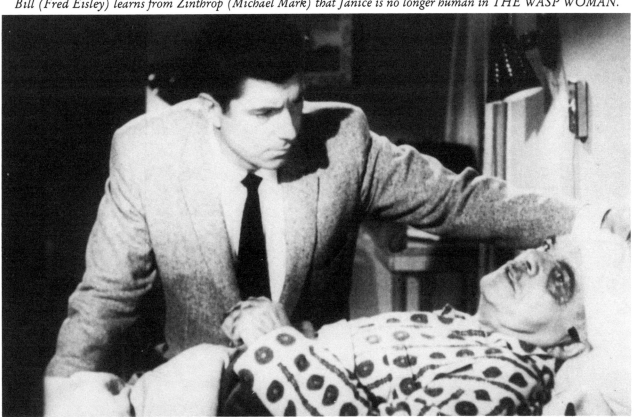

portraying Janice, he did not know that the prop man had filled it with water. The bottle hit Cabot like a tossed brick, but she maintained her acting equilibrium. Then the same dummy on props applied an excess amount of liquid smoke to Cabot's wasp mask. Two men behind the window Cabot crashed through caught her, but her face was so constricted by the mask that smoke filtering through the nostrils threatened to suffocate her. Cabot was doused with cold water, but had to tear off pieces of the mask to regain her breath — ripping away some face skin, too.

Corman obtained some very reusable music from composer Fred Katz, a member of the Chico Hamilton Quintet, all of whom had appeared in *The Sweet Smell of Success* (1957). Katz was the only member other than Hamilton to have his name mentioned in the film. Katz's jazz orientation and pursuit of originality have *Wasp Woman* music that was *on* to weirdness, but avoided shock or violence in most scenes — although the climactic tempo was strong.

Watching all of Susan Cabot's performances for Corman, it is hard to pick the very best since she was excellent in all of them. *The Wasp Woman* was probably Cabot's Immortalizer, since it asked the most of her versatility — and her tolerance to discomfort. Once an intimate of names like Frank Sinatra and King Hussein, Cabot had been married to Monte Hellman, the Director of *Wasp Woman*'s co-feature, *Beast from Haunted Cave*. Fred Eisley played Tracy Steele on "Hawaiian Eye" when he became Anthony, showing in *Wasp Woman* and "Eye" why he didn't deserve future crud-its like *Journey to the Center of Time* (1968) and *The Mighty Gorga* (1969). Barboura Morris, who stayed with Corman longer than any other actress, had a mellow, nurturing kind of sexuality until Corman started casting her in dowdy supporting roles.

Wasp Woman's author, Leo Gordon, wrote scripts that often featured his tall, husky-voiced brunette wife, Lynn Cartwright. As Irving's girl, Maureen, she spoke in a crude Brooklyn accent except when Maureen said to each caller in affectedly velvety tones," Good morning, Janice Starlin Enterprises". Frank Wolff of *Haunted Cave* was a wise-ass delivery man who saw through her airs and the doctor at Central Emergency was Corman.

When *The Wasp Woman* was shown to Allied Artists for TV syndication, Allied rejected it for being twelve minutes under playable length. Corman hired Jack Hill to write and direct the overlong honey ranch sequence, which clarified Zinthrop's identity and intent. Michael Mark reprised the role, but now suffered glaucoma. He had to memorize his lines as they were read to him. One of the masked beekeepers was future Beach star Aaron Kincaid. The footage is slightly disorienting to car experts. In a "1959" film, Barker drove a 1960 Ford Falcon Ranchero that was three years old at the time of its somewhat worn appearance. Hill also shot the detective agency's search for Zinthrop. He was the operative who answered the phone — sitting in Roger Corman's office.

Barboura Morris died of cancer in 1975. An unpleasant death was in Susan Cabot's horoscope too, but not a quiet one. After The *Wasp Woman*, Cabot left acting to marry Michael Roman and the birth of their son, Timothy Scott, left mother and child severely debilitated. Cabot recovered after eight months. Timothy required special hormone shots to help his deficient growth. Cabot returned to acting in mostly insignificant roles. Unsuccessfully, she tried to win the Susan St. James part on "McMillan and Wife". Cabot and Timothy had a volatile relationship that exploded on December 10, 1986, when twenty-two year old Timothy bludgeoned his fifty-nine year old mother to death with a pipe in her Encino, California home. An immediate suspect, Timothy told police he had been beaten unconscious by a long-haired Hispanic man garbed as a Ninja warrior. Timothy based his insanity defense on the hormone injections.

THE BEAST FROM HAUNTED CAVE

Filmgroup / Allied Artists, 1959

Executive Producer	Roger Corman
Producer	Roger Corman
Director	Monte Hellman
Screenplay	Charles B. Griffith
Associate Producer-Key Grip	Charles Hanawalt
Cinematography	Andrew Costikyan
Film Editor	Anthony Carras
Music	Alexander Lazlo
Assistant Producer	Kinta Zertuche
Production Coordinator	Beach Dickerson
Sound	Charles Brown
Technical Advisors	"Birdie" Arnold
	Ed Keene

The Beast created and portrayed by
Christopher *aka* Chris Robinson

Running time: 64 minutes

Cast: Michael Forest (Gil), Sheila Carol (Gypsy), Frank Wolff (Alex), Wally Campo (Bryon), Richard Sinatra (Marty), Linne Ahlstrand (Natalie), Christopher *aka Chris* Robinson (The Beast), Kay Jennings

Roger Corman had perfected his economy ingenuity to the point where he could shoot several pictures on the same locations or with the same studio sets. If a plot was especially viable, it would be told over again and made to fit a new background. South Dakota, Corman learned is a right-to-work state and its most interesting town is Deadwood. A living museum of lore, it was the place where Wild Bill Hickock was slain and two of its most memorable women were Calamity Jane and the cigar-smoking female gambler Poker Alice.

Corman went to Deadwood to film his World War II epic *Ski Troop Attack*, starring Michael Forest, Shiela Carol, Frank Wolff, Wally Campo and Frank Sinatra's cousin, Richard. All five were the leads in *Beast from Haunted Cave*, produced by Gene Corman but based on Roger's 1956 caper movie *Naked Paradise*, aka *Thunder Over Hawaii*. In the latter, an innocent yacht

Natalie (Linnie Ahlstrand) becomes a victim of THE BEAST FROM HAUNTED CAVE (1959).

owner's vessel was used by a gang to rob the payroll of a sugar plantation. A snag in the escape was a hurricane. In the change-of-venue *Haunted Cave*, a *Beast* was nature's justice. *Ski Troop* was only one kind of movie. *Beast from Haunted Cave* was an unorthodox film, a tangental monster movie and, because of setting, a modern western.

In Deadwood, Marty and Byron photograph the local administration building, then head for a ski lodge where their boss, Alexander Wood, and Alex's alcoholic mistress Gypsy Bollette are with ski instructor-guide Gil Jackson. Gil has been hired to take the gang on a cross-country trip through the Black Hills to his remote cabin, Happiness Lodge. Gil mentions a "cougar" that has been plaguing the area.

In a hotel room, the gang goes over its plan to rob the Deadwood gold deposit. Marty will plant a dynamite charge in the Broken Boot Mine outside of town. Meant to distract the people, it will be set to go off at nine o' clock tomorrow morning. Gypsy will be taken by Gil to the ski lift at eight thirty and keep him company while the job is being pulled. Once at Gil's place, the gang expects to be picked up by Tasser, a pilot who will fly them to Canada. Gil pays a visit to get money for food expenses and ask the group to reconsider going on a potentially dangerous journey. Just out of the tub, towel-wrapped Gypsy throws herself at Gil flirtatiously.

At a bar, Gypsy makes her attraction to Gil even more obvious, incurring Alex's jealousy. Marty combines business with pleasure by sneaking off with an obliging barmaid, Natalie. On the pretext of a casual exploration, he takes her to the mine. Marty ducks away from Natalie long enough to go to the nook where he will set the bomb and discovers pieces of a peculiar egg. Marty throws a prankish scare into Natalie, and as they get down to serious kissing, a shapeless beast attacks them. Shaken Marty returns to the bar alone. Alex hauls him into a back room and all Marty can tell him is that Natalie is dead. Alex beats up Marty, assuming the "cougar" had gotten her.

Gil meets the gang in the hotel lobby about a half hour before the bomb is to go off. The state police are in town investigating Natalie's disappearance. Per procedure, Gypsy goes to the ski lift with Gil while Alex, Marty and Byron park near the administration building. A watchman who finds the mysterious egg dies in the explosion. Responding to a siren, Alex Marty and Byron blow the bullion safe and put two gold bars into each of their knapsacks. With Gil in the lead, the trip begins.

Marty feels the presence of the lurking beast. Taking first watch at camp that night, he hears a strange animal wail. Lured away, Marty hears a woman moan and goes to a forked tree, where pale, half-alive Natalie is webbed in a giant cocoon. Natalie's eyes open and the beast lunges at Marty, whose wild rifle shots awaken the others. It was only the "cougar", he claims.

Marty (Richard Sinatra) and Alex (Frank Wolff) attend to injured Byron (Wally Campo)
in THE BEAST FROM HAUNTED CAVE.

The next morning, Gil finds odd snow tracks — left by the "cougar". The group reaches Happiness Lodge, where Byron has a comic fright encounter with Gil's Indian housekeeper Small Dove. Social relations in the cabin are strained when Gypsy dances with Gil, causing Alex to jealously attack Gil. When Gypsy slaps him, Alex strikes her back. The cabin radio mentions the robbery and the death of the watchman. Gil wonders why Gypsy stays with Alex, but she feels she is too much a part of Alex to ever leave him. Byron and Small Dove become semi-romantically involved. They hear the weird sound Marty heard earlier coming from the woods. With his rifle, Marty rushes out of the cabin to find the Beast. The Beast injures him with one of its lashing tentacles.

Another radio report warns of a coming blizzard. Gypsy is beginning to appreciate Gil's rustic, uncomplicated lifestyle and warns him that the gang intends to kill him. Gil plans to go to the authorities. He will send Small Dove back to her people and Gypsy will meet him at six-thirty tonight at the spot where the gang first saw the cabin. Marty leaves with a pair of snowshoes and discovers the entrance of the cave where the Beast lives. When Tasser comes, Alex tells Byron, Gil, Small Dove *and* Marty must go. Marty has become "dangerous".

To keep his half of the rendezvous, Gil goes out pretending he wants to hunt game for fresh meat. Gypsy cannot talk wealthy Alex into giving up crime and makes her departure. Byron sees Gypsy bidding Small Dove good-bye as she is about to escape on her skis. Small Dove is in the mood for passionate love when the Beast grabs her. Byron hacks away at the tentacle with a hatchet, then scoops up hot coals in a shovel and throws them. Afraid of fire, the Beast is repelled.

Alex hopes the Beast will be satisfied with Small Dove, but Marty knows who it is really after. Alex is concerned with nothing but the success of the robbery. Marty believes the beast hatched from the egg, which was probably exhumed by the mine workers. He mentions the cave. Gil and Gypsy face the peril of the blizzard until Gil suggests they hide in the cave, a "haunted cave".

Byron slips away to rescue Small Dove, reaching the cave first. Small Dove is pinned against a wall in a cocoon alongside Natalie's. Byron tries to free Small Dove, but the Best overcomes him. Alex and Marty set out to find Gil, Gypsy and Byron. Marty brings along two very pistols to light the cave. Imprisoned in a third cocoon, Byron tries to instill hope in Small Dove by telling her Marty should be along. They watch in horror as the Beast sucks Natalie's blood. Immediately, it turns on Byron and Small Dove.

Gil and Gypsy enter the cave. Gil fires his rifle at the Beast as Gypsy throws rocks at it. On Gil's urging, Gypsy flees into a passage where Alex and Marty seize her. Gypsy says that Gil made her come and that he is unarmed. Alex forces Gypsy to lead him and Marty to

Gil. Unnerved by the bodies of Byron, Small Dove and Natalie, Alex spots Gil high on a ledge and aims his rifle at him when the Beast wraps a tentacle around Alex's neck, killing him. The Beast charges at Marty, who downs it with two very pistol shots fired simultaneously. The prone Beast rouses long enough to mortally wound Marty. Two more flares immolate it. Gil leads Gypsy away.

Since Monte Hellman directed, the slowly-stirred, low-boil ingredients of *Beast from Haunted Cave* had the dry taste of studied existentialism found in his later films, notably *The Shooting* and *Ride in the Whirlwind* (1965). The plot was mostly Charles Griffith imagination working from Roger Corman's Hawaiian heist opus, which Griffith also wrote, and the Leo Gordon script of Gene's *Attack of the Giant Leeches* in its focus on sleazy people and a type of monster that sucked blood at gruesome leisure. Haunted Cave was also a more competent version of *The Astounding She Monster* in the way a stalking creature messed up the after math of an elaborate money scheme felon. With its tentacles, hard-to-figure biology, fondness for caverns and traumatic impact on a monster-aware man, Deadwood's "cougar" was a prototype Boogen, too.

For Alex, the emotional high of major theft was in the taking of things and considering the victims deserving marks for being so vulnerable. Alex had rescued Gypsy from a life of assembly-line trick-turning, taxing her in physical abuse for the privilege of being the kept woman of the great robbery brain Alexander Wood. Marty and Byron were basically nice guys who did not take their criminality beyond the call of duty. A Deadwoodite who left for awhile and came back, Gil had visited San Francisco to see most of what there is to see in the wider world. He "made the scene" in his own way, saving his happiest memories and foregoing the city temptations that jade and corrupt. While still entertaining the hollow motions of pseudo-sophistication, Gypsy yearned for the simple pleasures of high school innocence, coming out of these sobriety lapses when she reverted back to Companion Whore. Intriguing to Gypsy in his squareness, Gil was like a boy toy Mark Trail (complete with pipe).

Was the Beast some kind of arachnoid mutation or an Indian spirit put here to punish wicked whites? Just its mere existence was significant to Marty, who thought the thing meant to get him because he saw it. Unless it was for taking her to the mine, Marty could not take any real blame for Natalie's abduction. Alex didn't believe his story and Marty was hardly in a position to tell the police. Planting the bomb made him an accessory to the watchman's death and perhaps the Beast was angered by being deprived of the residential advantages of the blown-up mine shaft. By fixing on Marty, the Beast followed five prospective new meals, lugging immediate provision Natalie along to bait Marty. After wiggling out of the trap that reunited him with the girl he abandoned, Marty would handle his demon by taking the offensive. This diminished his worth as a henchman and made him expendable to Alex.

Gil, Alex, Marty and Byron found most of their danger to be caused directly or indirectly by the women: Natalie was used by the Beast to draw Marty away from camp, Small Dove's capture led would-be rescuer Byron to his doom, Gil's leaving with Gypsy prompted Alex and Marty to hunt them and when Gypsy told Alex that her escape was involuntary and Gil had no gun, she was effectively setting Alex up to be knocked off by Gil. The Beast, after claiming Alex, was rightfully exterminated by final casualty Marty — its greatest mental victim.

Roger Corman went to Paul Blaisdell, who demanded a pay hike and when refused, would not make the Beast. One day, Gene was called by Chris Robinson, an eighteen year old actor, who asked Gene to look at a two-hour makeup job of his. Bald, blue-skinned, one-eyed and smeared with stage blood, Robinson knocked Gene out of his socks.

In a library book on freak organisms, Robinson read about the wingless hanging fly. A fan of Lon Chaney, he related the microscopic, wingless and legless fly to Chaney's various amputee roles. Robinson envisioned the Beast, nicknamed Humphrass, as a seven-foot partially erect spider-like thing with eleven foot arms, black holes for eyes and a gaping mouth with uneven crooked teeth in the shapes of stalactites and stalagmites. Humphrass was fashioned out of plywood, thin aluminum stripping, chicken wire, sheets and muslin. Vinyl paint protected it from snow. Over putty and crepe hair, angel hair was added. Rather than money, Robinson was rewarded in two sets of billing that credited him as the creator and portrayer of Humphrass. Since shooting was done in below-zero temperature, the Beast was often photographed in segments and for its complete outdoor images, scenery shots were taken so interior ones of Humphrass could be superimposed — badly.

Michael Forest, who grew up in the area where *Beast from Haunted Cave* was made, carried Gil's stolid nature boy aura with understated bearing. Shiela Carol, as if convincing herself the film was high art, conveyed the deep and tawdry sides of Gypsy with a degree of caliber that marked her as someone for whom big things were in store. Disenchanted with a film career that lasted only a year, Carol returned to her real name of Shiela Nichols and took up horticulture. Frank Wolff devoured every nuance of bearish, boorish Alex and after *Ski Troop Attack* appeared with Michael Forest a third time in Roger Corman's *Atlas* (1960). Finding in Italy the appreciation that eluded him here, Wolff committed suicide in Rome in 1971 by cutting his throat with a razor.

Only a technician for *Haunted Cave*, Chris Robinson made his penchant for weird roles pay off for him as a scarred punk who made a decisive contribution to the story denouement of *The Young Savages* (1961). Robinson played Tech. Sgt. Sandy Komansky on "Twelve O'clock High", starred in a few exploitation films like *Stanley* (1972), which cast him as Seminole snake fanatic Tim Ochopee, and became a soap hearthrob as Rick Webber on "General Hospital".

Beast from Haunted Cave received routine quickie distribution in the States. However, it was one of the very few American horror films of the time to ever play in the Soviet Union.

Creature from the Haunted Sea (1961) reworked *Haunted Cave* as a gold-smuggling story in a tropical setting a la *Naked Paradise*. The gold was treasury currency Caribbean rebels stole from a corrupt dictatorship. The hoods were hired to transport it and invented their own sea monster to kill the guards and keep the bullion. A real monster happened along to up the body count. The hero was an undercover government agent. Isolation took place on a small island. While the submerged gold rested in its strongbox, the creature rested by *it* — its stomach a repository for eaten people.

THE KILLER SHREWS

Hollywood Pictures Corp., 1959	
Executive Producer	Gordon McLendon
Producer	Ken Curtis
Director	Ray Kellogg
Story-Screenplay	Jay Simms
Cinematography	Wilfred M. Cline
Film Editor	Aaron Stell
Music	Harry Bluestone
	Emil Cadkin
Music Supervisor	Harry Bluestone
Art Director	Louis Caldwell
Production Manager	Ben Chapman
Camera Operators	Harry A. Kokojan
	George Gordon Nogle
Camera Assistants	William John Rinaldi
	Harry L. Gianneschi
Set Decorator	Louise Caldwell
Sound	Earl Snyder
Sound Effects	Milton Citron
Music Editor	Gil Marchant
Makeup	Corrinne Daniel

Script Supervisor	Audrey Blasdell
Assistant Director	Edward Haldeman

McLendon Radio Pictures
Running time: 69 minutes

Cast: James Best (Thorn Sherman), Ingrid Goude (Ann Craigis), Ken Curtis (Dr. Jerry Farrell), Gordon McLendon (Dr. Radford Baines), Baruch Lumet (Dr. Milo Craigis), Alfredo De Soto (Mario), Judge Henry Dupree (Rook)

Filmed at the Lake Dallas Studio, *The Killer Shrews* and *The Giant Gila Monster* were executively produced by the late Houston tycoon Gordon McLendon. McLendon earned his wealth in real estate and ownership of a theater chain and some radio station, including Tijuana's XTRA, the original all-news stations. Instrumental in the rise of stone age Rock, creator of the Top Forty survey and well-versed in Oriental philosophy, economics and strategic metals, he furthered

(Above) THE KILLER SHREWS (1959).

Jerry (Ken Curtis) perches himself atop a house with a shotgun in THE KILLER SHREWS.

the growth of Texas drive-ins during the early sixties. Most of the players and technicians in McLendon's two films were Hollywood talent, including former musical cowboy Ken Curtis, who produced them. McLendon and Curtis also performed in *Killer Shrews*, which McLendon narrated.

Storm clouds gather menacingly above the trees of a small Gulf Coast island. Narrator: "Those who hunt by night will tell you that the wildest and most vicious of all animals is the tiny shrew. The shrew feeds only by the dark of the moon. He must eat his own body weight every few hours, or starve. And the shrew devours everything; bones, flesh, marrow — everything. In March, first in Alaska and then invading steadily southward, there were reports of a new species, the giant Killer Shrews."

Charter boat captain, Thorne Sherman, and his black mate, Rook Griswold, head to the island with crates addressed to Dr. Milo Craigis. A hurricane is coming. The boat anchors in a cove and on a forest trail, Thorne and Rook meet Craigis, his daughter, Ann, and Dr. Jerry Farrell, who carries a shotgun because of "animals". Ann is to leave, but Thorne will not depart or unload today. He accepts Craigis' cocktail invitation while Rook works on the boat. The fence gate of the Craigis compound is opened by a Mexican servant, Mario.

Thorne senses Ann's deep anxiety and is introduced to overly-preoccupied biologist, Dr. Radford Braines. The team hopes to isolate and identify genes to deal with the future problem of overpopulation. Worried about the hurricane, Thorne advises the opening of doors and windows. While Craigis opens the roof vents, Ann expresses hope she can leave tomorrow and extends a dinner invitation Thorne takes a raincheck on. The scientists are experimenting with shrews, hoping the reduction of their high metabolisms will lead to a race of smaller people. Radford presents a shrew that has lived twenty-eight days — one hundred twenty eight years in human terms. "How big do they get?" asks Thorne. Concealing another perception of "big", Craigis answers, "That's an adult." A window shutter blows open and Ann screams — only her fright is due to something other than storms.

Rook comes ashore with a gun and a check line from the boat he ties to a tree. Craigis tells Thorne that shrews are cannibalistic and eat three times their weight in food every twenty-four hours or they starve. Mario escorts Thorne to a bathroom to freshen up. Irked by Mario's hovering presence, Thorne wonders why everyone is so eager to see him set sail tomorrow. Ann reproaches Jerry for drunkenly freeing two escaped shrews when he left a cage door open. Ann tells Thorn that she wishes Craigis would go with her. Engaged to Ann, Jerry obnoxiously comments on her cozy position with Thorne.

Jerry is about to become shrew fodder in THE KILLER SHREWS.

Outside, some giant shrews chase Rook up a tree. Shouting for Thorne, he fires at them. Ann is mad at Jerry because two shrews charged them at the gate last night and he knocked her down getting inside first. The engagement is off. Jerry sees Craigis' projects as a big career move. Thorne is outside studying the weather when Ann calls him in for dinner. The shrews dine — on Rook — when the tree collapses and he falls to the ground.

Thorne wants to return to the boat, but Ann halts him at gunpoint. "No one opens that gate at night!" Talked into handing over the gun, Ann is about to tell Thorne "a true fairy tale — and you're right in the middle of it." Beyond the gate "there are two or three hundred *giant* shrews out there! Monsters weighing between fifty and a hundred pounds! And what's more, they are beginning to starve!" Six months ago, the escapees grew abnormally. The giants were not seen until Ann and Jerry were attacked last evening. In several days, the shrews will exterminate each other. A storm blackout darkens the house and candles are lit.

Jerry feels he should leave the island with Thorne instead of Craigis. Jerry hates Thorne. The shrews dig into a barn, scaring a penned-up horse. Hearing the noise of the threatened livestock, Thorne thinks it is Rook's voice and Jerry violently stops him from opening the gate. Craigis saw no need for contacting the Coast Guard. "The world is in no danger. This species does

not swim. And as far as the shrews are concerned, this island *is* their world." "Very soon, right here on this island," Radford informs Thorne, "There's going to be a miniature reproduction of an overpopulated world. And you'll see the importance of what we're trying to avoid." The shrews are nearing starvation point. "There's still some food on the island before they reach the crisis," hints Thorne. Exposed to rain, the adobe walls of the house will be soft enough for the shrews to dig in. Thorne puts all the men on watch duty. Intoxicated Jerry has Mario take his watch. A shrew enters through the kitchen window. Mario tells Throne he heard the shrew "singin'" in the cellar. The two investigate. Leaping out from under the steps. The shrew bites Mario's leg. Thorne shoots it and applies a tourniquet, but Mario dies. "In controlling the size factor," confesses Craigis, "we seem to have crossed some of the other characteristics." "You did a good job of it," snips Thorne. "I've been aware of it for quite some time, Captain!" Craigis fires back. An autopsy shows Mario died because the shrews ate poison which was assimilated into their salivary glands. Any shrew bite or scratch can be fatal.

During the eye of the storm, Thorne tosses the dead shrew over the fence. When none take the bait, he and Jerry head for the cove. Pointing the shotgun at Thorne's back, Jerry warns him to stay away from Ann and Thorne clobbers Jerry. Rook's remains are found. "They don't leave much, do they?" angrily whines Throne, holding

The castaways undergo tense momets in THE KILLER SHREWS.

Trapped in a barn, the castaways are cornered by the Killer Shrews.

James Best and Ken Curtis hunt Killer Shrews.
(Insert) A closeup of a two-hundred pound shrew.

up a piece of Rook's bloody shirt. The boat has drifted out. Having trailed them, the shrews chase Thorne and Jerry. Jerry tries to lock Thorne out, but Thorne bounds over the fence, beats Jerry up and is tempted to throw him to the shrews.

When Ann opens the kitchen door to get coffee, a shrew darts past her and bites Radford's leg before Thorne shoots it. Jerry unravels as Thorne fights other shrews trying to get in. Radford types his terminal symptoms before keeling over.

Thorne inverts four oil drums, ties them together and cuts eye slits into them so they can be used as a human tank. Perched on the roof of the house with the shotgun, Jerry refuses to accompany Thorne, Ann and Craigis as they duckwalk to the beach under the drums past nipping, clawing shrews. Deciding to follow, Jerry attracts more shrews that devour him. One shrew pokes its face under a raised corner of Ann's barrel and grabs her right boot. Once water begins to seep into the drums, Thorne, Ann and Craigis swim to the boat. "In twenty-four hours," calculates Craigis, "there will be one shrew left on the island and he will he dead of starvation. An excellent example of overpopulation." "You know something, doctor," says Thorne, holding Ann, "I'm not going to worry about overpopulation just yet."

Craigis' concept of population control was intriguing but seemingly cockeyed. How would the world agree to his vision of austerity? Wouldn't most things have to be rebuilt on a smaller scale? How would this affect any large people left? Even if miniature humans need less of most things, their number would still take up space if the actual birthrate continued to soar.

Though cheaply staged, the story perils were unmitigatedly fierce. The shrews were an army of eating machines that picked violent weather to attack *en masse*. The ground provided countless possible entrances, as did the walls of the house once the plaster covering the adobe was washed away. If not for vents, the closing of doors and windows would have made the house more vulnerable to the winds. The toxic elements that made the shrews poisonous were the scientists' fault and Jerry Farrell, the man who loosed the original shrews, was no one who could be counted on. The human tank itself could take the assaults of the shrews, but any critical slip in the balance of the drums would have tipped them over or given the shrews enough head access to pass infection.

Considered "racist" by a few were the consecutive demises of Rook and Mario. In the dichotomy of most film disasters, a few expendables must go regardless of race, creed or color. Admittedly, the terror of Rook was sadistically relished. A screaming obese black man dangling about the ravenous shrews must have delighted some of the redneck trade anticipating the shrew's consumption of dark meat. Thorne, at least, cared about Rook. It only followed that unimportant Mario, awkward Radford and cowardly Jerry were next.

Mostly, *Killer Shrews* has been panned for its notorious shortcut of using trained dogs as the poorly made-up shrews. Even if their face masks hadn't been phony, real rodents have squat, heavy bodies and move slowly on shorter legs. The shrew close-ups employing a model head were better because of quick editing and foreground distractions like the fence wood.

James Best was a resourceful, slightly shifty hero as Thorne, whose survival skills wouldn't have been so effective had he not learned to play by his own rules. Ken Curtis was rather monotonous as the yellow-all-over Jerry. By allowing themselves to be typecast as comic rubes, Curtis as Festus on "Gunsmoke", Best the Sheriff on "The Dukes of Hazzard", these actors lost

dramatic employability, finding public affection a lucrative substitute. Swedish Ingrid Goude had been 1957's Miss Universe. A luminary of the Yiddish theater, Baruch Lumet fathered director Sidney Lumet. If casting a Jew and a Swede as father and daughter was odd, Gordon McLendon made the cloddish idiosyncrasies of Radford more memorable by his own histrionic two left feet.

Killer Shrews was no milestone, but the more popular *Night of the Living Dead* (1968) abounded with reminders of it. Another regional film whose producers took large acting roles, *Living Dead* was also set in and around a secluded home. The exact number of imperilled was seven. The monsters ate flesh, spread infection, were prolific and persistent. The plots occurred in similar time spaces. Where *Living Dead* hero Duane Jones only threatened to feed his Jerry-like foe, Karl Hardman, to the ghouls, James Best was prepared to make Ken Curtis shrew food in earnest. Some of the stock music in *Night of the Living Dead* came from *The Killer Shrews*, matching several situations in their use.

An advancing shrew interrupts coffee time in THE KILLER SHREWS.

THE GIANT GILA MONSTER

Hollywood Pictures Corp., 1959		Script Supervisor	Audrey Blasdell
		Makeup	Corinne Daniel
Executive Producer	Gordon McLendon		
Producer	Ken Curtis	*Songs:*	
Director-Story	Ray Kellogg	"I Ain't Made That Way", "The Mushroom Song"	
Screenplay	Jay Simms	"My Baby, She Rocks"	
Cinematography	Wilfred Cline	Words & Music by Don Sullivan	
Film Editor	Aaron Stell		
Music	Jack Marshall	McLendon Radio Pictures	
Music Associate	Audrey Granville	Running time: 74 minutes	
Production Manager	Ben Chapman		
Art Director	Louis Caldwell	*Cast:* Don Sullivan (Chance Winstead), Red Grahem (Sheriff), Lisa Simone (Lisa), George "Shug" Fisher (Harris), Bob Thompson (Wheeler), Janice Stone (Missy Winstead), Ken Knox (Steamroller Smith), Don Flournoy (Gordy), Cecil Hunt (Compton), Stormy Meadows (Agatha Humphries), Howard Ware (Ed Humphries), Pat Reeves (Rick), Jerry Cortwright (Bob), Beverly Thurman (Gay), Clark Brown (Chuck), Grady Vaughn (Pat Wheeler), Desmond Dhooge (Hitchiker), Ann Sonka (Whila), Yolanda Salas (Liz Humphries), Gay McLendon, Jan McLendon	
Camera Operators	George Gordon Nogle		
	Harry A. Kokojan		
Camera Assistants	William John Ranaldi		
	Harry I. Ganneschi		
Special Photographic Effects	Ralph Hammeras		
	Wee Risser		
Set Decorator	Louise Caldwell		
Sound	Earl Snyder		
Sound Effects	Milton Citron		
	James Richard		

(Above) THE GIANT GILA MONSTER (1959) causes havoc and mayhem.

Gordon McLendon's second horror film was a teens-versus-monster story with some interesting Southwestern flavor and a positive depiction of hot-rodders. The youth angle accommodated McLendon's interest in rock music. Accenting the healthy was a bid toward family respectability. Routine as monster melodrama, but caring in its societal details and how the title beast affected them, *The Giant Gila Monster* occurred in a milieu where cars are an essential part of life. Linking the characters together, all were descriptive of their owners' identities. Invariably, the presence of cars was a lead-in to most encounters with the Gila monster.

Parked at William's Wash, Pat Wheeler and Liz Humphries are attacked by the Gila monster, whose foot knocks Pat's '40 Ford Coups into the bottom of a ravine. Their hot rod friends are at a malt shop waiting for latecomers to show up before going to a drive-in. Gordy and Gay appear. So does lovable drunk Horace Harris, owner of a pristine Deuce. Leader, Chace Winstead and his girl Lisa show up. She is the French ward of Pat's oil millionaire father. Pat did not come home for supper and the old man is worried. The kids go on ahead, expecting Pat and Liz to join them later.

Wheeler summons the Sheriff, who offhandedly suggests that Pat and Liz might have eloped. Wheeler considers Chace a bad influence on the kids, but the Sheriff defends him. Ever since his father was killed on one of Wheeler's drill rigs, Chace has been supporting his widowed mother and crippled kid sister Missy. Wheeler will have the Sheriff's badge unless Pat is found. The Sheriff talks to Chace, who works at Compton's gas station about the disappearance of Pat and Liz. Pat was a wild kid, but Chace does not believe he had any immediate wedding plans. Still entertaining the elopement theory, the Sheriff drops in on Liz's parents, Eb and Agatha, at their farm. He gives Harris a roadside sobriety check and is satisfied. Behind the Sheriff's back, Harris takes a nip.

Compton returns to the station with four quarts of nitroglycerin. Wheeler is sinking in a new well and needs it for fire prevention. Chace's dad taught him how to handle the stuff. Recklessly, Compton removed the nitro cans from their case when he stored them in a tin shed out back. Chace locks the shed. Over a party line, he hears an anonymous motorist phone the Sheriff about an empty smashed Pontiac sedan lying in a ditch beyond the old red schoolhouse twelve miles out of town. While Compton, who took it home to build a rock garden, gets the wrecker, Chace heads for the accident scene in his rod.

The Sheriff arrives at the wreck, meeting Chace, who has searched for the missing driver of the Pontiac in vain. The engine block of its smashed front end is still warm, there are peculiar skid marks at a right angle across the macadam and blood on the upholstery. The

Poor Compton (Cecil Hunt) encounters the Gila Monster!

The sheriff (Fred Grahem) and Chace (Don Sullivan) wonder about Compton's mysterious disappearance in THE GIANT GILA MONSTER.

223

A closeup of the "dreaded" Gila Monster.

Sheriff notices that one of the headlights on Chace's hot rod is out. He has been saving money for a partial down payment on leg braces for Missy. The doctors say she may walk again. The Sheriff lets Chace take a light from the Pontiac. He reports its engine and license numbers to the state police. A well-dressed hitchhiker tries to thumb Compton as he passes by in the wrecker. The hitchhiker removes a pack of cigarettes from his pocket, lights one and falls over in fright as the Gila monster strikes.

Headquarters say the Pontiac was stolen out of state and the plates were lifted instate. After helping the Sheriff photograph the skid marks, Chace goes on and sees the hitchhiker's upright suitcase on the side of the road. The Sheriff pulls up and finds the cigarette pack and the cigarette that was lit. Obviously, the hitchhiker did not take the car. Sneaking onto the Wheeler estate, Chace sees Lisa, who fears Wheeler may revoke her American sponsorship if he finds out that she and Chace are lovers.

While Chace is driving the wrecker the next afternoon, a Cadillac speeds by and its driver, seeing the Gila monster stretched across the road, swerves into a ditch. Still drunk from a party he was at, the driver describes a thing with pink and white stripes. Chace tows the driver and the Caddy back to the gas station. The driver sleeps it off in a back room and wakes up to hear Chace singing a rock tune as he hammers a bent fender. The driver gratefully accepts a cup of coffee and leaves forty dollars and a business card. Chace has just met Steamroller Smith, the disc jockey.

Wheeler demands a complete search of William's Wash. The Sheriff covers one end of a pass while Chace, Lisa, Gordy and Gay take another. Gordy and Gay go in one direction while Chace and Lisa explore the wash. Chace finds signs of something that has been dragged across the ground. Gordy and Gay make an urgent signal with Gordy's car horn. They have discovered Pat's car at the bottom of the ravine — empty. Chace gets the wrecker. Lisa is spooked by the sound of the Gila monster causing a small rockslide. With her help, Chace tows the car away.

Compton is driving back from the oil field with a new load of fuel. The Gila monster flicks it tongue and topples his exploding truck. At home, Chace finds Lisa with Missy, wearing leg braces Lisa had bought herself. Missy tries awkwardly to walk over to Chace. He sings her "The Mushroom Song". The Sheriff calls Chace about the oil truck wreck. Harris had talked to someone who had seen it explode at a distance. The Sheriff has a flat, so he, Harris and Chace pile into Chace's hot rod. Compton is nowhere to be seen around the still flaming wreckage of the truck. Privately, the Sheriff connects the human disappearances to some odd livestock thefts. The truck left the same kind of skid marks as the Pontiac.

The hot rodders are getting ready for a platter party at Hagartay's barn this Saturday night. Steamroller Smith announces over the radio that he will be there.

Ever-drunk Harris is cruising along in his Model-A when he sees a speeding passenger train. Playfully, he cuts across the tracks. Farther down, the Gila monster wrecks a trestle, causing the train to tumble into Williams' Wash. Frightened Harris does a brisk u-turn back to town as the Gila monster feeds on the screaming passengers. The state troopers take care of the disaster while the Sheriff tries to quiz incoherent Harris on what he saw. Harris can either go home to his wife or lock himself up for intoxication.

Chace is getting ready for the dance. Missy intends to spend the night at the Blackwell home and Chace will leave her there before picking up Lisa. The Sheriff calls, asking Chace if he still has a book on reptiles. In his office, the Sheriff tells Chace that he has talked to a zoologist who talked of how radical changes in diet can cause dwarfism or giantism. Scientists discovered the bones of some huge animals in Tangenyeka who grew from feeding on plants that absorbed salts from river delta water. In the Ukraine, a baby was born that weighed over one hundred ten pounds at ten months and was taller than its mother. Survivors of the train wreck describe the Gila monster to the state police, who passed it off as shock. Chace remembers what Smith had said about running into something with pink and white stripes. Until the party is over, the Sheriff wants Chace to keep this knowledge to himself.

While the party goes into full swing, Wheeler sees the Sheriff. He has heard about the Gila monster sighting and believes the creature is real. He accepts Pat's death, but feels that if the Sheriff had been more thorough in combing the wash, Compton would still be alive. Wheeler saw the Pontiac's white sidewalls on Chace's car. Considering this thievery and evidence tampering, he wants Chace arrested and will accompany the Sheriff to the dance to see this is done.

Steamroller Smith treats the party-goers to a demo disc with the voice of a mystery singer Lisa exuberantly identifies as Chace. Chace performs "The Mushroom Song" as the Sheriff and Wheeler arrive. The Gila monster attacks the barn and pokes a hole in the wall with its head. Everyone runs outside. The Sheriff repels the Gila monster with his shotgun. He has to get the state police and deputize Wheeler, who must arrest anyone who tries to leave. Chace has an idea. He and Lisa speed to the gas station, where Lisa helps Chace load his rod with the volatile nitro cans. They follow the Gila monster's trail of destruction to the Blackwell home — where Missy is. Chace searches the debris for her. He and Lisa cut across an open field where Missy is running, along with the Blackwells. Chace has Lisa hold Missy down while he steers the car straight at the Gila monster. He jumps out before their explosive collision.

The Sheriff, the state police, Wheeler and the other kids show up. Chace explains how he killed the Gila monster . . . lamenting the loss of his car. Humbled Wheeler apologizes to the Sheriff for the way he has behaved. With Compton gone, Chace is jobless, but Wheeler will give him one.

The Giant Gila Monster was really about Chace, the Gila monster a connecting element to all facets of his life. Rightful rewards for all his good deeds were the raft of benefits that kept coming his way. Success as a singer — only one accomplishment — was helped by the brash but ingratiating Steamroller Smith, a wanton (at first) parody of ultra-hip DJ's. Suiting his personality was his chintzilly-accessoried Caddy sedan with a vulgar Continental kit . . . tantamount to Dolly Parton wearing falsies. Destruction of the Gila monster was a supreme manhood test that demanded forfeiture of Chace's most cherished possession. However, one consolation — aptly timed — was the full recovery of Missy's legs. The last person to bestow privilege was former nemesis, Wheeler.

The Gila monster never interacted with people via superimposed or process shots. Only a prop foot placed any part of it in full sized reality. Twice, it effectively

swatted the camera, blacking out the screen. Most of the terrain miniatures meshed well with the location shots in Cielo representing Williams' Wash, a tangle of hostile underbrush. Like *Killer Shrews*, the film began with narration by Gordon McLendon describing the existence of unnatural life in some remote corner of America.

Audially foreboding, Jack Marshall's music used the theramin to create the sound of a ghostly whistle. Even though the audience knew what was loose, it helped sustain the mood of a mystery. Inflections of the score could be heard in Marshall's music for *Kona Coast* (1968).

One of the more sincere and agreeable teen horror stars, Don Sullivan made most moments of his brief career count. *Gila Monster* was both its height and its nadir. On an excerpt of the tune, "I Ain't Made That Way", Sullivan was in excellent voice with a good song. The intendedly sweet number, "The Mushroom Song" — the song that *would be* heard twice — suffered not only from quaint lyrics but the accompaniment of a ukulele. A stuntman and minor heavy in serials, Fred

The sheriff temporarily repels the Giant Gila Monster.

Graham was perfect as the Sheriff, creating a whole human being out of a character identified solely by his title. Graham later moved to Phoenix, where he directed the Arizona Motions Picture Development Board. Don Sullivan now lives somewhere in Ohio.

The Sons of the Pioneers included not only Ken Curtis but George "Shug" Fisher, who was a smile-a-second as Harris, the happy lush who practically lived in his car (to get away from Mrs. Harris, no doubt). *Gila Monster* followed the *Killer Shrews* pattern of casting a foreign ex-beauty queen. Former Miss France, Lisa Simone wasn't as Goude in the looks category as Swedish Ingrid, but managed a little more believability since her ethnic origin had some bearing on the identity of Lisa.

Two members of the McLendon family had bit roles, as did McLendon employee Yolanda Salas. The Gila monster just crawled through his part — except in one peppy instance when he appeared to be running to keep time with a fast beat of saxophone music.

The Giant Gila Monster and *The Killer Shrews* were intended for regional distribution in Texas only, but made such a big hit that they went into national distribution. Gordon McLendon saw to it the films had both Hollywood professionalism and the quality of local atmosphere Los Angeles studios can't duplicate. Unfortunately, when Larry Buchanan took it upon himself to make Texas a movie market, he had to settle for amateur talent on the production end. *His* versions of *Killer Shrews* and *Giant Gila Monster* would be better left uncontemplated.

The Giant Gila Monster advances on a barn full of teenagers.

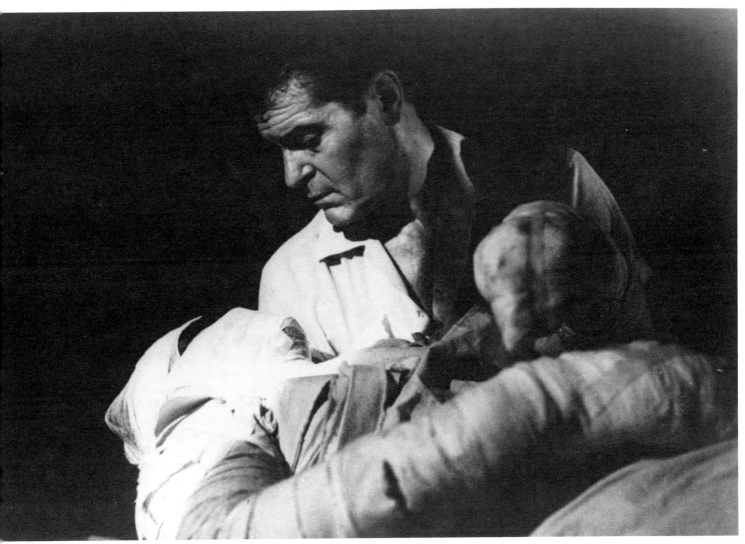

TERROR IS A MAN

Valiant, 1959
Reissued in 1965 by Hemisphere as *Blood Creature*

Producers	Kane W. Lynn
	Edgar *aka Eddie* Romero
Director	Gerrardo *aka Gerry* De Leon
Screenplay	Harry Paul Harber
Cinematography	Emmanuel I. Rojas
Film Editor	Gervasio Santos
Music	Ariston Auelino
Production Supervisor	Joseph Salzburg
Assistant to the Producer	Carpi Astunas
Production Coordinator	Artemu B. Tecson
Unit Manager	Mario David
Production Designer	Vicente Bonus
Assistant Director	Jose Dacumby
Assistant Cameraman	Ferdy Conde
Makeup	Remedio Amazan
Sound Effects Editor	Tony Gosaluez
Special Effects	Hilario Santos
Sound Engineer	Demetrio De Santos
Sound Technician	Pat Del Rosario
Sound Recordist	Pedro Nicolas
Assistant Film Editor	Rufino Cabrales
Laboratory Technician	Fred Lopez

Filmed at Premier Production Studios
Manila, Philippines
A Lynn-Romero Production
Running time: 89 minutes

Cast: Francis Lederer (Dr. Charles Girard), Greta Thyssen (Francis Girard), Richard Derr (William Fitzgerald), Oscar Keesee (Walter Periera), Lilia Duran (Selena), Peyton Keesee (Tiago), Flory Carlos (Beast-Man)

A distinguished Naval officer and fighter pilot in the Pacific during World War II, Kane W. Lynn helped develop motion picture production in the Philippines with Edgar "Eddie" Romero. The son of a Philippines ambassador to the Court of St. James, Romero had spent the war editing an underground

(Above) Dr. Girard (Francis Lederer) and his panther-like beast-man in TERROR IS A MAN (1959).

resistance paper and the Japanese put a price on his head. He entered films as a writer, winning the FAMAS award, the Philippine Oscar. Produced by Lynn and Romero, *Terror is a Man*, was a modest remake of *The Island of Lost Souls*, which had been done before in France in 1913 as *Ile d' Epouante (Island of Terror)*. The only American-released Filipino horror film made in black and white, *Terror*, to many, is the only good one.

One thousand miles off the coast of Peru is Blood Island. Lying unconscious in a rowboat is William Fitzgerald, who drifts to shore, where Dr. Charles Girard and his assistant, Walter, find him. Fitzgerald wakes up in Girard's home, meeting Girard. Walter says he is going out to find "the thing". An oil engineer from San Francisco, Fitzgerald was returning to the Sates when the freighter he was on, the Pedro Queen, blew up. While Girard and Walter take care of other business, Fitzgerald is attended to by a young native houseboy, Tiango. Girard's wife, Frances, has woken from an interrupted sleep. She knows "it" has escaped again. She heard it make cries, which sounded human. Frances hates the work that has absorbed two years of Girard's life.

As Frances returns to bed, a bandaged humanoid panther-like beast spies on her. The panther creeps into the native village, killing a man and a woman. All the terrified natives flee to their boats and move to another island except Tiango and his older sister, Selena.

Fitzgerald investigates the empty village and sees the fresh graves of the panther's victims. The panther is roaming nearby. Fitzgerald joins Girard, Walter and Frances. Girard and Walter are preparing a trap for the panther with sedated ground meat and covered pits. Fitzgerald is introduced to Frances.

At dinner, Girard reveals he gave up the wealth of his busy Park Avenue practice to come here. Fitzgerald will not be able to leave the island until the next supply boat comes two months from now. A disturbing noise is heard and Girard goes out with a gun. Frances fears the dark. The panther had been brought to the island and escaped last night. A nurse, Frances wants to leave when the supply boat finally comes. Fitzgerald is willing to help her. Girard and Walter return with the subdued panther. Fitzgerald turns in, but unease and curiosity bring him downstairs. Obscured by a partially closed door, Girard, Frances and Walter are doing laboratory work with the panther, who lies on an examination table. When the generator lights dim, Frances is sent to get candles. Fitzgerald ventures into the cage area where the panther is being kept. When Frances locks the door, she sees Fitzgerald and keeps him locked up, saying she is sorry.

Fitzgerald wakes up in his room to see Frances looking over him. He sees her the next day sunning on the beach. One of the graves, Frances says, is that if Tiango and Selena's mother. Fitzgerald shows passionate

Dr. Girard listens to Frances (Greta Thyssen) in TERROR IS A MAN.

interest in Frances, who holds back. Envious Walter looks on.

An evening storm aggravates group tension. Drunken Walter hints to Fitzgerald he knows a lot of lurid stories about Girard. Snooping in Girard's study, Fitzgerald sees biology books and anatomical drawings of a panther head being shaped into a human's. Cordial Girard explains he is researching the modification of the species — speeded-up evolution. The real force of evolution lies in the brain. An enlarged brain will alter cellular structure. Chemical injections can accomplish this. Later, while Girard is reviewing x-rays in the lab, the panther shows discomfort. On the porch, Frances sees Walter solicitously drape a blanket around Selena and they go off together for sex. Fitzgerald finally manages to seduce Frances.

Tiango gives Fitzgerald Aku-Aku, a local good luck charm. Girard asks Fitzgerald to help him move the panther. It thrashes wildly until Girard injects a sedative. Walter shows up and surgery begins. This is the panther's fifty-third operation. Afterwards, Frances comes to clean up the lab. She looks at the panther with sympathy. It responds to this. Walter makes a slimy pass, offering Frances "help". Wanting none, she is attacked by Walter. The protesting panther frees one arm until Walter straps it back down. Walter inflicts a cruel beating.

Selena asks Fitzgerald to help her and Tiango leave the island. Fitzgerald sees the bruise on her arm Walter had left. In the study, Fitzgerald and Girard discuss the panther. To Fitzgerald, it is a man — a man with a soul. Man breeds animals for his own purposes. Because man has too many phycological kinks, the panther will be a more suitable progenitor of a new human race. Girard shows photos of the panther how it looked before and how it appears now.

Girard teaches the panther to say the word "man". It sees Walter and breaks loose. Girard fixes a sedative. As the panther smashes things, Girard orders Walter to get a torch. Girard plunges the needle into the panther before Walter sets its bandages aflame. Girard and Frances extinguish the fire with blankets and the sedative takes. Walter wants Girard stopped and this leads to a fight between him and Fitzgerald. Walter grabs a gun and goes after the panther to kill it while the lights fade again. While they look for candles, Fitzgerald tells Frances they are leaving the island tonight. The panther appears in the hall, having killed Walter. It runs out into the rain and Fitzgerald and Girard chase it.

Tiango sneaks out and is missed by Selena. Doubling back, the panther kills her. Frances finds the body and locks herself in the study, where the panther claims her. Girard and Fitzgerald hear Frances' screams. They split up. Girard trails the panther, who is holding Frances, to a high clifftop. There, it warms to Girard's gentle coaxing until Fitzgerald shoots it. The panther

229

Dr. Girard catches a drunken Walter (Oscar Keesee) snooping about in his laboratory in TERROR IS A MAN.

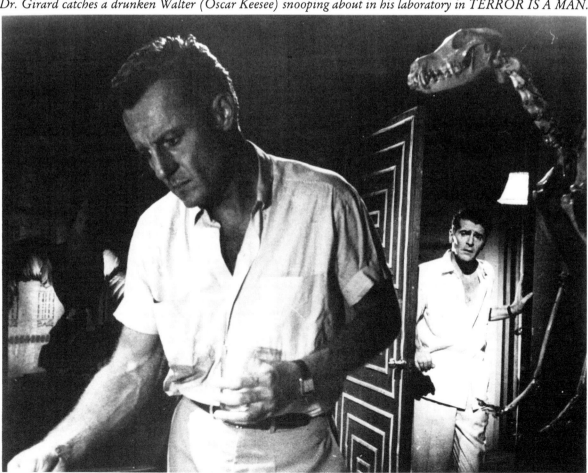

claws Girard's face and hurls him off the cliff. It staggers down the shoreline toward Tiango, who leads it to the lifeboat. Tiango pushes it out to sea, sending the panther on a one-way trip to oblivion. A new sun will rise soon.

Shunning the grandeur of its predecessor for clinical nastiness, *Terror is a Man* borrowed from *Lost Souls* its scientific theme and the circumstances for the hero's presence. Girard was a mellower Moreau, Fitzgerald a much calmer Edward Parker, whose second counterpart after Fitzgerald, Andrew Braddock, underwent animalization in *Lost Souls'* 1976 remake, *Island of Dr. Moreau*, which used the original title of H.G. Wells' story. The panther in *Lost Souls* was a desirable, near-perfect girl named Lota, cursed by recurrences of her beast flesh creeping back. Barbara Carrera in *Dr. Moreau* was the exotic but more ambiguous Maria. In *The Twilight People*, a 1972 *Lost Souls* spin-off Eddie Romero directed, Pam Grier was a literal panther woman from the neck up. *Terror is a Man* needed a more conventional heroine because Frances was a female equivalent of Moreau's guilty assistants.

Localized experimentation on just one animal gave the horrors in *Terror* more grimacing intimacy. What we saw was like the House of Pain photographed through a wider door without the rubbed-in salt of sadistic indoctrination . . . leastwise any from Girard. Walter was created to make a subordinate the Simon Legree of Blood Island. The panther was not simply one of many beasts but a unique something seeing dim light through the darkness of natural instincts it was being pulled away from.

But for its rather empty personal conflict, *Terror is a Man* started the Philippines' horror contributions off with good acting, intelligent direction by Gerry De Leon, good makeup and a mode of camera work that this film

justified, as Filipino films normally benefit from color to make the most of their location. De Leon, along with Eddie Romero and Cirio Santiago, is one of the directors responsible for the main bulk of Philippine exploitation films that came to the states in the sixties and seventies.

As long as Girard was supposed to be a cool pragmatist, the dry, measured theatrics of Francis Lederer served the role well. An actor in musical comedy, Richard Derr is remembered only as the male lead in *When Worlds Collide* (1954). Greta Thyssen, Miss Denmark of 1954, has worked with such unlikely people as the Three Stooges and John Casavettes.

Violence was strong in *Terror*, but not the raw ejaculatory carnage Eddie Romero would become noted for. What there was prompted a buzzer to herald every scene. Romero and Kane Lynn at this time specialized in war movies, handling most of their later productions through Hemisphere, founded by Lynn and Irwin Pizor. Valiant, the original distributor of *Terror*, went bankrupt and Lynn bought back the rights. When Hemisphere switched to horror full-time, *Terror* was reissued in 1965 as *Blood Creature*.

Terror is a Man told its own isolated story, but the setting, Blood Island, became the backdrop for a certified Blood Island trilogy starring John Ashley. The first entry was *Brides of Blood* (1968), where atomic mutation upset the whole ecology, turning a benign plantation owner into a girl-hungry fiend that the natives sacrificed their fairest maidens to. In *Mad Doctor of Blood Island* (1969), the chlorophyll treatments of Dr. Lorca made another affluent Blood Islander, Don Ramon, a violent vegetable man with a bent for dismembering people of both sexes. A direct sequel, *Beast of Blood* (1971) found Don Ramon still capable of mayhem even as a disembodied, electronically-maintained head.

230

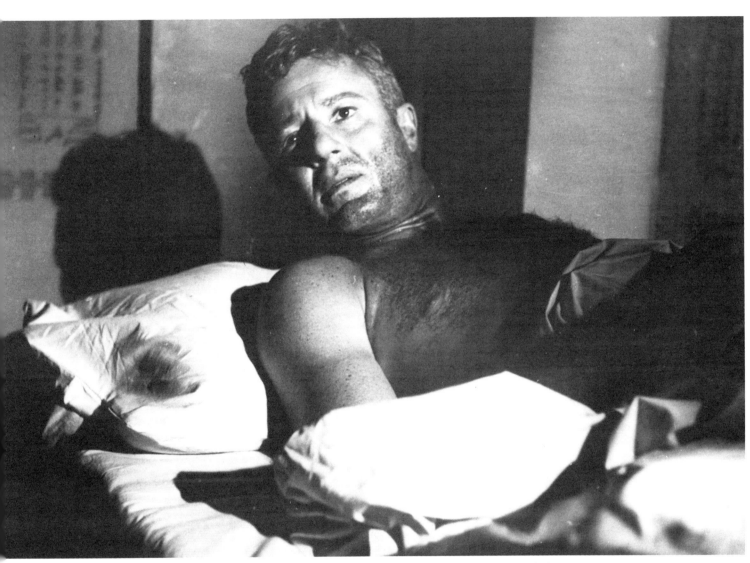
Dr. Girard awakens to a sudden surprise in TERROR IS A MAN.

HSD-12

THE HIDEOUS SUN DEMON

Pacific-International, 1959
Released in England as *Blood on His Lips*

Producer-Director	Robert Clarke
Co-Director-Film Editor	Tom Boutross
Screenplay	E.S. Seely, Jr.
Original Idea	Robert Clarke
	Phil Hiner
Additional Dialogue	Doane Hoag
Associate Producer-	
Production Manager	Robin C. Kirkman
Cinematography	John Morrill
	Vilis Lapeniecks
	Stan Follis
Music	John Seely
Assitant to the Producers-	
Art Director	Gianbattista *aka Richard* Cassarino
Assistant Director	Tom Miller
Assistant Film Editor	Ron Honthaner
Sound	Doug Menville
Makeup	Ben Sarino *aka Richard Cassarino*
Script Continuity	Deanie Follis

Song: "Strange Pursuit"
by Marylyn King

Clarke-King Enterprises
Running time: 72 minutes

Cast: Robert Clarke (Dr. Gilbert McKenna), Patricia Manning (Ann Lansing), Nan Peterson (Trudy Osborne), Patrick Whyte (Dr. Frederick Bickell), Fred La Porta (Dr. Jacob Hoffman), Peter Simuluk (George Messario), Bill Hampton (Police Lieutenant), Robert Garry (Dr. Sterns), Donna King Conkling (Suzie's Mother), Xandra Conklin (Suzie), Del Courtney (Radio Announcer), Pearl Driggs (Lady on Hospital Roof), Cass Richards *aka Richard Cassarino* (Policeman), Helen Joseph, Darryl Westbrook, Bill Currie, Fran Leighton, Bob Hafner, John Murphey, Tony Hilder, David Sloan

Robert Clarke's five percent share on the profits from *The Astounding She Monster* reached three thousand dollars when he decided he was ready to make *The Hideous Sun Demon*. Clarke and Signal Corps. friend, Phil Hiner, wrote a script called *Saurus* and to polish it up, Clarke attended the screenwriting class of USC teacher Melvin Wald. There, he met Robin Boutross and Vilis Lapeniecks. Clarke and co-producer Kirkman formed Clarke-King Enterprises. A friend of Kirkman, E.S. Seely, Jr., wrote the first draft of the actual *Sun Demon* script, titled *Terror from the Sun*. Industrial filmmaker Doane Hoag revised it, receiving credit only for additional dialogue. Tom Boutross would edit and co-direct. Vilis Lapenieks would share cinematography with John Morrill and Stan Follis. Starting money, equally divided by Clarke and Kirkman, was a mere ten thousand.

Alarm bells ring at an atomic research lab as ambulance men rush Dr. Gilbert McKenna from an accident scene to a hospital. Dr. Sterns, the head of the hospital, meets Gil's employer, Dr. Frederick Bickell, and co-worker Ann Lansing. Sterns is mystified because Gil shows none of the common symptoms of radiation poisoning. The accident occurred when Gil was unloading experimental isotopes from an electric train and the lid covering fell off. In love with Gil, Ann believes he had a headache, not a hangover. "I've warned him for the last time," threatens Bickell, "whiskey and soda mix — not whiskey and science!"

Gil recovers in good spirits. Wheeled to the hospital's solarium, he dozes off under the sweltering heat of the sun. An old lady sitting next to Gil turns and screams. Horribly changed, Gil runs back to his room. In a mirror, he sees a scaly face. "Oh, no — it can't be!" Gil smashes the mirror as a nurse runs in.

The condition fades, but could happen again. Sterns shows Bickell and Ann images of the fetus during its prenatal evolution — including a reptilian phase. He runs slides showing radiation-mutated insects. Solar rays trigger an aftereffect of the isotope — causing Gil's scaliness. There is nothing medicine can do for now. Gil can leave the hospital, but must avoid all sunlight. Psychologically, he isn't taking this very well. Bickell received a letter from him announcing his resignation from the project.

Gill moves into a gloomy seaside house. He goes to a nightclub for cigarettes and is entranced by sexy singer Trudy Osborne. Bickell tells Ann he has contacted radiation specialist, Dr. Jacob Hoffman, who will be arriving soon. Depressed Gil pores over textbooks looking for an answer. "Darwin never even scratched the surface," he thinks. "How could he?" Evolution backward to the age of the reptile. Half-human, half-lizard . . . and I'm the guinea pig to be locked up alone." Gil starts to compose a suicide note, balls it up, stares at the moon and suicidally approaches the edge of an inviting cliff. The beckoning of the water below is broken when Gil is startled by the faint laughter of some kids playing on the beach.

At the nightclub, Gil gets acquainted with Trudy. Her gangster boyfriend, George, reproaches her for standing him up. When George manhandles Trudy, Gil pummels him. He and Trudy speed to a secluded stretch of beach. Trudy gets her dress wet when she falls into the water. Gil starts a bonfire while Trudy wraps herself in a towel. Gil offers her his trench coat, pulling Trudy close as the towel slips down to her feet.

THE HIDEOUS SUN DEMON (1959).

Gil awakens to see the crack of dawn. Panicked, he abandons bewildered Trudy, racing for home, where Ann is looking for him. Gill arrives as the sun demon, bounding over the roof of Anne's car and taking a second story route to get inside. Down in the basement, Gil catches and crushes a rat. Ann finds Gil curled up in a closet, pitifully distraught. She urges Gil to hang on since Hoffman is coming, but he thinks his case is hopeless. "If you don't think of yourself," cries Ann, "think of the people who do." Gil apologetically takes weeping Ann into his arms.

Because of this morning, Hoffman urges Gil to stay indoors full time. Increased skin sensitivity brings on the attacks sooner and returning to normal takes longer. The research team has isolated the isotope and Hoffman will arrange for Gil to go to Hoffman's eastern clinic. Haunted by dream sounds of Trudy's music, Gil goes back to the nightclub. She is airing her displeasure over being run out on to George and his hoodlum buddies. Gil tries to apologize to Trudy, who throws a drink in his face. George and friends drag Gil out into an alley and beat him up until Trudy screams at them to stop. Trudy helps Gil away.

Instead of a hospital, Gil wakes up in forgiving Trudy's room. He doesn't want her to open some window curtains because sun "is bad for my eyes". Gil plans to stay here until dark, but someone knocks and it is George. Believing he and Trudy slept together,

George forces Gil to accompany him outside at gunpoint. "You're making a big mistake," warns Gil. As George tries to push him into the front passenger seat of his car, Gil lunges for the gun. From her window, Trudy sees the sun demon strangle George and scramble up the face of a cliff. As he runs through a backyard, Gil scares some kids and kills a fierce dog. Ann, Bickell and Hoffman are waiting for him at home. When she hears his car pull up, Ann runs to the front door — and into the face of the sun demon.

Normal again, Gil relates what happened and breaks down. Eventually, his transformation to the sun demon may be completely irreversible. The police pay a call. Kissing Ann good-bye, Gil flees while she tries to delay the cops. One cop in the driveway is run over and killed as Gil escapes in Anne's car. "He's dangerous only because he's a sick man," Hoffman tells Lt. Peterson. "Yeah, they all are," sneers Peterson. A city-wide search is launched for Gil. He runs into a truck at an intersection, but disappears.

Gil foots it to an industrial region and hides in a shack near some oil derricks. Suzie, an impulsive child, goes outside without her mother's permission. In her playhouse, the shack, she meets haggard Gil. His reluctance to go outside puzzles Suzie. "But sunlight is good for you," she says. Suzie goes back home to get Gil some cookies. Her mother has heard about Gil and Suzie is made to say where Gil is. Suzie's mother calls

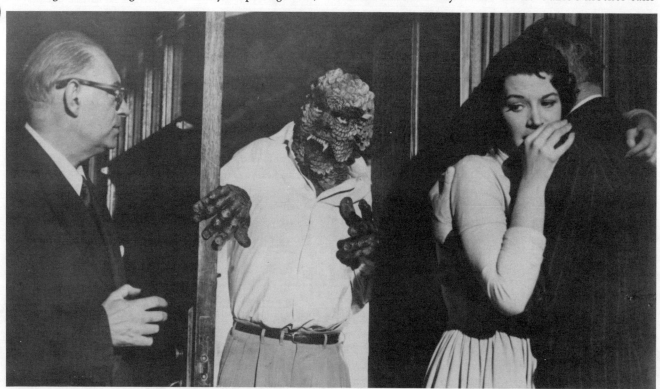

*The Hideous Sun Demon (Robert Clarke) forces his way into a house,
shocking poor Ann, while Hoffman and Bickell look on.*

A publicity still from THE HIDEOUS SUN DEMON

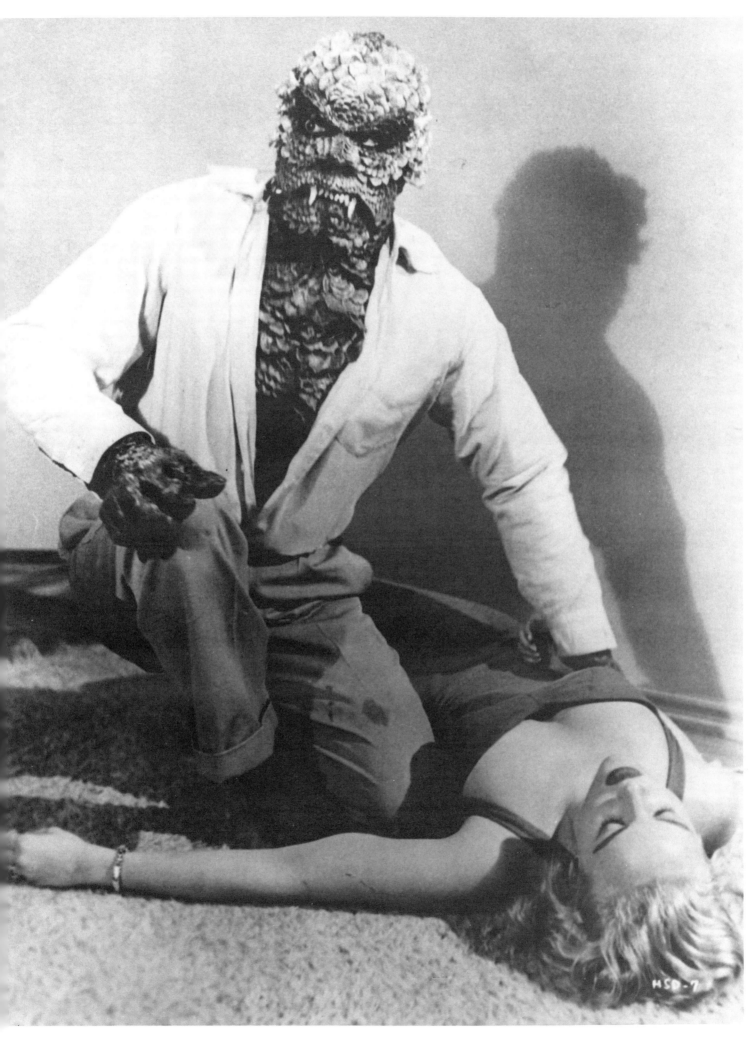

HSD-7

A brave policeman corners the Hideous Sun Demon.

the police while Suzie rejoins Gil. As Ann, Bickell, Hoffman and the police arrive, Gil lets Suzie go and changes again. One cop chases Gil into an old railroad building, where Gil leaps down and clubs the officer to death. Another cop pursues Gil to the top of a gas storage tank. Gil throttles the cop until ground fire picks him off and he plummets to the ground. Bickell tells Ann not to cry, then changes his mind. "The rest of us can only hope that his life was not a waste."

The Hideous Sun Demon had two surefire novelties in the Jekyll-Hyde genre: one, that normally purifying sunlight helped bring out the monster and, two, the monster was a Fallen Man. By soiling Gil with nasty habits, Clarke made some pointed observations about hedonism with no brakes. One vice in booze caused the isotope mishap. After his first attack, Gil could control his condition by limiting his free hours. It was potentially preventable until Gil resumed zigzagging in the fast lane, where he threw his options away on a passive but jinxy floozy. Trudy's association with music was out of *The Blue Angel* (1930), except that George and Gil's own self destructiveness were the active culprits.

Although each sun demon spell was temporary, the demon seemed to gain more dominance each time. Due to the nature of his violence, it seemed like Gil was performing actions of panic, when actually, the sun demon was exercising a passion for violence. This was

originally indicated in the basement scene with the rat. It was edited out of the TV version and even the Sun Demon videocassette. On the hospital sun roof, Gil had changed in a high, elevated, completely open spot. Coincidentally, the last spell saw Gil spend his last moments in a similar place atop the gas tank. With thudding literalism, he "hit bottom". There was not even the usual posthumous return to normalcy for someone who was a part-time beast. The cancer had eaten all of the patient except what parts of him it needed to move around.

Clarke wanted Jack Kevan to create the sun demon, only Kevan's fee of two thousand was too high. The very versatile Richard Cassarino designed the sun demon, making the first face mold from Clarke's head and the foundation of the monster suit from a wet suit. For makeup, Cassarino was billed "Ben Sarino". As "Gianbattista" Cassarino, he art directed and assisted the producers. As "Cass Richards", Cassarino was the cop on the gas tank. Clarke did all the sun demon scenes himself, including stunts. It was even he who threw the sun demon dummy off the top of the tank.

Three cameramen were hired because their personal schedules imposed a rotational system. Vilis Lapenieks had the most skill and devised the cleverest setups. In his longest, most fluid composition, the camera zoomed in on a flashing alarm box at the atomic lab, pulled back and tracked the ambulance men carrying Gil to their

The Hideous Sun Demon leaps onto Ann's car in an attempt to escape the police.

vehicle. As it took off the camera stayed on the ambulance until panning up to the sun, holding on same for the length of the credits as a filter made it a pale globe backed by medium gray. The mission of the ambulance was under scored by distant siren wails and urgent library music. The lead-up to Gil's first attack was an ominous montage of searing sunlight and perspiring skin taking on the hue of a tan. The results were joltingly shown in a close-up of Gil's clenched, scaly right hand, then a pan up to his mirror reflection.

Most other nose-rubbing mood scenes tended toward darkness. A sign that Gil had a medical problem was his habit of wearing sunglasses during night drives. Since Gil had never been shown having a normal Day life, being a Night person appeared to be natural for him. The beach scene with Gil and Trudy was done largely in silhouette against a pale horizon to show them as two vessels that moved in murky waters. For Gil, the Morning After was the price of Sin and when innocent Ann discovered him in the womb-like closet, Gil was curled up in an escapist fetal position.

The spookiest scene was Gil thrashing in bed as his mind replayed Trudy's song, "Strange Pursuit". A sub-layer of eerie music and dancing shadow patterns around the walls were effects that usually herald the start of a nightmare or the presence of an intruder. Some people get off on the jazz timed to Gil's beating.

Of course, a film as cheap and improvised as *The Hideous Sun Demon* is bound to make a few bad toe stumbles. One "mutant" insect in the slides was a grasshopper turned into a close-up of a spider (having enlarged both types of creatures, Bert Gordon might see an "homage" to him here). The collision with the truck had to be clarified in dialogue because of an abrupt cut from a stoplight to a ringing precinct phone.

Clarke is married to Alyce King of the singing King Family, whose distaff members made various contributions to *Sun Demon*. Alyce's youngest sister, Marylyn, composed "Strange Pursuit (a tentative production title, along with the British release title *Blood on His Lips*). Her vocal rendition was dubbed into actress Nan Peterson's mouth. Third sister, Donna,

played Suzie's mother. Suzie was her own daughter, Xandra Conkling. The mother of the women, Pearl Driggs, was the frightened old lady. Alyce, Marylyn and Donna were plugged in a radio station scene when a DJ said, "And now, we return you, once again, to the King sisters." Clarke later hosted the King Family TV specials. One showed scenes of the making of *The Hideous Sun Demon*.

To be expected of Vanity movies, the Star acted his every organ out, but Clarke had the heart to let Nan Peterson and Patricia Manning, two of the USC talent involved, have some good scenes. Manning was a slim, sweet-faced brunette, Peterson blonde, Monroe-looking . . . and not so slim.

Clarke had done a picture for the fledgling Pacific-International called *A Date with Death* (1959). Pacific agreed to release *Sun Demon* as as its co-feature. The company also handled *The Amazing Transparent Man* and Clarke's *Beyond the Time Barrier*, both directed in Dallas by Edgar Ulmer. When Pacific went bankrupt, the films were auctioned off and released by AIP is 1960. For both his efforts, Clarke failed to make any money. He recouped a little when *Sun Demon*'s T.V. rights were sold to M & A Alexander.

Gil's suicide attempt was almost a prophecy of Jerry Lewis' close brush with self-inflicted death. Troubled by a medical addiction in 1973, Lewis himself wanted to end it all until he, too, heard the laughter of children — his own. Clarke tried to make a psychic thriller in the late seventies called *Sorceress*, but the project was aborted.

The video rights of *The Hideous Sun Demon* were bought by Wade Williams. With both his and Clarke's cooperation, a company called Twenty Four Horses Productions planned to satirize it by adding comic scenes with new footage and re-dubbed dialogue. Clarke's son, Cameron, was to play Ishmael Pivlik, the inventor of an oral sun tan lotion whose experiment would explain the sun demon transformations. *Hideous Sun Demon - The Special Edition* was the title the film was known by until it was changed to *What's up, Hideous Sun Demon*.

238

A closeup of the Hideous Sun Demon.

NIGHT OF THE GHOULS

An Atomic Production, 1959
Alternate title *Revenge of the Dead*

Executive Producer	J.C. Foxworthy, Maj. USMC, Ret.
Producer-Director-Screenplay	Edward D. Wood, Jr.
Associate Producers	Marge Usher
	Tony Cardoza
	Tom Mason
	Paul Marco
	Walt Brannon
	Gordon Chesson
Cinematography	William C. Thompson
Editing Supervisor	Donald A. Davis
Music	Gordon Zahler
Art Director	Kathleen O'Hara Everett
Sound	Harry Smith
Assistant Directors	Ronnie Ashcroft
	Scott Lynch
Makeup	Harry Thomas
Costumes	Mickey Meyers
Accountant	John Jarvis

Running time: 60 minutes

Cast: Jeron Charles King Criswell *aka Criswell* (Himself), Kenne Duncan (Dr. Acula / Karl), James *aka Duke* Moore (Lt. Dan Bradford), Tor Johnson (Lobo), Valda Hansen (White Ghost / Shiela), John Carpenter (Insp. Robbins), Paul Marco (Ptl. Paul Kelton), Don Nagel (Sgt. Crandal), Jeannie Stevens (Black Ghost), Harvey Dunn (Henry), Margaret Mason (Martha), Marcella Hemphill (Mrs. Wingate Yates Foster), Tony Cardoza (Tony), Clay Stone (Young Man), Tom Mason (Foster Ghost), James La Maida (Hall), John Gautieri (Boy), Karen Hairston (Girl), Karl Johnson, Leonard Barnes, Frank Barbara, Francis Misitano, David De Maring (The Dead Men)

As both writer and director, Ed Wood could only function in the most hackneyed markets. Whether the topic was horror, porn or crime, everything he

(Above) Tor Johnson is Lobo in Ed Wood's NIGHT OF THE GHOULS (1959).

touched was branded with what some consider his genius and others derangement. Two things that kept Wood going were the support of his friends and the use of material from uncompleted films in his finished product. After working on *Hellborn*, a juvenile delinquency drama made in 1955 long thought to be *still*born, Wood wrote "The Final Curtain", the pilot for "Portraits in Terror", a tentative TV anthology show. "Final Curtain" concerned an actor cast as a stage vampire who experienced occult phenomenon in the theater after his last performance. A vehicle for him, Bela Lugosi was reading the script when he died.

"Final Curtain" was produced by Ernest Moore, brother of Wood regular Duke, who replace Lugosi. Its female vampire was Jeannie Stevens. She and sister Suzi were waitresses at a Hollywood donut shop Wood frequented and both had appeared in his 1948 musical stage comedy "Casual Company". Scenes from "The Final Curtain" and *Hellborn* turned up in *Night of the Ghouls*, aka *Revenge of the Dead*. Also incorporated was the character name Dr. Acula, the person Bela Lugosi was supposed to play in *The Vampire's Tomb* and chosen to be his moniker for a cancelled TV project. In *Night of the Ghouls*, Acula became the alias for Karl, an unscrupulous bogus medium. He worked in geographically altered *Bride of the Monster* territory and mentioned in passing were the aliens of *Plan Nine from Outer Space*.

Wood and retired U.S. Marine Corps. major, J.C. Foxworthy started Atomic Productions with *Night of the Ghouls* to be the first film of a multi-picture schedule. Among its six associate producers were Paul Marco, making his third appearance as Kelton, and Tom Mason, the Anaheim chiropractor who doubled for Bela Lugosi in *Plan Nine*, as well as Marco's agent, Marge Usher. Criswell, the narrator of *Plan Nine*, served as both narrator and leader of the dead. Lobo had survived the lab fire of *Bride*, and also back were Capt. Robbins of *Bride* and Lt. Johnny Harper of *Plan Nine*, under new identities. Robbins was now an inspector and Harper's name was changed to Lt. Dan Bradford.

Inside a crypt, Criswell rouses from his coffin repose and tells us, "For many years, I have told you the almost unbelievable, related the unreal and showed it to be more than fact. Now I tell you a tale of the threshold people . . . so astounding some of you may faint. This is the story of those in the twilight time . . . once human, now monsters in a world between the living and the dead. Monsters to be pitied . . . monsters to be despised . . ."

The East Los Angeles station for the L.A. County Sheriff's Department. Sgt. Crandal has talked to elderly Henry and Martha Edwards about their run-in with a ghost. "It was a nightmare of horror!" moans Henry. "Oh, that horrible face," wails Martha, ". . . and those long fingers!" Ptl. Kelton takes them to a waiting room where a hospital ambulance will pick them up. Prior to this, a teenaged girl ran from her pawing boyfriend under

the eyes of the Black Ghost. Both were killed by her.

Insp. Robbins impatiently waits for Lt. Dan Bradford, who shows up dressed in a tuxedo for an opera date he must delay until the Edwards' ordeal is investigated. "You're the only one with experience along these lines," insists Robbins. Henry and Martha, en route to a family medical emergency, drove past the cemetery near the mysteriously rebuilt Willows place. There, another female specter, the White Ghost, frightened them. Ordered to accompany Bradford to the house, Kelton cravenly balks. "Monsters! Space people! Mad doctors! They didn't teach me about such things at the police academy. Yet that's all I've been assigned to since I came on active duty. How come I get picked for these screwy details all the time? *I resign!*"

Reaching the Willows place first, Bradford is watched by the Black Ghost and hears her eerie cry. In the house, he meets Dr. Acula, who thinks Bradford wants a loved one risen. Down in the Resurrection Chamber, Bradford hears the cemetery clock tower toll midnight. The White Ghost, Acula's assistant, Shiela, sees the Black Ghost and screams. "She died over two centuries ago," Acula tells alarmed Bradford, "— the first I raised from the other side of the grave. She never left all these years." Bradford meets wealthy Darmoor, who is paying Acula to restore his wife, Lucille. Darmoor is granted a moment to see her shrouded body, surrounded by lit candles. Disfigured Lobo also inhabits the house.

Kelton arrives, glimpsing Shiela before he shoots at the Black Ghost. Frantically, he radios Operations. Robbins has gone home. Bradford, Darmoor and Acula share a seance table in the drape room with Maude Foster and her young fiancee. Acula invokes the spirit of Maude's husband, Wingate Yates Foster. Another helper, Tony, opens a casket. Foster reoccupies his risen body and tells Maude to get on with her life. While Tony talks to Acula, Bradford leaves through a side door.

Shiela tells Acula about Kelton and the Black Ghost. "*I am the one who creates ghosts around here!*" lectures Acula. "Me! *Me!*" He expects a big fifty-fifty payoff when Maude marries her lover, a gigolo working for Acula. Darmoor is about to be taken too. Bradford explores the upper levels of the house. Operations has contacted Robbins, who leaves for the house with Crandal. Bradford enters a room with a disturbingly lifelike female dummy. As he turns to leave, it suddenly smiles and beckons to him. Bradford is surprised by Acula and Lobo. Acula learns Bradford is a cop and has Lobo throw him into the locked Mortuary Room.

Kelton summons the nerve to enter the house. A warning light alarms Acula, who sends Lobo for the intruder. For Darmoor's seance, Shiela masquerades as a soul calling for Lucille's cousin Jeffrey. Kelton disrupts the ceremony until Lobo appears and takes three slugs in the chest before carrying Kelton away. "Again, a salute to the Prince of Darkness," proclaims Acula. "Always, there is an unbeliever to defile the supernatural."

Bradford breaks out of the Mortuary Room and sees wounded Lobo stagger by. He follows Lobo's trail of blood to a coffin where Kelton lies unconscious. Darmoor writes Acula a check for ten thousand dollars. "Barnum sure was right," chuckles Acula to himself.

Bradford revives Kelton. Acula plans to leave the house soon and abandon Lobo, thinking his wounds will be fatal. Unarmed, Bradford and Kelton return to the drape room. Lunging Lobo is shot down by Robbins and Crandal. Ptl. Hall is with them. "Foster" alerts Acula and Shiela to the law. While "Foster" tries to hold the cops off, Acula and Shiela flee to the Mortuary Room. "Foster" fires his gun at the cops and is killed. Hall gets winged in the arm.

Acula locks the door of the Mortuary Room, where he and Shiela face Criswell and five other living dead men. "You're not my actors," stammers Acula. "Your powers were even stronger then you realized," enlightens Criswell. "You have brought us back from the grave. Once every thirteen years, when called by a strong medium such as you, we are given a brief twelve hours of freedom from our pit of darkness. Those hours are almost gone. We must return to the grave. You will accompany us there." Losing his key, Acula is mobbed by the dead as Shiela slips away. Unconscious Acula is placed in a coffin. The lid is closed down on his face as he comes to and screams. The coffin is taken to the crypt.

Shiela loses herself in the woods, where the Black Ghost traps her. "It is time . . .," the Black Ghost decrees telepathically, "for you to join the others . . . in the grave." Hypnotized Shiela follows her. Near Acula's body are strewn skeletons. "Maybe the bodies have gone back to where they came from," volunteers Kelton. Bradford thinks Shiela is still around. "Unless . . .," guesses Kelton, "she's become a *real* ghost." Shiela vanishes into misty oblivion.

In his coffin again, Criswell says, "And now, we return to our graves . . . the old and the new . . . and *you* . . may join us soon."

The world of *Night of the Ghouls* was a place where monsters, aliens, mad scientists and ghosts could thrive in the same areas and touch the lives of some of the same people. Making some "creative" changes, Wood simply referred to Dr. Vornoff of *Bride of the Monster* as "the mad doctor" or "the old scientist". His house had been destroyed by lightning, but rebuilt completely by whoever owned it after Vornoff and before Acula. Lobo seemingly "went" with the house and now served Acula. Dick Craig of *Bride* was played by one-shot actor Tony McCoy. Since Duke Moore was a true Wood buddy, Wood made his renamed Lt. Harper the ostensible investigator of the Vornoff case.

Ghoul's narrative device of host Criswell *being* a ghost who participated in the story went "Inner Sanctum" one better. This was no more implausible than having Kelton be the only cop ever assaulted by several

types of monsters thanks to his "screwy details". In almost all of his films, Wood reflected the point of view of the police, usually making his gendarmes incompetent. *Night of the Ghouls* gave its cops a little more credit by implying the LAPD kept a secret file on occult occurrences and Dan Bradford was their reluctant ghost chaser. Kelton provided more humanized responses to the Unknown, his career zeal diminishing with each successive movie. The last person to be aware of real ghosts in *Ghouls*, Acula looked for wealth in the pose of a medium — only to have his unconscious summoning of the Deceased bring about the deaths of him and Shiela. The ghosts showed no malice for this couple, wanting only their company.

Both *Night of the Ghouls* and *Glen — or Glenda?* interpolated fact sensationalism with fantasy. Spiritual scams were the subject of *Ghouls* and Acula's illusions afforded the same absurdity as the narrative nonsense in *Glenda*, using such props as dancing bedsheets, a slide whistle, ukulele picks, a floating trumpet mute and a black Spirit Guide with a pith helmet. Somewhere, Acula found a bargain in skeletons. A skull occupied his crystal ball, skeletons sat on one end of the seance table, a closet skeleton scared Kelton, skulls adorned walls and all the dead who took out Acula were reduced to bones, except Criswell. Blonde like the White Ghost, the smiling mannequin offered a cute apparition in counterpoint to the dangerous spooks.

Marge Usher loaned her home for the interiors. The police station scenes were so minimal that there was only one "Wanted" poster (with Ed Wood's face) and the radio in the operations room consisted of only a microphone on a desk. Scenes in the Willows place showed more of the real house, largely a maze of dingy corridors. Dr. Vornoff's lab had originally been in the basement. For the renovated house, it was said to be in the attic. The "attic" was really the wings of the theater in "The Final Curtain". A flight of circular stairs could lengthen at the whim of a person's perception, a metal railing felt "alive" and an evening skylight admitted day.

The early narrative structure recounted the Black Ghost murders and the first appearance of the White Ghost in slightly unorthodox flashbacks. Between them was visual commentary on such everyday matters of juvenile delinquency and drunk driving, all in footage from *Hellborn*. Both its car wreck and a fight between Wood and Conrad Brooks were later scenes in Wood's *The Sinister Urge* (1961).

Kenne Duncan couldn't bring any Lugosian charisma to the role of Dr. Acula, but since Acula was a crook impressive only to the gullible, Duncan got by on con man believability. His "Final Curtain" monkey suit justified by the interrupted date, Duke Moore made Bradford casual enough so he could offset the uptight disposition of Robbins and the hysterics of Kelton. Harvey Dunn, the original Robbins, played Henry and his successor was John Carpenter. Paul Marco was allowed to show a more subdued side of Kelton and it was learned his first name was Paul. Valda Hansen was a sixteen-year old psychic — only not one who forecast the impossible like Criswell, who must have had a doozy of a hangover during the shooting of the prologue. Until *Ghouls* made it to tape, many thought Vampira played the Black Ghost instead of Jeannie Stevens, who was also the living dummy.

Despite vivid burn makeup covering over half his face, Tor Johnson wasn't as prominent a Lobo as he had been in *Bride of the Monster*. Tom Mason's Foster Ghost resembled Zacherle, and all of the living dead men were brawny hulks except David De Maring, who wore an unconvincing beard.

After Night of the *Ghouls'* initial previews, Wood considered dropping Criswell's scenes and putting in Lugosi footage. Supposedly unreleased because of an unpaid lab bill, *Ghouls* was offered to Allied Artists, but the financiers buried it as a tax write-off. A pseudo-adaptation of the film was A.C. Stephen's Wood-written horror nudie *Orgy of the Dead*. A more empirical deadmaster, Criswell reiterated his opening and closing lines from *Ghouls* — even mentioning its macabre occasion as a "night of the ghouls". Fawn Silver portrayed the Black Ghoul, a graveyard vamp who was more of a malevolent Elvira.

Once the Nostalgia Merchant issued *Night of the Ghouls* on videocassette in 1984, Wood mockers had another of his films to scorn and Woodphiles an unearthed treasure . . . to each their pleasure.

243

INDEX

251

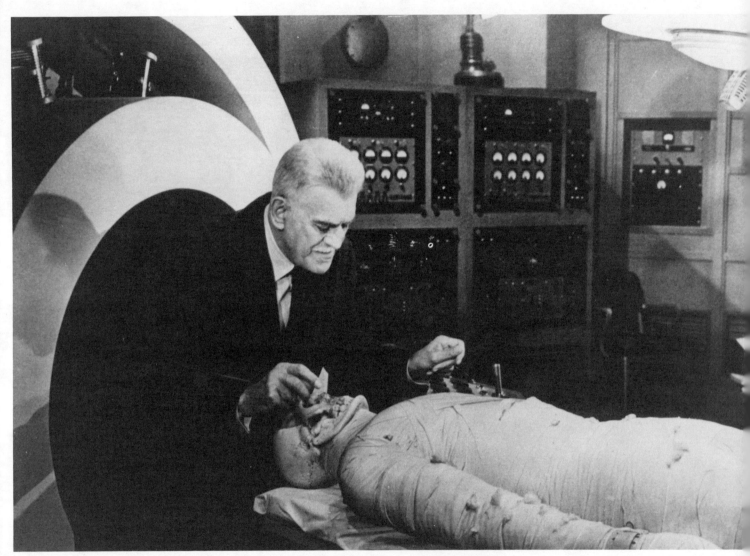

FRANKENSTEIN 1970 (1958).

THE MONSTER OF PIEDRAS BLANCAS (1959).